Inside the Neolithic Mind

DAVID LEWIS-WILLIAMS AND DAVID PEARCE

Inside the Neolithic Mind

CONSCIOUSNESS, COSMOS AND THE REALM OF THE GODS

with 104 illustrations, 29 in color

 Thames & Hudson

© 2005 Thames & Hudson Ltd, London

First published in 2005 in hardcover in the United States of America by
Thames & Hudson Inc., 500 Fifth Avenue, New York, New York 10110

thamesandhudsonusa.com

First paperback edition 2009

Library of Congress Catalog Card Number 2005900864

ISBN 978-0-500-28827-6

Printed and bound in Slovenia

Contents

Preface

The oldest monuments constructed with massive stones are in western Europe. Though modern visitors do not always realize it, these impressive structures – Stonehenge and Avebury in England, Newgrange in Ireland and Gavrinis in Brittany are four that readily spring to mind – are more ancient than the Egyptian pyramids, and they enshrine beliefs as powerful and as complex as those of the later Egyptians. The west European megalithic monuments date back to the early Neolithic period, arguably the most significant turning point in all human history. The full sweep of the period lasted from approximately 10,000 to 5,000 years ago – depending on the geographical region in question – and was the time during which agriculture became a way of life.

Yet those ancient west European monuments were not the first flicker of human interest in massive stones. It is now becoming clear that the use of megaliths in the building of what are surely religious centres of some sort goes back even further. At Göbekli Tepe and other sites in southeastern Turkey, even before the adoption of farming, people were carving large stone pillars, embellishing them with fine carvings of animals, birds and reptiles, and erecting them in semi-underground chambers. This was the time when the sort of fractious society that we know today was born in the Old World.

This is not a textbook designed to present all the excavation sites, researchers, facts, dates and pottery types of that intriguing time. Nor does it attempt to cover features of the Neolithic as they appeared in various parts of the world – the Americas, for instance. Rather, it is something at once more general and more specific.

Its generality is founded on the working of the human brain that, in all its electro-chemical complexity, creates what we call our minds. The neurological functioning of the brain, like the structure and functioning of other parts of the body, is a human universal. The specific contents of individual minds, their thoughts, images and memories, are another matter altogether; content is largely, but not entirely, provided by cultures as they are, or were, at specific times in human history. Content is therefore always changing. The way in which brain structure and content interact to produce unique life-patterns and belief systems is a key issue that we explore.

Specifically, we focus on two slices of the Neolithic, two contrasting times and places, both of which are in the Old World: the Near East and western Europe. By narrowing our focus, we can give some idea of the unity that exists within a seemingly broad diversity and suggest what it was that held the Neolithic together and gave it its essential flavour. We are therefore in some ways like miners, rather than geologists. Miners seek out the richest seams; there is no point in wasting time on uneconomic seams with only traces of the desired coal or precious metal. Geologists, on the other hand, study *all* the rocks and formations in their chosen region. They are the ones who write the indispensable 'textbooks' on which so many writers, and of course miners, depend.

The Near East, our first rich seam, was where agriculture and large settlements started, at least in the part of the world with which we are concerned. We consider sites such as Nevali Çori, Göbekli Tepe, 'Ain Ghazal, Jericho and Çatalhöyük (see Fig. 1). Like the even more famous ash- and lava-inundated Pompeii, these sites preserve evidence not only for the ways in which their inhabitants made a living, but, for our purposes more importantly, also for how they thought, what they believed and some of the rituals they performed. Their imagery and, for 21st-century Westerners, bizarre practices are valuable seams indeed – if only we can find a way to sink an exploratory shaft into at least some of their meanings. 'Meaning' is, of course, itself a difficult concept. We need to ask questions like: Meaning for whom? To what extent did Neolithic people actually formulate their beliefs? How did meaning articulate with action? Did action 'concretize' meaning?

We contrast the mud-brick and stone houses of the Near East with the massive stone monuments of Brittany, Great Britain, Ireland and Iberia, our other focus of attention. Atlantic Europe, whither farming spread from the Near East, certainly presents challenges, but it also opens up opportunities to archaeologists seeking thought-lives of the past and the ways in which belief systems articulated with daily life. Anyone who has crept down the narrow passage of the Gavrinis tomb in Brittany and marvelled at the varied ways in which each massive standing stone is fully covered with swirling, interlinked patterns and images will sense an enveloping conceptual universe, one that in some way motivated the builders to drag huge stones from distant sources, to raise them into place and then to carry their dead to the end of the elaborate passage. Meaning and action went hand in hand.

Contrasts between the sites of Atlantic Europe and those in the Near East enable us to ask further questions. In what ways did beliefs about the rock-immured dead of Gavrinis, Newgrange and other megalithic sites differ from beliefs about skulls buried beneath Near Eastern mud-plastered floors? Was there an underlying, not easily detected, bedrock of belief that expressed itself in contrasting ways? In geological terms, was there a subterranean chamber of molten rock that rose to the surface in different places to form batholiths, each similar to others in its origin but each shaped by the forces of erosion to display its own hills and valleys?

Today, many archaeologists are reluctant to seek generalities of this kind. They prefer to see each society as possessing its own unique culture, that is, the set of beliefs and norms that individuals learn from birth and with which they creatively interact. There is, of course, truth in the concept of the uniqueness of human cultures, but it is by no means the whole story. In his book, *The Blank Slate: The Modern Denial of Human Nature*, Steven Pinker writes, 'culture is crucial, but culture could not exist without mental faculties that allow humans to create and learn culture to begin with.'[1]

Yet, many archaeologists have tended to ignore those 'mental faculties' and have committed themselves seemingly irrevocably to the notion that environment (especially) and culture are everything. In line with contemporary, politically correct thought, they accept that all people are born with empty minds and that their environment and culture inscribe their nature on a *tabula rasa*, or a 'blank slate' – the popular phrase that Pinker uses in the title of his book. As he points out, to believe otherwise today is to court career disaster and to invite accusations of racism, elitism, sexism, endemic violence, genocide and a host of other ills. As a result of such pressures, many archaeologists uncritically believe that the influence of the (principally) natural and (secondarily) cultural environments are so powerful that innate human commonalities are of no importance. They therefore dismiss references to commonalities as superficial and worthless generalizations and, perhaps, a hangover from a now passé archaeological interest in finding 'covering laws'. Differences are what interest these archaeologists.

It is this position that lies at the root of the belief that ethnography describing varied societies around the world is a trap for archaeologists in their attempts to understand the past. The mental blank slates of the past would, according to this position, have been inscribed in ways entirely different from those of ethnographically observed peoples. If we project ethnography into the past, so the argument goes, we shall inevitably create a past in the image of the present, whether that 'present' be ethnographically observed small-scale societies or the unquestioned categories of the modern West. This, we argue, is a rather glib view that needs to be questioned. Is *every* facet of *every* culture unique and non-generalizable? We know that aspects of language and features of kinship systems, for instance, are indeed generalizable. Like so many platitudes – for that is what it has become – the doctrine of the utter uniqueness of every culture contains a grain of truth, but, ultimately, it blights the growth of archaeological enquiry. What we need is a method that will help us to access knowledge about the universal foundations of diversity. We need to ask: What anchors facets of human behaviour that turn up in culture after culture? What leads to these commonalities?[2]

As we have suggested, the human mind is an experience that is created by the working of the brain. The enormously complex neurology of the brain, its lobes, synapses and electro-chemical functioning, facilitates our thinking and our consciousness – in short, our minds. Now here is the pivotal point: the neurology and functioning of the brain create a mercurial type of human consciousness that is universal. And the ways in which that consciousness can be accommodated in daily life by human beings are not infinite, as world ethnography, spanning a multitude of cultures, indeed shows.

All of which means that we do not argue by naive analogy. We do not find something in the archaeological record, search the ethnography, pounce upon what seems to be a parallel, then declare that the human actions and beliefs that bring about the ethnographic instance must have been present in the past as well; before moving on to another archaeological feature to start the whole process all over again. That is the sort of arbitrary ethnographic analogy that has marred the archaeological literature;[3] we try to work differently. We propose certain principles that we derive from the universal functioning of the human brain. We then use ethnographic instances as *illustrations* of the ways in which that universal functioning can find expression. The ethnographic illustrations help us to see the practicality of our argument. We do not argue *from* them.

From the point of view of this book, an important issue is that the diverse ways in which communities come to terms with shifting human consciousness are sometimes recognizable in the archaeological record, as they are in world ethnography. Because we know (more or less) how the brain functions to produce consciousness, we can sometimes spot archaeological evidence for social strategies designed to accommodate that functioning *even though we may have never encountered strategies of that kind before in our own or in ethnographically recorded societies.* We are less constrained by the limits of ethnography than some commentators would have us believe.

In emphasizing the interaction between neurologically generated universals and cultural specifics we are not 'dragging in' an unnecessary factor – human consciousness – as some archaeologists may be inclined to think. (There are, of course, notable exceptions.) The omission of consciousness from explanations seems to result from researchers' own states of mind: when studying evidence for ancient beliefs, the mind is, rightly, kept alert, and entering any sort of dissociated state is eschewed. When reading what are highly perceptive accounts we often feel that the writers have stopped short on the very brink of saying something about human neurology and consciousness. As they pull back, they forget that ancient people probably sought to alter their consciousness to a greater or lesser degree – over and above the highly significant alterations that take place naturally and daily.[4] The universals of mercurial consciousness are present at all times. *All* religions have an ecstatic component, and *all* involve altering human consciousness to some extent by prayer, meditation, chanting and many other techniques. Indisputably, shifting consciousness is a factor with which *every* society, past and present, has to deal. Complex human consciousness is not an 'optional extra' that archaeologists can ignore. The assumption that *all* human behaviour can be accounted for on rational, ecological or adaptive grounds is unwarranted: extracting the means of daily material life from the environment is not always an entirely 'rational' matter.

In this sense, *Inside the Neolithic Mind*, though complete in itself, takes over from where *The Mind in the Cave*, a book that one of us published in 2002, left off.[5] That earlier book dealt with the oldest, well-documented manifestation of fully modern human behaviour to include abundant image-making: the striking Upper Palaeolithic paintings, carvings and engravings of western Europe. Here we move on from *The Mind in the Cave* geographically, temporally and conceptually. We examine the working of the Neolithic brain/mind in the Near East and in Atlantic Europe, our two foci.

We begin with a chapter entitled 'The Revolutionary Neolithic'. It deals with some of the explanations for why people gave up hunting animals and gathering wild plant foods (at least as a sole source of food) and started domesticating plants and animals. As we consider some of the sensational Near Eastern discoveries of the last decade, we make an initial attempt to get at the essence of religion.

Chapter 2 introduces common experiences known to every human being. We try to dispel the misapprehension that visionaries are exceptional, rather odd people. Here, we take up Pinker's contention by arguing that researchers should not ignore the functioning of the brain/mind when they examine ancient cultures. We show how people formulate common understandings of their various types of consciousness and how individuals manipulate those understandings in their relations with other people. We reject any kind of neurological determinism.

The third chapter looks more closely at the ways in which the functioning of the brain provides raw material for the fashioning of cosmologies. Although each society's cosmology is unique, nevertheless there are broad structures that derive from the brain. At the same time, in many societies there are people, we can call them 'seers', who believe that they can actually *see* and travel through the cosmos to capture insights hidden from ordinary people. For the former, the cosmos is not just a concept; it is a lived, explored reality.

Chapter 4 shows how people of the Near East began to construct exemplars of their particular cosmologies at the beginning of the Neolithic. Houses built for daily shelter and living could become, in certain circumstances, models of the cosmos, even to the extent that the dead could be buried in a chthonic realm believed to lie beneath living floors.

The last Near Eastern chapter (Chapter 5) links all this material on human thought, imagery and cosmological concepts to the mechanism that eventually led to the domestication of the aurochs (wild cattle). We cautiously circumnavigate the common explanations for animal domestication and argue that the taming of the aurochs was accidental, or perhaps we should say 'incidental' to other processes, ones that had to do with the sort of cosmology that made sense of the buildings and with the increasing social discrimination of the time.

Chapter 6 stands between the Near East and the west European Neolithic. It considers the role that myths play in clothing daily life with a sense of transcendent reality and how they weave history into realms that lie at the introverted end of the consciousness spectrum (see Chapter 2 for a discussion of the consciousness spectrum). We examine, first, the ancient Near Eastern myth of Gilgamesh and, secondly, a narrative that follows a Siberian novice shaman on a journey through the cosmos. A number of neurologically generated building-blocks turn up in both. We can now see that the human neurology we described in Chapter 2 manifests itself not only in the architecture and art of Near Eastern Neolithic structures but, more generally, also in some universal experiences that often provide turning points in mythical narratives throughout the world.

The next set of chapters takes the ideas developed in our Near Eastern studies and applies them to the megalithic monuments of the Atlantic seaboard, where the spread of Neolithic ideas reached the Atlantic barrier. In Chapter 7 we consider buildings, but on an altogether different scale from those in the Near East: the west European structures are truly monumental. As the ever-increasing popularity of Stonehenge shows, they can still seize people and make them respond in deeply moving ways (Pl. 15). The megalithic monuments were not, like the Near Eastern buildings, inhabited. Researchers have called them 'houses of the dead'.

To give a glimpse of the complexity of the period, Chapter 8 focuses on a cluster of Neolithic structures in Ireland. The Bend of the Boyne, a loop in that famous river, holds keys to the ways in which architecture, cosmology and the realm of the dead interlocked in megalithic monuments.

Chapter 9 considers the dark depths of a nether realm created by the human mind. Stone axes, for instance, may seem to be prosaic tools, but they are much more than that. We show how both Neolithic axes and the enigmatic motifs carved on the tombs were dredged up from a simultaneously material and psychic underworld. We also argue that different treatments of the dead, who in the Near East and in the megalithic monuments of western Europe were destined for that nether realm, illustrate the ways in which people engage with universal themes of social discrimination and how they link their discriminations to mentally and materially constructed cosmologies. We are dealing with an intricate, sticky spider's web of belief, myth and society with all its cross-cutting power relations.

But, as Othello warned of a highly symbolic handkerchief, 'There's magic in the web of it.' For Neolithic people, that 'magic' was belief in a neurologically generated and emotionally charged cosmology inhabited by supernatural beings and forces that influenced human life. Neolithic people were caught in a web spun by their own minds. Our final chapter draws together the threads that constitute that web, and we assess the role of mind and religion in society.

CHAPTER 1

The Revolutionary Neolithic

A famous biblical town where trumpets brought the walls tumblin' down introduces momentous themes (Fig. 1). The dramatic story of the Israelites' capture of Jericho was sufficient to make the site famous, and biblical archaeologists have, naturally enough, been intensely interested in it. In contrast to their attempts to 'prove' the historical accuracy of the Bible, we turn our attention to much smaller finds than city walls and to what the site tells us about changes in human life.

The Bible relates that, when Joshua was about to lead the Israelites into the Promised Land, he prudently sent two undercover agents to ascertain the strength of Jericho, a strategic town positioned on an important trade route. His spies found that the settlement was fortified by high, strong walls. Early biblical archaeologists hoped to find proof of these walls and also of the sensational, divinely occasioned manner in which they fell:

And it came to pass on the seventh day, that they rose early about the dawning of the day, and compassed the city after the same manner seven times ... Joshua said unto the

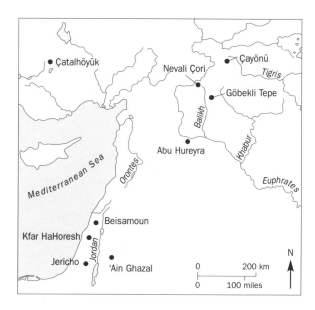

1 *Map of the Near East showing places mentioned in the text.*

people, Shout; for the Lord hath given you the city … So the people shouted when the priests blew with the trumpets: and it came to pass, when the people heard the sound of the trumpet, and the people shouted with a great shout, that the wall fell down flat … And they utterly destroyed all that was in the city, both man and woman, young and old, and ox, and sheep, and ass, with the edge of the sword. JOSHUA 6:15–16, 20–21

Therein lies a dispute. An absence of skeletons of oxen, sheep and asses from the excavations suggested that the walls archaeologists eventually found were far older than the time of the Israelites' occupation of the country: the level dated to a time before the domestication of animals. As with Heinrich Schliemann's celebrated 'discovery' of Homeric Troy, there was not just one settlement, but the remains of a whole series of towns piled one on top of the other. It was hard to tell which layer was the one that the biblical archaeologists most wanted to find. The matter was settled with the advent of radiocarbon dating in the 1950s: the walls of Jericho are definitely too old to be the ones described in the Bible.

Today Jericho is closely associated with the name of the British archaeologist Dame Kathleen Kenyon (Fig. 2). Her first season of excavation there was in 1952. She found a tell, or mound, that rises as much as 12 m (39 ft) above its surroundings; all in all, it covers about 25,000 sq. m (269,100 sq. ft). Pre-World War II archaeologists had sunk trenches and pits into the mound, but Kenyon's own excavations were much more meticulous. She showed that the site had been initially occupied as long ago as 10,000–8500 BC by sedentary hunters and gatherers. Then, between 8500 and 7300 BC, domesticated plants appeared alongside bones of wild game, and the town burgeoned. At that time, 3.6-m (11.8-ft) high perimeter walls were built, as well as an impressive circular stone tower that rose to a height of 8 m (26.5 ft). Another innovation appeared a little later: between 7300 and 6000 BC, people began to keep domesticated sheep and goats. The appearance of plant and then animal domesticates at what was originally a hunter-gatherer settlement was evidence for the so-called 'Neolithic Revolution' (see below) at Jericho.

Half a century after Kenyon's work, Jericho remains a key site in studies of the origins of farming. But some small finds there are even more astonishing than domesticates and city walls: in various ways, comparable discoveries run through the succeeding millennia of the Neolithic and suggest a kind of thinking that, at first glance, appears to lie outside of the ways in which people obtained their daily sustenance. To invoke a biblical trope, we may say that they show that people do not live by bread alone.

2 Dame Kathleen Kenyon: 'The most remarkable manifestation of customs which can best be explained in terms of cult practices might be called a Cult of Skulls.'[1]

Skulls beneath the floor

In 1953 Kenyon noticed the top of a human skull protruding from the side of an excavated trench. She was at first reluctant to sanction its removal. She wished to abide by the rules of excavation that she herself had helped to make the cornerstone of archaeological work: the sides of trenches and pits must be kept sheer and clean so that diagrams of the stratification can be accurately drawn. Eventually, she 'unwillingly' gave permission for the removal of the skull. As she says,

Only the photograph ... can convey any comprehension of our astonishment. What we had seen in the side of the trench had been the top of a human skull. But the whole of the rest of the skull had a covering of plaster, moulded in the form of features, with eyes inset with shells. What was more, two further similar plastered skulls were visible at the back of the hole from which the first had come. When these were removed, three more could be seen behind them, and eventually a seventh beyond.[2]

As often seems to happen in archaeology, the discovery was made at the end of a season's digging. Nevertheless, plans to leave the camp were at once suspended, even though 'the furniture had been all packed up, the kitchen cleared and the servants dismissed, the dark-room and repair room dismantled and most of the material packed up'.[3] Kenyon and her colleagues continued their excavation, living 'in considerable discomfort, sitting on the floor and eating picnic meals, while the photographer and repair assistant did wonders of improvisation'.[4]

As their work continued, they discovered that the skulls had been deliberately placed beneath the plaster floor of a house. It took five days to extract all seven of them. All had facial features – nose, mouth, ears and eyebrows – delicately modelled in clay, but the tops of the crania were left bare. One had its mandible in place; the rest had the missing jaw suggested by plaster fixed to the upper teeth. The interiors of the skulls were packed with solid clay. One specimen had bands of brown paint on the top of the skull, 'perhaps indicating a head-dress'.[5] In 1956, two more skulls were found beneath the same floor. It was a veritable charnel house (Pl. 7).

The plaster skulls enlarged on a pattern that had already come to light. Other houses had skeletons beneath their floors from which, in a significant number of instances, the skulls had been removed, apparently for further ritual treatment. Some severed skulls were in clear arrangements. In one case they were in a 'closely packed circle, all looking inwards, in another arranged in three sets of three, all looking in the same direction'.[6] In one find, there was 'an unpleasant suggestion of infant sacrifice' that seems to have jolted Kenyon: a collection of infant skulls still had the neck vertebrae in place, evidence that the heads were cut off and not merely taken from decayed burials.[7]

The Jericho skulls caused a sensation, but, since Kenyon's excavations there, similar finds have been made elsewhere in the Near East. For instance, at 'Ain Ghazal, an amazing site in Jordan (see Fig. 1), six plastered skulls were found. They were buried beneath house floors. In addition to the skulls, three 'masks' that had probably been attached to skulls were found in an outdoor pit dug especially for the purpose of receiving them.[8]

The Jericho skulls' eyes were emphasized in a remarkable way. Six of the seven skulls had eyes

composed of two segments of shell, with a vertical slit between, which simulates the pupil. The seventh has eyes of cowrie shell, the horizontal opening of the shells gives him a somewhat sleepy appearance. The state of preservation of five was excellent, but the other two were less good, one having little more than the eyes surviving intact.[9]

These shells had been transported some 50 km (31 miles) from the Mediterranean. The eyes of the Jericho plastered skulls were considered important enough for these exotic, and no doubt prized, items to be placed in skulls that were probably displayed in some way but that were ultimately destined for a context in which they would no longer be seen – a grave. Why did they use shells in this way? Their smooth, white surfaces and their origin in a remote (for Neolithic people) sea are, we believe, features that have not received enough attention. The Jericho skulls show that, early in the Neolithic, eyes and 'seeing' were important and were in some way connected with death and, perhaps, the sea. We return to these points in Chapter 3.

These, then, are fleeting glimpses of themes that we follow up in subsequent chapters. They thread their way through what is arguably one of the most momentous times of human history: those few centuries when people began to domesticate plants and animals, and, at the same time, to develop complex belief systems that, seemingly, focused on the dead. The finds we have described give some initial insights into the Near Eastern Neolithic.

The Neolithic period

A few words have migrated from professional archaeological jargon to daily usage. 'Palaeolithic' is one, but it probably takes second place to 'Neolithic'. Everyone has heard the word 'Neolithic', even if most people would be at a loss to define it. A few would know that it is concerned with the origin of farming and, as some writers more sensationally put it, the birth of civilization. But the less informed should not be overly concerned about their vagueness. Archaeologists, too, are still debating its exact meaning. Does it denote a period that can be fixed in time? Was it an event or a process? Does it imply a 'package' of features – farming would be one of them – that was adopted quite suddenly? Was the change to Neolithic life-ways a replay of a much earlier and, in western Europe, apparently comparably short time of innovation, the shift from the Middle to the Upper Palaeolithic?

That, much earlier, change-over in human history was characterized by the adoption of social and subsistence practices that have been labelled 'modern human behaviour'. Until quite recently, this change was called 'The creative explosion'[10] and 'The human revolution.'[11] The suddenness with which new tool types, new hunting strategies, complex burials and, above all, art appeared in western Europe seemed to justify the use of 'explosion' and 'revolution'. This burst of creativity was associated with populations of *Homo sapiens* who, some 30,000 to 40,000 years ago were living in western Europe side by side with anatomically more ancient groups of *Homo neanderthalensis,* famed Neanderthal Man.

Today, however, many researchers recognize that modern human behaviour emerged much earlier in Africa and was taken to western Europe, via the Near East, by *Homo sapiens* of the second 'out of Africa' migration.[12] The African emergence of modern human behaviour was spasmodic: behaviours were adopted in some parts of the continent and not in others, and some may have been adopted and then later abandoned. When the two species of *Homo* came to live in proximity to one another in western Europe, conditions were ripe for an efflorescence of cave art and beautifully carved portable objets d'art (that is how we tend to see them today), as well as new tool types, new raw materials and new social structures; all these had been nascent in the communities of *Homo sapiens* as they moved out of Africa, through the Near East and across Europe towards France and the Iberian Peninsula.[13]

Overall, there was thus no 'human revolution' but rather a staggered process. In the special circumstances of western Europe 40,000 years ago, that process culminated in the illusion of a revolution: there was a comparatively sudden efflorescence of art and an acceleration of change in tool types and raw materials.

By contrast, for many decades of research, the suddenness of the appearance of the Neolithic at places like Jericho, at least compared with the aeons of economic stasis or very gradual change that preceded it, appeared quite clear. There seemed to have been a relatively swift change-over from foraging to agriculture, together with the new norms of ownership and property that must have accompanied it. This apparently swift change was emphasized by the archaeologist Gordon Childe when he memorably added the highly charged word 'revolution'.[14] The 'Neolithic Revolution' was for him one of the few great changes in mode of production (to use a Marxist term – Childe was a Marxist) that preceded the Industrial Revolution that, millennia later, ushered in the modern world with its manufacturing, surplus production, trade and commerce. The notion of revolution and why Childe favoured the term are points that deserve attention because he influentially discussed the questions that are asked in most of our subsequent chapters: What generates changes in societies? Why did people domesticate plants and animals? Why did they make plastered skulls and other ritual objects?

A child of Marx

Vere Gordon Childe, probably the most written about of all archaeologists, was born in Australia in 1892. After taking his first degree at the University of Sydney, he studied classical philology at Oxford University. In the aftermath of World War I, he became involved in Australian left-wing politics and thus consciously forged a link between his own political philosophy and archaeological research. After a spell as Professor of Prehistoric Archaeology at the University of Edinburgh, Childe became Director of the Institute of Archaeology at London University, a post that he held until his retirement in 1956. He returned to Australia where, the following year, he died, apparently by his own hand. His body was found at the foot of a cliff in a part of Australia that he loved. He left a legacy of highly stimulating books that are still required reading for archaeologists.

The Left, following in Marx's and Engels' footsteps, had its own ideas of social change and human history. As a consequence of his reading of Marxist theory, Childe came to see social change as revolutionary. History was punctuated by social upheavals that resulted from class struggles: 'The history of all existing society is the history of class struggles.'[15] A small ruling elite appropriates the 'social surplus' that the lower orders of society produce, and this state of affairs lasts until, suddenly, the social relations that support the production of the necessities for life are no longer viable. They break down and a new social order emerges.

In the socially turbulent 1930s, some people considered these ideas to be dangerously radical, but, more positively, they were clearly a challenge to the racist archaeology of Nazi Germany. Well aware of the rise of fascism, Childe visited Soviet Russia in 1935, and, although he was impressed by Russian archaeology, he later came to denounce Stalinist policies as 'the marxist perversion of marxism'.[16] He was especially interested in the effects of technological innovations, and, as a Marxist materialist, he was not much concerned with beliefs and rituals, in Marxist terms, the superstructure of society. Plastered skulls and images were peripheral to the main business of life, which was class struggle. For him, ideology masked society's inequalities – an idea that is still partly valid today, though historians now recognize that ideology must be studied in its historical specificities.[17]

An issue that Childe confronted was: Why did people give up hunting animals and gathering plant foods as the fundamental way of making a living and take up farming? Today, we recognize that there is no simple, one-off answer to a question of such complexity, and debate about the origins of farming and its associated effects is conducted on a highly sophisticated level. No archaeologist doubts that there was a time when every person in the world either hunted, gathered or did both. Nature was humankind's larder, an essentially dependable storehouse of victuals from which people could draw food rations as they wished and, moreover, that kept food fresh and bountiful. Meat on the hoof in nature did not rot; plant foods did not wither and vanish – except seasonally, and people knew that they would return with the changing seasons. But, as we have seen, by at least 8000 BC people living in the Near East were starting to cultivate plants and to herd animals. Humankind had somehow crossed a Rubicon: there was to be no turning back. The historical trajectory that eventually led to the Industrial Revolution and today's threats of global extinction by war and climate change had been set in train.

Why, then, did people make the change from hunting and gathering to agriculture? First, we briefly examine this question from the point of view of traditional archaeological thought. Then we turn to recent discoveries at Nevali Çori and Göbekli Tepe, sites in southeastern Turkey. Here, a challenge is emerging to the most fundamental archaeological thinking of our time. Although the changes that took place were *revolutionary*, they were not a catastrophic 'package' that, in line with the French and Russian Revolutions, can be termed 'a revolution'. We therefore think of the Neolithic as revolutionary, rather than 'a revolution'. Perhaps we are seeing a 'revolution' in archaeological theory and method, not just an accumulation of 'facts' about the past.

Why agriculture?

On the one hand, agriculture seems to Westerners to be a Good Idea, an advance towards civilization. On the other, it could be pointed out that domesticated plants and animals are more prone to catastrophic disease, and, in any event, farmers work harder and longer hours than hunter-gatherers. Perhaps this change was humankind's first Big Mistake. How, then, can we explain the first farmers' 'decision'?[18]

By and large, some archaeologists suggest two moving principles: climate change and rising populations. In very general terms, it is argued that, as droughts intensified, food became harder to obtain and, at the same time, there were more mouths to feed. The first farmers were therefore acting rationally when they 'invented' farming as a response to the challenge that the environment was presenting, or they began to mimic nature and encouraged seeds to germinate near to their settlements. As a result, their religion and symbolic repertoire adapted to suit the new means of making a living. Change started in the economic infrastructure, and then the belief system was appropriately transformed.

This change-over can be seen at, for instance, Abu Hureyra, an archaeological site overlooking the Euphrates River (see Fig. 1). Archaeologist Andrew Moore and botanist Gordon Hillman found that the layered mound at Abu Hureyra had been occupied and abandoned, and then reoccupied. At about 9000 BC open forests were close to the settlement; people could gather nuts and fruits and stroll back to their mud houses. They also exploited wild einkorn wheat and rye. Sedentism thus came about before agriculture, in fact as early as the Natufian period, the time in the Near East that preceded the Neolithic.

After a few centuries, a drier climatic regimen caused the forests to retreat. The people of Abu Hureyra therefore concentrated on wild grasses that were still within walking distance of their homes. But even these more hardy plants eventually disappeared as the drought tightened its grip. By 8000 BC, Abu Hureyra was no longer a viable settlement site, and the people abandoned it. Three centuries later people returned and began to build new mud dwellings on the foundations of the old, decayed ones. Now they were depending not on wild plants but on domesticated emmer wheat, rye and barley. They were agriculturalists.

An advantage of seeds is that they can be stored in large quantities. People can therefore remain in one place for longer; they do not exhaust the natural foods within walking distance and then have to move on to other locations that can be exploited, as hunter-gatherers do. Sedentary life in villages and towns becomes possible. And so a chain of consequences, not all favourable, was triggered. Fields degraded natural soils, and erosion sometimes set in with disastrous results. If agriculture was indeed a form of human adaptation, it was sometimes questionably so. As fields grew in size, they demanded more water and, as a result, irrigation was developed in some parts of the world. There were also health hazards. Disease can rampage through closely packed towns with inadequate sanitation. Then, too, a starch diet can lead to tooth decay and other health problems. Mobile foragers have to keep their populations restricted because children are not easily transported from camp to camp, but sedentary populations do not suffer from this restriction. All in all, agriculture and its consequences were not an unmitigated success.

Some archaeologists offer a similar explanation for the domestication of animals. First of all, they look for environmental conditions that may have led to domestication. They cite such factors as growing aridity that could gradually change the kind of relationship between people and animals that existed when hunting was the norm. Many species of animals live in herds. Therefore all that people had to do was to control the herds to prevent them from wandering far off to seek water and grazing; they thus interfered with the natural patterns of breeding and genetic change. Keep one herd separate from all others, and domesticated species are the result. But why would people wish to do this?

One answer that springs to Western minds is that domestication of animals is labour-saving. But that is not necessarily true. Domesticated herds have to be tended, protected from predators and taken to pasturage. Then, as we have seen, disease can sweep through herds more disastrously than it does through scattered populations of wild animals. A different kind of explanation is that hunters became too effective and, as a result, diminished the wild species they pursued. The logical answer was to corral them and to allow them to breed, culling them only when necessary.

All these explanations combine environmental changes with human reasoning and ingenuity. In a view popular in the 1930s, the historian Arnold Toynbee[19] put forward a neat formulation: the environment presents a challenge and people respond to it. But, as is often the case with seemingly persuasive reconstructions of the past, it is not that simple. Challenge/response explanations run the risk of charges of teleology, that is, they use the end result as a cause. At risk of oversimplification, the argument can be set out thus:

— Domestication led to shorter distances that people had to walk to find animals or edible plants.
— Therefore people domesticated animals and plants so that they would not have to walk too far.

Labour-saving, a great Western obsession, did the trick.[20] Thus reduced to its bare bones, the argument is plainly illogical. A result of human action is used as its cause – an instance of teleology. Today few, if any, practising archaeologists would subscribe to this simplistic view, though it does seem to lurk behind more sophisticated versions of adaptation-to-environment explanations and therefore deserves some comment. By the 1960s, anthropologists had concluded that agriculturalists in fact work harder than hunter-gatherers.[21] Quoting the ethnographer Lorna Marshall, who worked with southern African San (Bushmen) in the 1950s, and other writers, Marshall Sahlins coined the phrase 'the original affluent society' to describe hunter-gatherers.[22] Lorna Marshall had written of these desert-dwelling people as enjoying 'a kind of material plenty', despite the popular view that hunter-gatherers lived on the brink of starvation and had no time over from their relentless subsistence activities to develop a rich 'culture'.[23]

How, then, can we approach the enigmas of the Neolithic? We accept that environmental factors cannot be ignored, and we grant that some people are indeed clever. But we need to explore a feature of human life and mentality that is commonly, though not universally, overlooked by archaeologists today – not just by Childe. In short, we go so far as to argue that, at least in some times and places, the domestication of plants and animals was an accident, a by-product of other activities.

In doing so, we align ourselves in large measure, if not entirely, with the French archaeologist Jacques Cauvin.[24] He neatly transformed Childe's phrase 'Neolithic Revolution' into 'Symbolic Revolution'. To the dismay of some archaeologists, he argued that major changes in thought (superstructure) *preceded* changes in subsistence (infrastructure): people changed their religion and symbolism *before* they became farmers, not as a result of becoming farmers. For strict environmentalists and adaptationists, this is heresy, but, somewhat ironically, there is hard, material evidence (rather than just theory) for the precedence of religion at this particular turning point in human history. As Cauvin says,

given that this chronological sequence is now indisputable, it is necessary to challenge and dismiss former materialist theories in which symbolic constructions were only derived 'superstructures'… the great civilizing changes of the neolithic were first anticipated and played out within religious and ritual contexts.[25]

Religion

Because 'religion' crops up frequently in this and subsequent chapters, it will be as well to say something about it at the outset of our discussion. What is religion?

To begin with, it is important to notice how our answer to this question differs from that of many other writers, because the distinction is fundamental to any real advance in knowledge about human behaviour. The language that some scholars use when they consider religion and cosmology shows whether they are grappling with difficult issues or simply skating around them in verbal arabesques. One example will suffice. Eruditely discussing tiered cosmologies in South America, Laurence Sullivan, an historian of religions, has this to say:

The multiplicity of world-planes and of qualities of space indicates the richness of manifest being. It demonstrates that known existence cannot be rendered by any single image. More important than that, this multiplicity proves that space itself is, in its essence, a manifestation of the meaning of existence in whatever form. Furthermore, the variety of perceptible spaces shows that human awareness, enriched by the imagination, can encounter multiple kinds of beings on its own terms ... In the very act of separating categories and modes of being, the human religious imagination constructs a cosmos and in coming to know something of the 'others', constitutes its own specific difference, the human quiddity, which is drawn to them all.[26]

Despite all the fascinating empirical information that Sullivan presents, we doubt whether phrases such as 'richness of manifest being', 'known existence', 'manifestation of the meaning of existence in whatever form', 'human awareness ... encounter[ing] multiple kinds of beings on its own terms' and 'human quiddity' have any meaning. Nor do we think that concepts such as 'human awareness', an enriched 'imagination' and 'the human religious imagination', all vaguely conceived, are able to account for something as specific as the widespread occurrence of tiered cosmoses, a point that we address in Chapter 3. These are examples of the theological practice of substituting one indefinable word or phrase for another. Writing of this kind explains nothing; it simply paraphrases.

In contrast to such writing, anthropologists, sociologists and philosophers have long grappled with the definition and explanation of religion. By and large those explanations have been either psychological or sociological. Psychological accounts see religion arising from the functioning of the human mind with its supposed innate tendency to seek 'spiritual' states, or comfort in a hostile world, or a bulwark against fear of death. Reacting to this view, Emile Durkheim famously denounced 'reducing' religion, which he saw as a social phenomenon, to a psychological one. Crudely put, the social explanation says that, in worshipping God, society is paying homage to a rarefied form of itself (an extraordinarily vague notion). No one would deny that religion plays a key role in many societies and that it is sometimes hard to distinguish between religion and politics, but it is its psychological and emotional components that trigger much of its appeal and that facilitate its potential reach to every member of a society.

Recently, Harvey Whitehouse distinguished between imagistic and doctrinal modes of what he calls 'religiosity'.[27] The imagistic mode, which is particularly associated with small-scale societies, centres on polysemic imagery, the multiple meanings of which are transmitted at episodic, often highly emotional, ritual occasions – such as initiation rituals. By contrast, the doctrinal mode of religiosity is associated with writing and the formulation of doctrines that can be imposed over a large geographical area. Doctrinal modes are also associated with large cult centres and the mobilization of large work forces. Whitehouse's distinction is valuable, but, for the moment, we need to point out that it does not explain why people everywhere, in imagistic and in doctrinal forms of religion, believe in gods, spirits and another realm of existence different from the one of daily life but interacting with it – on the face of it, all unlikely propositions. Categorizing religions is not the same as explaining why they exist.

One of the many writers who have offered definitions of 'religion' is the anthropologist Clifford Geertz, later a prominent figure in post-modern anthropology. In an influential article, he defined religion in a way that says much that is valuable and that we use in subsequent chapters, but, in our view, he nevertheless omits a crucial element. He wrote that religion is

(1) a system of symbols which acts to (2) establish powerful, pervasive, and long-lasting moods and motivations in men by (3) formulating conceptions of a general order of existence and (4) clothing these conceptions with such an aura of factuality that (5) the moods and motivations seem uniquely realistic.[28]

To be sure, all religions must inevitably work through a system of symbols (how could it be otherwise?), and we shall encounter such systems in subsequent chapters. But Geertz does not adequately explain *how* those systems and what he calls 'conceptions of a general order of existence' acquire 'an aura of factuality'. The missing element, the one that, fundamentally, provides the illusion of 'factuality', is the first of three dimensions of religion that we find it useful to distinguish: experience, belief and practice (Fig. 3).

Experience

Practice

Belief

3 The three interlocking dimensions of religion. Euphoric and transcendent religious experience derives from the human nervous system. Religious beliefs derive fundamentally from attempts to codify religious experiences. Religious practices lead people into religious experiences and manifest beliefs.

Religious experience, we argue, is a set of mental states created by the functioning of the human brain in both natural and induced conditions. We consider these conditions in Chapter 2. In some social contexts, people interpret these mental experiences as witnesses to the existence of cosmological realms (Geertz's 'conceptions of a general order of existence') and supernatural beings that can impinge on daily material life, an idea central to imagistic and doctrinal religions. In other, more secular, circumstances, people understand the same experiences, not as supernatural, but as some sort of aesthetic effulgence – Wordsworth's response to unexpected beauty, 'Ne'er saw I, never felt, a calm so deep!' Somewhere between supernatural and aesthetic experiences is the sense of being one with the universe. This state has been termed 'Absolute Unitary Being' – AUB. It is often the result of meditation: people in this state feel that boundaries between themselves and others (including the world itself) break down. The neurological foundation of AUB has been studied.[29] The sensations of religious exaltation, calm and AUB are wired into the brain.

When people interpret their neurologically generated mystical states as some sort of contact with supernatural, but to them very real, realms, we have what we argue is a distinguishing feature of all the phenomena that we recognize as 'religions': all religions entail some belief in supernatural entities, whether they be ancestors, spirits, gods or even less personal 'forces'. This point is easily exemplified. It is sometimes said that baseball is a religion in the United States of America. It has a pantheon of 'worshipped' heroes; its practice incorporates elaborate rituals; it is socially cohesive for its various 'sects', the teams and their supporters; it embraces a 'system of symbols' (badges, colours and so forth); it provides emotional catharsis and, we add, a sense of failure and despair that in other contexts causes many people to turn to religion. But to conclude that baseball is therefore a 'religion' is surely a distortion: rather, it is *like* religion in some ways. Baseball may well have some of the features of religion and perform some of its functions, but that does not make baseball a religion. If we claim that it is, we are using the word 'religion' metaphorically. Baseball is, we argue, markedly *unlike* religion in that all religions have some orientation to unseen realms, beings and powers. Religion posits the existence of supernatural things.[30]

Religious belief derives, in the first instance, from attempts to codify religious experiences in specific social circumstances. As we shall see, the mental, neurologically engendered, experiences that lie at the foundation of religion are common to all people; when they speak about them, others understand what they are talking about. Shared beliefs about, rather than idiosyncratic views of, those experiences, become a feature of society: people develop a set of fundamental, shared beliefs about the (neurologically generated) spirit world and a penumbra of debated extensions of those core beliefs. Thereafter, the elaboration of religious belief takes on a life of its own within a social structure that has its own tensions and divisions. The belief system thus produced need not in its every detail refer back to mental experiences. In literate societies, written scriptures become a canon to which people appeal for support of their own views.[31] Imagistic societies have no such 'court of appeal' and therefore far less religious strife. Essentially, then, religious beliefs are intellectually elaborated systems intended – again we add 'in the first instance' – to order and explain neurologically engendered religious experiences.

Religious practice includes rituals that are designed to plug into religious experience and to manifest religious beliefs. We should, however, allow that, for example, a requiem mass in St Peter's, Rome, is not representative of all rituals: the mass is highly formalized (in doctrinal mode), while in many other societies outsiders hardly notice some rituals, the ritual functionaries are not easily distinguished by accoutrements, and the place where the ritual is performed is not prepared in any way. It seems to be a matter of degree. In addition to rituals, religious practice also includes socially extensive projects that reproduce and entrench social discriminations, such as the building of cathedrals and monuments and, sometimes, the waging of crusades and genocidal war. For some, this is an uncomfortable view. Today people therefore often try to separate religious belief from religious practice by claiming that religious wars and persecutions (often triggered by individuals' religious experiences) are not true to the fundamental beliefs and experiences of a given religion (those who wage the wars, of course, claim that *they* are the genuine fundamentalists, in the strict sense of the word). By contrast, we argue that what we may see as ethically acceptable and unacceptable practices can simultaneously flow from religious experience and belief, and that a religion should be judged (we see no reason why religions should not be judged) not only by what its sages or (usually ambiguous) scriptures say its tenets are but also by what adherents *practise*. The social practice of a religion is inseparable from its systematized beliefs.[32] Experience, belief and practice are thus an integrated whole.

An individual's religion shifts between these three interlocking dimensions. For some, mystics and especially anchorites, personal experience is paramount, though it is, of course, always set within a specific, socially shared belief system and economic circumstances. Mendicant friars depend on the generosity of others who buy into the general tenets of the religion. Other religious practitioners, for whatever reason, emphasize belief: they are the theologians, medieval schoolmen and sophists who establish themselves as the arbiters of belief. Inevitably, they manipulate the systems of belief that they construct to include or exclude groups of people, as the Church Fathers did at Nicea. Religious belief is more divisive than religious experience. The third dimension of religion, religious practice, is an (often *the*) arena of society in which the widest range of people must necessarily take part, whether they have moving religious experiences or not, whether they fully understand the belief system or not. There are many reasons for attending mass.

It should now be clear that the three dimensions of religion that we distinguish are inevitably implicated in social, economic and political life. The degrees to which a religion is formalized, to which rituals are elaborated and socially deployed, to which there is a priesthood, to which that priesthood is exempted from daily labour, and to which it exercises political and economic power are, however, always historically situated and, unlike inherent (but culturally moulded) religious experience, cannot therefore be generalized; they must be studied individually.

This tripartite understanding of religion is a skeletal model that will acquire flesh and blood as we develop our argument. Bearing these briefly stated co-ordinates in mind, we can begin to navigate the admittedly perilous waters of the Neolithic with questions that shift some long-held beliefs about that period.

Stones, labour, ritual

Was Jericho really a centre of revolutionary Neolithic changes, as was long thought, or was it, as some archaeologists eventually began to believe, on the periphery? Did the Neolithic way of life develop farther to the north in the hilly flanks of the Fertile Crescent and then filter southwards, down to the Jordan valley and other parts of the Near East? Of course, one's answer depends on available evidence. And the last decade has brought to light a truly astonishing flood of discoveries. This new, we believe incontrovertible, evidence comes from the early Neolithic of the upper reaches of the Tigris and Euphrates.

Pre-farming sites like Nevali Çori, Göbekli Tepe and Çayönü (see Fig. 1) represent the beginnings of the change from hunting and gathering to farming and the establishment of villages and towns. The Urfa Province in south-east Turkey, where they are situated, slopes to the south and is drained by the Tigris and the Euphrates. It is a well-vegetated tableland with barren, limestone hills, in places covered with volcanic basalt. The diversity of the region and its climate of hot, dry summers and wet winters made it ideal for farming. But those conditions could not, of course, *cause* farming.

Nevali Çori was excavated in a (comparative) hurry because the area was threatened by the flooding of the new Atatürk Dam.[33] Work began in 1983 and had to be abandoned in 1991. Before inundation, researchers from the University of Heidelberg and the Archaeological Museum of Sanliurfa excavated five levels of occupation. All in all, they found 29 houses built of limestone chunks held together with a thick mortar of mud; new houses were erected on the foundation platforms of earlier ones. The houses were rectangular and had internal subdivisions. Of greater interest to our enquiry are the so-called cult buildings (Pl. 5).

One of the most long-lasting of the cult buildings (from at least level II onwards) was cut about 3 m (10 ft) into the slope behind it. It was almost square, 13.9 x 13.5 m (45.6 x 44.3 ft). In its earliest form (level II), two steps led downward into the interior, which was encircled by a bench of quarry-stone. The bench was interrupted by 13 T-shaped monolithic pillars. There were probably two further pillars in the centre, as is suggested by ones found in the building's successor, Cult Building III (Fig. 4). Along the southeast wall, the bench is interrupted by a 1.85-m (6.1-ft) section that is set back to form a niche, out of sight of the entrance. In one spot a podium was built on the bench; a large sculpted bird was buried in it.

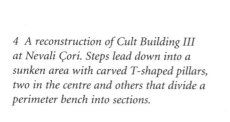

4 *A reconstruction of Cult Building III at Nevali Çori. Steps lead down into a sunken area with carved T-shaped pillars, two in the centre and others that divide a perimeter bench into sections.*

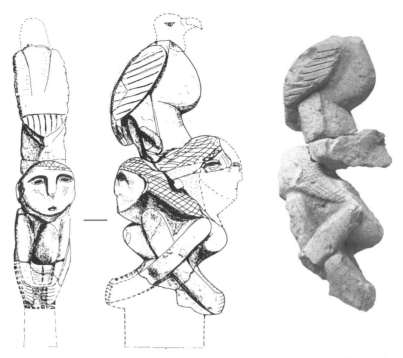

5 *A limestone statue from Nevali Çori, about 1 m (39 in) high. A bird, probably a vulture, perches on the heads of two back-to-back crouching female figures.*

These features were repeated, with additions, in the subsequent level III building. Here, there are ten pillars set in the encircling bench. The two in the centre of the room have relief decoration, including two bent arms, which join hands. There is also the head of a limestone carving of a snake built into the back wall of a niche. Harald Hauptmann, one of the researchers, comments: 'As a remnant from an earlier Cult Building, it appears to have shed its original magic and ritual spell onto this reconstruction as well.'[34] There was some supernatural continuity from one period to the next. Religious practice (the reconstruction of the cult building) ensured that continuity, but with, very probably, some changes in the web (or balance) of social relations within which belief was actualized.

Apart from the carvings on the pillars, there are 11 limestone sculptures. All were found 'interred' in the later Cult Building II–III.[35] One of them is a human head with large ears and a snake curled up on the back of it. Other themes include human figures with swollen bellies that may suggest pregnancy; some may be dancing. One intriguing piece of sculpture seems to combine human and avian features; while yet another has a human head, but the body of a bird. The bird theme is developed by a carving on a pillar: an apparently female head is in the clutches of a bird's talons. Another has two symmetrical human figures, back to back; a carving of a bird seems to have been perched on one of the heads (Fig. 5). Elsewhere on a pillar, two birds face one another, and, moreover, a vulture-like bird was sculpted in the round. Commenting on the carvings of birds, Hauptmann writes: 'The bird perched upon a human head may have represented the soul of a human or a connection between this world and the beyond.'[36] We agree in general terms, although we later suggest additional significance for the theme of flight.

Even more elaborate pre-farming structures occur at another site in southeastern Turkey. It is known as Göbekli Tepe. The German archaeologist Klaus Schmidt is excavating it. Discoveries of this magnitude are given to very few archaeologists.

Göbekli Tepe is on the summit of a hill strewn with Neolithic flint artefacts; it has a wide view over the adjacent countryside. There, in this commanding position, Schmidt found at least four circular structures partly cut into the limestone bedrock, a feature that made them semi-subterranean and rather like crypts (Pl. 6). Dating them proved difficult. But two radiocarbon dates from charcoal that had been part of, and covered by, infill when the structures were abandoned suggest that 9600 BC may be a fair estimate of their age. This conclusion places the structures in the very early period known as the Pre-Pottery Neolithic A (PPNA).[37] Confirmation of this date comes from later round structures of the succeeding Pre-Pottery Neolithic B (PPNB) Period that partly overlapped the depressions of the infilled older structures. The massive rock-cut structures at Göbekli Tepe were thus roughly contemporary with Nevali Çori and the first hunter-gatherer (rather than farming) settlements at Jericho.

As if rock-cut structures were not enough, Schmidt found that two huge stone stelae, or pillars, had been erected in the centre of each 'crypt', and as many as eight further pillars around the peripheries of each. They are rectangular and flat in cross section; each has a wider top section (Pls 2, 3, 4). Some of the pillars are as much as 2.4 m (8 ft) high and weigh up to 7 tons. Between the encircling pillars are stone-cut benches, as at Nevali Çori.

Most sensationally, Schmidt found that the pillars had images carved on them (Pls 2, 3, 4; Fig. 6). They include wild boar, gazelles, wild cattle, foxes, snakes and birds – no domesticated animals. Nor is there sign of any domesticated plants or animals in the deposits. These people were hunters and gatherers, albeit socially and economically complex.[38] One pillar appears to

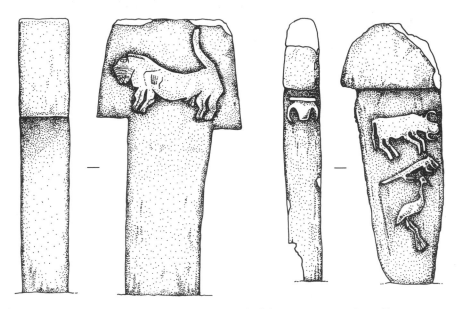

6 *Two carved pillars from Göbekli Tepe, that on the left measures 1.6 m (5.25 ft)
high and the one on the right 3.1 m (10.2 ft) high. A lion is depicted on one face of the
left-hand example, while the right-hand pillar has three figures on one face and aurochs
horns on one edge.*

have a human arm carved on it, and this feature, seen in association with the
armed pillar at Nevali Çori, seems to confirm the impression that the stone
columns are all somewhat anthropomorphic. Here was an early Neolithic,
pre-farming community that, like their Upper Palaeolithic predecessors in
Europe, most definitely had image-making as a practice that went beyond
practical matters of making a daily living – though such a distinction is probably ours rather than one made by the people themselves.

The pillars came from a quarry about 91 m (300 ft) away. There, the limestone bedrock was cut and the pillars shaped, at least to some extent. One
pillar still in place in the quarry would, had it been removed, have been as
much as 6 m (20 ft) long and would have weighed 50 tons. What drove the
people of Göbekli Tepe to make these pillars, to drag them to the rock-cut
structures, to embellish them with images and to raise them up?

Schmidt has found no traces of early Neolithic houses nearby. He therefore
concludes that Göbekli Tepe was a ritual centre to which Neolithic people
came for religious purposes. It may have been a site of intense religious experiences that reinforced beliefs and social networks. Perhaps 'pilgrims' came
regularly from as much as 100 km (62 miles) away, from a site known as Jerf el

Ahmar, where there are comparable round structures with benches and also images of animals, but no rock-cut structures with stone pillars.

While contemplating Göbekli Tepe, the English archaeologist Steven Mithen had an idea that supports what one of us had previously advanced for the domestication of cattle at Çatalhöyük and which, in general terms, followed in Cauvin's footsteps.[39] Mithen concluded that the religious beliefs embodied in the massive stone structures and associated carvings came before and eventually led to agriculture. How could this inversion of the sort of scenario that Childe would have recognized have happened?

Schmidt pointed out to Mithen some hills about 30 km (18.6 miles) to the south. These are known as Karacadag ('Black Mountains'). Phylogenetic DNA studies had shown that this area was the origin of domesticated einkorn wheat. To put the matter more forcefully, Karacadag was the place of origin of domesticated grain and therefore the origin of the Neolithic.[40] Mithen suggests that the switch to domestication came about as a result of frequent ritual and construction activities that took place at Göbekli Tepe, in our terms, religious practice. Large numbers of people, possibly measured in hundreds, would have been needed to make the Göbekli Tepe structures and pillars, and this would have necessitated the gathering and processing of much wild grain to sustain the workers. This activity would, in time, have resulted in fallen grain springing up, being gathered again and thus becoming domesticated. Mithen concludes that a drier climatic spell may not have been the trigger that set off Neolithic agriculture, as many researchers believe: 'It may have been a by-product of the ideology that drove hunter-gatherers to carve and erect massive pillars of stone on a hilltop in southern Turkey.'[41]

The good quality of Karacadag grain may have led workers returning home to take some with them to sow in their own gardens at Jerf el Ahmar and other settlements, eventually step-by-step even as far as Jericho itself. In addition to seashells and shiny obsidian that we know Neolithic people traded, the first domesticated strains of grain may also have spread across the Near East. Indeed, there is more obsidian at Jericho than one would expect for a town of that size; it may therefore have been a trading centre and one of its commodities may have been the Neolithic itself.

More than environment: preternatural seeing

The rock-cut structures and carvings at Göbekli Tepe and the highlighted eyes of the Jericho skulls point to an unavoidable part of human life, one that

Childe, as a Marxist, and more recent environmentalist archaeologists have tended to ignore, or, at any rate, to deprive of any causal influence. We suggest that 'conversion' from one belief system to another means accepting new understandings of the functioning of the human brain and the mental states that it produces (though, of course, the people themselves do not see it that way). What were once regarded as aberrant, meaningless mental states may, with a change in religious perspective, become central divine intimations. In short, we need to examine human consciousness, not just in the alert, problem-solving state that we cultivate today, but also in the more mysterious states that, in some circumstances, become the essence of religion.

Samuel Taylor Coleridge provides a useful introduction to those mystical states. He wrote romantically about his own brush with that segment of experience when he composed what he later called 'a psychological curiosity'. He left an enlightening description of that occasion.[42]

In 1797, he was living in a 'lonely farm-house' on Exmoor, southwest England. Having ingested an 'anodyne', almost certainly opium, he fell into 'a profound sleep, at least of the external senses'. In this condition, 'all the images rose up before him as *things* ... without any sensation or consciousness of effort' (his emphasis). Suddenly, his train of thought was interrupted by the arrival of the now-infamous but anonymous 'person on business from Porlock'. As Coleridge awoke he had 'a distinct recollection of the whole', but, when after more than an hour, the visitor (at last) left, he found that, 'though he still retained some vague and dim recollection of the general purport of the vision', all but 'some eight or ten scattered lines and images ... had passed away'. It was out of those recollections that he composed his frequently – and justly – anthologized 'Kubla Khan' (see box opposite).

The poem is of interest because it encapsulates, in a familiar setting, a number of points about the experiences of altered consciousness. Well-known words can be read with new eyes. The following are among the points that assume prominence in subsequent chapters:

- Images grade one into another.
- There is a subterranean river flowing through 'caverns measureless to man'.
- The river leads to 'a sunless sea'; water and subterranean spaces go together.
- A sense, or fear, of falling: 'that deep romantic chasm'; sinking 'in tumult'.
- There is a sense of floating.

Kubla Khan
Samuel Taylor Coleridge

In Xanadu did Kubla Khan
A stately pleasure-dome decree :
Where Alph, the sacred river, ran
Through caverns measureless to man
Down to a sunless sea.
So twice five miles of fertile ground
With walls and towers were girdled
  round :
And there were gardens bright with
  sinuous rills,
Where blossomed many an incense-
  bearing tree ;
And here were forests ancient as the hills,
Enfolding sunny spots of greenery.

But oh ! that deep romantic chasm
  which slanted
Down the green hill athwart a cedarn
  cover !
A savage place ! as holy and enchanted
As e'er beneath a waning moon was
  haunted
By woman wailing for her demon-lover !
  And from this chasm, with ceaseless
  turmoil seething,
As if this earth in fast thick pants were
  breathing,
A mighty fountain momently was forced :
Amid whose swift half-intermitted burst
Huge fragments vaulted like rebounding
  hail,
Or chaffy grain beneath the thresher's
  flail :
And 'mid these dancing rocks at once
  and ever
It flung up momently the sacred river.

Five miles meandering with a mazy
  motion
Through wood and dale the sacred river
  ran,
Then reached the caverns measureless to
  man,
And sank in tumult to a lifeless ocean :
And 'mid this tumult Kubla heard from
  far
Ancestral voices prophesying war !
The shadow of the dome of pleasure
Floated midway on the waves ;
Where was heard the mingled measure
From the fountain and the caves.
It was a miracle of rare device,
A sunny pleasure-dome with caves of ice !

A damsel with a dulcimer
In a vision once I saw :
It was an Abyssinian maid,
And on her dulcimer she played,
Singing of Mount Abora.
Could I revive within me
Her symphony and song,
To such a deep delight 'twould win me,
That with music loud and long,
I would build that dome in air,
That sunny dome ! those caves of ice !
And all who heard should see them there,
And all should cry, Beware ! Beware !
His flashing eyes, his floating hair !
Weave a circle round him thrice,
And close your eyes with holy dread,
For he on honey-dew hath fed,
And drunk the milk of Paradise.

 – If the poet could recapture his vision, all would cry, 'Beware!/His flashing eyes, his floating hair!'

Although it may not at first glance seem so, there is much in this last point
that is relevant to the rituals that took place at Jericho, Nevali Çori and
Göbekli Tepe. Eyes, properly stimulated to provide otherwise unattainable
insights, would inspire in others 'holy dread' and cause them to close their
own eyes; to submit to those believed to have preternatural sight; to shut out
realities of the diurnal world and to seek 'realities' of inner enlightenment.

To understand how such experiences as Coleridge's can influence human
behaviour and to see that they are far more common than is usually supposed, we need to enquire what happens in the human brain in visionary
states. We say 'states' because we are not dealing with a single, on/off, aberrant
mental condition that is experienced by only a few rather strange people but
with the fundamental, daily electro-chemical functioning of all human brains.
Moreover, 'anodynes' and 'the milk of Paradise' are not the only means of
access to visions, to 'seeing'; in some sense, 'visions' are also part of daily life.

Whatever influence the material environment may have on human behaviour, and we do not underestimate its power, all people have to live with and
to accommodate the products of their brains in a society of other brains and
bodies. That complex neurological and social accommodation makes them
what they are. Coleridge was not isolated on Exmoor. As he himself
recounted, he had been reading Samuel Purchas's travelogues, much admired
by the Romantics. Later, in 1817, Coleridge was delighted to encounter similar imagery in Henry Francis Cary's translation of Dante's *Inferno* with its
'brooklet, that descends/This way along the hollow of a rock' and caves with
'jagged ice'. In Purchas's narratives, he found plenty of material to feed his
desire for primitive mystery, exotic legends and an unfettered imagination
that broke free of Reason. Coleridge contributed handsomely to the Romantic Movement, but he was also a child of his time. Individual brains, whether
19th-century or Neolithic, must function within a web of social and conceptual relations.

Before we offer religious experience, belief and practice as possible stimuli
for the revolutionary changes of the Neolithic period, we must examine more
closely the functioning of the brain, for it is the organ that does the believing
and generates the emotions of rituals, not in esoteric isolation but in multi-
component social matrices.

CHAPTER 2

The Consciousness Contract

Jean-Jacques Rousseau (1712–1778; Fig. 7) was on the run for ten years. During that time he lodged with friends and patrons, often under an assumed name, and earned his living by means of clerical and tutorial appointments and by teaching music, a lifelong passion. Things had started well, at least from a literary point of view. He was born in Geneva and, after being brought up by various relatives, he moved to France where, in 1750, he won a prize for an essay entitled *Discours sur les Sciences et les Arts*. His real problems started in 1762 with one of the works for which he is best known, *Du Contrat Social*.

Readers of that book should have been prepared for his radical ideas. In *Discours sur les Sciences et les Arts* he had argued that civilization corrupted 'natural man' by promoting inequality, which it inevitably associated with idleness and suffering. Optimistically, Rousseau saw 'natural man' as an ideal. It was, however, John Dryden (1631–1700) who, in his play *The Conquest of Granada* (1670), coined what was to become a famous phrase:

> I am as free as nature first made man,
> Ere the base laws of servitude began,
> When wild in woods the noble savage ran.
> (PT 1, ACT 1, SC. 1)

Rousseau's ideas about the 'noble savage' broke forth lucidly and forcefully in the 'Social Contract'. The clarion call of his famous opening sentence was unmistakable: 'Man is born free, and everywhere he is in chains.' And so his incognito years of shifting abode began. His books were publicly condemned and burned. Warrants were issued for his arrest. He felt the constraints of the chains that he so roundly denounced.

The central ideas of the 'Social Contract' are now well known. Political rule should not be imposed by state or church but be ratified by common agreement. Whoever refused to 'contract in' would be forced to do so by 'the entire body: which means nothing other than that he shall be forced to be free'[1] – a splendid oxymoron. Every government would be provisional, and the people would regularly call it to account and consider renewal of its mandate. But

7 Jean-Jacques Rousseau: 'True Christians are made to be slaves; they know it and are hardly aroused by it.'[2]

Rousseau realized that the notion of common consent was flawed. He accepted that 'a single ambitious man among them, a single hypocrite' may get the better of the pious.[3] Here we have the seeds of much later social theory that sees society as the outcome of competing individuals, rather than a contract. So much for the secular arm.

Religion came in for scrutiny in his chapter 'Of civil religion'. 'No state,' Rousseau claimed, 'has ever been founded without Religion serving as its base.'[4] Institutionalized religion 'being founded on error and lies … deceives men, makes them credulous, and drowns the true cult of the divinity in vain ceremonial'.[5] More explicitly, and more dangerously, he proclaimed, 'Christianity preaches nothing but servitude and dependence. Its spirit is too favourable to tyranny for tyranny not always to profit from it.'[6] No wonder there was an outcry.

From a 21st-century position and as a prelude to further thoughts about the Neolithic, it is intriguing to look at Rousseau's notion that religion served as part of the 'base' for every state. In what is now a post-Marxist world, 'base' puts us in mind of Marxism's cornerstone: the fundamentals of all communities reside not in people's minds but in those relations between social groups that make production of the necessities of daily life possible – in Marxist jargon, the 'infrastructure'. The 'superstructure' of a society comprises the ideas, cosmology and ideology that oil the wheels of labour and production by concealing from the masses the fact that they are, in reality, being exploited. Hence Marx's famous 1843 dictum: Religion is the opium of the people. The pithy aphorism must have struck home, for Charles Kingsley (1819–1875), son of the parsonage, author of *The Water-Babies*, vigorous social reformer, contributor to *The Christian Socialist* and champion of muscular Christianity, wrote: 'We have used the Bible as if it was a constable's handbook – an opium-dose for keeping beasts of burden patient while they are being overloaded.'[7]

The other contract

Yet Rousseau was not a thoroughgoing atheist. 'Natural man,' he believed, had within him a religion 'without Temples, without altars, without rites, limited to the purely internal cult of the Supreme God and the eternal duties of morality.'[8] He allowed that there is 'Something pure' in the hearts of natural men. This, he said, is 'true Theism',[9] a 'purely internal cult' – but he did not say in exactly what sense it is 'internal'.

We approach this question of 'internal' feelings and religious experience from a perspective that explains why someone like Rousseau, despite all his reasoning, felt that there was Something, if not the God of traditional Christianity, in all people, and why such a notion is elaborated in a great many different ways in all human societies from the most 'natural' to the most 'civilized' – from Neolithic Jericho and Göbekli Tepe to 21st-century London and New York. We argue that a social contract is not the whole story; another, concomitant, 'contract' is necessary for human beings to cope with daily mental experiences, and it is out of this other 'contract' that notions of the ineffable and the three dimensions of religion flow: experience, belief and practice.

We therefore seek
- the experiential foundations of beliefs in supernatural realms and beings;
- the origins of cosmologies that represent both material and spiritual components of the universe;
- the origin of social distinctions that are based on esoteric knowledge and experience, and which therefore cut across brute force, age and sex;
- and also the ways in which these experiences, cosmologies and social distinctions can be marshalled in activities that we call religious practices.

In doing so, we point to a neurologically based *consciousness contract* in the earliest days of the Neolithic, one that people variously formulated and (sometimes violently) negotiated as the millennia passed. Using 'contract' more metaphorically than literally, we argue that every social contract is necessarily and intimately bound up with a consciousness contract. This second contract contributes substantially to theism and cosmologies. Like the social contract, it too has chains. 'Religion', or, as Rousseau would prefer it, 'Theism', was the first foundation for social discrimination that went beyond the criteria of age, sex and physical strength.[10] Importantly, it leads to an understanding of Jericho's skulls beneath house floors, rock-cut Göbekli crypts and other features of the Neolithic that we describe in later chapters.

The ineluctable brain

Some archaeologists express reservations about introducing notions of consciousness into accounts of past behaviour. With fine understatement, Colin Renfrew remarks that many writers see all research into past beliefs as 'an uncertain endeavour'.[11] How can we account for their reluctance?

Perhaps some sceptics believe the sort of approach we advocate to be (rather vaguely) associated with the hippie tendencies of the 1960s. That movement was an interesting social phenomenon, but it has nothing to do with the research strategy we practise – except in that it placed unusual (for Western society) emphasis on altered states of consciousness, states that hippie leaders misguidedly thought of as 'enhanced consciousness'. As a result, anything to do with altered consciousness seems, for many scientific researchers, bizarre, nebulous and peripheral to real life.

In making that judgment, they are in error. Neurological and neuropsychological laboratory research has supplied (and still is supplying) relevant information on human thought and consciousness. In ignoring this work, researchers deny themselves access to a bridge over troubled millennia. In what sense do we have a neurological bridge to the Neolithic?

Just as other parts of human bodies today are the same as they were during the Neolithic, so too is the general structure of the human brain and its electro-chemical functioning. Lest this statement seem simplistic and deterministic, we make explicit a key caveat. We distinguish between the fundamental functioning of the nervous system and the cultural milieux that supply much of its specific content. For example, we may perceive our skin to prickle in certain neurological circumstances, but the way in which a Westerner understands that sensation differs markedly from the way that a San hunter of the Kalahari Desert in southern Africa interprets it. For the Westerner, it is simply a meaningless experience; for the San hunter, it is the blood of an animal that he will soon kill – a good omen.[12] The neurological approach we prosecute in our research is thus in no way deterministic: *all* the stages and experiences of consciousness that we distinguish are mediated by culture. As this and subsequent chapters unfold, the central importance of a distinction between neurological universals and cultural specifics will become increasingly clear. Human beings are not automatons, slaves to their neural pathways.

At the same time, it will be evident that the many culturally specific ways of dealing with, or conceptualizing, shifting human consciousness are not infinite. There are some common construals, or understandings, of specific neurologically generated experiences. This observation is crucial. After all, differences between belief systems are not remarkable; one expects people living in, say, Siberia to have a different religion and cosmology from those in South America. What is remarkable is the empirically established existence of commonalities. Certain beliefs and experiences crop up in religions around the world. We argue that the commonalities we highlight cannot be explained in any other way than by the functioning of the universal human nervous system. That is why the ethnographic accounts we cite are not material for dubious, one-off arguments by analogy. On the contrary, they *illustrate* different *and* similar ways in which people understand and harness the fundamentals of human consciousness. Moreover, our ethnographic illustrations are so geographically diverse that they rebut the potential criticism that certain beliefs originated in some religious heartland and then diffused throughout the world; there is no clear centre from which ideas diffuse. They also open up a route to better informed, more varied interpretations of past human behaviour and its material residues.

We submit that it is impossible to discuss ancient religions and cosmologies in anything but a superficial, periphrastic way without recognizing the input of the human nervous system as it daily produces varied states of consciousness. As we remarked in our Preface, all religions have an ecstatic component, and, less dramatically, all involve altering consciousness by prayer, chanting, prolonged rhythmic dancing, and other techniques that we list below. Refusal to consider the role of consciousness in the past therefore effectively vitiates attempts to explain ancient (and modern) religious human experiences, beliefs and practice.

The strict separation between church and state that is advocated, if not practised, in the modern West is a comparatively novel, post-Rousseau position. Archaeologists are, generally speaking, part of this tradition. As a result, they accept that present-day governments should take decisions about economic matters, national defence, international relations and so forth rationally and without recourse to religion. If an American president announces that his decisions are guided by God, alarm bells start ringing. The associated assumption that rational decision-making and processes, such as sensible adaptation to the environment, can account for all past human behaviour is groundless. It imputes contemporary Western values to past societies. We must be more alert to the irrationality of the past (and of the present).

Elements of the consciousness contract

To dispel any notion that the forms of consciousness we discuss are 'special' or are experienced only by 'visionaries', 'mystics', 'saints', 'seers' and 'prophets', we begin with eight rather bizarre narratives that we label A to H. Before revealing their origins, we use them as diverse examples of human experience. We ask:
  – Do they have any common themes and images?
  – If so, why do they?

(A) Golden dots, sparks and tiny stars appear before my eyes. These sparks and stars gradually merge into a golden net with diagonal meshes which moves slowly and regularly in rhythm with the beating of my heart, which I feel quite distinctly. The next moment the golden net is transformed into rows of brass helmets belonging to Roman soldiers marching along the street below. I hear their measured tread and watch them from the window of a high house in Galata, in Constantinople, in a narrow lane, one end of which leads to the old wharf and the Golden Horn with its ships and steamers and the minarets of Stamboul behind them. The Roman soldiers march on and in close ranks along the lane. I hear their heavy measured tread, and see the sun shining on their helmets. Then suddenly I detach myself from the windowsill on which I am lying and in the same reclining position fly slowly over the lane, over the houses, then over the Golden Horn in the direction of Stamboul. I smell the sea, feel the wind, the warm sun. This flying gives me a wonderfully pleasant sensation, and I cannot help opening my eyes.

(B) [S]uddenly I saw a large green eye opening and closing. Also something very vague moving in the dark, like a train entering a tunnel or something similar, not very clear. Then, a landscape – outline of hills – very fluid – moving. A wolf's face grinning … View of a tree from under the ground – seen as if I were lying under the tree looking up through its roots.

(C) Brilliant rays of light. A great many geometric shapes. Something animate – could be a human but animal-like with big teeth. Forest – lots of greenery and flowers. A dragon. Many interwoven snakes. Prehistoric creatures. Birds.

(D) With the appearance of scenery and interiors I acquire a new faculty – that of travel. Though still aware that some aspect of myself remains in the body, I go on exploring expeditions through houses, streets and country lanes, or wander through the aisles of vast cathedrals … I once found myself, with an indescribable feeling of happiness and freedom, walking down a corridor built of transparent, iridescent planes set at angles to one another, rather as if I were inside a prism, though the arrangement of planes was more complicated than that …

(E) I was moving at high speed towards a net of great luminosity. The strands and knots where the luminous lines intersected were vibrating with tremendous cold energy. The grid appeared as a barrier that I did not want to move through, though for a brief moment my speed appeared to slow down. Then I was in the grid.

(F) We were never more wide awake, and the visions came whether our eyes were opened or closed … They began with art motifs, angular such as might decorate carpets or textiles or wallpaper or the drawing board of an architect. They evolved into palaces with courts, arcades, gardens – resplendent palaces all laid over with precious stones. Then I saw a mythological beast drawing a regal chariot. Later it was as though the walls of our house had dissolved, and my spirit had flown forth, and I was suspended in mid-air viewing landscapes of mountains … There I was, poised in space, a disembodied eye, invisible, incorporeal, seeing but not seen.

(G) He reported intensely illuminated and brilliantly coloured geometrics. After a time they took on the appearance of richly patterned carpets or mosaics. Soon they gave way to recognizable scenes: a chipmunk here, a dandelion there, all playfully displayed. They appeared like a slide show flashing about two feet in front of his eyes, but solid and three-dimensional, almost vivacious … The tunnel belched and geared its images, then inhaled and sucked Terry into its very center of light … Terry flew through an aurora borealis, under mandalas, over buildings, mountains, and giant lollipops. He saw many images repeating and multiplying … 'Oh my God,' exclaimed Terry, 'there's a bunch of eyeballs watching me! … There's a large one glaring at me from the center surrounded by smaller ones. They almost form a spiral.

(H) When you are learning to be a doctor, your teacher can take you to a big hole in the spirit world … The teacher shows you the line that takes you there. It looks like a white slanted line in the sky that goes underground … The underground place is called *n/um dom*. It means 'spirit hole'. The place in the sky is called *n/a'an*, meaning 'sky'. When I am in the dance and see the ropes, I can go either up or down … If I don't cool down, my body will disappear. The hot steam inside me leaves my body, giving me new eyes. The eyes can become any colour. I can change into another form and travel to other places. I once changed into a lizard.

I also see horizontal lines. They are coloured red, green, black, and white. The lines are connected to the Bushman doctors … The lines go in all directions.

For me, the lines are usually bright and shining. They pulse, like a pulsing smoke.

It would be easy to accept that all these accounts were provided by people under the influence of psychotropic drugs, and researchers have sometimes fallen into the error of assuming that visions and hallucinations are exclusively the product of hallucinogens and therefore of only limited relevance in untangling the past.[13] Indeed, all eight narratives seem to be intense hallucinations that are reminiscent of Coleridge's drug-induced vision of Xanadu. Yet that is not so.

Reports A to D are of vivid mental imagery experienced in an intermediate state between wakefulness and sleep.[14] They are known as 'hypnagogic' experiences. 'Hypnopompic' refers to comparable experiences encountered in awakening from sleep; it is customary not to distinguish the two and to use 'hypnagogic' to refer to both. Report E is an account of a near-death experience.[15] F and G describe drug-induced hallucinations (hallucinogenic mushrooms and cannabis respectively).[16] Ronald Siegel, who recorded narrative G, subsequently found that the vision of eyes derived from a training slide that he had used with his subjects.[17] H comprises statements given by two southern African San healers. Their altered states are induced by rhythmic dancing, auditory-driving (persistent, highly rhythmical sound patterns) and hyperventilation; they do not use hallucinogens.[18]

We have included four hypnagogic narratives because the state is not well known, even though it is part of everyday life. It is hard to say what percentage of the human population are hypnagogists. Some surveys suggest 70 and more per cent. But it is impossible to say if the remaining 25 or so per cent are unable to experience hypnagogia or whether they are untrained, or simply do not expect, to do so.[19] Many people experience hypnagogia, but dismiss the condition as mere dreaming. But hypnagogic experiences are not the same as dreams. Importantly, attending to hypnagogic experiences increases their duration and frequency.[20] People can learn to engage, control and prolong both their hypnagogic experiences and their dreams.[21]

An auditory component is not uncommon in hypnagogic experiences. The psychologist Andreas Mavromatis gives an example. The subject sees a ship at sea:

She cut through the water, making little waves that broke into foam … when quite suddenly and authoritatively a voice spoke on my right a little behind my pillow: 'There's no occasion to warn her. We've got one ship off already.'[22]

Another common feature of hypnagogia is synaesthesia, that is, sensations in one sensory modality being experienced in another. Through synaesthesia, people experience sounds as colours, or feel that they can touch music.[23]

Hypnagogic experiences are frequently so detailed and strange and include such peculiar transpositions of familiar and unfamiliar objects that those who experience them feel that they wish to draw their imagery.[24] Artists such as Max Ernst, Salvador Dali and René Magritte have succumbed to this urge. Dali consciously encouraged hypnagogia. He

is said to have trained himself to doze in a chair with his chin resting on a spoon which was held in one hand, propped by his elbow which rested on a table; in this position, when his muscles relaxed and he was on the verge of falling asleep, his chin would drop and he would wake, often in the middle of a hypnagogic dream or vision which he would then proceed to paint.[25]

In a similar vein, Magritte referred to his own paintings as 'the representations of half sleep'.[26] Hypnagogia is more important than is commonly supposed.

From the eight reports we have given we can reach two initial conclusions. First, we can see that human visions, or hallucinations, have much in common. Secondly, it is remarkable that, *despite the diversity of the means of induction*, the mental experiences of altered states are similar. We list some commonalities briefly:

– seeing bright geometric patterns,
– floating or flying,
– passage through a tunnel,
– transformations of one thing into another,
– transformations into animal forms,
– ability to see mercurially, though vividly.

A larger sample of reports would provide more repeated elements that we could add to this list. For instance, the image of shining helmets of the Roman soldiers walking in a line is known as 'polyopsia'. Mental images sometimes multiply rather like reflections in parallel mirrors that seem to trail off into infinity. Then, too, micropsia and macropsia, seeing things very small or large, are also common to the types of experiences we have illustrated.

Noting such commonalities, Ronald Siegel, together with many other neurologists and psychologists, concluded that 'These phenomena arise from common structures in the brain and nervous system, common biological experiences, and common reactions of the central nervous system to stimulation.'[27] Because the experiences are repeated and 'wired' into the human brain we can generalize and organize them into a model that will help us to understand the progression of altered states of consciousness in human beings – no matter what their particular culture or point in human history. Each historical instance will be a unique product of an interaction between human neurology and culture.

We cannot overestimate the importance of this understanding for the arguments we develop in subsequent chapters. We do indeed have a 'neurological viaduct' that carries us over the abyss of the centuries, and even millennia, to thought-lives and religious experiences that archaeologists have long considered beyond recovery. Those ancient experiences were neither random nor irretrievably unique.

A neuropsychological model

Altered states of consciousness may be induced by more means than the ones to which we have so far referred. A list would include:
- ingestion of psychotropic substances,
- hypnagogia,
- near-death experiences,
- intense, rhythmic dancing,
- auditory-driving (e.g., chanting, clapping, drumming),
- electrical stimulation,
- flickering light,
- fatigue,
- hunger,
- sensory deprivation,
- extreme pain,
- intense concentration (meditation),
- migraine,
- temporal lobe epilepsy,
- schizophrenia and other pathological conditions.

The ways in which these conditions work in practice are more subtle and interactive than a bald list suggests. Among the South American Bororo, for instance, the first call to a potential shaman may come during the chanting of songs associated with souls, or spiritual entities. Some of these chants are sung all night.[28] 'Suddenly while singing the potential shaman feels a chill creeping up from the stomach and into the chest.'[29] At the same time he (Bororo shamans are always men) may smell the odour of rotting corpses (associated with the *bope*, roughly, the principles of life and death) and *urucu* paste used to decorate the bones of the dead (a substance associated with *aroe*, spirits, in some ways the antithesis of the *bope*). In the days following this introductory experience, dreams begin, in which, accompanied by a small, beautifully decorated child, he walks down a 'wide, clean road towards a large water bird that suddenly changes into a person'. Or he may find himself and the child 'floating along just above the bottom of a river, surrounded by fish that change into people, and then back to fish'. In a subsequent definitive dream, he confronts a monster that turns out to be a spirit of someone who has recently died.[30] Here we see a combination of chanting and, later, a series of dreams leading a person towards becoming a shaman. The long road, the sense of floating underwater and people changing into animals are, as we later explain, neurologically wired experiences and are evident in the eight accounts of altered consciousness we have quoted. In addition, hallucinations are experienced in more senses than just sight: the initiate smells rotting corpses and *urucu* paste.

The overall structure of our neuropsychological model can be inferred from the eight statements we have provided.[31] We identify three potential stages through which people pass as they move into deeper and deeper levels of altered consciousness, no matter what means of induction they use (Fig. 8).[32]

It is important to note that the three stages we identify constitute an idealized *model* of the possible course of a person's experience of altered states of consciousness. We do not imply that all people always pass through all three stages.[33] Nor are the stages discrete; they grade one into another. Because the sequence is not ineluctable, some people move directly into Stage 3. Culturally informed expectations and interests may highlight one or other stage. If, for example, a culture places high value on Stage-3 hallucinations (which may include beings from myths), people seeking those visions may dismiss Stage-1 percepts as of no importance. We therefore re-emphasize the point that our three-stage model generalizes (this is what all models do) the progression of

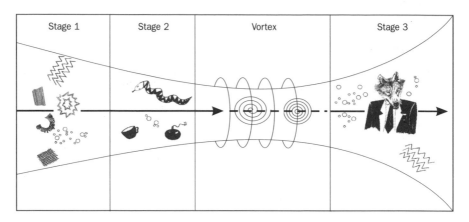

Stage 1	Stage 2	Vortex	Stage 3

8 The three stages of altered consciousness. As the human mind moves into deeper altered states, people's hallucinations shift from scintillating geometric forms through a narrow tunnel or vortex to bizarre full sensory hallucinations.

altered states: it does not imply that every altered state experienced by every person follows the full progression of the model from Stage 1 to Stage 3.

Stage 1

As statements A, C, E, F, G and H show, altered states often start with geometric mental images. Researchers have given these percepts various names: form constants,[34] phosphenes,[35] endogenous percepts[36] and entoptic phenomena.[37] We prefer the term 'entoptic', which means generated anywhere in the optic system, not necessarily within the eye itself, which would be 'entophthalmic'.[38] By and large, seven frequently repeated forms can be identified:

(1) a grid and its development into a lattice or expanding hexagon pattern;

(2) sets of parallel lines;

(3) bright dots and short flecks;

(4) zigzag lines, reported by some subjects as angular, by others as undulating;

(5) nested catenary curves, the outer arc of which comprises flickering zigzags (well known to migraine sufferers as the 'fortification illusion');

(6) filigrees, or thin meandering lines;

(7) spirals (see the section on the vortex below).

Because these forms are mercurial and appear in combinations, the seven categories are not rigid. Moreover, the percepts pulsate with bright light that is independent of any source in the subjects' environment. They rotate, expand, contract, combine and change one into another. They may be projected on to veridical imagery when the eyes are open, as many people know from experiencing migraine scotoma that obliterates parts of the visual field. (Migraine sufferers commonly report a scotoma comprising scintillating zigzags [5]; more rarely, they perceive lattices [1], whorls [7], funnels [7] and webs [1].[39]) The manner in which they seem to float on walls or ceilings is important.

In A we read of 'Golden dots, sparks and tiny stars' (type 3) that 'gradually merge into a golden net with diagonal meshes [type 1] which moves slowly and regularly in rhythm with the beating of my heart' (pulsating). The narrator of C reports 'Brilliant rays of light' (type 2) and 'A great many geometric shapes' (various types). E describes 'a net of great luminosity' and a 'grid' (type 1) that vibrated 'with tremendous cold energy' (pulsating). Another subject, F, spoke of 'art motifs, angular' (various entoptic types). The 'mandalas' of G are probably the circular, bright dots or discs of type 3. G also spoke of 'intensely illuminated and brilliantly coloured geometrics' (various types). The San healer, H, spoke of coloured 'horizontal lines' (types 2 and 6) that were 'usually bright and shining'; she added, 'They pulse, like a pulsing smoke.'

At this point, we note that, even though all people have the potential to see all the forms, cultural emphases may lead them to value some and to ignore others. People in societies that accord the experiences of altered states of consciousness important religious status therefore watch for, and try to cultivate, a restricted range of forms, the ones to which their religion ascribes emotionally charged spiritual meanings. Here religious belief begins to make sense of, and to give form to, neurologically generated, religious experience. Belief may fashion selected entoptic percepts into a system of symbols. The Tukano people of South America, for instance, take undulating parallel lines (type 4) to represent 'the thought of the Sun-Father'. An arc of several multicoloured parallel lines (type 5) is taken, understandably enough, to represent a rainbow, but in some mythological contexts that would be impossible for an outsider to guess, it is said to be the Sun-Father's penis.[40] As the hallucinating men speak of their visions, a kumú (a direct representative of the solar divinity who has esoteric knowledge) explains them and their accompanying sounds. The San, on the other hand, concentrate on brilliant lines (types 2 and 6) that they believe to be 'threads of light' that healers climb, or along which they float, to the Great God in the sky. A similar vision has been reported from Australia. An Aboriginal boy taking part in an initiation ceremony that involved looking at 'a large, bright crystal that stole the light from the dawn and dazzled their eyes' sank 'into a state of repose that was almost sleep'. Then he saw cords that 'seemed to rise into the air, and the old fellows climbed hand over hand up them to treetop height'.[41]

What Neolithic people in various places and at various times made of entoptic phenomena is a matter we discuss in Chapters 4 and 9.

STAGE 2

When people move into the deeper, second stage of altered consciousness, they try to make sense of the entoptic forms they are seeing by construing them as objects with emotional or religious significance.[42] In a normal state of consciousness the brain receives a constant stream of sense impressions. A visual image reaching the brain is decoded (as, of course, are other sense impressions) by being matched against a store of experience. If a 'fit' can be effected, the image is 'recognized'. In altered states of consciousness the nervous system itself becomes a 'sixth sense' that produces a variety of images including entoptic phenomena.[43] The brain attempts to recognize, or decode, these forms as it does with impressions supplied by the nervous system in a normal state of consciousness. The psychiatrist Mardi Horowitz links this process of making sense to the disposition of the subject:

Thus the same ambiguous round shape on initial perceptual representation can be 'illusioned' into an orange (if the subject is hungry), a breast (if he is in a state of heightened sexual drive), a cup of water (if he is thirsty), or an anarchist's bomb (if he is hostile or fearful) [original parentheses].[44]

This sort of construal seems to be taking place in the experience labelled A: the 'golden net' transforms into 'rows of brass helmets belonging to Roman soldiers'. In B, a bright, pulsating light becomes 'a large green eye opening and closing'; while in C 'geometric shapes' become 'interwoven snakes'. In F angular motifs 'evolved into palaces with courts, arcades, gardens … all laid over with precious stones'. The 'intensely illuminated and brilliantly coloured geometrics' of G 'took on the appearance of richly patterned carpets or mosaics'. If any of these experiences had been set in a religious context, the entoptic phenomena would have been construed as supernatural entities, beings or symbols.

VORTEX

As subjects move towards Stage 3, a more profoundly altered state of consciousness, they often experience a vortex or tunnel, at the end of which is bright light. On the internal surface of the vortex there is sometimes a grid, in the compartments of which appear the first iconic images of people, animals, monsters and so forth (Fig. 9).[45]

9 *As people pass through the vortex into the deepest stage of altered consciousness, they experience the first iconic hallucinations.*

Today, the vortex is popularly associated with near-death experiences (E) and is frequently discussed.[46] Examples abound. A child who was grievously ill and was rushed to hospital later recalled: 'I was moving through this … long dark place. It seemed like a sewer or something.'[47] Another person who had been near to death recounted his passing down a passageway: 'I floated on down the hall and out of the door onto the screened-in porch … I floated right straight on through the screen … and up into this pure crystal light.'[48] Less beatific experiences have also been recorded: 'It was like being in a cylinder which had no air in it.'[49]

The near-death phenomenon is by no means the only context in which a vortex is experienced. The hypnagogic experience described in B invokes the image of 'a train entering a tunnel or something similar'; while that in D describes wandering 'through the aisles of vast cathedrals' and 'walking down a corridor built of transparent, iridescent planes set at angles to one another'.

We dispel the possibility that these tunnel experiences may be unique to the Western culture from which all but one of our examples come by pointing out that shamans around the world frequently use similar imagery to describe their out-of-body travels to the spirit realm, regardless of the way in which they alter their consciousness. The San healer in narrative H, for example, spoke of 'a big hole in the spirit world' and of following a line 'that goes underground'. Similarly, a Sora shaman in India climbs down a huge tree that leads to the underworld: 'The path includes dizzying precipices on the descent to the "murky-sun country, cock-crowlight country".'[50] Descent to an underworld is indeed a common shamanistic experience, and Mircea Eliade collated a number of accounts of such journeys in his book *Shamanism: Archaic Techniques of Ecstasy*.[51] For instance, Siberian Yakut shamans' costumes had attached to them symbols known as 'Opening into the Earth' or 'Hole of the Spirits'; these enabled them to travel to the nether realms.[52] A Tungus shaman, also in Central Asia, sometimes descends to the underworld, a dangerous undertaking during which 'he goes into ecstasy' and 'goes down through a narrow hole and crosses three streams before he comes upon the spirits of the infernal regions'.[53]

Another Siberian shaman told of his initiation. His spirit guide, who was associated with a tree that the young man had cut down, took him to a hole in the earth.

My companion asked: 'What hole is this? If your destiny is to make a [shaman's] drum of this tree, find it out!' I replied: 'It is through this hole that the shaman receives the spirit of his voice.' The hole became larger and larger. We descended through it and arrived at a river with two streams flowing in opposite directions. 'Well, find out this one too!' said my companion, 'one stream goes from the centre to the north, the other to the south – the sunny side. If you are destined to fall into a trance, find it out!' [Parenthesis added].[54]

In Central America, the Maya were particularly sensitive to holes in the ground: 'To the Classic Maya, all natural openings into the earth, whether caves or cenotes (sunken waterholes), were portals to the Otherworld.'[55] In West Africa, a Bwiti man expressed the tunnel sensation in terms of his own environment: 'When I ate *eboka* (*Tabernanthe iboga*) I found myself taken by it up a long road in a deep forest until I came to a barrier of black iron.'[56]

A more complex interpretation of the vortex comes from the Colombian Tukano, who induce altered states by means of the hallucinogenic vine *yajé* (*Banisteriopsis caapi*), given to them, as Geraldo Reichel-Dolmatoff put it, by the Sun 'to serve as an intermediary so that through hallucinations people could put themselves in contact with all the other supernatural beings.'[57] They see the cosmos as two cones connected by a circular door, 'an image that leads to others such as "birth", "rebirth", the passage from one "dimension" (*turi*) to another while under the influence of a narcotic, and to similar shamanistic images'.[58] The South American Piro also speak of passing underground: 'He slipped into a big hole ... He went down into that hole. When he came out again, he was in another world by a shallow river.'[59]

Passing through 'portals' is an experience that is also associated with pathological conditions. A Western patient suffering from schizophrenia described his visions:

There were small suns and strange twilight worlds of lakes and islands ... An ancient cave, passage, or hollow ladder, seemed to connect new earths; perhaps this was such as Jacob saw, for it was an image of remote antiquity.[60]

A corollary of the vortex needs to be mentioned. One of the near-death experiences we cited recorded the sensation of being in a cylinder 'which had no air in it',[61] and the Siberian shaman spoke of 'two streams flowing in opposite directions'.[62] Similarly, a southern African San shaman said that he entered a wide river: 'My feet were behind, and my head was in front ... I travelled like this. My sides were pressed by pieces of metal. Metal things fastened my sides.'[63] The sensations of passing through a constraining vortex, difficulty in breathing, affected vision, a sense of being in another world, and weight-lessness are frequently interpreted as being underwater. In South America 'submersion in pools, springs, whirlpools, and rivers provides access to the underworld. The process by which one travels there is akin to drowning'.[64] Indeed, many shamans speak of diving into water. Lapp shamans, for instance, refer to altered states as 'immersion', and Inuit shamans situate the beyond in the sea.[65]

In Western clinical reports we read of passages, trains in tunnels, sewers and so forth; the ethnographic reports express the same sensations in their own imagery of holes in the ground, trees that link the sky (their foliage) to the underworld (their roots), subaquatic travel and so forth. Experiences of these kinds recall Coleridge's descent through 'caverns measureless to man' down to a 'sunless sea', 'a lifeless ocean', and the 'deep romantic chasm which slanted/Down the green hill athwart a cedarn cover'.

Together, all the descriptions we have given show that there is a common human proclivity to experience passage through a vortex. That commonality is clearly wired into the human nervous system and manifests itself in certain conditions of altered consciousness. Research has shown that this wiring is principally in the functional architecture of the striate cortex.[66] Small wonder, then, that passage through a tunnel and subaquatic travel will assume prime importance in both our Near East and Atlantic Europe chapters.

STAGE 3

Emerging from the vortex, subjects enter a bizarre, ever-changing world of hallucinations. People report somatic hallucinations, such as attenuation of limbs and bodies, intense awareness of one's body, polymelia (the sensation of having extra digits and limbs); zoopsia (seeing animals); changing into animals and other transformations. As long ago as 1880, William James, the American psychologist, philosopher and brother of the novelist, Henry, recorded the experiences of a friend who had ingested hashish; our observations are in square brackets:

Directly I lay down upon a sofa there appeared before my eyes several rows of human hands [polyopsia], which oscillated for a moment [pulsating], revolved and then changed into spoons [transformation]. The same motions were repeated, the objects changing to wheels, tin soldiers, lamp-posts, brooms, and countless other absurdities [some of these transformations appear to derive from entoptic forms 2 and 3] ... I became aware of the fact that my pulse was beating rapidly ... I could feel each pulsation through my whole system [somatic intensity] ... There were moments of apparent lucidity, when it seemed as if I could see within myself, and watch the pumping of my heart [preternatural sight]. A strange fear came over me, a certainty that I should never recover from the effects [heightened emotions] ... Suddenly there was a roar and a blast of sound and the word 'Ismaral' [aural hallucination] ... I thought of a fox, and instantly I was transformed into that animal. I could distinctly feel myself a fox, could see my long ears and bushy tail, and by a sort of introversion felt that my complete anatomy was that of a fox [transformation into an animal]. Suddenly, the point of vision changed. My eyes seemed to be located at the back of my mouth; I looked out between parted lips [somatic transformation].[67]

A feature of Stage 3 experiences like these is that the entoptic forms of Stage 1 persist, peripherally or integrated with iconic hallucinations. One subject found that the lattice, or grid form (type 1), merged with his body:

he saw fretwork before his eyes, that his arms, hands, and fingers turned into fretwork. There was no difference between the fretwork and himself, between inside and outside. All objects in the room and the walls changed into fretwork and thus became identical with him. While writing, the words turned into fretwork and there was, therefore, an identity of fretwork and handwriting. 'The fretwork is I.' He also felt, saw, tasted, and smelled tones that became fretwork. He himself was the tone. On the day following the experiment, there was Nissl (whom he had known in 1914) sitting somewhere in the air, and Nissl was fretwork [known as an 'after-image'].[68]

We can now summarize some points of interest that will assume significance in later chapters:
  – Entoptic forms may be projected onto surfaces and objects in the environment.
  – Subjects can themselves become an entoptic form.
  – Hallucinations are experienced in all senses.
  – The senses become confused so that one may smell a sound (synaesthesia).
  – After-images may recur unexpectedly some time after a hallucinatory experience.

Throughout all the accounts we have given we see an interaction between wired experiences that are activated in altered states of consciousness and the culturally specific content that is incorporated into those experiences. Human brains exist in societies.

We argue that it is out of the socially situated spectrum of consciousness, which we discuss in the next section, that religion develops. One could say that religious experience is, in the first instance, a result of taking the introverted end of the spectrum at face value – within a given cultural context.

The consciousness contract and society

Rousseau sought to devise a theory of how a society is structured and to explain how a just society could function by common consent. But there were niggling problems. These came out of his restricted notion of 'natural man'. He saw natural man as essentially rational: in an untainted state 'natural man' would see what was good for all and, apart from the 'single hypocrite' who would have to be forced to be free, could achieve justice for all. At the same time Rousseau believed that religion had formed a 'base' for every society the world had seen. It was easy for him to dismiss organized religion as he knew it in his time, but it was more difficult to explain away the universality of religious belief. A 'true Theism' that lodged deep inside every person was the best explanation he could find.

How does religion come to be such a potent force in communities? Can psychological and social explanations, which both have commendable points, be brought together? The answer lies in 'natural man', but in a more up-to-date formulation than Rousseau was able to achieve in the 18th century. 'Natural man' must, we now know, include human consciousness in all its shifting diversity.

Human beings are not either conscious or unconscious, as may be popularly supposed. Normal, everyday consciousness should rather be thought of as a spectrum.[69] At one end is alert consciousness – the kind that we use to relate rationally to our environment and to solve the problems that it presents. A little farther along the spectrum are more introverted states in which we solve problems by thought. Relax more and you are day-dreaming: mental images come and go at will, unfettered by the material world around you. Gradually, you slip into sleep and into the hypnagogic state, possibly with the vivid hallucinations that we have described. From there, you drift into normal dreaming, a world of changing forms and impossible circumstances.

These are all states that everyone experiences. But the introverted end of the spectrum can be intensified by the wide variety of means that we have listed: ingestion of hallucinogenic drugs, sensory deprivation, hunger, pain, auditory-driving, rhythmic dancing, intense concentration, certain pathological conditions and so forth. These means lead to the three stages of the neuropsychological model. Those stages are what most people think of as 'altered states of consciousness'.

We can now see that people do not have to resort to intentional induction in order to glimpse the highly 'altered' end of the spectrum. We all do it in dreaming, and many have the potential to do so in, for instance, hypnagogic states.[70] In addition, we may all pass through the three stages inadvertently if we happen to experience sensory deprivation, prolonged hunger, certain pathological conditions or any of the other triggering factors. Another realm of experience is, so to speak, always just around the corner.

Now, the important point is that some social relations are intimately bound up with states of consciousness. It is this proposition that solves Rousseau's dilemma concerning the place of religion in society. Every community of people has to come to terms with shifting human consciousness. Every community has to divide up the spectrum of consciousness and to place different values on its components – that is, to make shared sense of the diverse mental states that everyone experiences. It is, for instance, impossible to imagine a society that does not entertain some beliefs about what dreams are and what significance (if any) they have. Altered consciousness is therefore always situated in a social and political matrix. It is impossible to study altered states outside of a social context.[71]

Today, in the West we value alert consciousness and problem-solving cogitation. We do not value dreams. (Exceptions are, of course, a couple of schools of psychology that believe that dreams have a symbolic content.) Whatever inspiration may come to scientists in dreams, the answers to their research questions have to be rationally supported by mental activity at the alert end of the spectrum. Copernicus, Darwin, Einstein and Weber are enthroned in our pantheon. We know that this emphasis on rationality is not found in all societies, nor has it always been the case in the West. During the Middle Ages, people believed that God could communicate with them in dreams and visions; they did not laugh off their dreams as readily as we do (Pl. 1).[72] Dreams, visions and voices could be the foundation for disastrous military and political action, as Joan of Arc amply demonstrated. The Neolithic, we believe, must have been more like these societies than our own.

Along with the placing of different values on different kinds of consciousness goes a social concomitant. Because certain states are more highly valued than others, they are appropriated and defended by classes of people. In medieval Christianity, for instance, visions bestowed power, political as well as spiritual. The more intense forms of meditation and prayer were therefore the preserve of the clergy: it was they who, through extended prayer, solitary meditation, fasting, self-flagellation, repetitive ritual and chanting, altered their consciousness, and possibly even induced visions. In doing so, they entrenched or raised their status. The difference between monks and lay brothers in some monasteries was not just one of education: the monks through their chanting, fasting and incessant prayers were able to reach mental states considered closer to God than any that lay people could attain. Those few who could go beyond euphoria and dissociation to experience vivid visions were more likely to achieve positions of influence in the church and therefore in affairs of state as well. (Altered states were, of course, not the only road to power within the church.) When 'outsiders', such as adolescent girls, experienced visions of the Virgin Mary, they occupied an unusual, ambivalent social category and were investigated by the church. Sometimes the church found it politic to accept their revelations.

The inescapable need to accommodate shifting consciousness and the different values placed on segments of the spectrum means that, as we have seen, religion, long before the Christian era, was the first tool of social discrimination that was not founded on age, sex and strength.[73] New values entered human ethics. Importantly, it was the shifting nature of human consciousness that led people to suppose that there was another realm of existence and that beings in that realm interacted with people in the material world. The more a person, or group of people, inhabited the introverted end of the consciousness spectrum the closer they considered themselves to be to that other realm. That closeness distinguished them from ordinary people and was worth defending: access to 'spiritual' states was regulated. Religion and social discrimination went hand in hand.

Intrinsically, everyone does not have equal access to profound visionary states; it seems that some people are more likely than others to experience altered states. But everyone can understand what visions are because they experience dreams and the occasional 'other-worldly' incident, perhaps an elevating sense of Absolute Unitary Being (AUB, Chapter 1). Dreams are sufficiently emotionally charged to persuade people that the acknowledged seers of a community have access to powers beyond the ordinary. If dreams can frighten us, we can guess at the spiritual power that seers must possess to be able to confront visions.

Here we have a foundation on which the sort of church that Rousseau deplored can be built: religious and secular power inevitably becomes intertwined. In the largely unquestioning ethos of pre-Enlightenment Europe the threat of excommunication was sobering. Hell and the Devil lived not only in sermons and wall paintings in churches, but also in the brains and dreams of ordinary people, fed as they were by those sources of terror. No wonder, then, that some witches truly believed themselves to be in league with the Devil. They were victims of Christian doctrine.

At the beginning of the Neolithic, or perhaps at the end of the Upper Palae-olithic and in the Mesolithic (the period between the Upper Palaeolithic and the Neolithic), the interlinked social and consciousness contracts were chang-ing. Access to spirit realms was no longer through caves, as it was for the Upper Palaeolithic people of France and Spain, but through structures built above ground. The spirit realm itself, though, was not denied; it was too embedded in the brains of the people. But how it was structured – cosmology – was re-evaluated, refashioned and brought into line with a new social dis-pensation.

To form a better idea of how that new dispensation, the new, interwoven social and consciousness contracts of the Neolithic, functioned we examine the ways in which consciousness generates cosmology and how both are always situated in a specific cultural milieu. This is a rich seam that is well worth careful and meticulous mining. It is fundamental to a comprehensive, co-ordinated understanding of the Neolithic.

CHAPTER 3

Seeing and Building a Cosmos

Today, the study of the structure and functioning of the cosmos is a hot topic. It intrigues the general public, as well as physicists, astronomers and philosophers. Debate centres on such seemingly science-fiction concepts as black holes, worm holes and the 'big bang' that led to the formation of galaxies, solar systems, the night sky as we see it, and, of course, the earth itself. In the West, these debates are conducted principally (but not exclusively) by scientists and are based on physical and mathematical propositions. It was not always so.

The heat generated by contemporary debates is nothing compared with that produced in the 16th and 17th centuries in Europe when cosmology was largely the preserve of the Catholic Church. Today it seems odd that the church should have played such a role, but even in our present-day scientific milieu many people feel the tug of religious belief as they contemplate the cosmologists' hypotheses. Where, they wonder, in this vast universe is a place for God? Does the 'big bang' theory confirm a moment of divine creation? In extreme cases, creationists denounce everything but the two (contradictory) accounts of creation in Genesis, and demand that creationism be taught in schools. The importance of cosmology still extends beyond the purely scientific: the study affects people's lives at a deeper level than we sometimes allow.

The events that took Western thought from ecclesiastic cosmology to empirical observations of the solar system enshrine principles that apply to struggles that, we suggest, took place at the beginning of the Neolithic around 9,000 years ago. That is true especially of what is known as 'saving the appearances',[1] a notion to which we return below. There is always tension between a cosmology that arises 'spiritually' from within human beings, like the one that Catholic Church authorities favoured, and another that derives from people's observations of what they can see and measure.

The serious disputes began with Nicolaus Copernicus (1473–1543). He was ordained as a canon at Frauenburg, but preferred to spend his life studying at Italian universities and exploring the efficacy of mathematics in explaining the movements of planets. His *De revolutionibus* of 1543 revised

Ptolemy's (c. 100–c. 178) view that the earth was at the centre of the planets' orbits and proposed that the sun was, more or less, at the still centre. To argue that the earth moved seemed to many contrary to the teaching of scripture. The dispute that ensued was not merely one of better and better observations of planetary orbits but rather of two philosophical positions associated with the names of Pythagoras and Plato.

Copernicus was a Pythagorean. He believed that the mathematical relations that fitted the observed phenomena of the material world really explained why things are as they are. The solar system is actually as the mathematical formulations say it is. *Contra* this view is one that came to be favoured by the Catholic Church and that had a distant origin in the Platonic notions of perfect Forms in a realm removed from the everyday, ever-changing world.[2] According to this position, mathematical hypotheses, no matter how sophisticated, are fundamentally different from statements about the actual structure of the universe. Whilst it was acceptable for astronomers to evaluate competing mathematical formulations, the one they eventually favoured had nothing to do with the way things really are. The formulations remain abstract, perhaps elegant, mathematical statements. They merely 'save the appearances'; they are not physically true theories.

In the early 17th century, matters eventually came to a head when Galileo Galilei (1564–1642) began to adduce telescopic evidence for a heliocentric solar system (Fig. 10). Cardinal Bellarmine, one of Galileo's opponents, insisted that the astronomer's observations should be regarded as a mathematical formulation that had nothing to do with physical truth. But could it be a mere coincidence that a set of mathematical relations fitted planetary phenomena? As is now well known, Galileo was hauled before the Inquisition and forced to recant, a scandal that the Catholic Church has belatedly and pusillanimously tried to lay to rest.

The church's position derived from divine revelation in two ways. First, the overall biblical doctrine that 'Man' was the crown of creation and was made in the image of God meant that the earth, and not the sun, must surely be at the centre of the revolving planets – the cynosure of God's interest. Secondly, to this foundation were added, somewhat awkwardly, the visions of prophets and mystics. These revelations grew largely out of the notion that there are three levels of existence. Below is Hell, above is Heaven, and between the two is the level of the earth. So much could be inferred from various biblical narratives for which the mystics' visions, the experiential dimension of their religion, provided proof: the cosmological levels and their inhabitants could

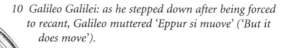

10 Galileo Galilei: as he stepped down after being forced to recant, Galileo muttered 'Eppur si muove' ('But it does move').

actually be *seen* by those to whom God chose to reveal the nature of his creation in dreams and visions. Because the biblical narratives are themselves saturated in visionary experiences, this sort of experiential confirmation should not have come as a surprise. But, even in this simple, tripartite concept of the cosmos, an awkwardness arose. Purgatory, a staging post for purification on the way to Heaven, was difficult to place in the three-tiered scheme of things (downward seemed the best option). To sort out this and related problems, medieval mystics like Hildegard of Bingen produced elaborate diagrams that purported to show just where multiple realms were situated, not only Purgatory but also realms inhabited by degrees of angels. The difficulty with placing Purgatory derives from the fact that it is a doctrinal creation, a construction of religious belief, whereas the three-realm cosmology is, we now argue, ultimately neurological in origin and thus derived from religious experience (Chapter 1).

Cosmological levels

Joan and Romas Vastokas, archaeologists who investigated a remarkable rock-engraving (petroglyph) site near Toronto, relate an Algonkian myth concerning the creation of the Midewiwin, an organization of North American shamans. The Great Spirit tells Shell and his assistant Bear that they must bring the Midewiwin from its birthplace in the bowels of the earth:

Earth made a great rumbling. As they came through successive layers to the top of the earth, the rumbling grew louder. Then they came out … The noise came down the layers of the *mide* Sky. At the last layer of the sky they paused, then met at the midpoint between Earth and Sky …[3]

The Vastokases point out that the Algonkian view of how the layered universe is structured incorporates shamanistic motifs. 'The Cosmic Axis is located at the very centre of the world and serves as the pathway through the openings in the layers of the universe.'[4] Those openings were made when Bear pushed the World Tree through the layers prior to the creation of the Midewiwin; he wished to provide a passage for shamans to traverse the universe. There are four layers above and another four below the level of the earth.

Imagery of this sort colours a great many creation myths throughout the world. It becomes a structuring principle that handles the notion of people and animals being transformed from a former existence into the present order. Connected, layered worlds are seen, for instance, in a Navajo myth that deals with an upwards migration through four levels. The dark First World was originally the home of First Man, First Woman and other beings. There were insects, plants and five mountains in this world. When the first beings tired of that world, they climbed the stem of a reed into the Second World, where further acts of creation took place. Then, conflicts with beings resident there caused the newly arrived proto-people to climb the reed into a Third World, which had 'light, rivers, springs and abundant life'. But further troubles and conflicts ensued, and the group once again climbed the reed. With difficulty, they reach the final level, this world.[5] In a survey of North American indigenous religion in general, Åke Hultkrantz, the Swedish ethnographer, ascribes such myths particularly to peoples of the Southwest, such as the Navajo, but goes on to identify the same imagery in rituals practised elsewhere.[6]

The Plains Indians' Sun Dance is an example. The central post, preferably an uprooted tree, represents the World Tree that has its roots in an underworld, stretches through the present world and has its top in the sky world – it is comparable to the Navajo reed. The three levels are marked on the post: an eagle at the top represents the sky, a buffalo skull represents this world and tobacco offerings at the foot of the post are destined for the nether world. The ritual itself replicates this three-part concept:

Dancers fast and dance around a sacred tree for hours each day. On the last day, those dancers who have opted for self-torture are attached to the tree by thongs tied to skewers that are pushed through deep gashes in the flesh of their chests or back. They must endure this agony throughout the 24 songs of the dance, which takes several hours ... A dance is considered to be successful if a participant experiences a vision during his protracted ordeal.[7]

Here, visions of passing through the cosmos are induced by extreme pain. As we have seen, pain is one of the many ways of altering human consciousness. The notion of a tiered cosmos structures not only religious belief and myth but also ritual.

Piers Vitebsky, Head of Social Sciences at the Scott Polar Research Institute, University of Cambridge, identifies a similar structure in Siberian cosmology. Siberian peoples believed that the universe was divided into three layers. 'Human beings lived on the middle layer, but the upper world, in the sky, could be reached through a small hole.'[8] As with the Algonkians, the upper world was subdivided into several levels, the number of levels depending on the closeness of the shamans' community to empires and courts. 'The lower world was likewise divided into several layers and was often considered the realm of the dead'.[9] Confirming part of the basic tripartite Siberian cosmos, Ronald Hutton, Professor of History at Bristol University, notes that, whilst the Samoyedic-speaking peoples conceived of a heaven of six tiers, and the tribes of the Altai spoke variously of three, seven, nine or more levels in the sky, the Buryats 'portrayed heaven with ninety-nine provinces, and a separate realm in the north for evil spirits'. Siberian cultures, he adds, were 'so mobile and dynamic' that generalizations are difficult.[10]

Nevertheless, one commonality is that the 'Siberian shaman's soul is said to be able to leave the body and travel to other parts of the cosmos, particularly to an upper world in the sky and a lower world underground'.[11] The shaman thus *sees* a tiered cosmos. Vitebsky adds a caveat: soul-travel is not found in all parts of the world. He therefore suggests that a broad definition of shamanism would 'include any kind of person who is in control of his or her state of trance'.[12]

We know that in many societies it is shamans and mystics who – ultimately – reveal the nature of the cosmos. The Siberian Tungus speak of three major levels: upper, middle and lower. When Sergei Shirokogorov asked them how they knew this, they replied, 'So the shamans say.'[13] The shamans visited and had actually seen the levels.

Among the Chukchee of northeast Asia beliefs in a tiered cosmos have a corollary to which we return in subsequent chapters. In general, they say that there are several worlds situated one above another, in such a manner that the ground of one forms the sky of the one below. The number of these worlds is stated as five, seven or nine.[14] All the worlds are said to be joined by 'holes situated under the Pole Star'. The interesting corollary is that the Chukchee map their multiple worlds on to living areas. In a folk tale, a young man is bereft of his senses by the machinations of an old witch. He 'rushes out of the sleeping-room, then out of the tent, *each of these representing a world*' (emphasis added).[15]

Something similar is experienced by the Desana of South America when they drink a brew made from the hallucinogenic vine *yajé* (Chapter 4). The house becomes the universe during the ritual so that the men's door becomes the eastern entrance to the earth we inhabit.[16] The house is thus transformed by people's altered consciousness; what they had built for daily use becomes an exemplar of the cosmos and movement through it becomes equivalent to movement through the cosmos.

Precolumbian inhabitants of Mesoamerica lived in a cosmos shaped by visions of mythological beings and events (Fig. 11). Although their universe was essentially tiered, each town or village had its own version: human settlement was formed by its own unique cosmology that incorporated local mountains, caves, springs and rivers, while the sun, the moon and the stars delineated its outer boundaries.[17]

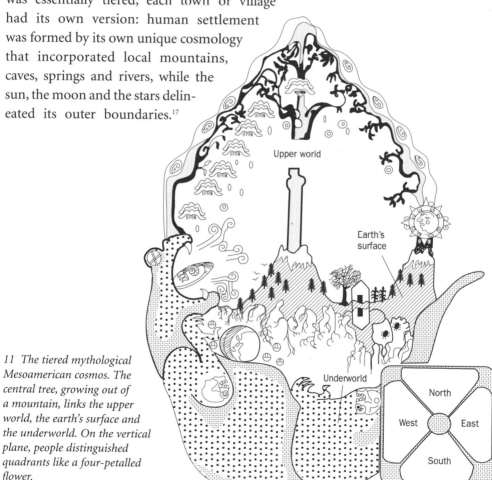

11 *The tiered mythological Mesoamerican cosmos. The central tree, growing out of a mountain, links the upper world, the earth's surface and the underworld. On the vertical plane, people distinguished quadrants like a four-petalled flower.*

Upper world

Earth's surface

Underworld

North

West   East

South

Nevertheless, all communities had shared larger visions. A watery, celestial, upper world of 9 or 13 layers arched over the earth's surface; below was an underworld of decay and death. In between, the level of daily life existed on a surface divided into quadrants of a terrestrial flower: north, south, east and west. The centre point sometimes required sacrifice to keep the cosmos living: if you wanted the gods to feed you, you had to feed them. Temples embodied the cosmos. The 14th- to 16th-century urban centre of Tenochtitlan had a huge temple at the ritual centre of quadrants; beneath the temple was the underworld filled with the sacrificial bodies of celestial and terrestrial animals. Temples were also oriented towards the daily turning of the heavens. The first temple at the Maya site of Cerros, for instance, was believed to be at the centre of the world: the vertical axis went from the sky, through the temple and into the underworld (Fig. 12). As Linda Schele and David Freidel put it, the temple

materialized the paths of power the king traveled through during ecstatic performance. Since the first temple functioned as the instrument that would convey the king as shaman on his sacred journeys, the builders designed it as a public stage. The rituals that enabled the king's journey into the sacred world would be enacted in public spaces so that the full community could witness and affirm their successful performance.[18]

How do shamans accomplish this sort of transcosmological travel?

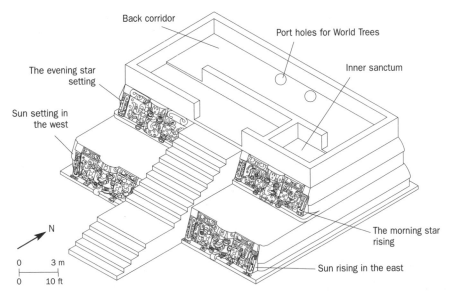

12 A reconstruction of the first temple at the Maya site of Cerros, Yucatan Peninsula, Central America. Temples of this kind placed religious beliefs within a tiered cosmos.

I bear you on eagles' wings

South American Tapirapé shamans speak of travelling through the cosmos in a canoe. Like the Siberian shaman's horse, a feature of the open steppe, the canoe is clearly related to the riverine life of the Amazon Basin. The Tapirapé also speak of changing into birds and flying through the cosmos. Flight is globally a more common trope than canoe travel.[19] Other South American people, the Tupinamba of Brazil and the Caribs of Guyana, ingest a hallucinogen that helps a shaman's soul to leave his body and fly.[20] Similarly, a recurring shamanistic dream among the South American Bororo is one of soaring very high above the earth like a vulture, accompanied by the soul of some living person, often but not always a shaman. The dreamer sees 'a curiously altered but perceptually vivid world, in which "things are very little and close to one another"'.[21]

North American Inuit also speak of shamanistic transformation from human to bird, and they carve ivory shamanistic bears in a flying posture.[22] In Siberia, Khanty drum rhythms facilitated shamanistic flight. Shamans 'were able to fly faster than a speeding arrow and pierced the sky on drums, flying to the golden residence of the sky god Torum'.[23] Then, too, in southern Africa, 19th-century San spoke of their shamans transforming themselves into birds.[24]

After summing up these sorts of beliefs about the shamanistic tiered cosmos, James Pearson, who has expertly synthesized the literature on shamanism, comments on the kind of 'magical flight' that is achieved in trance states:

the special skill of the shaman is his ability to journey between the mundane world, where the rest of the community is confined, and the spirit realm ... When the shaman enters an altered state of consciousness, he is truly transformed, attaining the capacity for supernatural flight ... When he travels to the spirit world, he becomes the powerful animal or creature whom he calls on for supernatural aid.[25]

Mircea Eliade reached a similar conclusion in his 1951 survey of world shamanism: 'All over the world, indeed, shamans and sorcerers are credited with the power to fly, to cover immense distances in a twinkling, and to become invisible.'[26] Joan Halifax provides a more florid description:

To the heavens, to the well at the end of the world, to the depths of the Underworld, to the bottoms of spirit-filled lakes and seas, around the earth, to the moon and sun, to distant stars and back again does the shaman-bird travel. All the cosmos is accessible when the art of transformation has been mastered.[27]

The widespread nature of such flights is indeed striking. Vitebsky comments that 'there are astonishing similarities, which are not easy to explain, between shamanistic ideas and practices as far apart as the Arctic, Amazonia and Borneo, even though these societies have probably never had any contact with each other.'[28] Worldwide, there are tiered cosmological levels and people who fly between them. How can this situation be explained?

The neurology of flight

We have already noted that reports of altered states of consciousness often include the sensation of travelling through a hole or tunnel (Chapter 2). In one that we cited, a child's near-death experience 'was moving through this … long dark place' that seemed 'like a sewer or something'.[29] We also saw that a San trancer spoke of 'a big hole in the spirit world' that leads to an underground place' (H).[30] These experiences parallel the Algonkian tree, the Navajo reed and the Chukchee's holes under the Pole Star. In Chapter 2, we argued that they derive from the sensation of passing through a vortex that is wired into the human nervous system, a functioning of the brain that recent neurological research has located in a precise spot in the brain.[31]

Now we note another feature of those reports. The first of the hypnagogic experiences that we recounted in Chapter 2 (A) recorded flying 'over the lane, over the houses, then over the Golden Horn in the direction of Stamboul'. In drug-induced states, subjects spoke of their spirits having 'flown forth', of being 'suspended in mid-air viewing landscapes of mountains' and being 'poised in space' (F). Another spoke of flying 'through an aurora borealis, under mandalas, over buildings, mountains, and giant lollipops'.[32] As we have seen, shamans worldwide in their altered states frequently fly not only to spirit realms but also to other parts of the material world.

We therefore argue that descent into a tunnel and flight to a realm above (or through the real world) are both sensations wired into the human brain and are activated in altered states of consciousness.[33] Sometimes the vortex and flight experiences combine, and a person may experience 'flying under the earth'.[34] Beliefs in magical flight and vortex travel seem to be inextricably linked to beliefs about a tiered cosmos. How else could it be? Both sets of beliefs are generated by neurological mechanisms.

A difficulty may seem to arise when we recall that, although shamans talk of travelling between layers of the cosmos, they also describe the way in which spirit beings and influences are present in this world as well as above and below. Spirits are *here*, not exclusively *there*. This widespread belief leads Vitebsky to conclude that space is a metaphor for 'the otherness of the spirit realm. If we see spirits around us, then this realm is not geographically removed ... Space is a way of expressing difference and separation, but the shaman's journey expresses the possibility of coming together again.'[35]

The problem of *how* the spirit realms can be spatially removed and, at the same time, immanent in the material world is resolved by a further understanding of human neurology. Flight and tunnel-travel, to be sure, suggest space, but the sensations of flight and underground journeys are experienced within the brain, that is, inside one's head. Then, too, hallucinations, as we have seen, are frequently projected onto a person's immediate environment – outside of one's head: hallucinations (perhaps of spirit beings and animals) are therefore also part of this world.

That at least some people who experience visions are aware of this duality of transcendence and immanence is evident in an explanation that a Huichol shaman gave to Joan Halifax:

There is a doorway *within our minds* that usually remains hidden and secret until the time of death. The Huichol word for it is *nieríka. Nieríka* is a cosmic portway or interface between so-called ordinary and nonordinary realities. It is a passageway and at the same time a barrier between worlds [emphasis added].[36]

In summary, we can say that both neuropsychology and world ethnography show that the near universality of belief in a tiered cosmos and in movement between the levels may be ascribed to the functioning of the human nervous system in a variety of altered states. The vortex leads through a tunnel or some such construal down to a nether level, while flight leads up to a realm in or above the sky. This conclusion does not mean that each and every member of a community experiences the full gamut of altered states. Rather, those who do thereby acquire high status and are in a position to 'naturalize' their experiences, to proclaim their irrefutable reality. Those who do not experience states at the fully hallucinatory end of the consciousness spectrum manage to glimpse in their dreams something of what the visionaries experience. That is their reassurance.

The eyes have it

We now explore in more detail a key implication of beliefs concerning the tiered cosmos, one we have already hinted at. Because the levels are created by the nervous system and are related to various forms of consciousness, people who experience those 'visions' believe that they can actually *see* the levels. That, after all, is how they know what they are like and what beings or animals inhabit them. Although all the senses have the potential to hallucinate, people speak the most about sight. Seeing becomes especially vivid as it reveals 'worlds upon worlds' and the seer passes through realms; transcosmological travel and preternatural sight go hand in hand. The experience is, at least potentially, a human universal.

This conclusion is supported by the accounts of altered states of consciousness that we gave in Chapter 2. Speaking of 'a wonderfully pleasant sensation', a person who experienced hypnagogia said, 'I cannot help opening my eyes' (A); the desire to see was overwhelming. Another subject reported seeing 'a large green eye opening and closing' (B). A man who had taken marijuana involuntarily recalled a picture he had seen and exclaimed, 'Oh my God … there's a bunch of eyeballs watching me!' (G). Another who had ingested hallucinogenic mushrooms went even further: he *became* 'a disembodied eye, invisible, incorporeal, seeing but not seen' (F).

Ethnographic accounts of shamanic experiences from around the world incorporate similar ideas.

In the jungles of South America, a Colombian Barasana shaman spoke about his 'inner seeing' as he traversed the cosmos. He put it like this: 'This is how the shamans travel, as they see with their thoughts and cross between the levels of the world.' 'Seeing with their thoughts' is a strikingly apt phrase.[37]

The Chukchee have a word to denote such shaman's statements about cosmology. It is *eñe'ñilimä lo'o* and means 'things seen by a shaman'. A shaman's 'seeing' is sufficiently distinct to warrant a special word. His preternatural sight is induced by the consumption of hallucinogenic fly-agaric mushrooms. Once he is in an altered state, the mushrooms appear to him in semi-human form and lead him 'through the entire world, showing him some real things, and deluding him with many unreal apparitions'.[38] These sights become his *eñe'ñilimä lo'o*.

The visionary quality of a potential Chukchee shaman's eyes is said to be striking. A young man destined to be a shaman may be recognized even in his teens by his gaze, which

is not turned to the listener, but is fixed on something beyond him. In connection with this, they say that the eyes of a shaman have a look different from that of other people, and they explain it by the assertion that the eyes of the shaman are very bright, which, by the way, gives them the ability to see 'spirits' even in the dark.[39]

Even in death a shaman's eyes are emphasized. Edith Turner, an anthropologist at the University of Virginia who specializes in symbolism and ritual, found this emphasis when Kaglik, an Alaskan Inuit elder, told her that he had once worked for archaeologists. In 1939 he had excavated a shaman's grave and found the skull 'with ivory eyes set into the eye sockets'.[40] Thereafter Kaglik carved masks with ivory eyes. 'Them's shaman's eyes,' he said, tapping one of his masks. Then Turner realized that the laughing mask was an effigy of himself, his own 'gleaming slit eyes and high cheekbones'.[41]

Wenceslas Sieroshevski, a late 19th-century Pole, who was exiled in Siberia for 12 years, was also intrigued by shamans' eyes. After his return to the West, he wrote about Yakut shamans:

The pupil of his eye was surrounded by a double ring of a dull green colour. When he was practising his magic, his eyes took on a peculiar, unpleasant dull glare, and an expression of idiocy, and their persistent stare, as the author observed, excited and disturbed those upon whom he fixed it.[42]

This reaction was also that of the Australian anthropologist Peter Elkin. Writing in 1945 of Aboriginal 'men of high degree', he confessed that their 'shrewd, penetrating eyes ... look you all the way through – the lenses of a mind that is photographing your very character and intentions'. He goes on to say:

I have seen those eyes and felt that mind at work when I have sought knowledge that only the man of high degree could impart. I have known white people who almost feared the eyes of a *karadji*, so all-seeing, deep, and quiet did they seem.[43]

Sometimes shamans treat their eyes to enhance their greater prominence. John Hitchcock, who studied shamanism in Nepal, experienced the penetration of a shaman's 'charcoal-smeared eyes ... opening wider and wider'. To enable himself to see a witch, the man had pronounced a spell over some pieces of charcoal and crumbled them in his hand. He smeared the dust on his eyelids. 'In the near darkness this makes his eye sockets seem even deeper set and his dark eyes still more dark and large'.[44]

On another continent altogether, one of the southern African San healers whom we quoted in Chapter 2 and who induced his altered states by dancing, hyperventilation and auditory-driving reported: 'The hot steam inside me leaves my body, giving me new eyes. The eyes can become any colour' (H). That was in the 20th century. In the 1870s, another San man told the Bleek family about a shaman who was especially known for his ability to make rain.

This man struck fear into people 'because his eyes used to shine like a beast-of-prey's (eyes): a cat's eyes were small (in comparison)' (original parentheses).[45] They were so large that they were like an ostrich's eyes.[46] Lions, especially those who behaved strangely, were believed to be marauding shamans in feline form.[47] Lions' eyes glint in the darkness beyond a campfire.

On the other side of the Atlantic, in South America, a Desana *kumú* (a priest-like shaman) is said to have 'an interior light, a brilliant flame that shines and unveils the intimate thoughts of all people who speak to him'. This light is seen in his eyes, in his 'penetrating glance'.[48] For the Waiwai, another South American people, this brilliance is related to the person him- or herself. The 'eye-soul' is said to be 'the small person one always sees in the other's eye'.[49]

Together, these accounts of the power and brightness of a shaman's eyes recall Coleridge's words: 'Beware! Beware!/His flashing eyes, his floating hair!' In his 'anodyne'-induced vision the poet felt himself transformed. His eyes filled those around him with fear; power flashed from them and demanded submission. The intense eyes of a visionary cause others to close their own eyes 'with holy dread'.

'Seeing' in the Neolithic

Evidence for similar beliefs and experiences is to be found at 'Ain Ghazal, the early Neolithic village that we mentioned in Chapter 1 and that we consider in more detail in Chapter 4 (see Fig. 1). As at Jericho, the inhabitants of 9,000 years ago kept goats and cultivated cereals. But the most striking discovery at 'Ain Ghazal was a number of extremely fragile clay statues (Pl. 9; Figs 13, 14). Each about 1 m (3.3 ft) tall, they were part of what Denise Schmandt-Besserat of the University of Texas, Austin, calls 'an explosion of symbolism' that also included animal figurines, tokens of various shapes, motifs painted on walls and floors, and human skulls modelled with a partial plaster covering (a practice to which we return in a moment).[50]

The statues, 32 in all, were found in two closely packed caches. The older, comprising 13 full-body statues and 12 one-headed busts, was dated to 6750 BC. The second cache was dated to approximately 6570 BC, that is, there was a gap of about 200 years between the two. The second comprised two full statues, three two-headed busts (a form not found in the first cache) and two fragmentary heads. They were made on reed armatures comprising bundles tightly bound with twine and then plastered over. Lime plaster was also used

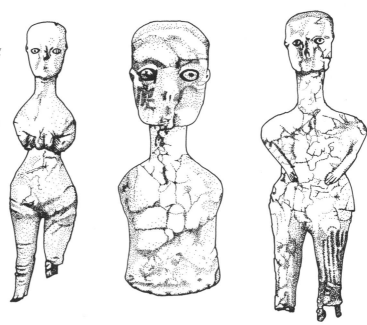

13 'Ain Ghazal statues from Cache 1 (6750 BC). The staring eyes are outlined with bitumen. The accomplishment of supernatural seeing seems to have been an important feature of these figures.

to cover house walls and floors, and in the modelling of skulls. The statues and the busts, it was found, were all made so that they could stand up and be viewed from the front. Both caches were carefully laid in specially dug pits beneath the floors of long-abandoned houses. As Schmandt-Besserat points out, they were 'not under habitation floors but segregated from the living'.[51]

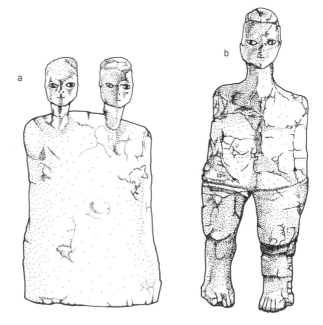

14 'Ain Ghazal statues from Cache 2 (6570 BC). At this time, two-headed figures make their appearance. Heights: a 85 cm (33.5 in); b 107 cm (42 in).

Although breasts and arms are sometimes shown, the makers' principal focus was on the heads. The faces are highly stylized and disproportionate.[52] The noses are short and upturned. The nostrils are suggested by vertical lines; the mouth is simply a horizontal line; no lips are shown. The face was treated with ochre to give it a 'silky finish'.[53] On all the figures, the eyes are disproportionately large and set far apart. The eyeballs bulge slightly and are surrounded by marked oval ridges of black bitumen.[54] The eyes of the earlier cache figures tend to be rounder than the more almond-shaped eyes of the later group. They also have a thin filament of 'an intense green pigment'. Their irises (or pupils, it is not clear whether the painted middle of the eye represents the iris or the pupil) are round and contrast with the diamond-shaped irises of the later group.[55] Schmandt-Besserat believes that the diamond-shaped irises or pupils give the Cache-2 statues 'an eerie, alien, or feline look, distinguishing them from the more benign figures of Cache 1'.[56]

Comparison of the two caches suggests that 'Ain Ghazal statues underwent some stylization. The older ones have single heads extending from 'carefully smoothed, human-shaped torsos'. The later cache has figures with two heads projecting from a quasipyramidal, rough base.[57] But, significantly, the focus on the eyes does not change. They remain the key feature of the statues.

Painstaking work by scientists at the Conservation Analytical Laboratory of the Smithsonian Institution separated the statues and fixed and restored the crumbling clay. What did their meticulous labour reveal? The University of California, Santa Barbara, archaeologist Brian Fagan is a writer of immense archaeological knowledge and experience, yet he was stunned when he saw the restored figures in the Smithsonian:

Androgynous and near life-size, the 9,000-year-old plaster figures gazed wide-eyed across the centuries, as if possessed with boundless wisdom. It … felt as if their eyes were following me around the room – their impact upon me lingers still.[58]

What could these staring statues have represented? Schmandt-Besserat considers various possibilities: ancestors, malevolent or beneficent 'ghosts' involved in exorcism or divination rites, and gods and goddesses, probably associated with concepts of fertility. She favours the last explanation, arguing that such beings were probably part of a new ideology that accompanied the development of agriculture.

Jacques Cauvin also noted the attention that the makers gave to the eyes. He suggests that 'The eyes and their expression evoke that which is most subjective and specifically psychic in the human being.'[59] True – at least in some sense. But we argue that, if we can envisage social and consciousness contracts set in a tiered cosmos, we can go further in explaining the prominence of the eyes of the 'Ain Ghazal figures.

We follow Schmandt-Besserat in drawing attention to a feature of supernatural beings as they are described in much later Babylonian and other texts, some as recent as 2000 BC. Some of these beings had two heads, like some of the 'Ain Ghazal figures: they expressed 'infinite beauty, omnipresence, and wisdom'.[60] One text that describes the creation of Marduk, the greatest Babylonian deity, speaks of his four eyes and four ears.[61] In another, we read of 'four eyes for limitless sight and four ears hearing all'.[62] In yet another text, we read:

> Four were his eyes, four were his ears.
> When he moved his lips, fire blazed forth.
> Each of his four ears grew large
> And [his] eyes likewise, to see everything.[63]

Comparable supernatural seeing and hearing were probably characteristics of the personages that the 'Ain Ghazal figures represented or, perhaps more likely, embodied. Their ability to 'see' was beyond anything that ordinary human beings could experience. They were frighteningly omnipercipient.

This ability seems to be again emphasized in some of the plastered skulls from Jericho (Chapter 1) and other Near Eastern sites.[64] Post-mortem skull removal as part of burial practices seems to have had a long history in the Near East, having started as early as 10th–9th millennium BC and lasting until the end of the 7th millennium BC.[65] The modelling of some adult skulls was a temporally and geographically restricted practice that grew out of this tradition. Eyes were represented in various ways: cowry shells embedded in the plaster (Jericho), bivalve shell fragments embedded in the plaster and partly covered with plaster eyelids (Jericho); hollow, open cavities narrowed by plaster eyelids (Beisamoun, see Fig. 1); 'coffee-bean eyes' created by the attachment of plaster eyelids (Kfar HaHoresh) (Fig. 15, Pl. 7).[66] An 'Ain Ghazal skull seems to have had eyes outlined with bitumen, as do the statues from this site. An example exhibited in the Israel Museum, Jerusalem, has been described as a 'nearly sleeping' face.[67] Open or closed, the eyes were important.

All in all, there was a generally shared Near Eastern pool of knowledge about how to make plastered skulls; although there were local traditions as

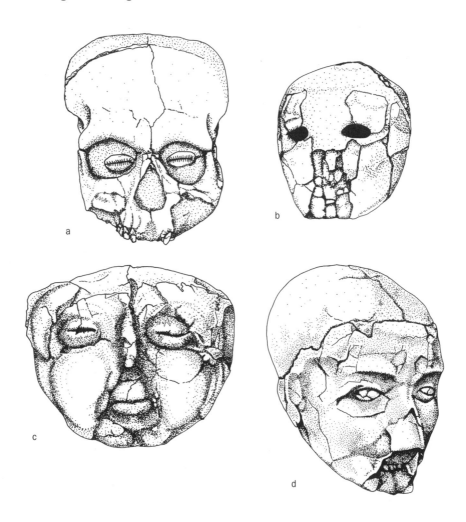

15 *Plastered skulls are a feature of the Near Eastern Neolithic.* a *Jericho;* b *Beisamoun;* c *Kfar HaHoresh;* d *Jericho. Seashells are used as eyes to emphasize the importance of seeing in death.*

well. In one remarkable instance (a Beisamoun skull), the plaster covering the skull included crushed calcite crystals that would have been specially mined from veins in limestone. The substance does not seem to have had any technical advantage. Its glittering appearance was what the craftsman was after: 'The surface of the modelled skull was probably polished (with fine sand or ash) to burnish or buff the calcite crystals, thus amplifying the shine of the object' (original parenthesis).[68] Of particular interest is the suggestion that the use of crushed calcite in the making of some of these 'spiritually oriented' skulls 'acted as a preliminary framework on which the technological knowledge for producing later daily performing [pottery; i.e., in daily use] was gained'.[69] This sort of development from 'spiritual' to 'practical' is a theme that will recur in Chapter 5 where we consider the domestication of the aurochs.

A final significant point is that many of the skulls were buried in caches ('skull nests'). Some were found in carefully contrived arrangements. When arranged, it seems that it was not so much the overall configuration that counted (whether they were in circles or rows or arcs) as the fact that they faced in the same direction. At Nevali Çori three pits were found in each of which were two skulls: in all three cases, the skulls faced one another. As we have seen in Chapter 1, a circle of skulls at Jericho were, in Kathleen Kenyon's phrase, all 'looking inward', and a further three sets of skulls were placed so that, within each cluster, they were all 'looking in the same direction'.[70] This congruence of direction, we believe, may indicate that the skulls were 'looking' in the same direction, that they were 'seeing' in death as they did in life, but with greater percipience and sharing their perceptions.

Seeing from above by means of flight may be a special type of supernatural vision. It is suggested by some of the Neolithic images we mentioned in Chapter 1. At Nevali Çori, a piece of sculpture seems to combine human and avian features, while another has a human head, but the shape of a bird. One of the pillars has a carving of a bird that seems to be perched on a human head. Elsewhere on a pillar, two birds face one another. Moreover, a vulture-like bird was sculpted in the round. At Çatalhöyük (Chapter 4), there is a wall painting of two cranes facing one another with heads raised (Pl. 14).[71]

Recent excavations at this site have added to the number of bird bones that James Mellaart found. Amongst these was the left wing of a crane; it was associated with a complete cattle-horn core. Nearby, were two wild goat-horn cores, a dog's head and a stone macehead. By studying cut marks on the crane wing, Nerissa Russell and Kevin McGowan were able to conclude that the wing was not waste from normal butchery.[72] Probably, they argue, the wing was part of a ritual costume used in dances that may have mimicked cranes' dances; these 'animal rituals' involve breeding pairs and also whole groups. As we pointed out in Chapter 1, Harald Hauptmann suggests that birds may have represented 'the soul of a human or a connection between this world and the beyond.'[73] We enlarge this suggestion by noting the universal importance of flight and the kind of seeing that it permits. Add to this the significance of the vultures we discuss in Chapter 4, and it becomes clear that Neolithic bird symbolism was highly complex.

Buried twice over

The removal of skulls from human remains, their treatment and, presumably, subsequent display or reburial are points that raise far-reaching issues concerning ritual.[74] We comment on a few because they will be raised again in our chapters on the megalithic tombs of Atlantic Europe.

Why did Near Eastern Neolithic people perform such elaborate and multi-stage burial practices? A commonly advanced, and indeed attractive, answer is that the rituals created social cohesion and thereby contributed to the society's adaptation to its environment.[75]

This is what is known as a 'functionalist' explanation. It is based on the problematic, rather naive assumption that all things work together for the good of society. Moreover, as anthropologists and sociologists have pointed out, it has logical problems. Take, for example, the statement:

– The function of periodic ritual pig slaughter in some Pacific societies is
   to regulate escalating pig populations.

Reformulated, this means:

– The function of x is to do what it does.

The statement is thus purely descriptive rather than explanatory.[76] The word 'function' could be omitted without harming the sentence (x does what it does). If we observe that people collectively participate in rituals, and we then go on to conclude that rituals – or myths, or kinship, or political structures – exist to hold society together, we are falling into the functionalist trap. One could hardly argue that these institutions exist to tear society apart. If they did, there would soon be no society. So we can say, with little fear of contradiction, that rituals, mythology and other institutions hold society together.

It is a short step from this observation to add that they exist *in order to* achieve solidarity, as if people consciously invented them for that purpose. As Cauvin puts it, 'collective ceremonies of a religious character ... must have served as a strong cement for the psychological cohesion of these sedentary groups'.[77] We are wading deeper and deeper into a logical morass. At the very least, we must distinguish between the people's own various (emic) views of the institutions of their communities and the (etic) explanations that anthropologists formulate – and, we should add, all too often formulate within the value structures of their own cultures. People in small-scale societies do not invent rituals in order to hold communities together.

An extension to the statement we have given as an example appears in numerous archaeological and anthropological works in accordance with the writers' theoretical positions:

– The *adaptive* function of ritual pig slaughter is to regulate pig populations.

We are still left with the basic statement that the function of x is to do what it does, but now we have added an unobservable assumption: that the ritual killing promotes adaptation to the environment.

If we still wish to allow that rituals and so forth may have had a positive social function, we must ask: Positive for whom? As soon as we do this, the simple functionalist explanation falls apart. Rituals and beliefs benefit some people more than – and often at the expense of – others, even if those 'others' are persuaded to accept the necessity for them. Our conclusion seems inescapable: Whole societies were not, in concert, consciously concocting rituals to keep their communities together; they were performing them for other reasons. What were those reasons?

To break out of the functionalist tautology we suggest that Neolithic people practised serial burials for mythological and, importantly, cosmological reasons, not simply because those religious practices were adaptive to environmental conditions. We suggest that their view of the cosmos entailed multiple stages of post-mortem existence that were lived out in multiple cosmological levels analogous to those we find in small-scale societies worldwide. The living had to 'help' the dead from one stage to the next with a series of sometimes widely spaced mortuary rites. In doing so, the living were able to tap into the supernatural percipience and power that the dead exercised during their lives and which was probably enhanced in death. If we had the opportunity to ask Neolithic people why they were processing the skulls, they would have given an answer along these lines (not that they were consolidating their community – the etic view).

Still, that would be only half the answer. It is clear that only some corpses were selected for exhumation, disarticulation, special treatment and reburial. It is also clear that, although the people of a community generally went along with their customs, it was certain powerful people, those believed to have insight into spiritual matters, who kept the customs alive, explained them and decided on whom extra ritual was to be lavished. Were the selected dead believed to have had (and still to have after their demise) powers similar to those possessed by the people who made the decisions? Probably. The hierarchy of the dead in some ways paralleled (and reinforced) the hierarchy of the living. We thus see that social cohesion cannot be separated from social division: they are two sides of the same coin. It is also probable that degrees of social power, or influence, among the living were related to the spiritual stages and cosmological levels that the long-drawn-out burial rites dramatized. The delay necessary for corporeal decay before exhumation paralleled the continuity of power among the living.

A less eirenic reading is also possible. Çayönü is a site in southern Turkey that was, in its early stages, contemporary with the oldest occupation of Jericho and the rock-cut structures at Göbekli Tepe. By 8000 BC it began to display complex architecture that included a cult building of special interest (Fig. 16).[78] It had a rectangular plan, but in its early phases it also had an apse at one end. Beneath the floor were no fewer than 66 human skulls and the remains of a further 400 people. Understandably, the building has become known as 'The House of the Dead'.

There were stone columns in the room and a large, flat stone that seemed to invite description as an 'altar'. This interpretation was supported when close examination of it revealed traces of both human and animal blood. In another building, archaeologists found a large stone slab that was decorated

16 'The House of the Dead', a 'cult building' at Çayönü. Excavators of buildings like this one often find that the layout of the building changed from time to time.

with a carved human head; it, too, had traces of human blood, as did a stone slab in yet another building. Commenting on the Çayönü finds, Brian Hayden, an anthropologist and archaeologist who has studied the socially complex hunter-gatherers of the American Northwest Coast, points out that the skulls were primarily of young adults, male and female, a fact that counts against their being of ancestors who died naturally at an advanced age.[79] Hayden notes that a high ratio of young individuals is an indication of 'controlled killing'.[80] He cites a comparable pattern at Çatalhöyük, where skulls show a high incidence of head wounds among males and there is also evidence for wounds on men's arm bones.[81]

It seems that an ancestor cult may not be the whole answer. Some of the skulls in Near Eastern Neolithic sites may have been trophy heads or from sacrificed victims (cf. Moche sacrifice and dismemberment[82]). Hayden feels that the second of these possibilities is less likely because human sacrifice is usually associated with complex societies that have marked differences in wealth and power. The victims are commonly war captives, slaves, children or the very poor. He does, however, note that at Jericho, 'Ain Ghazal and Çatalhöyük infants were buried beneath thresholds or in walls. Such positions for burials are so unusual that it is hard to resist the suggestion that they were offerings of some kind, perhaps to protect the house and its inhabitants. At Jericho we also saw that Kathleen Kenyon discovered a group of infant skulls with vertebrae still in place (Chapter 1).[83] The heads had been removed from intact bodies, not from decayed skeletons.

Moreover, the discovery of human and animal blood on what may have been altars cannot be ignored. It seems probable that sacrifice, whether of animals or people, was part of Neolithic contact with the supernatural. With Hayden, we reject the notion that Neolithic rituals and cult building arose to cement social relationships or as a result of some sort of spiritual enlightenment. The practices and the architectural structures in which they were performed probably point to social discriminations, to a hierarchical society in which an emerging elite manipulated surplus wealth and controlled what could and could not be seen. All this happened within a generally accepted tiered cosmology through which the dead passed stage by stage. It also seems likely that intensely altered states of consciousness, that is, ways of traversing the cosmos, were reserved for elites and were experienced in cult buildings. Regionally, some sites, such as Göbekli Tepe, may have been foci of elite groups that were extending their influence beyond the village level. Finally, it seems likely that the elite controlled transition to spirit realms by means of sacrifice: they had the power to send people, whether sacrificed children, specially selected individuals or captives, in to the other world and, by effecting such cosmological and supernatural transitions, to benefit the living.

Saving the appearances

If we are correct in concluding that beliefs about a tiered cosmos, spiritual travel between levels, seeing preternaturally and both transcendence and immanence are wired into the human brain, we may begin to enquire about possible changes in cosmology between the Upper Palaeolithic and the Neolithic. What led up to the Neolithic cosmology and practices we have described? Were the changes that came about in the early stages of the Neolithic in some ways comparable with those that Copernicus, Galileo and others effected in Western cosmology? A more difficult question is: Were those changes as traumatic and as contested? We suspect the answer is Yes.

One difficulty that confronts such an enquiry is that we know little about Upper Palaeolithic and Mesolithic cosmology in the Near East. Our best evidenced regions are in France and Cantabria where deep limestone caves afforded Upper Palaeolithic people an opportunity to explore an underworld in their minds and, literally, in caves. Still, allowing for geographical distance and a general absence of deep caves in the Near East, we hazard a few tentative observations.[84]

During the west European Upper Palaeolithic, people made small carvings on antler and mammoth ivory, some of which were used as pendants while others were part of spear throwers and other implements. More intriguingly, they explored deep limestone caves and, relying on flickering tallow lamps and torches, made images by various techniques on walls, floors, ceilings, stalactites and stalagmites. A persuasive explanation for this behaviour is that they believed that the caves led into a subterranean level of a tiered cosmos.[85] There, in the dark, silent passages and chambers they sought spirit animals in visions that bestowed supernatural power and status. Those visions may have been triggered by sensory deprivation in the Stygian, silent, chilly caverns, by the ingestion of hallucinogens, by pathogenic conditions or by other means.

People went into the caves believing in the existence of a bestiary of special animals that was probably also celebrated in their mythology, and this predetermined 'theology' created expectations of what they would 'see'. It is important to remember that there never was a time when Upper Palaeolithic people made images of whatever took their fancy; right from the beginning of the period, the painted, engraved and carved images derived from a fairly narrow range of animal subjects, some of which seem to have been subsequently numerically emphasized at different times of the Upper Palaeolithic. The making of subterranean images from about 35,000 years ago must therefore have been an extension of a pre-existing belief system. They believed in a suite of subterranean spirit animals and beings *before* they started to make images of them in caves.

Some visions of these preternatural animals were 'fixed' with a few deft painted or engraved strokes on the walls on to which the functioning of the brain projected them. This 'fixing' was done either in a lightly altered state of consciousness or, after having returned to an alert state, as they sought to recreate and control their fleeting visions. The images are therefore not pictures of animals seen outside the cave, as is often supposed: there is never any painted suggestion of a ground surface (the hoofs often 'hang' as the animals float on the rock wall), nor of grass, trees, rivers or indeed anything in the natural world. Rather, the fixed visions often blended with the form of the rock, a natural nodule, for instance, being used as an animal's eye. Others appear to be entering or leaving the rock surface, sometimes via cracks or fissures, while still others are only partially drawn, the rest of the image being created by shadow when one's light is held in a certain position. Many images were thus intimately set in and part of the rock face (not as part of a depiction of the outside world), and light and darkness complemented one another in a fecund way. The rock wall, floor and ceiling constituted a permeable 'membrane' between the vision seekers in the dark passages and an animal-filled spirit realm that lay just out of normal sight.

Other images were made by groups of people; they are large, impressive animals. Some required the construction of scaffolds to reach the desired surfaces. These striking images are usually in large chambers where groups of people could have congregated to perform rituals in the presence of powerful spirit animals. This kind of communal image may have helped to prepare vision seekers for what they would 'see' when they penetrated more deeply into the mental and physical vortex and thus into the depths of the nether realm or realms. In sequences that probably involved dancing, beating on stalactites, music, imitation of animal sounds and dramatic revelation of already existing paintings, vision seekers stocked their minds with emotionally highly charged mental images. The caves were alive with the sounds and visions of potent spirit animals.

For Upper Palaeolithic people physical travel through caves was probably identical to psychic travel through the tiered cosmos. The tiered cosmos in the mind was verifiable by visionary experiences that could be had anywhere but, especially, by climbing down through the subterranean labyrinths to see the fixed visions of predecessors, some probably believed to have been made by the spirits themselves. Religion was thus not something separate from real caves; rather, the material and the spiritual were inseparable.

To this understanding, we add the highly significant fact that Upper Palaeolithic people did not bury their dead in deep caves. It seems that passageways and chambers were the realm of spirit animals but not of the human departed. Some people were buried in the entrances to caves, in often quite large rock shelters. The dead, frequently provided with items from the world of the living, were thus on the *threshold* of the nether tier of the cosmos; they were in a mediatory position, neither completely absorbed into the lower tier or tiers of the cosmos nor still part of everyday life.[86]

What happened to this sort of cosmology and religion at the end of the Upper Palaeolithic is a puzzle. Was there a 'paradigm shift'? Thomas Kuhn influentially developed this concept of change in science in his book, *The Structure of Scientific Revolutions*. Like Gordon Childe in his discussions of the Neolithic, Kuhn turned to the notion of revolution. He argued that major changes in scientific thought come about comparatively suddenly and are characterized by the overthrow of a whole theoretical paradigm. In a period of what he called 'normal science', researchers answer questions within the parameters of the paradigm – what he calls 'puzzle-solving'. Then anomalies begin to appear. Scientists try to accommodate these anomalies by adding a rider or two to their propositions. But, despite their efforts, the anomalies sometimes accumulate to a critical point at which the whole paradigm of normal science is overthrown and a new paradigm is accepted by the scientific community. Underlying this thought we can see the Marxist notion of increasing incompatibilities between the relations of production and the means of production leading to political revolution. Kuhn's prime example was the Copernican Revolution, though he allowed that this 'revolution took about a century and a half'. He called it 'revolution by degrees'.[87] We are, in effect, following him when we write of 'the revolutionary Neolithic', rather than the 'Neolithic Revolution'.

Today, philosophers of science express reservations about the wide applicability of Kuhn's view of change. We need not go into them now. Instead, we note that, though ideas about what was at the centre of the solar system changed from the earth to the sun, there were observational continuities, some carry-overs: there were still planets that moved through a pattern of stars; there were still orbits.

So, was there a paradigmatic, revolutionary (if by degrees) change at the end of the Upper Palaeolithic? What major changes can we observe in the archaeological evidence?

In the Neolithic, people constructed exemplars of the cosmos above ground, as we show in subsequent chapters. In doing so they escaped from the highly varied intricacies of the labyrinthine subterranean passages and chambers that Upper Palaeolithic people negotiated. Each cave is different from all others in its topography. Neolithic people eliminated the variable labyrinth and replaced it with more predictable and simpler structures of their own design. In doing so they gained greater *control* over the cosmos and were able to 'adjust' beliefs about it to suit social and personal needs.

In some instances, Neolithic people buried their dead, or selected dead, beneath the floors of living areas, as did the people of the Upper Palaeolithic in the rock shelters where they lived. In other instances (in western Europe), they placed their dead deep in constructed exemplars of the cosmos – unlike the Upper Palaeolithic practice of reserving the depths for images of, principally, spirit animals. Furthermore, they sometimes exhumed the dead, dealt with the bones in various ways and then reburied them; sometimes they cremated the bones. They thus exercised greater control over the dead and kept them 'active' for longer.

These are some of the changes that we discuss in subsequent chapters. As we do so, we shall see that the people of the Neolithic were dealing with the same wired experiences of human neurology as their Upper Palaeolithic predecessors. In other words, there were still planets, stars and orbits. They were just being differently conceived. Perhaps one could use a metaphor and say that Neolithic people developed new 'mathematical' formulations to 'explain' the neurologically generated tiered cosmos, but these merely 'saved the appearances'. They did not challenge the fundamentals of a tiered universe; they did not say, 'There are no spirit worlds.' The ability to do something so radical lay far in the future.

Neolithic people did not – could not – challenge the tiered nature of their universe: it was wired into their brains. Nor could they ignore notions of passing through a vortex and flight: those experiences, too, were 'hard-wired'. So the new, 'above-ground' arrangements for representing and for accessing the tiers of the cosmos, arrangements that sometimes necessitated major construction, became an acceptable way of accommodating a burgeoning new social and religious dispensation *without jettisoning the fundamental structure of the cosmos*. This shift, we suspect, could not have been accomplished without bitter trauma. People have too much invested in a cosmology to abandon it without a struggle. Cosmologies are an integral part of societies.

Social change

We must therefore ask what transformations of society could have accompanied the changes in cosmology? How did the social contract articulate with the consciousness contract?

A clue to an answer may be found in South America. Christopher Crocker argues that Amerindian shamanism moved between two domains that contain antithetical cosmological principles.[88] This sort of difference was brought about by social change. Much of the change characteristic of South America is caused by the presence of Christian missionaries and by white commercial endeavours. We do not, of course, wish to imply that the Neolithic was in every way comparable to 20th-century Amazonia. Still, there are points that may well lead us towards some understanding of what happened socially as cosmology changed from Upper Palaeolithic hunter-gatherer versions to the forms that came to be associated with larger Neolithic settlements and agriculture.

Stephen Hugh-Jones, a Cambridge University anthropologist who, with his wife Christine, studied South American peoples, identifies two kinds of shamanism:[89]

Horizontal shamanism (HS) is comparatively democratic, though this does not mean that all shamans are equally respected and feared; some are indeed considered more powerful than others. HS is associated especially with the forest and depends on individual shamans contacting the spirits by means of hallucinogens. In a trance, shamans make contact with Jaguar. There is thus an emphasis on personal experience. The experiential dimension of religion is paramount. This kind of shaman is believed to provide game and to ensure animal fertility. HS is also associated with hunting, fishing and warfare. HS shamans also tend to perform ad hoc rituals for the benefit of individuals.

In *vertical shamanism* (VS) the principal component is esoteric knowledge that is revealed to and transmitted within a small elite. Here, the dimension of religious belief becomes prominent. By contrast with HS, VS is more associated with the house than the forest. VS shamans are more associated with forest fruits and vegetable fertility than with animals. Another difference is that, while HS practitioners use hallucinogenic snuff, VS shamans use the hallucinogenic vine known as *yajé*. There remains a strong element of experiential religion, but VS practitioners learn to become shamans by being taught an esoteric canon of belief and myth. They are thus *essentially knowledgable*: either they themselves can *see* or they learn from those who can. They perform regular ceremonies on behalf of the community, rather than ad hoc rituals in response to individual requests for healing. They play a major ceremonial role in rites of passage. Older and often physically inactive, they are respected rather than feared, as are HS shamans. Their high status overlaps with secular roles; politics are more important to them.

We suggest that the hunter-gatherer religion of the Upper Palaeolithic was probably dependent on *some form of* HS. During the Neolithic, some of the features that Hugh-Jones describes as characteristic of VS began to appear. It was these features that enabled people eventually to build large towns and to construct massive monuments. By emphasizing knowledge and learning, VS practitioners became more like a priesthood with powerful political influence, the ability to command large numbers of people, and the authority to orchestrate rituals such as disarticulation and reburial.

Yet, at the same time, they had to 'save the appearances' of the tiered cosmos. The continuing neurologically generated experiences that we have described provided repeated reinforcement of beliefs about a tiered cosmos. Not *everyone* travelled through the layers, but enough people did, while others saw flashes of it in their dreams and felt the impact of the seers, to make the fundamentals credible, indeed irrefutable. This complex of culturally situated neurology provided material for manipulation and the forging of new social and consciousness contracts. But Neolithic people could not escape what was wired into their brains.

CHAPTER 4

Close Encounters with a Built Cosmos

One of the principles that help us to understand the interaction between the materiality of Neolithic daily life and more abstract concepts of cosmological and religious belief is the notion that when people of that time built structures, cosmology was never far from their minds. They lived in a tiered cosmos that was *real* – whatever its specific details at different times. Sensations of moving through a subterranean passage to a nether world and also flying to higher realms to encounter beings and animals were wired into their brains. Even in houses designed principally for daily living, the cosmos was enveloping, simply because all life was played out in it, and the level on which people lived was only a part of the whole. What we call the supernatural was not something separated from daily life; it intruded continuously. Nor could the supernatural be separated from the very structure of the cosmos.

To illustrate just one of the many complex ways in which cosmology can invest architecture we turn to the Barasana Indian people who live in the densely forested Vaupés region of Colombia.[1] Stephen and Christine Hugh-Jones have written the most detailed account of the symbolism of Barasana structures, and it is on their meticulous and insightful research that we draw.[2] We do not, of course, imply that Near Eastern Neolithic beliefs were identical with those of South American Indians; we merely show, in one immensely illuminating instance,

– how the neurologically generated tiered cosmology can be embodied in structures that people build,
– how the results of their labour reproduce and sometimes modify beliefs about the cosmos and
– how labour and buildings unite religion, social structure and cosmology.

The Barasana thus illustrate how social and consciousness contracts can come together in architecture and the demarcation of space that architecture inevitably creates.

Replicating and regulating the cosmos

All Barasana life and thought centres on the *maloca,* or longhouse. Early Christian missionaries realized this and burned down *malocas* not because they were dwellings, but because they were intimately associated with (supposedly evil) Barasana beliefs about the universe and were sites of religious rituals. Daily life, cosmology and religion were one. As Stephen Hugh-Jones puts it, the Barasana 'do not see their kinship, marriage and social organization in isolation from a wider religious and cosmological order'.[3]

All members of a kinship group comprising a number of brothers and cousins (some of whom are regarded as brothers) live together with their families in a *maloca* (Fig. 17). One *maloca* may house more than 30 people, of whom probably somewhat fewer than 15 will be adults. Each *maloca* is set in its own manioc garden and is one or two hour's travel from other *malocas.* The Barasana subsist on cultivated manioc, combined with the spoils of hunting and fishing. The largest houses are sometimes 24.4 m (80 ft) long and 12.2 m (40 ft) wide; they have tent-like gabled roofs that reach almost to the ground. Inside, there are divisions that separate the sleeping areas of families. The front of the house is the men's area and the back, separated by a screen, is associated with women and their activities. Amongst the Tukano, a nearby group comparable to the

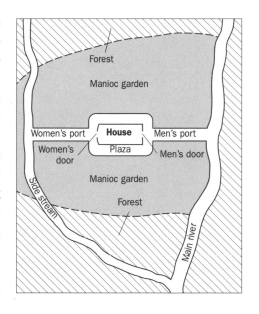

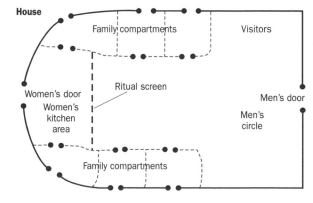

17 *Barasana longhouses, or* maloca*s, are positioned in relation to rivers and manioc gardens. Partitions within the houses separate families, and also the men's ritual area from the women's space. Men's graves are dug in the centre of the house, women's at the entrance to family compartments.*

Barasana, the men drink *yajé* and experience their ritual altered states of consciousness in the front part of the *maloca*, while the women, out of sight behind the screen, sing to 'animate' the men:

> Drink, drink! This is why we were born.
> Drink! Drink! Because this is our task.
> By drinking they will know all of the traditions of their fathers.
> By drinking, they will be brave.
> We will help them [lineation added].[4]

Overall, the *maloca* is a microcosm of the sort of universe that we have described as being neurologically generated: as Stephen Hugh-Jones says, 'the roof is the sky, the house posts are the mountains that support the sky, and the floor-space is the earth'.[5] Beneath the floor of the house is the nether world.

In this conception, the vertical cosmological axis is supremely important. Every day at noon, the sun's rays re-establish it as they fall directly to earth, and it is, moreover, repeatedly 'emphasized in shamanism and ritual'.[6] Religion and shamanistic altered states of consciousness are intimately bound up with cosmology. In the roof of the house is a small vertical post (easily missed by those unfamiliar with Barasana life) that represents the vertical cosmological connection within the *maloca*; it is called 'the Sun's post'. Suspended between the roof and the floor are ritual objects, collectively known as 'macaw feathers' – instruments of transcosmological flight. Christine Hugh-Jones points out that these 'correspond to the mediating tree and mountain layer between earth and sky which, appropriately enough, was the home of the macaws that [according to Barasana myths] were obtained for ritual ornaments'.[7]

Death leads to the lower realm of the cosmos. Graves are dug into the floor and are thus in the underworld. The body, in a foetal position and with a gourd over its face, is placed in a canoe that is cut in half and doubled over; it provides the deceased with transport through the subterranean river. Geraldo Reichel-Dolmatoff, who studied South American people some years before the Hugh-Joneses, pointed out that a doubled canoe is hexagonal, a geometric form associated with quartz crystals, one of the shamans' power objects used in transcosmological travel.[8]

A man is buried with feather headdresses, monkey-fur tassels and so forth, while a woman is accompanied by her basket, mirror and other personal possessions. The grave is dug in the centre of the house for a man and by the entrance to the family compartment for a woman. It is deep and has a side chamber for the coffin. Once the grave is filled, a shaman performs a cleansing ceremony. If a dead person was important, the people move to another, newly built, *maloca*. The building of a new *maloca* may be the responsibility of a shaman, who may also be a headman. He has authority to command the labour necessary to clear the forest for a new manioc garden and to construct the *maloca*.

So much for the vertical axis. The horizontal axis of the cosmos is also present in the structure of *malocas*. The major east–west horizontal beam on which the Sun's post rests is called 'the Sun's path'. Ideally, each *maloca* is oriented along an east–west axis, though terrain (especially the locations of rivers) and individual decisions mean this is not always so. The men's door represents the Water Door in the east; it leads to the river and the important canoe landing place, and hence to contact with other *malocas*. The west door is the women's door. The women's kitchen area is separated from the men's area by a ritual screen: importantly, the structure of the *maloca* restricts what different groups of people can and cannot see. The centre of the house is the centre of the world. Because the earth is thought of as bisected by a river, the house, too, is conceptually bisected by a river that is said to run from east to west.

Christine Hugh-Jones's diagrams neatly sum up and illustrate the way in which each *maloca* is an exemplar of the cosmos (Fig. 18). The *maloca*, its setting in the landscape, and the cosmos itself are reflections one of another. In Hugh-Jones's diagram, the cosmos is shown as having five levels – two above the earth and two below. The higher one above the earth is the same as the lower one beneath: it is the path of the sun.

The way in which *malocas* replicate the cosmos is reflected in rituals. When supernatural *He* beings enter the house, accompanied by men playing trumpets, they do so through the east door (the *e* in *He* is pronounced as in 'egg'). It is especially at the major dance sequence known as '*He* House' that the *maloca* becomes the cosmos and the people inside become *He* people, or first ancestors. This transformation is achieved 'through the powers of the shamans, hallucinogenic drugs and contact with sacred ritual objects'[9] – in other words, through the same altered states of consciousness that generate concepts of a tiered cosmos. People thus *see* their beliefs. A shaman's soul can leave his body at any time and experience the supernatural world, but this is especially true during *He* rituals.[10]

The origin of *He* beings and the cosmos itself is enshrined in myth. In the beginning, there was only one universe, which was a house occupied by Yeba,

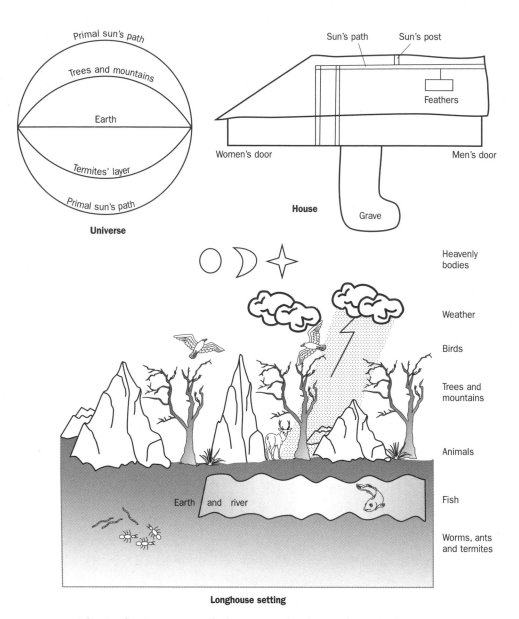

18 *The tiered universe surrounds the Barasana longhouse. The levels of the universe are reflected in the structure of the house. The sun's path represents the upper tier of the cosmos; the grave is dug into the nether world.*

the original ancestor of the Barasana, who was himself a jaguar ('Yeba' means earth). His sons were the ancestral anacondas. In due course, each of the sons became a father in his own house with his own sons. These were the *He* people. In each present-day kinship group, society is thought of as being only two generations in depth, and each *maloca* reproduces the mythical structure. History and myth are telescoped; they are, to all intents and purposes, indistinguishable. United, they fuse the material and supernatural worlds, as do the shamans' altered consciousness and transcosmological journeys. Throughout the world, many myths are shot through with the imagery of altered states (Chapter 6).

As the Yeba myth suggests, jaguars are avatars. They are also conceived of as 'mediators between the three cosmic divisions of the world, between life and death, between the human world and spirit world of the ancestors, and between nature and culture'.[11] These are also the attributes of shamans, who exploit altered states of consciousness to accomplish a number of things:
- They travel between cosmological levels.
- As killers and curers, they control the passage between life and death in the human world.
- They mediate between the worlds of human beings and spirits in their rituals and mental travels.

Powerful shamans are called 'jaguar' and are believed to be able to change into jaguars at will. Moreover, they are believed to keep jaguars as other people keep dogs, and they become jaguars at death. Not surprisingly for so important an animal, we find that the jaguar is cosmologically placed: the eagle is the predator of the sky, the jaguar the predator of the earth, and the anaconda the predator of the water, the underworld. Each creature is, in its own way, a mediator. Eagles stoop to the land and catch fish in rivers; jaguars swim and climb trees; anacondas come out of the water on to land. It is believed that, if an anaconda wishes to eat birds, it simply sheds its skin and becomes an eagle.[12] The mediating creatures can transform one into another. It is also important to notice that these principal animals of Barasana mythology are intimately associated not only with the tiered cosmos, and therefore with the architecture of the *malocas*, but also with shamans and the experiences of altered consciousness. These are only some of the many interrelationships of which the Barasana speak. Their symbolic system is indeed highly complex yet closely integrated. The key to its complexities is an understanding of shifting human consciousness. Indeed, the consciousness contract includes cosmology.

So close a relationship between the built environment and conceptual cosmology is not restricted to the Barasana. One further and very brief example will suffice to make our point. The Bororo, also of South America, see the village as mapping 'the principles which organize the relations of all beings and processes'. The divisions of the village do not merely order the flux of daily life: 'they reflect and impose the laws by which the whole cosmos is regulated'. The Bororo 'perceive the village as *the* manifestation of transcendent reality' (original emphasis).[13] The whole cosmos, so to speak, comes down to earth.

Bearing in mind what we have learned from Barasana and Bororo architecture and cosmology, we start our exploration of Near Eastern cosmos-articulating architecture at 'Ain Ghazal, the site that yielded the large, staring statues (Chapter 3). Those statues must surely have had cosmological implications. Indeed, we find hints about cosmology at 'Ain Ghazal that are more fully expressed at other sites and, as subsequent chapters show, even on the far side of Europe in the great megalithic tombs.

'Ain Ghazal architecture

In the 1970s, bulldozers constructing a new motorway on the outskirts of Amman, Jordan, uncovered an archaeological site and thereby posed the sort of problem that faces 'developers' in so many parts of the world, but perhaps especially in the Near East. Eventually, in 1982 archaeologists led by Gary Rollefson and Zeidan Kafafi were able to do something about the threatened heritage. They found that the new road, which ran along the west bank of the Zarqa River, cut a 600-m (1,970-ft) swathe through the site. Ancient remains were found on both sides of the river. It is estimated that the west-bank part of the site covered about 10 ha (25 acres); on the east bank there was a settlement covering approximately 1.5 ha (3.7 acres).

The overall results of the 'Ain Ghazal excavations are summarized in Table 1, which also sorts out the potentially confusing naming of time periods to which we must refer. As Rollefson points out, the settlement saw 'an unprecedented history of uninterrupted habitation in the Levant for more than 2,000 years'.[14] The table shows how architectural and demographic fluctuations characterized the settlement. Of especial interest to our enquiry are certain features of, and changes in, architecture, because it is here that we shall discover evidence for the articulation of social and consciousness contracts.

Neolithic settlement at 'Ain Ghazal began in the Middle Pre-Pottery Neolithic B Period (MPPNB), between 7250 and 6500 BC. By the end of the MPPNB there may have been as many as 750 people living in the settlement. At the beginning of the subsequent Late Pre-Pottery Neolithic B (LPPNB), about 6500 BC, there was what the excavators call 'a population explosion'. This sudden expansion is thought to have been caused by an influx of people from other Near Eastern villages, such as Jericho, where environmental degradation caused by ill-advised land-use led to their abandonment. Consequently, 'Ain Ghazal expanded across the Zarqa to the previously uninhabited east bank. By 6000 BC there were approximately 2,500 people living at 'Ain Ghazal.[15]

The first houses of the MPPNB Period were built with rectangular stone walls and lime-plastered floors. They were in tightly knit clusters, each group being separated from others by several metres. Circular hearths were sunk into the floors. The excavators believe that each group of houses was associated with a specific kinship group, perhaps a single, nuclear family.

The increased population of the LPPNB Period brought changes to this comparatively simple layout. People now built what seem to have been much larger two-storey houses. It is thought that these buildings suggest a shift away from small family groups to more extended families that shared labour and resources to cope with exacerbated degradation of the environment. The conditions that caused people to leave their original homes and move to 'Ain Ghazal were catching up with them. As we have already had occasion to remark, if agriculture was an adaptation, it was not entirely successful. There was a Neolithic ecological backlash.

In the Pre-Pottery Neolithic C Period (PPNC) the large buildings were abandoned and replaced by small, single-room, single-storey structures. This shift, the excavators argue, is indicative of a move back to the nuclear family as the core of social organization.

So far, we have sketched a fairly unremarkable sequence (at least for the Near East) from which we can infer little about the people's beliefs and rituals. But archaeologists made more informative finds. Over and above such essentially domestic architecture (like the Barasana *malocas* and 'Ain Ghazal houses) many societies have special buildings that lead directly and exclusively to access to the spirit realm. These structures, to which names such as 'temple', 'shrine' and 'church' are variously given, exert influence beyond the nuclear family and embrace larger communities that come together to celebrate and to contact supernatural levels, beings and powers. Some of these ancient structures are among the most impressive architectural creations of humankind.

Buildings of this kind have been found at 'Ain Ghazal. During the LPPNB the people began to build rectangular structures with a semicircular apse at one end (Fig. 19). There are three or four in all. They are smaller than the houses of the MPPNB Period: floor space averages 7.5 sq. m (80 sq. ft). The

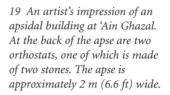

19 An artist's impression of an apsidal building at 'Ain Ghazal. At the back of the apse are two orthostats, one of which is made of two stones. The apse is approximately 2 m (6.6 ft) wide.

apse seems to have been a focus of interest, because in one instance the centre of the arc is marked by an orthostat (large standing stone) and what the excavators describe as 'two large stones mimicking another orthostat' (Fig. 19). The attention of people entering the apsidal buildings was directed, or controlled: they were led to see what the designers of the structure intended them to see – the curved space of the apse and the adjacent orthostats. Guided (or controlled) sight is a key feature of religious experience, belief and practice that will crop up in subsequent chapters. It is important to note that these exceptional, apparently religious buildings preceded 'palaces', that is, secular exceptional buildings. Houses remained all much the same size, and so give no indication of social differentiation. Changes in religion came before, and probably led to, the development of institutionalized, hierarchical societies.[16]

20 The orthostat in the doorway of the 'Upper Temple' building at 'Ain Ghazal. The singular standing stone is in stark contrast to the rest of the wall.

In addition, researchers found two small circular buildings (Fig. 21). Each focused on a central hole and had subfloor channels. The floors had been replastered many times, possibly in the performance of repeated rituals. They are so small (less than 5 sq. m/54 sq. ft) that they could hardly have been houses. The excavators think of them as 'shrines'. One of these was the fourth and final design in a sequence that began with a rectangular building with an apse. It therefore seems that the circular buildings evolved out of the apsidal structures. Rollefson and Kafafi suggest that they were 'specially dedicated to cult activity, possibly overseen by a shaman or priest who was associated with a particular kinship unit'.[17]

What we believe are key architectural elements are repeated in two much larger (20 sq. m/215 sq. ft and more than 36 sq. m/388 sq. ft) rectangular structures that the excavators call 'temples'. They probably served a communal function. In the smaller of the two there is a red-painted hearth; it is

21 A circular 'shrine' at 'Ain Ghazal with a central hole. It is the last of four stages of alteration to a structure that began as an apsidal building. The room is about 2 m (6.6 ft) in diameter and the hole about 60 cm (23.6 in) wide.

Table 1 The archaeological sequence at 'Ain Ghazal

PERIOD	DATES	DOMESTIC BUILDINGS
Yarmoukian (Late Pottery Neolithic)	5000 BC	Isolated single rooms. Large courts.
	5500 BC	
PPNC (Pre-Pottery Neolithic C)		Small single rooms. Single-storey buildings. Courtyards. [*Nuclear families*]
	6000 BC	
LPPNB (Late Pre-Pottery Neolithic B)	Population explosion: 2,500 people on 12 ha. Leads to environmental stress.	Large two-storey houses. Twice the size of MPPNB settlement. [*Extended families*]
	6500 BC	
MPPNB (Middle Pre-Pottery Neolithic B)	750 people on 5 ha.	Small clusters of free-standing buildings. Close together. Lime-plastered floors. [*Nuclear families*]
	7250 BC	

surrounded by seven stones, another three standing stones and 'a large anthropomorphic orthostat' in the eastern wall – quite a complex arrangement. Standing stones, or whatever they represented, were clearly important to the people of 'Ain Ghazal, as they were at Göbekli Tepe.

Special Buildings	Burials	Skulls and Statues
	No burials. Outside cemetery?	
	Subfloor burials. No decoration in graves. Fully articulated skeletons.	
Apsidal buildings with orthostats in key places. Small, circular shrines. Two 'temples'. Three standing stones and orthostat. Hearth and 'altar'. Six orthostats.	Little evidence for burials.	
	Burials subfloor or in courtyards. Disinterred and decapitated. Rubbish pits with articulated skeletons. 30% of burials adults. Infants, articulated in rubbish pits. Minority of burials beneath floors, walls and in doorways.	Plastered skulls: four in one pit. Eyes: bitumen outlines. Animal figurines. Flint in two cattle figurines. Few goats, yet mainly bones of goats. 6570 BC: Two statues. Three two-headed busts. 6750 BC: 13 statues. 12 busts.

The larger 'temple' is even more elaborate (Pl. 8). It has two rooms, in one of which is an 'altar made up of two large limestone slabs supported by six orthostats',[18] apparently set in pairs, against the centre of the eastern wall. In addition, there is an unpainted hearth in front of the 'altar'; it was once surrounded by seven flat stones. This sort of feature makes one wonder about the hearths in houses: did they serve a practical *and* a ritual function? We suspect that, whatever its exact nature may have been, the symbolism of fire, a transforming agent, was inevitably present in domestic contexts. There was probably no decisive separation between domestic activities and ritual.

Arrangements of stones similar to the 'Ain Ghazal 'altars' have been found at other Near Eastern MPPNB and LPPNB sites. For instance, in the so-called Cult Building at Çayönü, a site we mentioned in Chapter 3, human skulls were deposited on the floor. In addition, many human skeletons were found in a pit, together with aurochs skulls and horns (that is, parts of wild animals were deliberately associated with human remains). Most strikingly, traces of human, aurochs and sheep blood were found on a large stone 'table' or 'altar'. Human and aurochs blood residues were also found on a long flint knife. In another Çayönü structure, the Terrazzo Building, there was a circular stone basin in the northwest corner. Traces of human blood were detected on the rim.[19] As we saw in Chapter 3, the implication of both human and animal sacrifice is hard to avoid. Sacrifice, both human and animal, is posited on a notion of transition between cosmological realms: the sacrificial person or animal is 'sent' from one part of the cosmos to another (see also Chapter 5).

At another site, Kfar HaHoresh (see Fig. 1), the theme of human and animal associations is taken further. The excavators found a large but shallow pit in which human and gazelle bones had been arranged so that, when seen from above, they represented an animal.[20] In addition, a plastered human skull from Kfar HaHoresh was found in a cache and in association with a headless gazelle carcass, as if the human head took the place of the animal's missing head.[21] The implications of these finds are far-reaching. A unity of opposites is built into the way in which sacrifice bridges the cosmos: human beings and animals, so different in this world, are united – or transmuted into one another – by cosmological beliefs, as they are in Stage 3 hallucinations (Chapter 2). Whether there were human and animal sacrifices or not, the interaction in some Neolithic ritual contexts of human beings and animals and, moreover, their combined cosmological implications seem clear.

Perhaps the most informative feature of the large 'Ain Ghazal 'temple' is at the door between the two rooms. It is 'a screen wall [that] would have blocked any view of activities in the eastern room to anyone standing in the western room' (parenthesis added).[22] So we find not only focused vision (on to orthostats in apses and altars) but, simultaneously, *restricted* vision. The ritual activities that took place within this building were posited on 'seeing and not-seeing', as were activities in Barasana *malocas*. The immediate implication is one of social distinctions. Indeed, distinctions between what can be seen and what cannot be seen and by whom are features of ritual buildings right through the Neolithic and beyond, even into medieval cathedrals with their sanctuaries and elaborate screens.

What of the people who frequented these special buildings? Over 100 human burials have been found at 'Ain Ghazal, most in the rich MPPNB Period. Adults were interred in courtyards or beneath house floors. It seems that, after an intervening period, they were disinterred and decapitated.[23] Treatment of the dead was a serial, not a one-off, event. Others, including a majority of infants, were simply buried in rubbish pits; their heads were not removed. This difference almost certainly reflects social distinctions: bodies of powerful (however that word may be understood) people were placed beneath floors, while less significant people were buried elsewhere. Of great interest are a few infant burials that were placed beneath floors, walls or in doorways. They seem to have had a significance that related to the built structure itself, perhaps as offerings to secure good fortune.

At this stage in our argument, we summarize some architectural features together with their cosmological and social implications; these associations increase in importance in the remainder of this and in subsequent chapters. They are:
- standing stones that emphasize the vertical dimension of the tiered cosmos;
- holes sunk into the floor and subfloor channels, also indicative of verticality;
- hearths that suggest transformation by fire;
- structures that guide what people can and cannot see;
- sacrifice as cosmological transition;
- an implication of ritual being associated with social differentiation.

A number of these features are found at what is the most elaborately symbolic Neolithic site in the (broadly conceived) Near East. It is situated on the Konya Plain in southern Turkey.

Çatalhöyük

In her acknowledgments of assistance in the celebrated Jericho excavations Dame Kathleen Kenyon named such luminaries of the day as Lady Wheeler, wife of the famed researcher and popularizer of archaeology, Sir Mortimer Wheeler. Also listed is one 'J. Mellart (1952–53)' (sic). James Mellaart was himself soon to make even more sensational discoveries, and Sir Mortimer Wheeler was to write the preface to his subsequent book.

Mellaart first saw the double mound now known as Çatalhöyük in 1952, but it was not until 'a cold November day in 1958' that he was able to make 'its more formal discovery' (see Fig. 1).[24] Where the prevailing southwesterly wind had exposed the surface he found 'unmistakable traces of mudbrick buildings, burned red in a conflagration contrasting with patches of grey ash, broken bones, potsherds and obsidian tools and weapons'.[25] At that time it was widely believed that there were no Neolithic remains on the Anatolian Plateau in southern Turkey. Çatalhöyük was soon to refute this belief spectacularly. Here was evidence not only for a Neolithic settlement of sophisticated architecture, but also for advanced art – wall paintings, figurines and moulded animal heads. Mellaart concluded: 'Every year the study of the origins of civilization in the Near East becomes more complex and thus more human.'[26] He was right, and in extensive ways that he could not have foreseen.

Mellaart's work at Çatalhöyük ended in 1964. New excavations were begun in 1993. Led by Ian Hodder, then of Cambridge University, now of Stanford University, an international and multi-disciplinary team is currently producing more and more highly detailed evidence both to confirm and refine Mellaart's original findings (Pl. 10). Hodder sums up the excitement of this remarkable new endeavour: 'we are on the edge of a new type of understanding of a mythical world deeply embedded in a complex social system ...'[27]

> ... more complex and thus more human ...
> ... a mythical world deeply embedded in a complex social system ...

Both Mellaart and Hodder sensed that views of the Neolithic are shifting away from austere artefact analysis to an understanding of beliefs and rituals, in short, to a cognitive archaeology. Today, Çatalhöyük is perhaps best known for its richly decorated rooms and plaster-covered bulls' heads – the so-called 'bucrania' – that, significantly, recall the human plastered heads from various Near Eastern Neolithic sites. They are evidence indeed for a 'mythical world'.[28]

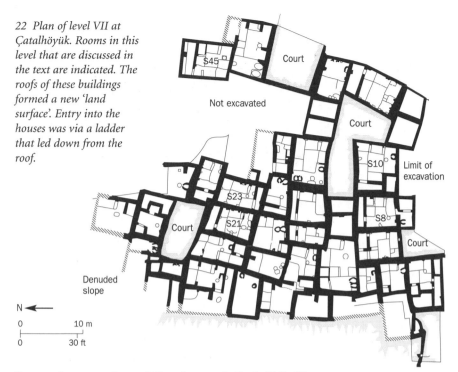

22 Plan of level VII at Çatalhöyük. Rooms in this level that are discussed in the text are indicated. The roofs of these buildings formed a new 'land surface'. Entry into the houses was via a ladder that led down from the roof.

Cosmology and architecture at Çatalhöyük

The 15-m (49.2-ft) high mound that rises above the Konya Plain comprises the remains of layer after layer of mud-brick houses. We shall consider these structures in some detail in the light of what we have learned about the tiered cosmos that is the neurological heritage of all human beings. We ask: Does that neurological heritage make sense of and, in doing so, co-ordinate the diverse finds at Çatalhöyük? Was a consciousness contract, together with its cosmological implications, embedded in Çatalhöyük architecture?

Apart from completely immured rubbish dump areas, there were few spaces or walkways between the self-contained groups of rooms, at least in the part of the settlement so far excavated (Fig. 22). In effect, the roofs of the town created a new land surface, probably, we argue, a replication of the cosmological level on which people lived their daily lives. Each complex of rooms was entered through the roof by climbing down a wooden ladder set on the south wall, or, possibly, via a shaft at the north end.[29] The recent excavations show that in some rooms a bench was constructed to facilitate entry from above.[30] The rooms to which the ladders led may have been naturally lit, if at all, by small, highly positioned windows and, in some cases, possibly by light shafts.

23 James Mellaart's reconstruction of the north and east walls of S.VI.A.8, showing platforms with bulls' horns along the edge, columns, wall panels, bucrania, an image of a bull cut into the plaster and a hearth. Above: third phase; below: fourth phase.

Some rooms, generally those farthest from the entrance, were richly decorated. Mellaart called these rooms 'shrines' (Fig. 23), but today the distinction between so-called shrines and living-rooms seems less and less clear-cut.[31] We therefore abandon the use of 'shrine'.[32]

This decision is important because it helps to avoid an imposed distinction between sacred and secular concepts, spaces and relationships. Such a distinction makes sense to modern Westerners, but, as we have already seen, it is by no means universal. As a result, it lands us in another dilemma. Rather than use 'house', another word with unwelcome restrictive connotations, we prefer the more neutral word 'structure'. It seems probable that domestic and ritual activities were not rigidly – spatially or conceptually – separated. There was probably a dynamic, creative *amalgam*, a seamless conceptual fabric, of what Westerners see as 'sacred' and 'secular'. As Jonathan Last rightly remarks, 'obsidian [tool] manufacture is as likely to have been a shamanistic practice as painting walls'.[33]

Recalling what we learned from the Barasana *malocas* and what is implied by the 'Ain Ghazal buildings, we argue that movement through the spaces created by the Çatalhöyük structures was almost certainly meaningful and socially contextualized. Access between rooms was afforded not by full-length doors but by small porthole-like openings (72–77 cm/28–30 in high) through which people were obliged to crawl. Similar openings sometimes led to much smaller chambers behind richly decorated rooms. Entry into a complex of rooms thus entailed, first, descent into a dimly lit area; secondly, having descended, people had to crawl or bend low in order to move from one walled space to another and thus deeper into the structure. To understand the way in which the people of Çatalhöyük conceptualized their buildings and the experiences that they engendered we consider the significance of deep limestone caves, such as the ones in France and Spain with their Upper Palaeolithic painted and engraved images.

At Çatalhöyük, descent, limited light and the need to crawl through small openings between chambers are akin to the experience of moving through limestone caves. This suggestion is not as fanciful as it may at first seem. Such caves occur in the Taurus Mountains, only a couple of days' travel to the south.[34] That the people of Çatalhöyük knew and explored them is shown by pieces of stalactite and limestone concretions from them that were found in the structures. Some of these were partially carved; others, suggestive of breasts, udders and human figures were left uncarved. Although the data are sometimes imprecise,[35] these pieces were deposited in some decorated rooms together with 'cult statues'.[36] Stalactite, along with blue or green apatite, was also used to make necklaces. Mellaart saw an implication of these finds: 'It does not require an overdose of imagination to imagine a host of deities, humans and petrified animals in the grandeur of one of the stalagmitic caves, of which plenty were available in the Taurus Mountains'.[37]

Certainly, the presence at Çatalhöyük of broken-off stalactites suggests cosmological and religious beliefs about an underworld to which caves afforded one mode of access. In bringing stalactites to the structures at Çatalhöyük people may have been taking parts of that *natural* underworld to their own *built* underworld. The flat-topped buildings with their entrances from above may therefore have paralleled limestone caves in certain ways and yet, at the same time, created conceptual distance between human-made structures and the natural caves: they were similar to, but not identical with, caves. What ultimately mattered was 'the cave in the mind' – the neurologically engendered vortex and religious experiences.

We can now consider some architectural details at Çatalhöyük. Vertical and horizontal features recall Barasana *malocas*: they seem to have both expressed and, by their very manufacture and use, moulded beliefs about a tiered cosmos.

First, we examine *verticality*.

This dimension was powerfully suggested by the wooden ladders that gave access to dimly lit rooms. In many societies with a tiered cosmos ladders are associated with spiritual transcosmological travel. In the 1940s Alfred Métraux discovered the significance of ladders among South American Indian groups. Among the Caribs, novices seeking to become shamans have hot pepper rubbed into their eyes. Thus blinded and in great pain, they receive hallucinogenic tobacco juice and experience visions. In the land of the spirits, the novice is told, 'You will climb to heaven on the ladder of Grandfather vulture.' He then climbs a twisting ladder and so reaches the first level of the upper cosmos.[38] On another continent, Sora Indian shamans shoot a succession of arrows to create a ladder down that the soul of a dead person can climb to the underworld.[39] As a material symbol rather than just a vision, Siberian Tungus shamans take a young larch tree and cut off its branches and leaves. They then fix two cross beams to make a 'ladder' up that a shaman can climb to the upper realm.[40] Reports like these recall a well-known biblical passage. Jacob dreamed of 'a ladder set up on the earth, and the top of it reached to heaven; and behold, the angels of God ascending and descending on it' (GENESIS 28:12). Though described in only one biblical verse, that transcosmological ladder has entered Western imagery.

Mircea Eliade, in his compendious synthesis of shamanistic practices and beliefs around the world, comments that there are 'countless examples of shamanistic ascent to the sky by means of a ladder'.[41] Of particular interest, given the geographical location of Çatalhöyük, are ancient Egyptian beliefs. The *Book of the Dead*, a collection of funerary texts found on tomb walls, sarcophagi and in papyrus rolls, records: 'I set up a ladder to heaven among the gods.' The gods also 'made a ladder for N., that he might ascend to heaven on it'. Amulets representing ladders have been found in Egyptian tombs.[42] Ladder symbolism is a theme that continued through Christian writings, and Dante described a ladder rising to the highest celestial sphere.

Whilst the Çatalhöyük ladders provided perfectly mundane access to the buildings, that function does not preclude them from having further significances, any more than daily living precludes Barasana *malocas* from representing the cosmos. Given the widespread association of ladders with a tiered cosmos, we must not ignore the possible symbolism of the Çatalhöyük ladders, especially in view of the nature of the rooms to which they led, details of which we give in a moment.

Then, too, verticality was emphasized by columns set in the walls (see Fig. 23). Mellaart believes that the form of these columns evolved from the structure of timber houses.[43] This is particularly clear in the earlier levels[44] where wooden posts of juniper and oak were separated by brick panels that did little to support the building.

There are no juniper trees on the Konya Plain; the nearest juniper forests are in the valleys of the Taurus Mountains. Wooden posts and beams are therefore further evidence for contact with the region of the limestone caves. At a later time, there was much less emphasis on timber, but the builders did not abandon the visually prominent vertical lines of columns; wooden posts were replaced by skeuomorphic mud-brick pillars engaged against the walls. As we have pointed out, trees are sometimes associated with vertical spiritual journeys; columns, even though the later ones were not wooden, may have continued to emphasize the *axis mundi*.

A number of features confirm the importance of columns, both timber and brick, beyond any structural function or aesthetic fashion. The builders sometimes emphasized pillars by using red paint,[45] a colour that almost certainly had symbolic connotations, perhaps of blood and sacrifice, and therefore of transition. In one instance, parallel zigzags that give a diamond chain effect further embellished two pillars against a north wall;[46] in the centre of each diamond is a dot.[47] (We return to these intriguing patterns shortly.) In another case, when one room[48] was built on top of its predecessor,[49] the builders duplicated the central post set in the north wall, together with a plaster ram's head that seems to support the post but in fact served no structural function.

This sort of repetition is characteristic of cult continuity, a common but not inevitable feature at Çatalhöyük.[50] Plaster bulls' heads, which we come to in a moment, are, however, more frequently associated with columns than are rams' heads. They are at the feet of columns or set in positions on them.[51] By contrast, images of felines are never associated with columns, only with the panels between them. Finally, shorter columns frequently marked the edges of low platforms that subdivided the floors of rooms; plaster bulls' heads, often moulded around frontal bones and horn cores, surmounted these stumpy columns, as if guarding them (Pl. 11; and see Fig. 23). As our Barasana illustration and the central pole in the Plains Indians' Sun Dance (Chapter 3) suggest, certain selected animals are tied into notions of the cosmos and its replication in architecture. Each animal has its place in the structure of the cosmos and hence in the house as well.

The construction of platforms within Çatalhöyük rooms, a feature of other Near Eastern Neolithic sites as well, was, we argue, a further expression of cosmic and social verticality: they subdivided the floors into discrete levels, some of which were painted red. The dead, or, rather, selected dead, were buried beneath these platforms.

The spaces created by the platforms were probably socially significant, though not rigidly so. As people moved around in the rooms, they were obliged to step (or avoid stepping) from one level to another, physical movement thus repeatedly emphasized, and sometimes no doubt challenged, social distinctions and the place of those distinctions within the overall verticality of the cosmos. In some instances, moving from one floor level to another entailed stepping past bucrania that were liminally situated on the edge of the step. The cosmos and its animals were embedded in the house.

Thus there seem to be two modes of verticality. First, columns, frequently associated with bulls' heads, and ladders reach from floor to roof of the structures. Secondly, platforms set at different heights subdivide the floor. As bucrania sometimes support and embellish columns, they also mark the edges of platforms: there is a distinct, visible link between aurochs heads and *edges* between levels. There is therefore an implication: bulls' heads were physically associated with liminality and movement on the vertical axis of the cosmos. They were associated with transition between levels, in other words, with spiritual journeys in a tiered cosmos. They were comparable to the jaguar in Barasana cosmology and shamanism.

Notions of *horizontality* are set within and defined by the vertical framework: one could say that horizontality 'opens up' some of the implications of the vertical axis. The frequent division of the plastered panels between columns into three horizontal levels strikingly portrayed this dimension (Pl.

12). The lowest level is often painted red, certainly more often than any other level. Elaborate painted patterns are also usually associated with the lowest level. Whilst bulls' heads were placed within the horizontal levels, the inter-columnar panels are pre-eminently the place of the so-called 'goddess' figures. The ways in which people made and related these figures to the panels deserve comment.

Apart from one apparently highly stylized exception,[52] female figures were not modelled on vertical posts. Secondly, animal heads are solid and moulded in clay; often, especially in the later levels, the makers set actual skulls, horns and jaw bones in the plaster. By contrast, they made female figures of plaster moulded on bundles of reeds;[53] this technique recalls the making of the 'Ain Ghazal statues (Chapter 3). Notwithstanding technological considerations, the different materials and the different ways of gathering them (on the one hand, plaster and parts of animals and, on the other, plaster and reeds) are suggestive of social, possibly gender, distinctions in the process of production.

Further, the different materials and construction techniques mark distinc-tions between the verticality of the posts and the horizontality of the panels. While posts are associated with bull and other imagery only, the panels carry diverse animal imagery and, virtually exclusively, female figures. Bulls, especially, control the columns; then they share the panels with other animals and female figures.[54] We can thus detect a general conceptual pattern with cosmological associations, even if we cannot be precise about the exact mean-ings of the various images.

At this point, we can summarize the explanatory power of our suggestion that Çatalhöyük architecture related to neurologically generated tiered cos-mology. Again we ask: Does this hypothesis make sense of and co-ordinate otherwise disparate features of the structures?

- The notion of verticality may have been linked to the *axis mundi*, the transcosmological route travelled by, and probably the preserve of, rit-ual specialists, who may have been members of most Çatalhöyük families rather than a priestly class or rare spiritual figures.
- Burials beneath floors were probably let into the subterranean realm.
- The columns were embellished with bulls' heads. Bulls were probably the ritual specialists' pre-eminent (though not exclusive) spirit-animals, the power of which made transcosmological travel possible.
- At the same time, notions of cosmological horizontality were reflected in the usually tripartite division of intercolumnar panels and differentiat-ing platforms.

– Both panels and platforms may have been associated with the three principal divisions of the cosmos or, possibly, with subdivisions of the lowest level of the cosmos; the second of these possibilities is suggested by the fact that platforms were encountered *after* descent into the 'subterranean' rooms. What seem to us to be contradictions may not have been so to Çatalhöyük residents.

– The levels of the cosmos that the panels opened up were associated with bulls and with female imagery, the so-called goddesses.

All in all, descent into the structures took people into a complexly constructed level of the cosmos that had social implications.

Permeable walls

We can now take our argument a stage further. The walls at Çatalhöyük were, in themselves, clearly of great significance. They were not only painted; they were also moulded so that three-dimensional images were an integral part of the vertical surfaces. What does this evidence imply?

We have already referred to moulded plaster heads of rams and, especially, bulls. There are also what appear to be moulded breasts. Some of these contain beaks of vultures, fox teeth and, in one instance, a weasel skull. Other animal parts moulded into the walls included jaws of wild boars.[55] Importantly, all these forms, especially the animal heads, are not only part of the walls: they also *look out* from the walls. From a certain point in the history of Çatalhöyük onwards, the use of horn cores and skull bones increased, and the bulls' heads were constructed around these parts of actual animals. As time passed, it seems that animals came to emerge more and more 'literally' from the walls. Simultaneously, the moulded bucrania became more and more like the plastered human skulls of other Near Eastern Neolithic sites; in death, (some) human beings and (some) animals were treated in comparable ways.

Most of these three-dimensional mural images were replastered many times. In one of the rooms,[56] 1.8-m (6-ft) long facing leopards were replastered at least 40 times, during which process they began to lose their original sharp outlines.[57] Replastering was also practised on female figures. Some images were replastered up to a hundred times.[58] Renewal of images by means of the very substance of the walls themselves was, we argue, a meaningful act, not just an aesthetic refurbishing. The fact that, in the case of the leopards, and indeed other images as well, the patterns painted on some layers of plaster were similar to but not identical with those on earlier layers suggests repeated appropriations and re-creations of the images. The *act of making* and *remaking* was as important as – or, perhaps, more important than – the finished image.

Over and above imagery integrated with walls, additional features and evidence for other practices are of interest because they point to the mediating role of the walls. Walls stood between not only spaces but also states of being.

Many rooms had red-painted niches cut into the walls, seemingly to receive some sort of object. These niches were present in even the earliest decorated room that Mellaart found.[59] We suggest that they may, in a broad sense, parallel the Upper Palaeolithic practice of placing objects in the walls of caves.[60] In the Palaeolithic case, it seems that animals moved two ways through the walls: they appeared out of the walls to vision questers, and people passed pieces of them back to the spirit realm behind the walls.[61]

Then, too, the importance of actually 'getting into' the walls is powerfully suggested by a remarkable brick burial.[62] The body of a prematurely born child was wrapped in fine fabric together with a 'tiny bit of bright shell and a small chip of obsidian' and then enclosed in a brick that became part of the wall of the decorated room. The shell, associated with other burials as well, may have referred to a subaquatic nether world (as we have seen, the neurologically generated vortex is frequently accompanied by sensations of immersion), and was possibly in some general ways symbolically linked to the shell eyes of the Jericho skulls. Obsidian, probably from the slopes of the volcanoes Göllü and Nenezi Dag, may similarly have referred to an underworld that spewed forth fire and molten rock (Chapter 9). Also stuck between bricks (though not exclusively so) were 'crude clay figurines, mainly of animals but including clumsy and highly schematized human figures'.[63] As the changing architecture at 'Ain Ghazal suggests, so too at Çatalhöyük, practices came and went as the years passed.

Finally, the importance of walls and movement of various kinds through them is powerfully suggested by what happened when a room was abandoned.[64] Not only were the plaster figures defaced by having their hands, feet and faces broken, but the small porthole-like 'doorways' between rooms were bricked up. Any further emergence of figures from the walls, as well as the possibility of human beings or, more probably, spirit beings crawling through walls, was thus both literally and symbolically terminated before a new room was built. Clearly, there was more to these structures than mundane living quarters.

In sum, the evidence we have outlined suggests that the walls of Çatal-höyük structures were ritually important. They were, we argue, thought of as permeable interfaces between people in the building (and therefore already in a lower level of the cosmos) and a spirit world that lay behind the walls. They were like 'membranes' between components of the cosmos; behind them lay a realm from which spirits and spirit-animals could emerge and be induced to emerge. Images could, by oft-repeated ritual replastering and repainting, be coaxed through this mediatory surface; each replastering and repainting may have been a new celebration and enactment of the emergence of spirit-animals and 'goddesses'. Other replastering may have been intended to conceal the images, perhaps for a ritually determined period. In addition, objects and offerings of various kinds were placed in the walls; there was a two-way traffic. The important point is that control of the spirit world and its inhabitants was socially significant and needed to be repeatedly demonstrated. Such demonstrations may have been conducted by spiritual leaders within families, rather than by any sort of priesthood.

These observations suggest that small undecorated chambers behind the walls of some highly decorated rooms were not exclusively storerooms or granaries (though grain and other evidence for domestic activity were found in some) and lightshafts, but retreats reached by crawling through walls and where solitary religious experiences could be induced, perhaps by sensory deprivation, away from the rich imagery of other areas.

Did all these divisions and images have social implications? Contact and movement between the divisions, vertically and horizontally, was probably controlled. It seems likely that the built environment of Çatalhöyük was a place where people, by moving between demarcated areas, made statements about their social statuses, in the same way that a Christian priest makes a statement about his status when he moves into the sanctuary of a cathedral. Significantly, the ways in which Çatalhöyük people thus built up their social statuses were related to the tiered structure of the cosmos itself. Cosmology and society went hand in hand. There is nothing exceptional about this suggestion. We have shown it to be the case with Barasana *malocas* and other ritual contexts.

We have by no means exhausted the complex symbolism that Mellaart's excavations revealed and that Hodder and his associates are still uncovering. As we have implied, within the processes of moving between areas and their associated social statuses, control of altered states and their communally sanctioned imagery probably played a significant role. This last point becomes clearer when we consider further the kinds of images that have been found at Çatalhöyük.

Imagery in a built cosmos

Mellaart found that Çatalhöyük imagery comprises both representational and geometric motifs. The two kinds of imagery can be understood in the light of their location in a built, but neurologically generated, underworld. Imagery should not be abstracted from its physical and conceptual contexts and analysed simply as 'pictures in a book'. It is always implicated in social and consciousness contracts. We deal first with representational imagery and then move on to geometric motifs.

So-called 'Goddesses'

Perhaps the most celebrated imagery at Çatalhöyük, along with the bucrania that we have already discussed, are the so-called 'goddess figures'. Mellaart was especially struck by them and wrote of a Great Goddess who 'became associated with the process of agriculture, with taming and nourishing domesticated animals, with ideas of increase, abundance and fertility'.[65] His and other writers' proliferating language reflects the impact that the notion of a female 'Goddess' has on some modern Westerners. Moving to (rather vague) African ethnographic analogies, Jean-Daniel Forest suggests something different. He argues that kinship relations underwrite the Çatalhöyük murals and figurines: exchange of females links patrilineal lineages and generates a principle whereby the female begets the male.[66] Ian Hodder emphasizes the contexts of Çatalhöyük imagery and also turns to African analogies, the Nuba of Ethiopia and to Mary Douglas's influential and insightful work on pollution.[67] He sets up a structuralist group of oppositions:

male	inner (back)	death	wild
female	outer (front)	life	domestic[68]

We consider this kind of analysis in more detail in Chapters 5 and 6. For the present, we note Mary Voigt's detailed analysis of Near East Neolithic figurines. Like Hodder, she emphasizes context and suggests that 'fertility' may be too vague an interpretation of the figurines. She suggests that '"abundance" and an assured supply of food and offspring ... makes good sense based on a significant shift in the subsistence economy of tenth to eighth millennium sites in Turkey'.[69]

We feel that these sorts of interpretations of imagery are enticing but problematic. One cannot argue that Neolithic people consciously made 'goddess' figurines and reliefs in order to make statements about 'fertility' or 'abundance', or about the exchange of females linking patrilineal lineages, or about a generating principle whereby the female begets the male. Asked why they made and kept the figurines, they would not have replied in those terms. Rather, they would have responded with a myth or some other explanation internal to their thought-lives and cosmology, not with abstract concepts that are essentially Western. In general terms, those concepts *may* in some unformulated ways have underlain, rather than triggered, the making of figurines, but they were not the reason why people made them. We therefore content ourselves with noting what we think are some important features of the images.

A particularly interesting example[70] is a female figure that was covered with painted patterns in red, black and orange that extended beyond the figure itself on to the panel.[71] Mellaart believes that the pattern represents a dress or veil thrown wide, perhaps in a dramatic gesture of revelation. That may or may not be correct; either way, the extended pattern causes the figure to blend with the wall. Indeed, Mellaart himself, referring to another female figure that is set between pillars,[72] writes of the 'effect of coming through a door to show herself'[73] – an apt description in view of the ideas that we have developed about the walls as 'membranes' between built spaces set in the nether world.

The association of female figures with the underworld is also implied by carvings of stalactites that appear to represent a 'goddess'. They recall a much earlier manifestation of the same idea: the 'vulvas' of Upper Palaeolithic art. These inverted U-shapes are carved into the walls of many Franco-Cantabrian caves. Sometimes, too, clefts in the rock were coloured with red ochre. Although these vulva forms are often taken to refer to a concept of fertility, a different explanation can be given. Some features of Upper Palaeolithic art suggest that spirit-animals came out of the walls of the caves.[74] The walls themselves were thus, in a sense, *giving birth* to spirit-animals. It was to the fecundity of 'membranous' mediatory walls that the Upper Palaeolithic vulva motifs referred, not to 'fertility' as conceived by some in the modern Western world. It seems probable that some aspects of this more focused notion were present, no doubt in transmuted form, at Çatalhöyük.

At the same time, we note that spiritual transcosmological travel is sometimes thought of as a journey into the womb.[75] Depictions of female genitalia therefore do not *necessarily* stand for fertility and birth, as Westerners are apt to believe. Notwithstanding the notion of the Çatalhöyük female figures being in what is often taken to be a birth posture, we should allow that some may have been associated with the neurologically generated sensation of passage through a tunnel, but construed as *entrance* into the womb. Certainly, the female figures may have had little to do with 'fertility' as it is commonly conceived today by some writers on 'goddess' figurines.[76] Later we suggest another understanding.

THE GREAT HUNT

In addition to female figures there are more complex representational wall paintings that appear, at first glance, to be realistic scenes in the sense that they depict happenings observable in the material world of the Konya Plain. A great 3.4-m- (11-ft-) long frieze,[77] for instance, appears to depict a hunt (Pl. 13; Fig. 24), as do other friezes in the same room. The frieze was plastered over and renewed at least three times.

By carefully removing layers of plaster one at a time Mellaart was able to show that the earliest of the three paintings is polychrome and depicts, on the right, two stags and a fawn together with at least ten hunters with bows and slings.[78] A possible narrative reading of the scene is, however, problematic because a number of figures to the left are apparently dancing. With the exception of a man holding a circular object (probably a drum) and a bow-man, who holds a sling, these left-hand figures all face away from the hunt on the right. The drum is a typical shamanic instrument; insistent, rhythmic sound alters consciousness and carries both drum players and some listeners into the spirit world. The making of a shamanic drum, its decoration and taking into use are often accompanied by complex rituals. The drawings on Siberian drums usually represent the tiered cosmos that their use mediates.[79]

The way in which the figures in the panel are dressed is also important. A number of the dancers wear leopard-skin garments; two figures, said by Mellaart to be acrobats, are naked.[80] Two central figures are headless. In view of other paintings to which we come in a moment, Mellaart suggests that these acephalic figures represent ancestors, 'great hunters of the past ... invoked to partake in the hunting-rites of the living'.[81]

An association of headless figures with what appears to be a dance and also with a hunting scene implies a somewhat, though not entirely, different reading. In many societies the hunting of meat-producing animals is inextricably bound up with the acquisition of the animals' supernatural power. For the southern African San, the eland antelope provides not only meat but also

24 One of the Çatalhöyük wall paintings (S.A.III.1) shows a deer hunt. The figures to the left seem to be dancers; one holds a drum; two are headless. A panel like this suggests that hunting was more than a merely practical undertaking.

more potency than any other creature. When hunting eland, the Ju/'hoansi San use the respect word *tcheni*, dance, because acquisition of that antelope's potency will facilitate an especially efficacious trance, or healing, dance.[82] Set in a constructed nether world, the Çatalhöyük hunt frieze may depict a similar conception, one that did not distinguish decisively between 'materiality' and 'spirituality'. It may therefore not be a daily-life 'scene' as we generally understand the word. As Mellaart argues, the headless figures may well represent the dead, though not simply concerned ancestors: more probably, they were ancestors who, in the lowest level of the cosmos, continued to be involved in the control and acquisition of animal power.[83] Perhaps they are headless because their skulls had been removed for ritual treatment.

VULTURES AND EXCARNATION

The interpretation that takes headless figures to represent the dead is supported by a further set of wall paintings, the remarkable vulture scenes (Fig. 25).[84] In these paintings large, carrion-eating vultures (*Gyps vulvus*, the Griffon vulture) are associated with small headless human figures. The figures lie on their left sides, as do many of the burials beneath the floors, both at Çatalhöyük and elsewhere. Skulls separate from bodies were also found in some of the highly decorated rooms. The relative positions of the vulture and human images seem to imply that the vultures are responsible for the mutilation of human corpses. At Nevali Çori, this theme is developed by a carving on a pillar: an apparently female head is in the clutches of a bird's talons.[85]

Mellaart interprets the Çatalhöyük scenes as depicting excarnation (removal of flesh from the skeleton) prior to burial, a practice for which he claims to have found evidence at Çatalhöyük, though recent work suggests that excarnation was rare.[86] This may well be so, but, as in the case of the headless dancers, there is more that is immediately noticeable. As Mellaart points

out, the legs of some vultures are clearly human.[87] We have seen that therianthropy (combination of human and animal forms) is a common component of shamanistic and other beliefs, many of which are associated with altered states of consciousness. It therefore seems likely that the vultures are another blurring of the distinction between 'materiality' and 'spirituality': they are not merely scavenging birds, but rather beings associated with excarnation and disarticulation, a practice that requires further comment for it will engage our attention in later chapters on the Neolithic of Atlantic Europe.

In some instances of ethnographically recorded excarnation and the severing of skulls from bodies the practice is a ritual enactment of the 'death' and 'rebirth' of a shaman.[88] Reduction of a novice to a skeleton and

25 *The Çatalhöyük wall painting (S.VII.8) that shows vultures and headless human figures. Vultures may have been associated with the removal of flesh from skeletons, either literal or spiritual.*

dismemberment is a widely reported shamanistic spiritual experience; it precedes reconstitution of the fully fledged shaman's body.[89] For example, the clinical psychologist Richard Katz found that some southern African San shamans say that their 'body parts become separated' when they are in an altered state of consciousness.[90] When asked to draw themselves, some San shamans drew separated zigzags and spirals. Pointing to a zigzag with legs attached, an experienced shaman said that this was his spinal cord; seven adjacent but separate zigzags were, he said, the rest of his body. Katz concluded that the image that shamans have of their bodies 'is determined more by their own inner states than by external anatomical criteria ... as body lines become fluid, body parts become separated.'[91]

Because so many shamans around the world report dismemberment and skeletalization as components of their initiation into shamanic status, it seems that the sensation, or hallucination, of one's body coming apart in an altered state of consciousness is, like the sensations of entering a vortex and flying, wired into the human nervous system. This important implication has wide application in the Neolithic. Some people living at Çatalhöyük and other Near East sites who entered altered states probably experienced reduction to a skeleton and dismemberment. Exactly how they understood these experiences and precisely why they valued them would have been culturally and historically situated. As we have seen, the wired brain is always embedded in a cultural milieu. That actual (rather than hallucinatory) excarnation was rarely practised at Çatalhöyük probably suggests that it was a form of special treatment reserved for selected people.

It is crucial to note that the full range of 'hard-wired' experiences and imagery of altered consciousness always constitutes a *potential* resource. People are *able*, but not obliged, to select from them as they build up their belief systems and related social statuses. We must therefore distinguish between psychic (neurologically generated) experiences of excarnation and ritualized enactments of the practice. It seems that, at a particular time in the history of Çatalhöyük,[92] some religious specialists chose to emphasize the mental experience of dismemberment even beyond the literal practice of excarnation by making, in no doubt complex ritual circumstances, wall paintings of therianthropic vultures and headless human beings. Significantly, they placed them on the interface between themselves and a spirit realm.

The apparent rarity of images of dismemberment suggests that it was not a common run-of-the-mill ritual. Only some ritual specialists attempted to differentiate themselves from those who emphasized other components of the

Çatalhöyük ritual complex and the neurologically wired experiences of altered consciousness. Altered states afford a range of experiences from which cultural predilections and personal choices can select some that they deem key to religious and social status. By making excarnation paintings on the membranous walls – behind which the spiritual experiences of reduction to a skeleton and of dismemberment were believed to take place – a specific group of ritual specialists (perhaps in a single extended family) was, we argue, able to further the process of social differentiation and establish for itself a special status vis-à-vis other groups that did not emphasize excarnation. The limited number of vulture scenes, compared with, say, bucrania, suggests that the group that associated itself with (conceptual) excarnation and therianthropic vultures was ephemeral: it did not last for the duration of settlement at the site. Çatalhöyük religion was neither monolithic nor static; on the contrary, it was a dynamic engine for change.

HANDS-ON EXPERIENCE

Before we come to the apparently non-representational – but highly significant – art of Çatalhöyük, there is a category of images seeming to lie between the representational and non-representational: handprints. At Çatalhöyük there are both positive and negative prints.[93] Positive prints are made by coating the palm and fingers with paint and then pressing the hand against a surface. Negative prints, or more correctly 'stencils', are made by placing the hand against a surface and then coating it and the surrounding area with paint. When the hand is removed, an image remains.

The positions of the Çatalhöyük handprints clearly had significance. In one instance a small child's hand-imprint was made on the body of a female figure;[94] in another, there are larger handprints on bulls' and rams' heads.[95] In one of the so-called shrines,[96] handprints were placed around a bull's head, while in yet another room[97] handprints are associated with a pattern of squares (Fig. 26)[98] and with a net-like pattern, zigzags and diamond chains. More examples could be given. Far from being randomly scattered, Çatalhöyük handprints were systematically integrated into a malleable symbolic complex. They were not idle daubings.

Although the image of a hand no doubt had significance as the residue of a specific ritual and person, we argue that the processes of production of those images mattered a great deal, as did the act of making plaster reliefs. Moreover, the paint used for making handprints was probably itself not merely a technical material, as Westerners may think of paint, but rather a powerful

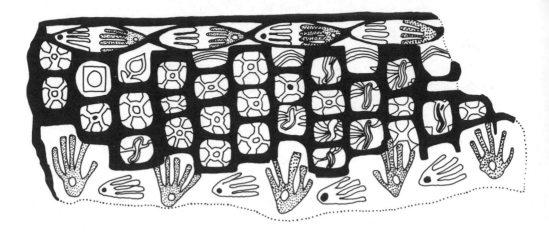

26 Çatalhöyük wall decoration (S.VI.B.8), which includes paintings of hands and what appear to be stylized flowers. The grid-like design is reminiscent of the neurological vortex (see Fig. 9).

substance that effected or enhanced contact with the supernatural.[99] Hand-prints were therefore a product (not necessarily the end-product) of a ritual sequence that entailed, in the case of positive handprints, preparation of a powerful substance, application of it to a human hand, and pressing of the hand against the surface from which forms of animals sprang. In the case of negative prints, paint was applied over both the hand and the adjacent wall surface. As a human hand was painted on to the wall, it was also painted *into* the wall; it disappeared behind the paint. This seems to have been the signifi-cance of handprints in the deep Upper Palaeolithic caves of western Europe. People were placing their hands on the cave walls, which were probably a 'membrane' between them and the spirit realm into which the cave itself led.[100] Whatever other, no doubt numerous, connotations Çatalhöyük hand-prints may have had, they are, we suggest, evidence for and symbols of manual, as well as mental, contact with the spirit world.

GEOMETRIC IMAGERY

The association of some handprints with grids and other forms brings us to the apparently non-representational geometric imagery of Çatalhöyük. In addition to 'chequerboards' (one of which surrounds a niche surmounted by a boar mandible)[101] and net-like patterns (one of which is around the head of a bull, also just above a niche in the same room), there are zigzags and dia-mond chains on a bull's head,[102] diamond chains that are not associated with representational imagery,[103] horizontal zigzags (Fig. 27, above),[104] vertical zigzags,[105] crenellations (Fig. 27, below),[106] and cross hatching to create triangles,[107] so-called kilim patterns, some of which are also cut into the plaster.[108]

If we accept the hypothesis that altered consciousness probably (almost certainly) played a role in Çatalhöyük religion, we must go on to consider the possibility that these motifs derived from entoptic phenomena (Chapter 2). The people of the time must have had the potential to 'see' these very forms. Certainly, they are comparable to the geometric visual percepts generated by the human nervous system in Stage 1 of the model of altered consciousness (Chapter 2).

If we are correct in thinking that, like so many other peoples around the world, those living at Çatalhöyük selected and valued certain geometric mental percepts, then we may conclude that 'chequerboards', net-like patterns,

27 Wall paintings from two Çatalhöyük rooms (above S.VI.A.66; below S.A.III.8). The motifs include horizontal zigzags, crenellations and quatrefoils. Some of the motifs are similar to the forms in the grid in Figure 26.

zigzags, crenellations, diamond chains and cross hatching are consistent with a neurologically generated worldview that included
- a tiered cosmos,
- the mediation of cosmological realms along an *axis mundi*,
- visions of those realms,
- spirit-animals,
- supernatural personages,
- concepts of supernatural potency,
- reduction to a skeleton and dismemberment.

Unity of belief and experience

As we have repeatedly noted, visions cannot be separated from social contexts and consequences. The multifaceted nature of a neurologically generated 'spiritual' complex opens up numerous forms of social and personal manipulation: there are both social and consciousness contracts. There are maintained 'givens' but also variations.

When certain people at Çatalhöyük moved down into the constructed underworld and then (both literally and spiritually) through the walls, the movements of their journey and the existing imagery primed their minds for what they would see if they themselves experienced altered consciousness. Deliberately designed architectural space, a conceptually constructed underworld, and a selected vocabulary of visual motifs were implicated in the reproduction (but also potential subversion) of the social order.

Our notion of consciousness and social contracts thus brings a range of diverse features at Çatalhöyük and other Near Eastern sites into a co-ordinated and, within its own terms, rational framework. There is coherence in Neolithic diversity. The tiered cosmology is, however, an overarching belief system; it should not be taken to imply that *every* image or figurine is *directly* related to altered states of consciousness. On the contrary, the richly resonant motifs probably did not all have precisely the same focus of meaning.[109] What their foci and connotations may have been is a topic for further research.[110] That research will have to consider wider issues, including the mythology that gave coherence to Neolithic life (Chapter 6).

CHAPTER 5

Domesticating Wild Nature

The architecture and imagery that we have described have together begun to reveal something of another world, one very different from the world we inhabit today. We wonder if, language aside, it would be possible to converse with the people of Jericho, 'Ain Ghazal, Göbekli Tepe, Nevali Çori and Çatal-höyük. If we could be transported back over the millennia to an 'Ain Ghazal apsidal building or to a dimly lit Çatalhöyük room, to sit in front of a bull's head, would we find any topic of common interest? Would we be able to understand the inhabitants' conversation, or would we be repeatedly jolted by what to us would seem wildly illogical leaps? Probably conversation would be difficult. If we were to ask for an explanation for a feature of their rituals, they would, as we have pointed out, almost certainly respond with a myth. Would we have any way of understanding that myth, or would it appear inconsequential and bizarre? Our cerebral speculations would be very different from our Neolithic friends' sense of wonder, awe and, perhaps, terror, because our sense of causality and our categories of thought would be different.

In this chapter we try to narrow the communication gap by building on the notion of combined social and consciousness contracts. First, we consider some concepts that we take for granted. One of the widest divergences between us and Neolithic people would be between the connotations and symbolic associations of (apparently) quite simple words, such as 'death', 'birth' and 'wild'. We therefore attempt to uncover what might have been some early Neolithic associations of these three commonly used English words. In doing so, we open up a chink in the curtain of time.

Secondly, we show that, reformulated, the meanings and connotations of 'death', 'birth' and 'wild' provide ways of thinking about a question that has been central to our discussion. It is the great archaeological enigma of the domestication of the aurochs, the wild cattle of the Palaeolithic and the Neolithic. We see that breaking out of restrictive concepts of Western thought administers a sharp tap on our mental kaleidoscope. Suddenly, the pieces assume new patterns. Domestication was not the kind of problem many researchers assume it to be; it was something else altogether.

In considering domestication, we draw together many of the themes that have run through our chapters so far:

– categories of thought;
– relationships with animals;
– neurologically engendered mental experiences;
– a tiered cosmos;
– mental imagery.

Dying to the world

'Death' in many consciousness contracts means 'transition to the spirit world *by whatever means*'. An example from southern Africa illustrates this point. Richard Katz found that, when a Ju/'hoan (!Kung) San ritual specialist falls to the ground in deep trance, he is said to have 'died' (Fig. 28). That 'death' is thought to be, in its essence, identical with physical death: the spirit leaves the body and journeys to the spirit world. Pushing his San informant, Kau Dwa, Katz asked, 'Does that mean really die?' 'Yes', Kau Dwa replied, 'It is the death that kills us all,' but 'healers may come alive again.'[1]

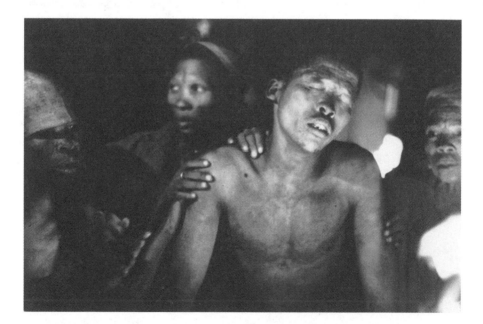

28 *A 1950s southern African San shaman falls into a deeply altered state of consciousness. Women and other dancers take care of the man because his soul is believed to have left his body.*

Katz wrote: 'The Kung say that healers are in great danger at this time. Their soul might wander away or be taken by the spirits.'[2] It is in this condition that they achieve the kind of preternatural sight that we have described. It is 'something like X-ray vision' and can see into a person's body or enable a shaman to see at great distances.[3] They can see the boiling potency inside other ritual specialists.[4]

But how can an altered state be 'death'? Katz remarks, 'I struggle to maintain my Western notions of reality.'[5] His conceptual categories were being shattered; they were inadequate for grasping San thought. He was forced to accept that the notion of spiritual *transition* between a material world and a spirit world infuses the San concept of 'death'. It is not (so much) decay of the body after physical death that matters to the San. For them, 'death' is not annihilation but rather enhanced sight: the dead are seers. Indeed, around the world, ritual specialists' mastery of 'death' – their ability to return from the spirit world – gives them social status and respect and, in some instances, political influence.

The Amazonian Piro hold comparable beliefs. The anthropologist Peter Gow points out that the theme of death is crucial: 'Dying, in Piro thought, is not the negation of life, but a further mode of ontogenesis.'[6] Death is thus one of a series of transformations. Piro ritual specialists also cross over into the dimension of death: they see 'other beings … hallucinatory experience [is] a new way of seeing'.[7]

Those who possess skills of this kind are commonly known as shamans, a word that we continue to use with reference to the southern African San hunters and gatherers and to other societies around the world where the Siberian Tungus word has become accepted. We are less certain about its use in incipient agricultural societies. We therefore use the more neutral phrase 'ritual specialist' or, recalling one of the principal accomplishments of such people, 'seer'.

Bearing ideas of this kind in mind, we suggest that descent into the lowest realm of the cosmos as constructed at some Neolithic sites was, in certain circumstances, itself probably a form of 'death' in the sense of transition between cosmological realms. At Göbekli Tepe rock-cut structures are sunk into the bedrock; at Çatalhöyük people climbed down ladders and through small openings between twilight rooms; at 'Ain Ghazal hearths sunk into floors may have led, by the transmutation of fire, to another, lower level of existence. Yet descent was not always, or entirely, passage through the cosmos. People may well have 'died' when they entered a 'deep' and highly decorated room at

Çatalhöyük, but at the same time they were simply entering part of a dwelling; as we have pointed out, entry into the spirit world and entry into the house are not mutually exclusive concepts. Similarly, the Barasana *malocas* are simultaneously dwellings and models of the cosmos (Chapter 4). It was therefore appropriate that both Barasana and Çatalhöyük dead, or, rather, certain dead, should be buried beneath floors and, at Çatalhöyük, that vultures performing the service of dismemberment and excarnation (whether actual or spiritual) should appear on the walls of rooms.[8] The cosmos enveloped all life.

It is within the same cosmos that we must briefly return to a special kind of death that we have mentioned in earlier chapters: sacrifice. Further comment on it is needed now to fill out the notion of death.

Sacrifice, a worldwide custom, has spawned a vast literature, especially in theology, where ideas of a bargain with deities, propitiation and substitution of an animal for a human being frequently recur (Fig. 29). Here we are not concerned with formulations of this kind. We find them unsatisfactory in that they do not dig deep enough; they seem, especially in Old Testament instances, to interpret practices in the light of much later notions of salvation and symbolism. Abraham does not seem to have found the concept of human sacrifice strange or intrinsically abhorrent (GENESIS 22:1–14). He fully expected to kill and burn his son Isaac at God's behest. Yet, he told his attendants that he was going to 'worship' and that both he and the boy would return. Human sacrifice was part of his religious thinking. The substitution of a ram for his son as prefiguring the sacrifice of Christ is, of course, a later gloss that masks the horror of the incident.

We think it more profitable to situate sacrifice within the tiered cosmos. If we do this, we see that sacrifice, both human and animal, is posited on a notion of transition between cosmological realms. This view is reconcilable with that put forward by Henri Hubert and Marcel Mauss[9] in the last decade of the 19th century and later developed by Victor Turner.[10] These writers divide the act of sacrifice into three stages: in Turner's formulation, separation, liminality and incorporation. We think of separation from one part of the cosmos; a liminal phase during which the victim may be dismembered and imbued with supernatural potency; and incorporation of the victim into another level of the cosmos.

Sacrificial transition, this process of cosmological breakthrough, is in the hands of a ritual specialist who is believed to hold keys to other realms. Sacrificers themselves are thus empowered by the act of sacrifice. It is they who

29 The Sacrifice of Isaac by Mantegna (c. 1490–95): 'And he said, Take now thy son, thine only son Isaac, whom thou lovest, and get thee into the land of Moriah; and offer him there for a burnt offering upon one of the mountains which I will tell thee of.... And Abraham lifted up his eyes, and looked, and behold behind him a ram caught in a thicket by its horns: and Abraham went and took the ram, and offered him up ... in the stead of his son' Genesis *22:2, 13.*

send a human being or animal from the material world into a spiritual dimension. They control 'death' as cosmological transition. Their bloody demonstration of this power enhances their own and their fellow ritual specialists' social influence.

What supernatural beings in the other world make of the proffered person or animal is a separate matter. Some peoples, like the ancient Maya, believed that sacrifices fed the gods: 'sacrifice is a two-way exchange between people and gods, involving the consumption or absorption of soul and flesh by both humans and supernaturals'.[11] Blood was of huge significance. The Moche of ancient Peru also dismembered their sacrificial victims, each body part being imbued with supernatural energy and meaning.[12] The plastered heads found at Near Eastern Neolithic sites (Chapter 1) probably imply something like the Moche transformation of body parts into sacred objects, the power of which would be felt among the living.

Different societies understand the role of sacrifice in different ways. The important point is that sacrifice, initiated by people (though believed to be ordained by gods), bridges divisions of the cosmos and thereby affects daily

life. Therein lies its power to move people emotionally, and it is on this foundation that elaborate rituals and myths, variously interpreted by theologians
and historians of religions, are constructed.

One brief example will suffice to illustrate these points. Early 19th-century
Christian missionaries in Central Asia described Altaic sacrifice. The *kam*, or
shaman, erects a new tent at a chosen spot. In it, he arranges a young birch tree
(*axis mundi*) so that it protrudes through the upper opening of the tent; it is
stripped of its branches and notched to form a ladder. A sacrificial horse is
then chosen, and the shaman ensures that it is acceptable to the spirits. He
then hands it over to a 'head-holder' and shakes a birch branch over its back to
force its soul to leave its body and prepare itself for its journey to the spirit Bai
Ülgän. He performs the same ritual over the 'head-holder' so that his soul will
accompany the horse's soul on its 'celestial journey'. Later he kills the horse. Its
skin and bones are displayed, and its flesh is eaten ceremonially, the best
portions being reserved for the shaman. At the same time, offerings are made
to the ancestors and tutelary spirits.[13]

Death is therefore a complex concept, moulded by individual societies.
Certainly, it has an unassailable physical reality, but, beyond that, it is a construct that societies build up. The same is true of the antithesis of death,
though now the fundamental reality of the concept is in doubt.

Born-again seers

For communities that exist in a tiered cosmology with the possibility of inter-
level travel, 'birth' is usually more than parturition. It involves notions about
the cosmological origin of a child's spirit, as well as the 'birth', or 'rebirth', of
ritual specialists who are destined to master altered states of consciousness
and to use their ability on behalf of their communities – but at the same time
to establish their own social status as those who are seers, who can see things
denied to ordinary people.

Cross-culturally, the birth of children is associated with diverse sets of ritual observances and contingent nuances of belief. But some births are more
significant than others. Shamans and seers are sometimes said to inherit their
abilities from one of their parents. Perhaps more commonly, they are said to
be chosen by the spirits, the call coming to them in a dream, vision, omen or
severe illness. Either way, their passage into their new status as a transcosmological traveller is spoken of as death and rebirth. As Piers Vitebsky puts it,
'The theme of death in the shaman's initiation is complemented by a rebirth,

1 Hieronymus Bosch's
(*c.* 1450–1516) *The
Ascent of the Empyrean*
is one part of a triptych
in the Doge's palace in
Venice. The souls of the
saved float weightlessly
to a 'tunnel' on the way
to heaven.

2 (Above left) Göbekli Tepe stela 33. Cranes are depicted on the column and on the capital. The undulating lines represent snakes and, possibly, water.

3 (Above right) Göbekli Tepe, Enclosure C, pillar 12. The upper part of the pillar has images of five birds carved against a lattice background. The lower part of the pillar, still partly buried, shows a wild boar and the head of a fox.

4 (Left) Göbekli Tepe, Enclosure D, pillar 33. Between the decorated sides of this pillar (snake heads and chevrons) are two sets of descending snakes and what appears to be a beetle or a spider. A second 'beetle' is below the section illustrated.

5 (Opposite above) A rectangular temple at Nevali Çori. A second pillar stood where there is now a hole. The bench was originally divided by stone pillars.

6 (Opposite below) Göbekli Tepe, Enclosure B, with its two central pillars and benches between the perimeter pillars.

7 (Right) A plastered skull from Jericho with cowry shell eyes. This is one of a cache of skulls discovered by Kathleen Kenyon in 1953.

8 (Below) A 'temple' at 'Ain Ghazal with an altar against the rear wall. An unpainted plaster hearth is in front of the altar.

9 (Opposite) 'Ain Ghazal statues from Cache 1 (6750 BC). The prominent staring eyes are outlined with bitumen. The legs of the standing figure are decorated with vertical stripes.

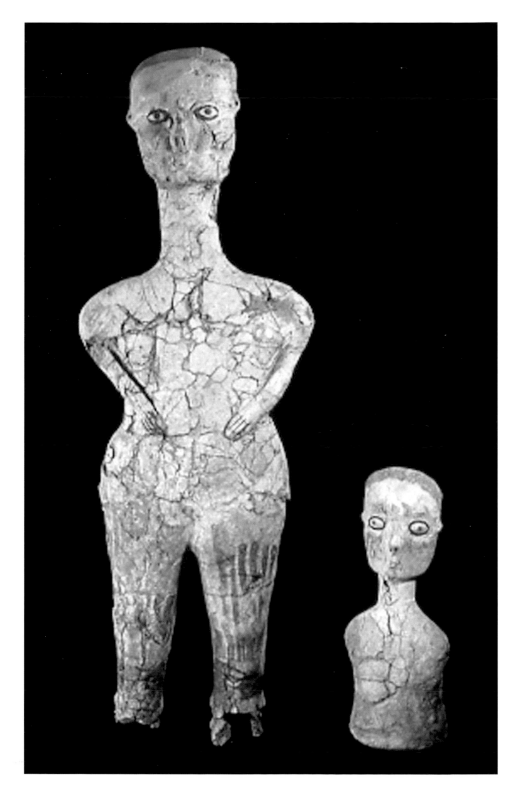

10 (Left) New excavations at Çatalhöyük, led by Ian Hodder, are enlarging and refining knowledge of the site. Çatalhöyük is rich in evidence for the thought-lives of early Neolithic people.

11 (Opposite below) Three bucrania piled one above the other at Çatalhöyük. The large curved aurochs horns are clearly visible. Bull motifs are common at the site.

12 (Below) Zigzag geometric motifs painted in horizontal bands at Çatalhöyük. The bands emphasize the notion of horizontality that is also expressed by the platforms in the rooms (see upper left of Plate 10).

13 (Above) The Çatalhöyük wall paintings include numerous animated human figures. This one is in a panel that depicts many human figures grouped around a wild bull. The man carries a bow and may be wearing a leopard skin at the waist. Compare this figure with those in the deer hunt panel (Figure 24).

14 (Left) A Çatalhöyük wall painting depicting cranes. Discoveries at the site suggest that people made crane costumes to wear in rituals. These birds perform complicated mating dances. Compare this painting with the carvings on stela 33 at Göbekli Tepe (Plate 2).

and the shaman's movement through cosmic space is sometimes explicitly likened to a return to the womb.'[14]

Examples of this kind of thought abound. For instance, the Alaskan Inuit believe that the passage leading into an igloo is symbolic of the vagina. Consequently, their word *ani* means 'to go out of an igloo' *and* 'to be born'.[15] Then there is an extension to this notion. Amongst the same people, a shaman who is about to fly away during a trance is bound down with a seal-line that represents the umbilical cord.[16] His passage to the spirit realm is like birth, but he has to remain connected to his earthly abode. Were there no link, he might never return. The widespread nature of such beliefs is explained by human neurology: as we have seen, both passage through a vortex (that can readily be construed as birth) and flight are hard-wired into human brains.

At Çatalhöyük, female figures that are apparently giving birth to horned bulls suggest the complexity of Neolithic notions of 'birth'. At the very least we can say that 'birth', as a general concept, meant more to the people of Çatalhöyük than bringing human children into the world. The 'birth' of spirit-animals in a lower cosmological tier (the highly decorated rooms) seems to have been part of a complex conceptual and symbolic order, the outlines, but not necessarily the specifics, of which we can discern in some shamanistic traditions. The 'subterranean' birth of animals from human figures at Çatalhöyük may well have been related to the 'birth' of shamans whose power creatures were to be those very animals and into whose form they could change. As Barasana shamans *are* jaguars, Çatalhöyük shamans may have *been* bulls. This point will become clearer in the next chapter when we discuss mythology.

What then of those 'wild animals' that were born of women and that people encountered in other realms? What of the wild bulls' heads? These questions bring us closer to the enigma of animal domestication.

'Nature' and 'the wild'

Today the Romantic notion of 'Nature', together with the importance of wild animals as embodying that concept, is high on the Western list of priorities. Nature is seen as something pristine and pure, something that can easily be spoiled by human beings, who have treacherously betrayed their natural heritage. Rousseau would have approved. In some rather vague ways, Nature is thought to 'show up' the supposed impoverishment and superficiality of our civilization. Atavistically, we are frequently urged to recapture a lost communion with Nature.[17] In some ways, Nature is the spirituality of our times. But, Nature of that kind is a notion constructed by Western people, rather than a universal given. Can we assume that Neolithic people entertained similar ideas about Nature? The answer to that question must surely be no.

Ian Hodder rightly allows that 'wild' and 'natural' are concepts constructed within social processes.[18] They are 'people-made'. As Hodder puts it: 'society is dialectically created out of its own negative image'. The 'wild' is in virtually all its aspects the opposite of human society. A particular notion of 'wild' as one of the elements in the backwards-and-forwards (dialectic) process between the 'wild' and humanity is evident in his interpretation of the prominent female imagery of Çatalhöyük. He cites three features:

- the presence of 'death-dealing beaks, tusks and teeth'[19] in moulded plaster representations of human breasts,
- the relationship between female figures and leopards, and
- the female figures that are apparently giving birth to animals, including wild, horned bulls.[20]

He then sums up the implications of these points by arguing that women appear to be associated with danger and wild animals.

So far so good: his inference from the archaeological evidence seems logical. But he does not leave it there. He goes on to argue that male figures in the wall art and the grave goods of male burials suggest a male association with hunting.

But how was hunting regarded at that time? Do we have here another of those apparently simple yet actually elusive concepts? Almost certainly. Hunting was, Hodder continues, taken to 'mean' control or subjugation of the 'wild'. From here, it is a short step to reading Çatalhöyük symbolism in terms of male–female relationships, an absorbing concern of contemporary Western society that much archaeology today 'naturalizes' by apparently repeatedly finding evidence for it in the past. Putting his reading in general terms, Hodder argues, with good reason, that 'the process of domestication (control of the wild) is a metaphor and mechanism for the control of society'[21] – especially, that is, for men's control of women. Unfortunately, he does not explain *who* saw 'the process of domestication' as a metaphor for the control of women: the people of Çatalhöyük themselves, or the archaeologists who study them? Even if we allow that the process was in some way a metaphor, we have to concede that the metaphor could not have *caused* domestication. For the people of Çatalhöyük, the metaphor would have been post hoc, a retrospective gloss.

Still, Hodder has put forward an intriguing, ingenious notion. We have, however, to take care that we are not turning a current Western interest into a universal, social 'law'. Referring to this sort of danger, James Whitley, archaeologist at Cardiff University, remarks: 'When students learn to "apply" theory, what they actually "apply" are … interpretations … such all-purpose interpretations … circumvent the tedious business of undertaking contextual analysis, or testing specific models against the available evidence.'[22] So, whilst we concur that domestication was, in a sense that we shortly develop, a 'mechanism for the control of society', there are aspects other than gender that require consideration if we wish to form some idea of 'the (Neolithic) wild'. To get at those aspects we return to the consciousness contract.

In tiered, shamanistic cosmologies, wild animals frequently come from god or a Lord of the Animals. Some animals are richly imbued with supernatural potency, the very potency that shamans need to reach god and the spirit world. This is the potency that San shamans see boiling in others' bodies, and the potency that is implied by *tcheni* (dance), the respect word that hunters of eland antelope use. Hunting is therefore more than meat-acquisition, or what we would call a material technology. It entails interaction with and acquisition of supernatural potency and is therefore hedged around with ritual observances. By 'hunting' potency as much as meat, those engaged in the dance-hunt on the walls of one of the Çatalhöyük rooms[23] were, we suggest, interacting with one of the lowest tiers of the cosmos, the ultimate seat of supernatural potency and the locus of archetypal spirit-animals.

Wild animals thus have spiritual counterparts that inhabit, for the most part, another tier of the cosmos and that can become spirit guides or helpers. We recall that the Barasana say that their shamans keep jaguars as ordinary people keep dogs; that is, they 'domesticate' spiritual jaguars.

It is perhaps in terms of concepts like these, rather than as signifiers of 'danger' and 'death', as we generally understand those words, that the beaks, tusks and teeth set in moulded breasts at Çatalhöyük should be seen. It was the *mouths* of wild creatures that were being associated with breasts.

Why such an unlikely connection? In shamanistic terms, the answer is straightforward. From supernatural breasts at the 'birth' of a shaman there flows supernatural potency, as we shall see in the next chapter. Then, too, the mouths of wild animals give forth the sustaining potency that shamans seek and that enables them to perform their tasks. In numerous societies, breath is taken to be some form of spiritual essence, even a soul.[24] The symbolism of beaks, tusks and teeth is, however, still more complex and exercises great emotional heft. Beaks, tusks and teeth also inflict death and dismember-ment. Life-giving essences and 'death' (in all its complex meanings) come together and thus create a powerful emotional nimbus around mental and graphic images of spirit-animals.

Domestication of the aurochs

The concepts of 'birth', 'death' and 'wild' and the constructed mythical world, or worlds, of the Neolithic were, we contend, the context for far-reaching changes in relationships between people and animals.

In Chapter 1 we briefly noted some of the problems that we encounter when we try to construct hypotheses to explain how it was that people came to abandon hunting and gathering as their way of life and turn to the domes-tication of plants and animals.[25] We need not rehearse them here, save to note that Mellaart ascribes the domestication of the aurochs and other animals at Çatalhöyük to 'food-conservation and the production of milk and, in the case of goats and sheep, hair and wool'.[26] In line with much thinking on this issue, he sees domestication in terms of increased productivity and security. There are problems with this reasonable approach. Domestication no doubt did lead, later if not immediately, to easier availability of milk, animal fibre and so forth. However, whether greater security of production was also attained is a moot point; even though they can support higher populations, domesticated animals are more susceptible to disease and the vagaries of nature than are wild animals. A desire for secure production was not necessarily the reason why people tried to domesticate animals, as many accounts imply. As we have pointed out, there is a teleological trap here (Chapter 1). With absolutely no idea of what an agricultural way of life was like, how could early Neolithic people evaluate it, decide it was worthwhile and then aim for it? Cause and effect are confused in this kind of argument. In any event, appeals to prin-ciples such as efficiency of production and access to products mask social processes and the role of sentient human beings, not to mention the mythical world in which they operate.

These logical problems were noted a long time ago and then rather forgot-ten. At the end of the 19th century and the beginning of the next, Eduard Hahn, a German geographer, dismissed the current explanations for the domestication of cattle and argued that 'The economic uses of the animal would have been a by-product of a domestication religious in origin.'[27] He believed that cattle were originally corralled and domesticated to have a supply available for sacrifice. The animal was selected because its 'gigantic curved horns resembled the lunar crescent'.[28] Hahn's ideas were more recently summarized by another geographer, Erich Isaac, who agreed that 'irrational forces' were important in some major technological advances.[29]

We take a comparable view. While we concur that religion, not rational economics, was the key motivating factor, we highlight a special kind of relationship between some human beings and animals and argue that *the domestication of animals was already conceptually embedded in the worldview and socio-ritual complex we have described before people began actually herding the aurochs.*

In place of ecological imperatives and ineluctable forces of capitalist optimization, we point to the building up of social status and so link the domestication of animals to aspects of human history, cosmology and myth. There was, we argue, a creative, dynamic interplay between the cosmology and imagery of the Neolithic, their social concomitants and the domestication of animals. In short, domestication of the aurochs came out of interaction between the Neolithic social and consciousness contracts.

This is, we believe, a more human scenario than those conventional in the literature on domestication. It should, however, be borne in mind that we do not suggest that the domestication of animals took place in the same way in all parts of the world; we are concerned here with one instance only, the Near Eastern Neolithic. Another caveat is in order: present work at Çatalhöyük suggests that domesticated cattle were not a central part of life at the site, despite the prominence of bull imagery.[30] Consequently, it is the initial stages of the process of domestication that we now describe.

Owning animals

The social statuses and supernatural capabilities of hunter-gatherer shamans are, as we have seen, often posited on relationships with spirit-animals from which they derive potency, their enabling 'electricity'. These relationships afford a measure of control over real animals. Often, shamans are believed to have the ability to guide the movements of animals into the hunters' ambush, and, by tricking or placating a Lord of the Animals, to ensure the reproduction of the animals and their release to the hunters. One of the ways in which this three-cornered spirit-animal/shaman/real-animal relationship can develop is well illustrated by beliefs recorded in the 1870s in southern Africa.[31]

The /Xam San of the central part of the subcontinent distinguished several overlapping categories of shaman, one of which comprised shamans of the game, *ɵpwaiten-ka !gi:ten*.[32] Some shamans of the game wore caps made from the scalps of springbucks (a medium-sized southern African antelope) sewn so that the ears stood up;[33] these caps often appear in rock paintings (Fig. 30).[34] Tānō-!khauken, a woman who was a healer and a shaman of the game, explained that the springbuck would follow the wearer of such a cap wherever he or she went. The cap thus afforded its wearer control over the movements of the game.[35] More than that, it was visible evidence for that ability – it made a social statement and people respected those who had the ability.

Tānō-!khauken went on to give further information. She said that she kept a castrated springbuck 'tied up' by means of a thong so that it did not 'wander about'.[36] She said that she could untie the springbuck and send it among wild springbuck so that it would lead the herd to the place where her people were camped. Tānō-!khauken described this 'domesticated' springbuck as her 'heart's springbuck'.[37] It is highly improbable that she was speaking of a tamed and trained springbuck; the species is insufficiently tractable. More probably, she was referring to a spirit-springbuck that was her 'animal helper'. Her phrase 'heart's springbuck' probably means just that: a springbuck experi-

30 *Southern African San rock painting of a bowman wearing a cap with antelope ears. One arrow with an iron point is set in the bow, another, with a bone point, is held in the hand that is drawing the string. He also has three extra arrows for rapid shooting.*

31 Diä!kwain, a San man who, in the 1870s, provided detailed accounts of his people's beliefs and rituals: 'Then the old woman said, "O ≠Kame-an, take my old cap, keep it and see whether the springbok do not follow the cap to the place to which it goes".'

enced in her 'heart'. She said that she 'owned' (with connotations of 'controlled') not just this one springbuck but also springbuck in general.[38] The verbatim phonetic transcript of this passage is important because it shows that the /Xam used one word (*/ki*) to mean both supernatural possession of a spirit-animal and ownership of real flocks and herds.[39] Diä!kwain, the narrator who told about Tānō-!khauken, said of his mother, ≠Kame-an, that she did not own flocks of sheep and goats: 'For those [wild] springboks they were those of which mamma made her flocks'[40] (Fig. 31). Wild animals thus became akin to domesticated animals through the notion of shamanic */ki* in a way comparable to that in which South American Desana shamans kept spiritual jaguars.

Another, and highly significant, component of this sort of 'ownership' is evident in Tānō-!khauken's account of how her spirit-springbuck assumed materiality in unfortunate circumstances. She said that Diä!kwain's father, Xā:ä-tin, inadvertently shot a springbuck that turned out to be her 'heart's springbuck', the one that she 'owned' and controlled, the one that she had sent among the wild springbuck. Near disaster followed. Diä!kwain's elder brother, K"obo, fell ill as a result of eating the meat of this springbuck. But Tānō-!khauken, also being a healer, was able to save him. She claimed that it was her intervention as a healer that snatched him from death.

What happened in this remarkable incident? The invisible 'heart's springbuck' turned into a real animal and became visible proof of Tānō-!khauken's powers as a shaman of the game and, as subsequent events showed, also as a shamanic healer. This demonstration of her rather intimidating shamanic status was taken a stage further when Diä!kwain's mother made her a new eared cap from the scalp of the killed springbuck. (We do not know if all eared caps were believed to come from spirit-antelope.) She was thus able to continue her role as one who could control the movements of antelope herds. All in all, this series of events confirmed and enhanced Tānō-!khauken's own social status and prestige and, by extension, that of /Xam shamans in general.[41]

This account highlights four points about relationships between shamans and animals:

 – Supernatural potency was believed to derive, in part, from supernatural animals.
 – These spirit-animals gave shamans at least partial control over wild animals, as a food (and probably ritual) resource.
 – Shamans were believed, under certain circumstances, to cause their spirit-animals to mingle with and be *indistinguishable from* real animals.
 – Such incarnated spirit-animals were taken to be visible and tangible proof of a shaman's powers and hence confirmation of his or her social status.

Neolithic 'spirit-animals'?

We do not, of course, claim that these generalized points were present at the beginning of the Neolithic exactly as they were among the 19th-century /Xam San. Nevertheless, we argue that shifting relationships between spirit-animals and real animals, an important part of the ways in which shamans build up their statuses, were a factor in the domestication of animals.

To trace this relationship in the historical trajectory of domestication at Çatalhöyük we go back to the 7th-millennium BC site of Suberde near Lake Sugla in the foothills of the Taurus Mountains. Ninety per cent of the animal bones here belonged to wild sheep, pig and red deer; the remaining 10 per cent were aurochs, goat, wolf, fox and tortoise.[42] Small pigs may have been the only species domesticated at Suberde. By contrast, the Konya Plain surrounding Çatalhöyük 'teemed with wild life' as late as 6000 BC. Aurochs (*Bos primigenius*), a pig (*Sus scrofa*) and red deer (*Cervus elaphus*) attained maximum size for these species in this favourable ecological niche. Mellaart suggests that it was the presence of these great herds that attracted people to the grasslands of the plain. He may well be right, though not entirely for the reasons of subsistence he puts forward.

World ethnography suggests that the shamans of a community do not all seek power relationships with one species only. For instance, some may claim relationships with dangerous animals, such as jaguars, while others may relate to birds. At the beginning of the Neolithic, this kind of differentiation held the potential for competition and social struggle between individual ritual specialists and among small groups of them. It is possible, though far from proven, that some Neolithic ritual specialists in southern Anatolia may have placed their faith in more readily controlled species, such as sheep, goats and pigs, that can be corralled comparatively easily and so could have become visible evidence of their potency. Indeed, sheep and goats seem to have been domesticated at Çatalhöyük.[43] But the flocks of sheep and herds of swine would, we argue, have soon lost their mystique: they would have become 'ordinary', whereas shamans need to derive their potency from 'out there', beyond society; domestic animals are a rather dreary part of human society. Some ritual specialists, who were competing for social status, therefore put their faith in larger and physically more potent wild animals, in this instance the aurochs. Around the world, large and physically powerful animals, such as bears and felines, are associated with shamans. The status of influential Çatalhöyük ritual specialists may therefore have derived from the vast herds of aurochs on the Konya Plain, not from corralled, smaller species. The attraction of the plain consisted not only in its potential meat supply, but also in the physical manifestation of supernatural potency and status in the proud herds of wild aurochs.

A new struggle was thus initiated. Ritual specialists, who were also seers (they could *see* spirit-animals), concentrated more and more on aurochs bulls as incarnations of supernatural potency. Plastered skulls of these animals were fixed to columns and edges of platforms, thus marking their guardianship of the vertical *axis mundi*, the route between layers of the cosmos.

Spirit-bulls were believed to be amongst real herds as well as in the underworld, and people's religious leanings may have been in some ways divided between the stalagmitic caves of the Taurus Mountains and the real herds of the Konya Plain – as the range of finds at Çatalhöyük suggests (Chapter 4). In their efforts to demonstrate more and more unequivocally their relationship with spiritual animal potency, seers provided an impetus to controlling – both supernaturally and literally – the animals of the plain. As Tänö-!khauken's 'heart's springbuck' went into the springbuck herds, so spirit-aurochs may have been believed to mingle with the wild herds, probably indistinguishably to the untutored eye. As social negotiation and struggle developed between competing ritual specialists and various kinds of people who were themselves not seers, it became more and more imperative for them to demonstrate their power. As time went by, real skull bones and horns (perhaps from animals believed to be spirit-animals) rather than plaster models were increasingly incorporated into the built cosmology of Çatalhöyük. Animals and their potency were being brought more and more forcefully into domestic space.

Another practice was also open to the ritual specialists of Çatalhöyük. Non-real relationships between them and animals were depicted in wall art. As we have seen (Chapter 4), one panel depicts people apparently baiting a herd of red deer (see Fig. 24). On an adjacent wall, people surround a large bull, just over 2 m (6.6 ft) in length. One of the 'hunters' wears 'a pink leopard skin with black spots, and is waving a club or mace, and both are headless'.[44] Some of the figures wear what look like 'bonnets' of leopard skin, but it seems that some of the figures were intended to be acephalic. Mellaart found no evidence that their heads had flaked off the plastered wall. He takes the mural to depict a bull hunt and adds that it is probably not a case of 'bull-worship'.[45] But, if we bear in mind what we have said about shamanistic hunters and their complex relationships with animals, the relationship may well be more than simple hunting, though it is true that 'worship' would probably be an inappropriate word.

The 'deer hunt' scene bears out this conclusion. Mellaart remarks that, although their significance is obscure, the wall paintings 'were not art for art's sake, but had a ritual meaning'.[46] His view is supported by the dancing figures and the presence of what is apparently a drum. So, too, the headless figures must recall the apparent excarnation being carried out by the painted vultures and the headless burials beneath the platforms in some rooms. Post-mortem (perhaps not always post-mortem) decapitation was an important reflection of transition to the spirit world.

There are also significant statuettes that point to non-real human/animal relationships. Some depict a woman seated on a 'throne' with a leopard on each side. One of these shows her hands resting on the animals (though the hands themselves are now missing; Fig. 32). These relationships point to a desire to control and to be associated with these potent animals in unique, inimitable ways, ways that cannot be duplicated by ordinary people with real animals; it was the seers, and only they, who could 'tame' wild animals.

We should also recall here an aspect of the burials that we mentioned in the previous chapter. Human beings and animals were in various ways 'com-

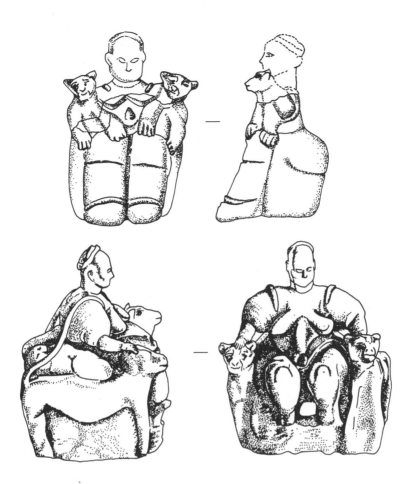

32 *Two seated female figures, previously said to represent goddesses, found at Çatalhöyük. These clay statuettes show close relations between women and leopards.*

bined' in death: both were interred and their bones were sometimes inter-mingled. We think especially of the arrangement of human and animal bones at Kfar HaHoresh that, together, formed a profile of an animal (Chapter 4).

There were thus good reasons for corralling aurochs, ones that had little to do with making subsistence easier. What would be the value of corralled aurochs for the seers? A number of advantages could have followed. Once controlled, aurochs herds made greater display statements. The prestige of the seers was thus enhanced and dramatized. In addition, corralled aurochs could provide animals for sacrifice. These sacrifices would, reasonably enough, be presided over by seers, for it was they who established contact with, and stood between, supernatural worlds. At the same time, as sacrifices made contact with the supernatural, they facilitated the control of meat distribution and feasting, ritual practices that, in numerous societies, are intimately bound up with social structure.[47]

Spin-offs of ritual and cosmology

We can now draw together some of the strands of our argument. Bearing in mind what Jacques Cauvin[48] and Steven Mithen[49] have argued, we suggest that the production of meat was a by-product, not a consciously formulated end, of social processes. These processes, though not easily discerned, are not necessarily lost. They probably involved the definition and social appropriation of certain altered states of consciousness – the social and consciousness contracts came together. As we have repeatedly remarked, the spectrum of consciousness is a resource that is manipulated in specific historical circumstances. The people at Çatalhöyük constructed a cosmology (derived in part from 'hard-wired' experiences of certain altered states) and reproduced that cosmology in architecture and images. Ritual specialists, appropriating and exploiting the experiences of altered states, asserted themselves by modifying, or elaborating, that cosmology and by manipulating a symbolic vocabulary. This manipulation extended beyond the fields of iconography and hallucination to herds of actual animals with whom spirit-animals were believed to consort. Economic behaviour can therefore not be divorced from symbolic behaviour.

Eventually, we suspect, the mystique and potency of corralled aurochs herds evaporated. Too many people came to possess animals, and the notion of wild, powerful spirit-animals was weakened. As the last shamans of the west European Upper Palaeolithic gradually painted themselves into a subterranean corner that afforded little opportunity for further manœuvre, so Neolithic seers eventually corralled themselves. New sources of spiritual potency, other than now-domesticated animals, had to be sought. Classic animal-shamanism was left behind. Çatalhöyük, it should be recalled, was a precocious and early Neolithic town. The common pattern in the later Neolithic of Anatolia and the Near East does not include the elements that we have considered here as consistent with a classic shamanistic hunter-gatherer society. Elsewhere, especially in western Europe, other kinds of imagery came to the fore.[50]

CHAPTER 6

Treasure the Dream
Whatever the Terror

This chapter stands between our discussions of the Neolithic in the Near East and the different ways in which that period manifested itself in Atlantic Europe. Our chief concern here is to show that the elements of consciousness and cosmology that we have discussed find their way into myth. Myths are set within the cosmology of the people who give allegiance to them; indeed, myths reproduce, or reinforce, that cosmology every time they are recounted, simply by taking the cosmos for granted as a framework for the origins, events, journeys, transformations and beings that the myth describes. Because knowledge of cosmology often derives in large measure from the experiences of seers – those who travel through and see the cosmos – it is understandable that their neurologically generated experiences will turn up in many myths.

As we have pointed out, Neolithic people almost certainly explained the tiered cosmos and their various rituals by narrating myths. Those tales are now lost. Though we cannot retrieve them, we can formulate some idea of what they may have been like. We can understand the power and essence of Neolithic myths, if not their stories and protagonists.

But what is a 'myth'?

Deep meanings

A universally accepted definition of myth is another of those elusive goals that researchers have not yet attained. We can offer only a few remarks on some of the fascinating research that has been done on mythology.

The popular view that myth is unverifiable and, for the most part, incorrect history need not detain us.[1] Many myths do indeed incorporate historical events, but there is much more to them than fantastically embroidered history. Some writers therefore go on to speak of myths as sacred narratives and thereby differentiate them from folktales. But the notion of a distinction between sacred and secular does not exist in many societies. Some people laugh uproariously at what we may see as sacred tales of creation (the San of southern Africa are an example), but their jocular reception of those myths does nothing to reduce the power and effectiveness of the narratives in their original social settings. Other writers suggest that supernatural transformations, amusing or not, are indicative of 'true' myths, a notion with which we have some sympathy, but which is, as we shortly show, incomplete.

All researchers, however, agree that myths are socially situated – groups of people define themselves in part by the myths with which they associate themselves. For instance, Christians are defined as those who believe in the birth, life, death and resurrection of Jesus; Jews identify with the Old Testament narratives concerning God's chosen people; Muslims are defined as those who accept the events recorded in the Koran. Social groups and myths go hand in hand. As Ian Hodder put it in his account of Çatalhöyük, life there was lived in 'a mythical world deeply embedded in a complex social system' (Chapter 4).[2] This point shows that, contrary to a once popular view, myths do not merely explain origins and events in the natural world, such as why the sun rises and sets. It is incorrect to suppose that a natural phenomenon is at the heart of every myth. Society itself is more significant in understanding a myth than natural phenomena.

Another point of agreement between researchers is that it is not easy to discern the 'true meaning' of a myth. Many say that the 'meaning' of a myth is elusive because it is contingent on who tells it to whom and under what circumstances. We agree.[3] We also believe that the meanings (they are multiple rather than single) of myths are not readily discernible on their narrative surfaces: they are not parables or fables, which illustrate simple moral principles.[4] Rather, we lean (slightly) towards the French anthropologist and philosopher Claude Lévi-Strauss (born 1908), who, along with the innovative Swiss student of language, Ferdinand de Saussure (1857–1913), was a father of the philosophical research programme known as structuralism. In short, Lévi-Strauss believes that meaning is locked up in the 'deep structure' of a myth.[5]

What exactly that 'deep structure' is and how we can distil meaning from it are difficult matters. Lévi-Strauss sees the structure of myth as comprising multiple binary oppositions. These oppositions constitute one source of the 'mythemes' that, for him, are the building-blocks of myth. The oppositions can be arranged in sets:

life : death

up : down

male : female

right hand : left hand

light : darkness

All such oppositions boil down to the great, all-encompassing binary opposition culture : nature, the fundamental dilemma with which Lévi-Strauss believes humanity wrestles. Are we animals or more than animals? (Early Neolithic people in the process of domesticating animals were probably concerned with this issue.) We can also see in this simple table that the binary oppositions of myth are tinged with cosmology. This, as we shall see, is a significant point.

To get at the binary mythemes of a myth, Lévi-Strauss says that researchers must virtually do away with the narrative and arrange the oppositions in sets that show how one is a transformation of another. Thus, in the example we have given, the right hand may come to symbolize men, and the left, women. Then a structuralist interpreter may go further and notice that life, as it appears in the myth, is frequently associated with the right hand. The implication now is that women are associated with death, and this connection may explain why a society has avoidance customs (taboos) that men must observe in their relations with women. Similarly, the Amazonian Piro myths speak of relations between the living and the dead as between people and white-lipped peccaries (a kind of wild pig).[6] Sets of oppositions can be read horizontally and vertically. Lévi-Strauss makes the study of myth still more complex. He argues that the task of discerning mythemes should be tackled not in one version only but through multiple versions, when they are available[7] (e.g., the two accounts of creation in Genesis Chapters 1 and 2, and the four Gospels[8]). Moreover, myths become nested in other myths; sometimes a myth may split into two. In its various versions, a myth may, for instance, speak of a protagonist moving up and down in vastly different contexts, such as along the course of a river or up a ladder into the sky.[9] Each of these apparently different tales may simply be an alternative way of talking about, for instance, life : death or culture : nature.

Why all these transmuting binary oppositions? Lévi-Strauss makes two points. First, he claims that this binary mode is how the human brain works. Secondly, he argues that the oppositions deal with (rather than solve) a contradiction in human life (e.g., we are part of nature, yet distinct from it). If the contradiction is real (as in the we : nature example), it will never be overcome.

Then myth 'grows spiral-wise until the intellectual impulse which has produced it is exhausted'.[10] The oppositions remain.

Today, writers express serious reservations about Lévi-Strauss's structuralism, and scholars have indeed moved on from his insights. The brain does not
work like a binary computer. Hard-line structuralism is now rightly seen as
presenting too rigid a framework, one that does not allow for human action.
Myth should be seen as a resource on which people can draw, not a structure
that is imposed on them.

Nevertheless, researchers are, perhaps, in danger of dispensing with the
baby along with the bathwater. In this chapter we therefore remain alert to the
general idea of 'deep structure', though we think of it rather differently from
the great French savant. To begin with, we agree that much of the sense of a
myth is wrapped up in its non-sense (contradictions, transformations and so
forth), rather than in its narrative – though narrative is obviously important,
particularly in a protagonist's movement between symbolic and cosmological
spaces.[11] But we go on to deny myth a life of its own: myths do not think themselves through people's minds. As Lévi-Strauss himself insists, myth is
language and therefore exists in its telling and retelling. Individual people
reproduce myths in ways of their own choosing.

Overall, our aim in this chapter is to make two principal points that will
help us to understand the kind (though not the specific details and narratives) of mythic framework within which Neolithic people lived:
  – Many myths derive from, or have in them elements of, a consciousness
    contract.
  – Their narration is embedded in a social contract.
To follow up the first of these points we suggest that part of the 'deep structure' of a myth consists in neurologically engendered building-blocks. As
Steven Pinker points out (Preface), the human mind/brain is not a blank
slate: neurology is ever-present.[12] From this starting point, we try to untangle
the psychological and the social aspects of myth, two viewpoints from which
different schools of researchers approach myth, as they do religion itself.

In the first instance, the consciousness contract (what one might call the
psychological component), together with its associated tiered cosmology,
supplies building-blocks, episodes that we believe constitute part of the
'deep structure' of a myth. Importantly, these building-blocks trigger profound emotions. People frequently and repetitively recount myths in what are
emotionally charged circumstances and places. It is these heightened contexts
that facilitate the evocation of 'deep' meaning from what may, to outsiders,

seem a trivial narrative studded with bizarre events. Emotion, closely allied to shifting consciousness, internalizes myths and burns them into people's minds.

The social contract, on the other hand, is the arena of manipulation: people and groups of people tell myths in ways and with emphases that suit themselves in particular contexts and at particular times. The building-blocks can be articulated in various combinations and transformations. Myths are thus malleable – even those that have been committed to writing and constitute sacred scripture, as the schismatic history of the Christian Church shows. It is often said that a canon of sacred scripture stabilizes a religion, but in fact it may simply constitute a foundation for dispute and enhanced bitterness.

With these ideas in mind we consider what may have been some of the features of Neolithic myths. We look for neurologically generated building-blocks that provide narrative turning points and construct a 'deep structure' that wells up from human consciousness and people's eternal struggle to make sense of its spectrum within given social circumstances. A key point here is that these mythical building-blocks are consonant with the Neolithic architecture and imagery that we have discussed. Neolithic communities lived in a seamless (though malleable) conceptual and material whole. Tensions that arise between, on the one hand, conceptual, experiential and social components of religion and, on the other, their material concomitants constitute a key to understanding the development of the Neolithic through the millennia. The ways in which those tensions played themselves out in specific instances will become clearer in the chapters that follow.

We begin by considering some features of the oldest Near Eastern myth that we have, *The Epic of Gilgamesh*. It dates from the 3rd millennium BC, and thus antedates the Homeric epics by at least one and a half thousand years, but post-dates the Neolithic by some four or five millennia. Clearly, it is unlikely that it was a Neolithic narrative in the form that has come down to us. Still, there are intriguing elements in the Gilgamesh epic that seem to be relics of much earlier times, and, in any event, it is to the shaping of the universal, neurologically generated building-blocks rather than narrative that we give special attention.

Then, to show more concretely how cosmology, architecture and imagery came together in Neolithic thought patterns, we turn to an Avam Samoyed (Siberian) narrative.[13] Whilst not a Neolithic myth it is set in the 'non-sense' realm of myth, and the protagonist encounters mythic personages. Broad parallels between it and *The Epic of Gilgamesh* will be apparent.

Gilgamesh, King of Uruk

The most complete version of *The Epic of Gilgamesh* that we have today comes from cuneiform clay tablets excavated from the library of Ashurbanipal, the last great king of the Assyrian Empire (reigned 669–631 BC) (Fig. 33). Versions of the epic were, however, widely known throughout the Near East, as finds from Anatolia and elsewhere show. Scholars piece together the narrative by correlating tablets from various archaeological sites.[14] Unfortunately, the tablets and fragments of tablets are scattered in museums throughout the world – a truly epic jig-saw puzzle.

Today, *The Epic of Gilgamesh* is best known for its tale of a great flood. Uta-napishti, whose name means 'He Who Saw Life', tells the story to Gilgamesh as if it had happened to him, but it seems already to have been a myth of great antiquity. Biblical scholars have seen this episode as an early precursor of the story of Noah's flood, even to the release of birds to seek out dry land (Fig. 33). (The biblical narrative is in fact a blend of two sources; GENESIS 6:5–9:17.) But there is a great deal more in *Gilgamesh* that is of interest.

Gilgamesh himself is semi-divine by ancestry: he is two parts god and one part man.[15] He thus bridges, or mediates, the binary opposition between

33 A fragment of Tablet XI, an Assyrian version of
The Epic of Gilgamesh *(c. 650 BC). Ellipses indicate missing or untranslatable words.* Roman *indicates insecure decipherments.*
'*On Mount Nimus the boat ran aground …*
When the seventh day arrived –
I brought out a dove, setting it free:
  off went the dove …
  No perch was available for it and it came back to [me].
I brought out a swallow, setting it free:
  off went the swallow …
  No perch was available for it and it came back to me.
I brought out a raven, setting it free:
  off went the raven and it saw the waters receding.
  It was eating, bobbing up and down, *it did not come back to me.*
I brought out an offering and sacrificed to the four corners of the earth.'[16]

The Epic of Gilgamesh 'He who saw the Deep'
A summary

Semi-divine Gilgamesh, King of Uruk, tyrannizes his people. To mitigate his superhuman energies the gods create Enkidu, who is brought up in the wild with animals. A prostitute seduces him and directs him to Uruk. Meanwhile Gilgamesh dreams of an axe that he places at his mother's feet: 'like a wife I loved it, caressed and embraced it'. His mother, the goddess Nísun, explains that the axe is a friend whom he will love and who will be his equal.

The prophecy is soon fulfilled. Enkidu arrives at Uruk and fights with Gilgamesh but in the end accepts Gilgamesh's supremacy. To find fame and fortune the two, who are now firm friends, set out on a journey to the Forest of Cedar, despite advice not to do so. They seek the help of Shamash, the Sun God, and his wife, Aya.

On the journey, the two heroes conduct rituals to provoke dreams. Gilgamesh has nightmares, but Enkidu assures him that the dreams are favourable. Shamash advises Gilgamesh to attack Humbaba, the ogre of the forest and guardian of the cedar. Aided by blinding winds that Shamash sends, Gilgamesh and Enkidu kill Humbaba and begin felling trees in the sacred groves. Enkidu selects one especially fine cedar to fashion into a door for the temple of Enlil, god of wind, earth and universal air, who separated the heavens from the earth and took possession of the earth as his domain.

Back in Uruk, Gilgamesh provokes the goddess Ishtar, who, through the aid of her father, Anu, sends the Bull of Heaven to kill Gilgamesh. But Gilgamesh and Enkidu prevail and kill the bull.

A dream alerts Enkidu to his imminent death. He dreams of being dragged down into the nether world. He falls ill and dies. Bitterly, Gilgamesh laments his passing and selects grave goods to accompany Enkidu to the nether world.

Oppressed by this intimation of mortality, Gilgamesh searches for Uta-napishti, who has the secret of immortality. His journey takes him to the nether world at the end of a long, dark tunnel. Eventually, he finds the ferryman, Ur-shanabi, and his crew of Stone Ones. After killing the Stone Ones, Gilgamesh and Ur-shanabi cross the Waters of Death. Uta-napishti tells Gilgamesh how he survived the Deluge and was given immortality. Gilgamesh tries to go without sleep for a week, but his failure to do so reminds him again of his mortality.

Gilgamesh returns to Uruk and shows the ferryman the walls of the city. These, he says, will be his enduring monument.[17]

material and spiritual realms. In the material world, he is king of the walled city Uruk (present-day Warka). As a semi-divine hero, he kills the great Bull of Heaven and takes its huge horns back to his palace, where he hangs them on the wall, in a manner reminiscent of the Çatalhöyük bucrania.

All Gilgamesh's adventures take place within the tiered Sumerian cosmology. Seeing the cosmos, both in reality and in dreams, is important throughout the epic. Indeed, the first line of the poem reads: 'He who saw the Deep, the country's foundation.'[18] 'Seeing' and wisdom are intimately linked. This point is implied by the Near Eastern Neolithic finds that we have discussed.

From the point of view of the cosmology of the epic, the sun, personified as a beneficent god, Shamash, traverses the tiered levels (as it does for the South American Barasana and other peoples). In the ancient eloquence of the myth, we read:

> O Shamash, all the world longs for your light …
> in a hollow voice feeble man calls out to you …
> when his family is far away and his city far-off,
> the shepherd boy fearful of the open field comes before you …
> the caravan which marches in dread,
> the trader, the pedlar with his bag of weights.
> Guide and beacon who constantly passes over the infinite seas,
> whose depths the great gods of heaven do not know;
> your gleaming rays go down into the Pit,
> and the monsters of the deep see your light [lineation added].[19]

The heavens are thus distinguished from the underworld, the realm of the dead, which, we are told, is reached by a road that runs 'into the mountain'. The notion of entering a cave and passing underground is thus suggested. When Gilgamesh takes an oath, he swears by 'the heavenly life, by the earthly life, by the underworld itself' – all three of the cosmological levels.[20] Sumerian cosmology may be summed up thus:

upper realm : beneficent Shamash

middle realm : the level of human life

nether realm : the dead and frightening creatures

Further insights into transition and death are revealed in the account of Enkidu's tragic end. He was reared with wild animals and was 'as swift as the gazelle'.[21] He was Rousseau's natural man. While Gilgamesh is semi-divine by ancestry and so bridges the human : spirit opposition, Enkidu bridges the human : animal opposition. But Enkidu was seduced by a harlot from, significantly, the city; he lost his innocence and began to be tamed. The animals rejected him, so he learned to wear clothes, to herd sheep and to be antagonistic to the lion and the wolf. The construction of 'wild' and 'tamed' categories (nature and culture) is clear.[22] At last, he reached the city of Uruk where he

met Gilgamesh and became his alter ego. Together, their personalities constitute a set of parallel oppositions that can, as Lévi-Strauss would urge, be read
horizontally and vertically:

Enkidu : Gilgamesh
nature : culture
wild : civilized

These oppositions reveal a particularly interesting aspect of the meaning of
bulls. We have seen that, at Çatalhöyük, bulls' heads were placed on points of
transition and on columns that suggest the *axis mundi* joining cosmological
levels. In *The Epic of Gilgamesh* we see a transmutation of this linking symbolic function. When 'wild' Enkidu first meets 'civilized' Gilgamesh, they
fight. Their colossal struggle is expressed in highly significant imagery:

Mighty Gilgamesh came on and Enkidu met him at the gate. He put out his foot and
prevented Gilgamesh from entering the house, so they grappled, holding each other like
bulls. They broke the door posts and the walls shook, they snorted like bulls locked
together. They shattered the doorposts and the walls shook.[23]

Their conflict is presented in terms of violent bull imagery (nature) that
endangers 'civilized' architecture. Bulls thus stand symbolically between the
major oppositions that Gilgamesh and Enkidu represent. This insight probably enlarges our appreciation of the complexity of Near Eastern Neolithic
bull imagery: meanings are seldom unitary.

Further aspects of what Enkidu's life symbolizes have been suggested by
scholars who argue that it represents the stages by which human society
evolved from hunting to pastoralism to urban life.[24] The learned, literate
Sumerians must surely have been aware of this historical progression, though
they would probably have expressed it in myths and without knowing the
time-depth involved. Enkidu may thus represent the process of Neolithiciza-
tion, a process that was probably even more important in early Neolithic
societies than it was in the later times of the epic. It seems probable that at
sites such as Göbekli Tepe and 'Ain Ghazal myths featured protagonists who
mediated the hunting : farming dichotomy and did so within the tiered cosmology of the time. Their cosmological exploits were probably linked
symbolically to the animals carved on the Göbekli stone pillars. Myth and
cosmology were thus consonant with architecture.

As Enkidu lay dying, he realized what he had lost (his 'wildness') and he
cursed his educators. He went down to the realm of the dead, darkness and
numerous gods. Devastated by the loss of his friend, Gilgamesh lamented.

The writer of the epic records: 'seven days and seven nights he wept for Enkidu, until the worm fastened on him. Only then he gave him up to the earth'.[25] His funerary rites were thus episodic in ways that recall Near Eastern Neolithic practices. Here, in the epic, we have an echo of excarnation and delayed burial.

Speaking of his own forthcoming death, Gilgamesh said, 'Immolation and sacrifice are not yet for me'.[26] We see that the notion of death as sacrifice was part of Sumerian religious belief and practice. When Gilgamesh does eventually lie dead, his body is 'stretched on the bed, like a gazelle that is caught in a noose'. The simile is significant. It recalls the combined human and animal burial at Kfar HaHoresh in which the bones of the two species were arranged so that, when seen from above, they represent an animal. At the same site, a plastered human skull was associated with a headless gazelle carcass, as if the human skull took the place of the animal's head (Chapter 4) – culture : nature, and permutations of that opposition.[27] Even Gilgamesh, part human and part divine, was implicated in the human : animal opposition and its mediation in transition to the nether realm of death.

More about the underworld was revealed to Enkidu in a dream.[28] In that realm, the dead 'are clothed like birds with wings for covering'. There, too, was

an awful being, the sombre faced man-bird … His was a vampire face, his foot was a lion's foot, his hand was an eagle's talon. He fell on me and his claws were in my hair, he held me fast and I smothered. Then he transformed me so that my arms became wings covered with feathers.[29]

Dreams, a key component of the consciousness contract, clearly held huge significance. To prepare for one of Enkidu's revelatory dreams Gilgamesh performed immolation: he scattered sacrificial meal on the ground and said, 'O mountain, dwelling of the gods, send a dream for Enkidu, make him a favourable dream.'[30] Here, again, the gods are associated with the upper realm. The dream came, and it revealed the cosmos and its transforming beings.

Transformations leading to a unity of animals and people characterized the spirit world – as we have come to expect of a realm initially created by altered states. Avian transformation recalls the role of birds in Neolithic sites: flight embodies spiritual experience and leads to another world. At Nevali Çori, it will be remembered, there was a stone carving of a human head apparently in the clutches of a bird's talons, and a stone pillar with two symmetrical human figures, back to back, and with a carving of a bird perched on one of the heads. Another carving combines human and avian features

(Chapter 1); while at Çatalhöyük there is a suggestion that the wings of cranes were parts of ritual costumes, and there are wall paintings of vultures apparently scavenging on human remains (Chapter 4). Along with sacrifice, flight, as epitomized by birds, was part of the spirit world and transition to it.

The Epic of Gilgamesh also shows that, at least at the time of its currency, religion – founded on access to other realms – was under the control of a hierarchy of people to whom the epic refers as 'high priests and acolytes, priests of the incantation and ecstasy'; there were also priestesses and 'servers of the temple',[31] as well as administrators and a vast work force to tend the temple's herds and fields.[32] Enkidu sees parallels of real-world priests in 'the house of dust', that is, in the underworld. During the Neolithic, religious centres were probably a comparable mixture of religious and economic activities, and, in the earliest periods, priests may not have been full-time specialists.

The theme of priestly ecstasy and altered states of consciousness, apparently induced by chanting ('incantation'), may be taken up in another Sumerian poem, *Bilgames (Gilgamesh) and the Netherworld*. A version of it was appended to the Ninevite recension of *The Epic of Gilgamesh*. In Nancy Sandars' controversial account, Enkidu descends to the underworld to bring back

a mysterious and perhaps shamanistic drum and drumstick that Gilgamesh has let fall into it. In spite of warnings he breaks all the taboos and is held fast, 'for the Underworld seized him'; but a hole is made in the earth's crust so that he (or his spirit) may return and describe what he has seen [original parenthesis].[33]

The rhythmic drum, a hole in the surface of the earth, travel to the underworld, and a return having actually seen parts of the cosmos that are hidden from ordinary people are now for us familiar features of religious experiences achieved through altered states of consciousness. Other scholars do, however, dispute part of this translation. They give the Sumerian word *pukku* as ball or hoop, rather than drum.[34] Andrew George, Professor of Babylonian at the School of Oriental and African Studies, London, argues persuasively that the passage should be seen in the light of Sumerian ballgames: in a Sumerian cultic lament human heads, severed in battle, roll like 'heavy *pukkus*'.[35] Here the word clearly means balls rather than drums or hoops.

Whatever the correct translation, we see that descent into the underworld is probably again associated with the vortex. Along with flight, passage through a hole or tunnel to the lower realm is repeated again and again. These are both 'non-sense' building-blocks.

At this point we can discern what we believe may be the origin of some of the binary oppositions that Lévi-Strauss argues are intrinsic to myth: ultimately and in their simplest ur-forms some key oppositions derive from human neurology, and it is on these that 'myth-makers' (Lévi-Strauss's *bricoleurs*) build more abstract oppositions – permutations build on permutations.

flight : vortex

up : down

condor : anaconda

life : death

gods : spirits

Heaven : Hell

good : bad

exogamy : endogamy (in some societies)

This list omits 'in-between' elements, the mediators and transitions. Often myths posit mediators of oppositions, and these become the focus of ritual attention and, sometimes, awe. In a famous example, the Lele of the Congo Basin respect the pangolin (scaly anteater) because it appears to mediate the categories of land : aquatic creatures.[36] In Christianity, Christ, who mediates the major God : Man opposition, is the principal focus of ritual (and doctrinal) attention. So it is that Gilgamesh and Enkidu, each in his own way a mediator, are foci of attention.

The passages from Gilgamesh that we have examined echo our earlier discussions. In the epic we can see the role of altered consciousness and how its generation of a tiered cosmos provides a framework for mythical narrative, transition and mediation and, further, for situating daily life, as well as religious practice, within a wider whole. We also see that ranked 'seers' were part of that religious practice. Comparable themes probably came together in the mythical thought and narratives that must have clothed and given coherent meaning to Neolithic buildings, symbols, images, rituals and daily life. Though our approach differs from Lévi-Strauss's notion of 'deep structure', we too are pointing to something about myth that is indeed 'deep'. (We take up the notion of depth in Chapter 9.)

The cave of the Reindeer-Women

In recounting the Samoyed narrative for comparison with *The Epic of Gil-gamesh*, we do not imply that the beliefs it enshrines were held in an identical way in the Neolithic. Although the Siberian beliefs clearly derived in part from universal, neurologically wired experiences of altered consciousness, those experiences were socialized, explored and manipulated in historically specific ways. The Samoyed account nevertheless shows that widened under-standings of a tiered cosmos, subterranean birth of animals, and historically contingent notions of 'death', 'birth' and 'wild' (Chapter 5) help to bring Neolithic symbolism into clearer focus.

We divide the Samoyed narrative into nine stages.

STAGE 1

Unconscious for three days during an attack of smallpox, a Samoyed man felt himself carried 'into the middle of a sea'. There, the Lords of the Water gave him his shamanic name, Huottarie (Diver): he was one who could travel underwater. Thereafter, he jour-neyed up to a mountain where he met a naked woman, who was probably the Lady of the Water, and he began to suckle at her breast. She said, 'You are my child; that is why I let you suckle at my breast. You will meet many hardships and be greatly wearied.'[37]

Transformation of the novice takes place in an aquatic underworld, and he becomes a 'Diver', one who plunges through the cosmos. We also see that the initiation of a shaman was thought of, at least in part, as a kind of birth and suckling. The Lady of the Water's milk contributed to the development of his shamanic powers. One thinks of the moulded breasts on the walls of Çatal-höyük and the female figures apparently giving birth to horned bulls. The 'birth' represented by those female figures may have related, in part, to the 'birth' of a shaman in the spirit world (at this point in the Samoyed narrative, paradoxically an upperworld cave like Coleridge's 'miracle of rare device', 'A sunny pleasure-dome with caves of ice !'). The breasts related to the suckling of a novice, one of the means by which he obtained potency. The apparently 'death-dealing' bones and teeth in those breasts may have referred not to death and danger, as we may prosaically understand those words, but to the power of the wild 'out there' and so to supernatural potency: both mouths and breasts are orifices through which 'life-essence' escapes. The connection between this potency and the concept of birth and suckling will become apparent in a moment.

STAGE 2

Then the husband of the Lady of the Water, who was the Lord of the Underworld, gave the initiate his two guides, an ermine and a mouse, to lead him to the underworld. There he encountered the men of the Great Sickness (syphilis), the Lord of Madness, the Lords of all the nervous disorders, and evil shamans. Thus he learned of the diseases he would later cure. Still accompanied by his guides, he came to the Land of the Shamanesses, who strengthened his throat and voice. He was then carried to an island in the middle of the Nine Seas where a young birch tree rose to the sky: it was the Tree of the Lord. As, flying with the birds of the seas (ducks, a swan and a sparrow-hawk), the initiate left the place of the tree, the Lord of the Tree told him to make three drums from one of its branches, one for each of the major rituals he would later conduct (caring for women in child-birth, curing the sick and finding men lost in the snow).[38]

The verticality of the tree, joining as it did earth and sky, suggests that it was the *axis mundi*: the initiate continued to move between levels of the cosmos. In this concept, we have suggested, lay the significance of trees and the posts embellished with red paint and bulls' heads at Çatalhöyük and the other indications of Near Eastern cosmological verticality. That the initiate's drum (its rim) was made from a branch of the Tree of the Lord implies a connection between drums and the *axis mundi*. Drums are, as we have pointed out, common shamanic instruments: their insistent beating induces altered states of consciousness and thus passage along the *axis mundi*. Speaking of supernatural travel, Yakut shamans say, 'The drum is our horse'.[39] Horses convey people through space, and the sound of their hoofs resembles drumming.

STAGE 3

Clasping the branch the initiate resumed his flight. He came to an endless sea where he found trees and seven stones. The stones spoke to him one after the other. The first had teeth like bears' teeth and a basket-shaped cavity. It told him that it was the earth's holding stone: it prevented the fields from being blown away. The second stone served to melt iron.[40]

Here we have a combination of water and stone that will assume importance in later chapters. For the present, we note the significance of stones as oracles: they link the initiate to supernaturally vouchsafed information about cosmology. One of the stones is like a mouth and has a hollow in it. We recall the standing stones at Göbekli Tepe, 'Ain Ghazal and other sites. Working in west European Neolithic tombs, Aaron Watson, an archaeologist at Reading University, found that ritually produced sounds can 'induce enormous stones to appear to shake and become alive'.[41] This is a point to bear in mind when, in the following chapters, we consider megalithic tombs. Without drawing a specific analogy, we suggest that this part of the Samoyed narrative opens up ways of thinking about stones in the Neolithic as, in various ways, bridging realms.

STAGE 4

His guides led him to a high, rounded mountain. There he entered a bright cave that was covered with mirrors. In the middle of it was 'something like a fire'.[42]

From an upper level of the cosmos, the initiate descends into the lower level via a cave. He continues to alternate between levels of the cosmos. The images in the mirrors and their brightness suggest the hallucinations that appear on the sides of the 'tunnel', or vortex, that leads to deep hallucinatory experiences, and also the initiate's participation in his own projected hallucinatory imagery, both well-documented experiences (Chapter 2).[43] The reflecting walls, with their imagery, also recall the decorated rooms of Çatalhöyük, in some of which polished obsidian mirrors were found in burials. Reflections (disembodied images, unreal like hallucinations) and death were associated.

STAGE 5

In the cave, the initiate saw two women, naked but covered with hair, like reindeer. The underground chamber in which they were was lit, not by a fire as he at first thought, but by a light that came from above, through an opening.[44]

Note the therianthropic nature of the women and their association with the underworld: these are women-animals. Again, the dimly lit, decorated rooms of Göbekli Tepe and Çatalhöyük, as well as other sites into which people descended, are suggested by 'a light that came from above'.

STAGE 6

One of the women told the initiate that she would give birth to two reindeer that would become sacrificial animals, one for the Dolgon and Evenki, the other for the Tavgi, all three being Samoyed groups. She also gave him a hair to use 'when he shamanized for reindeer'.[45]

Giving birth to sacrificial animals thus had dual significance. First, 'birth' was a source of supernatural potency. Secondly, the 'birth' of the two reindeer had social significance: social divisions (between the Dolgon, Evenki and Tavgi) were being 'naturalized' in the initiate's experience. At the same time, the ambivalence of 'the wild' was being created.

STAGE 7

The other woman would also give birth to two reindeer, but these would be 'symbols of the animals that would aid man in all his works and also supply his food'.[46]

The Samoyed reindeer here are comparable to the Çatalhöyük aurochs in the process of domestication and, of course, to other species in so many shaman-istic communities. The subterranean births recall the female figures in Çatalhöyük that appear to be giving birth to bulls. The creation of and the closeness between spirit-animal helpers and real animals is clearly brought out by this episode of the Samoyed account: for shamanistic people, animals remain a mystery (in the religious sense of the word: an inexplicable, divinely revealed truth) with great power. That power needs to be accessed and har-nessed so that it can aid man in all his works.

STAGE 8

From the cave of the Reindeer-Women the initiate went to another mountain with another cave. In it, he met a naked man working a bellows. The man caught him, 'cut off his head, chopped his body into pieces' and threw everything into a cauldron. He suf-fered death and dismemberment. His body boiled in the cauldron for three years. Later, the man put the shaman's bones together again and covered them with flesh. 'He changed his eyes; and that is why, when he shamanizes, he does not see with his bodily eyes but with these mystical eyes. He pierced his ears, making him able to understand the language of plants.'[47]

Here we encounter divisions within the underworld – 'another cave' – that recall the differentiated spaces of so many Near Eastern Neolithic sites. The screen wall between the two rooms of the 'Ain Ghazal 'temple' is an example of demarcated space. As we have suggested, the wall paintings of vultures at Çatalhöyük, the practice of excarnation on some bodies and the plastered skulls were probably manifestations, directly or indirectly, of the widely reported shamanistic experience of dismemberment and restoration. The three years in the cauldron in the Samoyed narrative may parallel the time a body was allowed to decay before it was disinterred for further ritual treat-ment in Neolithic times. When restored, the initiate had 'mystical eyes': he was a seer. As we have repeatedly remarked, preternatural sight seems to be suggested by the eyes of the 'Ain Ghazal statues and by the shell eyes of plastered skulls.

STAGE 9

The candidate found himself on the summit of a mountain, and finally he woke in the yurt, among his family. Now he can sing and shamanize indefinitely, without ever growing tired. When he wishes to perform his shamanistic rituals, 'he mentally turns toward the cave' of the Reindeer-Women.[48]

The way in which, as a fully fledged shaman, he turned 'mentally' towards the cave of the Reindeer-Women when he wanted to perform shamanic interventions shows that he relived or recaptured or re-created some of the experiences that made him a shaman in the first place. In a similar way, Neolithic religious specialists (whether we call them 'shamans' or not) probably returned, literally as well as in their religious experiences, to their built environment, places where those spiritual experiences could, sometimes by the induction of altered states of consciousness, be repeatedly relived. In caves, apsidal buildings with orthostats, semi-subterranean rock-cut structures like those at Göbekli Tepe, and in embellished rooms the underworld was re-created and contacted.

'Abstract' myth

This is a slightly simplified version of the rich Samoyed narrative. Nevertheless, it shows that the modern Western concepts of 'death', 'birth' and 'wild' need to be expanded if we are to understand the Neolithic symbolic code and the social processes associated with it. Rethought in terms of a tiered cosmos, altered states, transcosmological travel, and animal potency and control, these concepts bring the complexity of Near Eastern Neolithic architecture and imagery into clearer focus. Moreover, the 'mechanism for the control of society' of which Hodder writes and its role in the domestication of animals is better understood.[49] That 'mechanism' was a historically specific form of religion that explored a tiered cosmos and engendered a complex symbolic and social order that was variously constructed, both literally and metaphorically, at Neolithic sites.

The Samoyed narrative, like *The Epic of Gilgamesh*, gives us a tantalizing glimpse of what the Near Eastern mythical world may have been like. To get away from their specificities, we must try to conceive of an 'abstract' myth, a suite of content-free, neurologically generated experiences and images. These building-blocks were set in narrative matrices peculiar to 'Ain Ghazal, Göbekli Tepe or Çatalhöyük: narratives were the mortar that held the building-blocks together in meaningful patterns. We do not underestimate the importance of narratives, as Lévi-Strauss perhaps does, but we must face the fact that those of the Neolithic are now lost. Sumerian cuneiform tablets do not reach that far back. Although Neolithic narratives may be beyond our grasp, the crucial building-blocks are not, and it is they that afford the most acute insights into past religious experiences and the beliefs that were built on them. To contextualize them, we need to comprehend them in the archaeological contexts of specific Near Eastern sites.

This endeavour suggests what we believe is a fair summing up of the essence of life and belief in a Neolithic world so different from our own. How did religious experience, belief and practice come together to fashion the social and emotional fabric of ordinary people's daily lives? How did people combine blinding insights into the cosmos and its supernatural inhabitants with the emotions of daily life? Simply put, how did people who believed in the sorts of things we find in Gilgamesh and the Siberian narrative manage to get from day to day? Perhaps there is a clue in *The Epic of Gilgamesh*. After Enkidu had related his awesome dream of the underworld, Gilgamesh expressed his apprehension of life with its mix of fear and hope:

Strange things have been spoken, why does your heart speak strangely? The dream was marvellous but the terror was great; we must treasure the dream whatever the terror.[50]

Materiality and symbolism

We saw that James Mellaart wrote that the study of the Near Eastern Neolithic was becoming 'more complex and thus more human',[51] and Hodder urged 'a new type of understanding of a mythical world deeply embedded in a complex social system'.[52] Though written nearly 30 years apart, both statements point to Neolithic complexity and human action. Above all else, the evidence we have considered suggests the importance of complex thought patterns, some neurologically generated, as a resource on which sentient actors could draw and that they could manipulate. In exploring those patterns, we have adumbrated an overarching yet dynamic tiered 'mythical world' that brings to light connections between cosmology, architecture, human movement in built spaces, imagery and domestication: there was an intricate process of mutual construction.

The details of the trajectory of Near Eastern Neolithic thought through the millennia of the period still need to be worked out, and, as excavations at various sites continue, they will doubtless be filled in and modified. They will, as we have tried to do here, diminish the gap between materiality and symbolism. The materiality and symbolism of so much in the Neolithic will be shown to have had a dynamic interrelationship that led to changes through time as human beings engaged with, constructed and reconstructed the articulation between their material and conceptual environments.

We have seen that, in addition to being living spaces, the Near Eastern Neolithic structures were manifestations of the cosmos and were thus related to mythology – as, throughout the world, many other buildings, tombs and alignments were to be in succeeding millennia. Earlier, during the west European Upper Palaeolithic, caves had been part of a visible and, at the same time, invisible universe that people adapted and embellished.[53] In the Neolithic, on the other hand, people constructed a model of the cosmos in which the 'cave in the mind' played an even more defining role. As a result, human control of the conceived form of the cosmos increased markedly. Cosmological control created a more flexible and effective mechanism for social control. How could this be?

Constructing a cosmos with its concomitant mythology is, in Marxist terms, a function of the 'intellectual means of production'. For an elite to control society effectively, they must seize control of the material *and* the intellectual means of production, though they may never manage to do so totally. In unprecedented and innovative ways, groups of Neolithic people manipulated cosmology and the states of consciousness that provided them with the fundamental building-blocks for religious experience, belief and practice. Seers thus gained political power and economic influence as well as religious domination. Therein lies the real, innovative essence of the Neolithic: expression of religious cosmological concepts in material structures as well as in myths, rather than the passive acceptance of natural phenomena (such as caves), opened up new ways of constructing an intrinsically dynamic society.

In the following chapters we move from the Near East to the European Atlantic seaboard and investigate the ways in which that essence was expressed in huge megalithic monuments that recall, though exceed, those at Göbekli Tepe. In doing so, we must unfortunately leap-frog the complex developments of the central and eastern European Neolithic.[54] We ask: Do the great Neolithic structures of western Europe embody any of the beliefs and cosmological concepts that we have discerned in the generally much less impressive and enduring Near East buildings and rituals? Were any of the fundamental Near East Neolithic tropes expressed in west European megalithic chambered tombs, circles of standing stones, stone- or embankment-demarcated avenues, circular wooden structures, multi-stage burials, and whirling imagery laboriously carved into the great stones?

CHAPTER 7

The Mound in the Dark Grove

The 'mound' in the title of this chapter recalls the Near Eastern 'tells' (Arabic for a hillock or mound) of mud- and stone-built villages piled one on top of another. But the association of the word with a 'dark grove' suggests a different kind of mound that is found in the forests of Atlantic Europe and that has associations with Druids and mystery. Far from the dusty sites of Nevali Çori, Göbekli Tepe and Çatalhöyük, the bosky hills of Brittany, Iberia, Britain and Ireland were centres of another Neolithic architectural flowering, our second – and markedly contrasting – focus of exploration. What was the connection, if any, between the two regions?

> And did those feet in ancient time
> Walk upon England's mountains green?
> And was the Holy Lamb of God
> On England's pleasant pastures seen?[1]

William Blake (1757–1827), the rather eccentric engraver, poet and mystic, was convinced of a link between the land of the Bible and 'England's green and pleasant land'. He was delighted with Arch-Druid Chyndonax's writings. William Stukeley (1687–1765), who adopted this bizarre title and name as part of his Society of Roman Knights, toured England and published splendid volumes that illustrate and meticulously describe ancient monuments, many of which he believed to be the handiwork of Druids (Fig. 34). After having been secretary to the Society of Antiquaries, this friend of Isaac Newton had a mind-changing experience, was ordained as a Church of England clergyman and came to believe that the Druids had proclaimed in England the true, patriarchal religion. The religion of Abraham and Moses, he believed, was brought to England by Phoenicians accompanied by priestly Druids. In Ireland, similar beliefs flourished. Dolmens (megalithic tombs from which the covering mound has been eroded) were called 'transcript(s) of the ancient patriarchal altar, as recorded in the holy writ'.[2] Stukeley went further and argued that Stonehenge and Avebury, huge circles of standing stones that seem to imply impressively choreographed rituals, provided all the proof

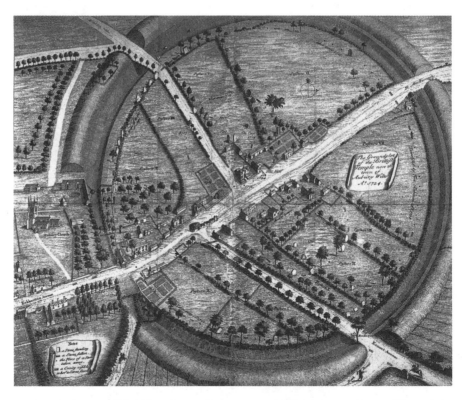

34 Self-portrait of William Stukeley as Chyndonax, 1740. Of the Rollright stones (Pl. 16) Stukeley said: 'a very noble monument; the first antiquity of this sort that I had seen; and from which I concluded these works to be temples of the ancient Britons … Nought pleased me better.'[3]

necessary. Thus began the whole Druid saga that flourishes even today.

Blake, much impressed by all this, called for his 'bow of burning gold' and his 'chariot of fire' and vowed that he would not sleep until Jerusalem had been built in England. After all, Abraham and Noah were, according to him, Druids. Here was a potent mixture of mumbo-jumbo, lunacy, social reform and patriotism.

Yet, behind all the nonsense, there is a small grain of truth. The west European Neolithic did indeed originate in the Near East and spread from that

35 Stukeley's ground plan of Avebury, Wiltshire. He made the drawing in 1724 and entitled it 'The groundplot of the British Temple now the town of Avbury Wilts'.

heartland to the Atlantic seaboard of Europe – though neither Israelite patri-
archs nor Druids had anything whatsoever to do with it. At one time,
researchers thought that the great tombs of western Europe may have had
their origin in the megalithic buildings of Mycenae, but radiocarbon dating
changed that view: the Mycenaeans flourished in the eastern Mediterranean
from about 1700 BC; the oldest west European megaliths date as far back as
4800 BC. The Pyramids at Giza date from mid-3rd millennium BC. Still, European agriculture as a way of life did originate in the Near East.

Our concern is not so much the steps, routes or means (such as migration
or the transmission of ideas or both) by which the Neolithic spread through
Europe; that is a highly complex matter that scholars are still debating. Some
wonder if the spread of the Neolithic was a replay of the much earlier (40,000
BC) migration of communities of *Homo sapiens* into a Europe that was occupied by Neanderthals. Rather than going into all these issues, we are more
concerned with architectural and artistic contrasts between two geographical
extremes of what many researchers see as a single, though by no means uniform, archaeological period.

In this chapter, we concentrate on some of the architectural achievements
of Neolithic Atlantic Europe (we deal with image-making in a later chapter).
In doing so, we follow the lead of Colin Renfrew, formerly Disney Professor of
Archaeology in the University of Cambridge, who coined the phrase 'cognitive archaeology'[4] and provided a perceptive impetus to studies of west
European Neolithic monuments.[5] Bearing in mind the relationship between
architecture and cosmology that we noted at various Near Eastern sites, we
put forward a number of hypotheses:

– The west European monuments reflected and at the same time constituted, with greater or lesser elaboration, a culturally specific expression
   of the neurologically generated tiered cosmos.
– That cosmos was mediated by a complex system of symbols through
   which people represented and engaged with it.
– The neurologically wired concepts of flight and passage through a vortex
   help us to understand the ways in which the massive stone monuments
   of the west functioned in their social and mythical contexts.
– The ways in which the monuments were laid out reflected and controlled social distinctions that were, in turn, related to neurologically
   wired concepts.

We assess evidence for these general propositions and see how well they co-
ordinate and explain different kinds of Neolithic architecture. The concept of

'proof' is inappropriate in discussions of this kind. The best that researchers can hope for in all archaeological explanations beyond the trivial is that they provide a persuasive account that articulates at the finest level possible with the available evidence.

To illustrate this sort of articulation, we choose two sites, neither among the best known. They introduce types of Neolithic monuments and also some of the principles – cosmological, religious and social – that gave the structures meaning and practical impact on people's lives. We begin with a multi-component site that encapsulates themes that we noted in the Near East and that, somewhat transmuted, appear in western Europe. It provides a useful, if rather unusual, starting point for our exploration of a few of the many and varied megalithic monuments of western Europe.

Bryn Celli Ddu

'The Mound in the Dark Grove' is a translation of the Welsh 'Bryn Celli Ddu'. It is the name of the best-known megalithic monument on the island of Anglesey, Wales (Pl. 17; Figs 36, 37). Like so many other Neolithic monuments, it lay unregarded for thousands of years. Excavations begun in 1865 were not satisfactory, but the work of more modern archaeologists in 1928–1929 began to reveal the complex history of the site.[6] Despite this work, some researchers still feel unsure about the sequence.[7] As we outline the principal features of the monument, readers will begin to notice similarities and

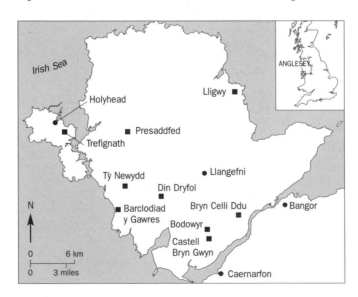

36 Anglesey, an island off the Welsh coast, has numerous Neolithic monuments.

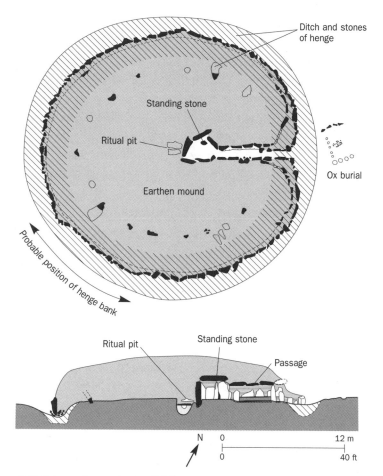

Ditch and stones
of henge

Standing stone

Ritual pit

Ox burial

Earthen mound

Probable position of henge bank

Ritual pit

Standing stone

Passage

N

0   12 m

0   40 ft

*37 Bryn Celli Ddu, an impressive Neolithic monument in Anglesey. Only a portion of the
mound has been reconstructed so that other features are not obscured.*

differences between it and the Near Eastern structures that we described in
earlier chapters.

Bryn Celli Ddu began in Middle Neolithic times as a henge monument.[8]
Like other henges throughout Great Britain and Ireland, it comprised a circular bank with a ditch on the inner side. The ditch measured 21 m (69 ft) in
diameter and was some 1.8 m (6 ft) deep and 5.2 m (17 ft) wide. At first,
the 1920s excavators did not recognize the ditch and bank as an earlier monument than the megalithic tomb beneath the now-prominent mound; that key
realization came later.[9] The sequence at Bryn Celli Ddu intriguingly reverses
that found elsewhere and, in doing so, illustrates our proposition that the
Neolithic was a period of change and contestation.

HENGES

The word 'henge' has a curious history. It derives from the most famous of all British Neolithic monuments, Stonehenge (Pl. 15). The name of this massive historical icon derives from the Old English words 'stone' and 'henge', the second of which means 'hinge' or 'hang' and may suggest a gallows.[10] The 'hanging' stones are, of course, those set on top of the huge vertical stones to form lintels. In this respect Stonehenge is unique: no other monuments have lintels resting on a circle of standing stones.[11]

Then, in 1925, an unrecognized type of monument was discovered. Squadron Leader G. S. M. Insall was flying over the area around Stonehenge when he spotted a circular shape in a ploughed field; the wheat growing over the circle was of a darker hue than that elsewhere. Its shape reminded him of nearby Stonehenge, which, from the altitude at which he was flying, was clearly visible with its alignment supposedly pointing towards the summer solstice. Archaeological investigation on the ground showed that the new discovery was a circular bank and ditch with a causeway entrance. Within the circle was a large number of (filled in) post holes that had formerly held wooden posts (archaeologists do not agree if the posts in this and other henges supported roofs). The monument was immediately dubbed Woodhenge, even though there was no sign of stones, let alone 'hanging' ones.[12] Alerted to this 'new' kind of monument, archaeologists soon found others throughout the British Isles.

What else do henges have in common with Stonehenge? Do they all have alignments? Some researchers believe that the henge of the Bryn Celli Ddu monument, which is on a low rise, is aligned not with any celestial body but with the rocky knoll and a solitary standing stone that is between the two, though nearer the knoll than the tomb. Both the knoll and the standing stone are to the northwest of the mound. Rocky outcrops are rare in the area. The notion of alignment at Bryn Celli Ddu is intriguing. There are many indisputable alignments in Neolithic western Europe as at Stonehenge itself, but we are unable to convince ourselves beyond any doubt that this particular proposed three-point alignment was intentional.

Henges like Bryn Celli Ddu and Stonehenge have sometimes been seen as defensive, but the placing of the ditch inside, rather than outside, the bank seems to suggest some other purpose. By contrast, later Iron Age hill-forts have the ditch on the outside of the bank, thus making access more difficult for attackers. (Ironically, the eponymous Stonehenge has the ditch outside the bank.) Moreover, henge monuments, such as the beginnings of Bryn Celli

Ddu, usually have one or more causeways across the ditch. Like the position of the ditch itself, they tend to negate the suggestion that henges were defensive structures. On the contrary, the openings through the banks and ditches seem to have been deliberately left as approaches to whatever took place within the circle, or, perhaps simultaneously, to allow the effects of those activities to reach out into the world beyond the circle.

If there was no practical advantage in having a ditch within a bank, we must conclude, along with most archaeologists, that henges were built, at least in part, for ritual purposes – that is, as a place for religious experiences and practices. Some writers have gone so far as to use the phrase 'open-air sanctuaries'. They may not be entirely wrong. A ritual interpretation is confirmed at Bryn Celli Ddu by evidence for a circle of 14 standing stones inside the ditch. Many of these no longer exist, but some do remain. Archaeologists determined the positions of the missing ones by finding evidence for the holes that were dug to hold them erect. The stones certainly did not have a practical function. Indeed, their very erection seems to have been steeped in ritual, for small deposits of burnt human bone and shattered quartz (as we shall see, a highly significant substance) were placed at the base of some of them. In one instance, there was the almost complete cremation of a girl of about 15 years.[13] Death, possibly by sacrifice, was related to the Neolithic architecture of Atlantic Europe. We can already begin to detect a pattern that included symbols (such as the quartz) and cosmological transition (death). We should also remember that newly constructed banks in limestone country would have stood out, a brilliant white against their green surrounds.

Many people's first reaction is therefore to accept without question that the activities that took place within henges constituted some form of ritual. Solemn Druidical ceremonies, as the modern imagination has constructed them, spring to mind – venerable bearded men in long robes invoking the influence of heavenly bodies along the lines of Stukeley's ideas. On the other hand, most archaeologists argue, probably correctly, that the activities were economic as well as religious: people went into henges perhaps to offer sacrifices *and* to trade goods and animals, and to maintain social relations between scattered groups of people. As in the Near East, economic and religious activities were probably not clearly differentiated. Religion was an integral component of daily life, not a gloss on it. Neolithic people could not imagine life without religion.

How, then, did the building (not just the use) of henges impact on daily life? The construction of a henge must have required a great deal of planning and organization and, of course, labour, but the people had earlier passage tombs (described later) to show that large-scale building was humanly possible. If groups of people came together to construct henges, as they must have done to build the rock-cut structures at Göbekli Tepe, leaders of some sort must also have had to co-ordinate the work force and arrange adequate food supplies. Bones found at henges in Great Britain show that hunting was a significant food source. In addition, it seems that there must have been some specialist activities over and above the sheer labour required to build such large monuments. Someone, or some group, had to decide to build the henge, to lay out its circular form, determine where the causeways should be, command the necessary labour and so forth. A picture of a complex society is emerging, but there is no indication that people were settled at or in the henges. Unlike the 'temples' at 'Ain Ghazal, henges were not integral parts of extensive settlements. More like Göbekli Tepe, they were probably points of social and religious congregation.

But, by itself, the invoking of unspecified 'ritual' or 'religion' would be both too narrow and too vague an interpretation. As we have seen, ritual practices and notions such as death must be situated in a specific cosmological and social context; they are not universal. A crucial question therefore is: Did henges relate in any way to Neolithic cosmology?

To answer that question we begin by noting that, for modern viewers, the circular ditches of henges recall moats. This impression may not be as fanciful as it at first seems. The archaeologist Colin Richards has persuasively suggested that the ditches of henge monuments in Orkney, off the north coast of Scotland, were intended to be filled with water and thus to create a microcosm of the land : water relationship that he, probably rightly, argues was part of Neolithic cosmology.[14] As part of his analysis, he identifies what were probably 'elements' in Neolithic thought: earth, water, fire, air. Henges thus became microcosms of Neolithic cosmology. The central areas were surrounded by water (the ditches) and earth (the banks); air and the notion of height and the heavens were emphasized by circles of standing stones, in Orkney some rising to 5 m (16.4 ft); fire occupied a central position and was contained within monumental hearths. Richards cites Mircea Eliade's broad argument that people need to pin down a sense of place and, especially, a node that provides 'a centre, an *axis mundi*, to the world'.[15] We have already encountered the notion of an *axis mundi* that is neurologically generated and that joins the levels of a tiered cosmos.

Other monuments associated with water are found in Ireland. One of these, an enclosure near Ballycarty, a few miles from Tralee in County Kerry, has a clearly defined internal rock-cut ditch. It is approached across a cause-way and through an entrance on the west.[16] The interior seems to have been deliberately constructed to retain water. Another enclosure not far away has an interior some 2 m (6.6 ft) below the exterior ground level.[17] Michael Connolly and Tom Condit, who described these and other similar Irish monuments, conclude that they 'appear to be associated with a water cult'.[18] It could be objected that the ditches of many henges in limestone or chalk terrain do not fill up with water. Moreover, some henges, such as Durrington Walls in Wiltshire, are constructed on slopes.

Still, those may not be significant objections. Ditches could well have been *symbolic* of water, and, even if not perennially filled with it, they are soggy at some times of the year. Their shape is suggestive of a river bed, and at least puddles gather in the bottom of them during heavy rain. A circle of water (river) that has to be crossed may well have been part of Neolithic cosmology.[19] It is certainly a common notion. Crossing a river is overcoming an obstacle separating two regions. One has simply to recall not only Charon ferrying the dead across the subterranean river Styx to the Elysian Fields, but also that 'one more river to cross, and that's the river of Jordan', and, of course, Lethe, submersion in the waters of which brings oblivion. In the Sumerian narrative, *The Epic of Gilgamesh*, the 'waters of death' are crossed by the ferryman, Ur-shanabi and his crew of Stone Ones (Chapter 6).[20]

But rivers divide *and* connect: a circular river may suggest a cosmologically isolated spiritual region and, at the same time, its proximity to the material world. The second phase of construction at Bryn Celli Ddu (the megalithic tomb that we describe in a moment) confirms and amplifies these cosmological implications of a circular ditch.

PETRIFIED BEINGS?

Within the Bryn Celli Ddu henge was a circle of large standing stones. Monuments of this kind are widely found in the British Isles and are well known to the public. They are also usually steeped in local traditions. The Rollright stone circle some 20 miles (32.2 km) northwest of Oxford, for instance, was said to be the bodies of a Danish king, Rollo, and his men who were turned to stone by a witch – or variations on this tale (Pl. 16).[21] More interestingly, this monument was the first to be seen by Stukeley, in 1710; it was Rollright that started him on his quest. Later, he wrote of it,

'There are many different opinions concerning these venerable pieces of antiquity, many fabulous stories retold of them. I cannot but suppose them to have been a Heathen Temple of our Ancestors, perhaps in the Druid's time.'[22]

Dated to at least 2500 BC, the Rollright circle is 31 m (101.7 ft) in diameter and comprises about 77 blocks of local oolitic limestone, as Stukeley put it, 'corroded like wormeaten wood by the harsh jaws of time'.[23] There is, however, doubt as to the exact number of original stones; some broke through the millennia and local people added the pieces to the ring. It does, however, seem clear that there was a stone-marked entrance through the northern part of the perimeter. The least weathered sides of the original stones seem to have been arranged to face inwards, thus presenting a relatively smooth wall. About 73 m (239.5 ft) outside the ring stands the King Stone, 2.4 m (7.9 ft) high and 1.5 m (4.9 ft) across. Farther from the circle, some 360 m (1,181 ft) to the east–south–east, are the remains of a megalithic burial chamber. It is known as the Whispering Knights: the clustered standing stones lean confidentially towards one another.

In recent times, some researchers have sought stellar, lunar and solar alignments at Rollright. Best-known of these writers is Alexander Thom, who was a professor of mechanical engineering at Oxford; he also made sensational archaeo-astronomical claims for Stonehenge.[24] Many such alignments of Neolithic monuments are today questioned: for example, Thom's claim that, from the centre of the Rollright circle, the King Stone is aligned with the 1750 BC rising of Capella, a date that is too late for the building of the monument. Still, whatever may be the case at Rollright, Bryn Celli Ddu or Stonehenge, some alignments were intentional.

But what of the great stones themselves? As we have seen, some in the Near East are indeed shaped somewhat like human beings and seem to have arms. It is, moreover, worth noting that, in *The Epic of Gilgamesh*, Ur-shanabi's ferry is crewed by what Andrew George translates as 'Stone Ones'.[25] Sandars gives the cuneiform phrase as 'holy things, the things of stone'.[26] When Gilgamesh confronts Ur-shanabi, he takes up his axe and draws his dirk:

> Like an arrow he fell among them,
> in the midst of the forest his shout resounded.
> [...]
> They took fright, the Stone [Ones, *who crewed*] the boat,
> who were not [*harmed* by the Waters] of Death.[27]

The Stone Ones, guardians of transition, cannot keep the hero out, even though they are themselves immune to the Waters of Death. Are these 'Stone Ones' to be compared with the carved standing stones at Göbekli Tepe and with those at Bryn Celli Ddu and indeed throughout western Europe? It is likely that *part* of the significance of standing stones was that they represented, or embodied, beings of some sort. We investigate this intriguing possibility in Chapter 9, where we consider the 'substance' of stone.

MEGALITHIC TOMBS

Towards the end of the Neolithic, the people who were using the Bryn Celli Ddu henge and stone circle (or, perhaps, others who moved in from elsewhere) brought about significant changes. They erected a megalithic passage tomb in the centre of the ring. In doing so, they reversed the usual sequence, for megalithic tombs are usually older than henges.

We use the common term 'tomb' because the massive structures were undoubtedly repositories for the dead, but we argue, along with other archaeologists, that they were more than 'tombs' in the modern sense of the word. They were also places where the dead were revisited and where people maintained long-term relations with them: they were religious and social foci.

The Bryn Celli Ddu tomb has features that are repeated, with variations, in a great many passage and chambered tombs in Brittany, Iberia, Ireland and Great Britain (see Fig. 38). We describe them in a moment.

After constructing the tomb with huge stones, some of which were probably dragged from the nearby outcrop of rock, they covered it with a large stone and earth mound that extended as far as the older ditch and obscured the circle of standing stones. Material for the mound came from the bank, and some of the standing stones probably went towards building the tomb. Some appear to have been deliberately damaged before being covered by the mound. Three now-recumbent stones seem to have been intentionally broken by having other heavy stones dropped on them.[28] These features may suggest conflict between old and new (or, rather, even older but now reasserted) beliefs and their respective adherents. As we proceed, it will become evident that tension and conflict, rather than pacific Druidical rituals, were at the heart of the west European Neolithic. Yet there was also continuity. The builders of the megalithic tomb could have ignored the henge and built their tomb elsewhere, but they valued some sort of continuity along with the changes that they were effecting. A special place in the landscape remained important, even though its precise significance and its relationship to society changed. Religious and cosmological revisions must have some connection with the past if people are to accept them.

Around the perimeter of the Bryn Celli Ddu mound the builders placed a ring of large kerbstones. The edge of the new monument, which was the same in general shape (circular – elsewhere passage tombs are contained in long mounds; Fig. 38) and which more or less coincided with the earlier henge, was thus clearly marked. One could argue that the kerbstones served the practical purpose of containing the mound and preventing it from slipping down. But elaborate decorations on kerbstones, such as those at Newgrange, Dowth and Knowth in Ireland, suggest rather that the edge of the mound was *conceptually* as well as practically significant.

The kerbstones show that the precise demarcation of a special circular place, at Bryn Celli Ddu originally imprinted on the landscape by the ditch and bank, remained important. People were mapping ideas on to the landscape. What were those ideas? As later thinkers and scientists, such as Copernicus and Galileo, drew diagrams of the solar system, so Neolithic people constructed monuments that not merely represented their ideas of the cosmos but that *embodied* those concepts. The distinction between an astronomer's diagram and the actual solar system is abundantly clear to us. We suggest that the distinction between Neolithic concepts of the cosmos and their henges and tombs was far less clear-cut.

The construction of the demarcated mound at Bryn Celli Ddu that caused the destruction of the circular henge bank perhaps reflected, reified and re-asserted older Neolithic cosmology and beliefs, as they were on Anglesey. Do we have any idea of what those beliefs may have been?

Of one thing we can be sure: the reasserted cosmology concerned, in large measure, the dead. As we have seen, henges were not burial grounds, although burials are sometimes found in them. If the henges were in some ways models of the cosmos, their significance did not, literally, embrace numerous remains of the dead. By contrast, the earlier megalithic monuments were built to contain human remains and to facilitate continuing rituals that related to the dead. Why would the dead have increased in importance, as evidenced by the building of large tombs, then apparently declined as people constructed henges, and, finally, at Bryn Celli Ddu, returned to a central position? The renewed centrality of (selected but numerous) dead in massive stone tombs was probably associated with social changes that involved a resurgence of interest in establishing the political role of ancestors and thus emphasizing social continuities related to the landscape on which the tombs were imprinted.[29]

These tombs are supremely important to our investigation because their essential shape appears in various expressions all over Atlantic Europe. They thus point to widely held beliefs – with local variations and repeated adjustments. Fundamentally, a megalithic tomb comprises an inner chamber and a passage that leads out from it to the perimeter of a covering mound.

Archaeologists have expended much energy in classifying megalithic tombs according to shape, size and so forth. Sometimes the passage or the end chamber may have smaller side chambers, thus giving it a cruciform shape. End chambers without side alcoves are known as undifferentiated tombs. Those with demarcated spaces at the entrance are called 'court tombs' (Fig. 38). Classificatory work of this kind illustrates a curious principle in archaeological research. When we cannot explain, we classify – in ever-increasing detail.[30] Though understandable given the daunting nature of research, the whole task of classification can become self-defeating. Classification demands the selection of criteria. Necessarily, the selection of criteria is done 'blind': in doing so, researchers may emphasize features that had little or nothing to do with the significance that the items being classified had for their makers and users. Unless researchers luckily hit on criteria that were significant, each classification moves them further and further away from the original meaning of the items. But once researchers have some grasp of that meaning, they can construct a much more instructive (and probably simpler) classification.

Leaving aside any attempt to place Bryn Celli Ddu in a classification of monuments, we consider the sections of the tomb that we believe had cosmological meaning. We start at the perimeter and then move towards the centre (see Fig. 37). Each part helps us to glimpse the sort of religious practices that people performed in them.

The circle of kerbstones bends in towards the entrance to the passage, which faces northeast. Attention was thus focused on the entrance as an approved way through the ring of kerbstones, just as causeways were approved routes through banks and across ditches to henges. Hearths and what seems to have been a spread of white quartz pebbles were placed at the entrance. Moreover, hearths were also found built up against the kerbstones on either side of the entrance: fire marked and framed the transition to the interior. Fires and quartz were thus both related to death as it was conceived in the cosmology of these Neolithic people.

In addition, burials of an ox and a cremated human being were found in front of the entrance.[31] The ox burial was enclosed by a stone and timber rectangular structure. The timber posts may have supported a platform of some kind. As in the Near East, rituals involved both animal and human remains. Elsewhere in western Europe (Brittany, Jersey), horse bones have been found interred with human remains. They have been interpreted as prestige goods, or the remains of feasts.[32] In Britain in the Cotswold-Severn tombs, cattle bones are common and seem to have been treated similarly to human bones in the same context.[33] These are highly significant finds, but we believe that we can go further and explore possible cosmological and spiritual associations.

The complex way in which the Bryn Celli Ddu entrance was arranged shows that the demarcation of space with its implications of cosmological and social differentiation was important to the builders. As we have suggested, they were constructing an 'existential diagram' of their beliefs. The entrance, a transitional zone between the tomb interior and the outside world, was thus a place for rituals that involved sacrifice and, possibly, transmutation of the dead by fire. In the same way that fire transmutes raw meat into food,[34] so it changed the dead into spiritual, non-material beings. Fire speeds up the natural processes of decay and excarnation by birds and animals. We suggest that the concept of death at Bryn Celli Ddu was comparable to, though not necessarily identical with, the Near Eastern beliefs we discussed in Chapter 5: death was conceived of as passage between cosmological realms. Cosmological transition, death and the structures themselves formed a conceptual triad.

We now move from the perimeter towards the centre of the tomb. The passage that leads to the inner burial chamber is narrow, being about only 0.9 m (3 ft) wide; it is 8.2 m (27 ft) long. Halfway down it there are two large stones opposite one another: they divide it into two sections, an inner and an outer. The inner part was roofed with large stones. The outer section was probably not roofed. The inner passage is about 1.5 m (5 ft) high. There is a low shelf or bench along the northern side that may have been used for placing human remains. It recalls similar benches in the Near East, such as those in the Göbekli Tepe rock-cut, semi-subterranean structures. On the southern side of the passage, just inside the portal stones, two upright stones are set in niches.

38 (Opposite) These three types of Neolithic tomb, as well as passage tombs (Fig. 37), all use huge stones to delineate space, and probably also social divisions.

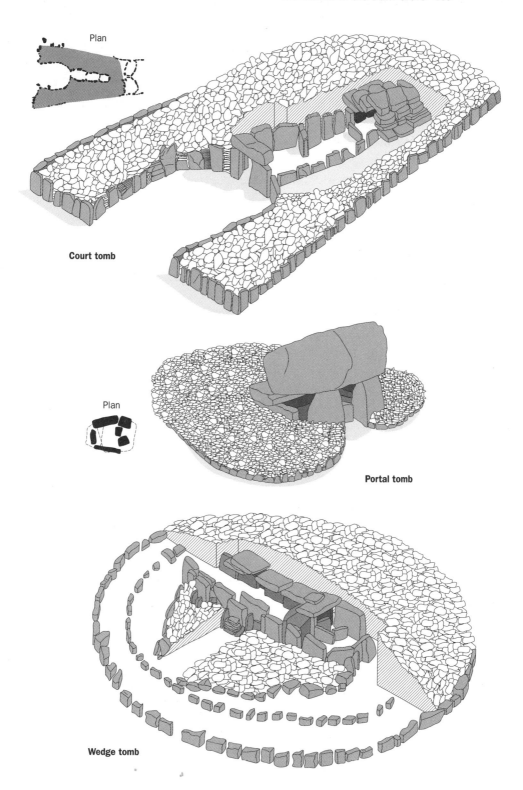

Plan

Court tomb

Plan

Portal tomb

Wedge tomb

The unroofed, outer section was eventually filled in. When that happened, the inner section was left clear but inaccessible because of the filled outer part. The infill included some burnt human bones. The inner edge of the blocking was marked by a row of quartz boulders. There was quartz at this point of transition and, as we have seen, outside the tomb itself and in the holes dug to receive the earlier circle of standing stones. A clearly meaningful pattern, a conceptual template, continues to emerge (see Fig. 37). We already have indications of the sort of system of symbols that Clifford Geertz identified as integral to religion (Chapter 1).

The polygonal chamber at the end of the passage is about 2.4–3 m (8–10 ft) wide. It is roofed by two huge capstones. Today, we marvel at the enormous amount of labour and ingenuity that must have been required to raise such large stones into place. Of particular interest is a large standing stone somewhat off-centre in the chamber. It is more or less circular in cross section and was carefully dressed. It does not reach the roof and therefore served no structural function. In essence, it is no different from those that in an earlier phase had stood in a circle within the henge ditch. Indeed, it may in fact be one of them. Standing stones in the chambers of megalithic tombs are rare, but not unknown. They show that it was not just the *circle* demarcated by the standing stones that was important to the builders. The stones themselves were *individually* significant. The tomb as an emblem of the overall cosmology *becomes* that cosmology.

Excavations in the chamber and in the passage revealed the presence of human bones, both burnt and unburnt. Funerary practices were clearly varied and complex, perhaps intended to achieve a variety of ends. Details could not be established for Bryn Celli Ddu, but an interesting sequence was discovered at the Ascott-under-Wychwood chambered tomb in the English Cotswolds. There, skeletons were excarnated (as in some Near Eastern sites), bleached by exposure to sunlight for some months and broken. Bones from different skeletons were mixed and then transferred to the tomb.[35] Researchers do not know if this sequence was duplicated at the Anglesey tomb, but something like it seems to have been practised.

In the Bryn Celli Ddu chamber, there were two flint arrowheads, a stone bead, and limpet and mussel shells. The shells point to the significance of water and the sea. (On one of the wall stones on the south side of the chamber there is a shallow pecked spiral design, but this may be a modern addition.)

DEEPER THAN A TOMB

Two of the most interesting features of Bryn Celli Ddu are located a metre or so behind the innermost wall of the burial chamber (see Fig. 37). They were covered when the mound was constructed over the tomb. One is an oval pit (about 1.2 m/4 ft in diameter and 1.4 m/4.5 ft deep) that was positioned at the centre of the earlier henge. The centre of the overall circle thus remained important, while the manner of approaching it and its precise significance were refined and changed. The pit was cut through a grassy layer that had formed in the centre of the henge and was probably dug by the tomb builders before they started on the main construction work.[36] A ceremony that related to the old henge thus seems to have marked transition from it to the construction phase of the new tomb.

What actions could have formed part of that ceremony? Excavations showed that fires were lit in the pit. Moreover, an adult human ear bone was found at the bottom of it. The significance of the ceremony that led to the placing of a human ear bone in a pit is not clear, but it is worth noting that ear bones are conspicuous in later Bronze Age burial barrows on Anglesey.[37] We suggest that the ear bone, coming as it does from within the skull, may have been associated with the spirit of the deceased, perhaps even with his or her ability to hear. If other human parts, such as eyes, were also placed in the pit they would not have survived. After the ceremony, the pit was filled in with the soil that had been dug out, and finally it was covered with a large flat stone that was set about 0.6 m (2 ft) below the surface, thus boxing in the remains of the ritual. At the centre of Woodhenge, the monument that Insall spotted from the air, archaeologists discovered the burial of what seemed to be a girl about three-and-a-half years old (there was also an adult burial in the ditch). Her skull had been split in half and the parts placed in such a way that the excavators at first thought that they had uncovered two burials. The split skull at once suggested human sacrifice, but it has since been shown that the skull in fact separated along natural sutures. The damage was not done by a stone axe.[38] This child burial seems to have been related to the henge, not to the construction of a subsequent megalithic tomb, as at Bryn Celli Ddu. The henges at Woodhenge, Bryn Celli Ddu and elsewhere were associated with death, but they were not burial grounds.

The second interesting feature that the excavators uncovered is only a metre from the pit. It is a standing stone on which meandering and spiral patterns were pecked, or hammered. The carvings extend from one face to the other, thus uniting the surfaces (Pl. 18; Fig. 39). The undulating lines are

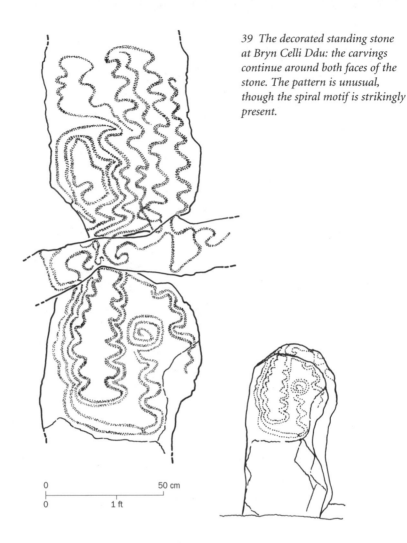

39 The decorated standing stone at Bryn Celli Ddu: the carvings continue around both faces of the stone. The pattern is unusual, though the spiral motif is strikingly present.

0 ——— 50 cm
0 ——— 1 ft

comparable to an element of a more complex design at another Anglesey tomb, to which we come in a moment.[39] Others seem to relate to motifs in megalithic tombs in Ireland and Brittany and raise questions about far-flung contacts, another point to which we shall return.

As we have pointed out, the Bryn Celli Ddu tomb is dated rather later than similar monuments elsewhere in Great Britain and Ireland. Researchers think that the demolition of the earlier henge and the construction of the anachronistic tomb may represent a kind of 'Neolithic Reformation' that re-established older religious practices that had ceased to exist in other parts of Atlantic Europe.[40] Perhaps in a similar way to that in which some Cotswold-Severn tombs were apparently built to look as if they were beginning to collapse, the builders were appealing to the authority of supposedly long-dead ancestors.[41] Probably, Anglesey came increasingly under the unwelcome influence of a Neolithic polity, the centre of which was elsewhere. To assert their threatened independence, the people of Bryn Celli Ddu 'resurrected' the central role of their ancestral dead who had turned the first sod and thus laid claim to their territory.

It is clear at Bryn Celli Ddu that the Neolithic was not as monolithic as some of its monuments literally are: it was a time of change during which monuments were built and refashioned, closed up and then rethought as henges were built, often near to them. It is hard to believe that such back-and-forth changes were not accompanied by social strife. As we shall see in the next chapter, the three dimensions of religion that we identified in Chapter 1 – experience, belief and practice – were probably implicated in this conflict and were expressed, in part, by means of the sort of carvings that are on the stone next to the pit at Bryn Celli Ddu. There is only one carved stone at Bryn Celli Ddu, but other monuments have many more than just one. One of these is about 17.7 km (11 miles) to the west of Bryn Celli Ddu and is spectacularly situated on a cliff-guarded promontory overlooking the Irish Sea.

Barclodiad y Gawres

The fanciful name of this tomb, Barclodiad y Gawres, 'The Giantess's Apronful', derives from local tradition. The mound looks like a pile of stones dropped on the headland. Although known for centuries in a badly degraded form, it was not until the early 1950s that it was carefully investigated.[42] The archaeologists made some sensational discoveries. At the end of their work they reconstructed the tomb, and it is in this form that it is known today.

Like Bryn Celli Ddu, Barclodiad y Gawres comprises a narrow passage (about 7 m/23 ft long) leading to a chamber (Fig. 40). The chamber and the passage are formed by huge stones set vertically. Many of these remain; the presence of others has been inferred from the holes dug to receive them. All the large stones that form the passage and the chamber were set in prepared holes and then supported by piles of large boulders. An absence of stone holes at the entrance to the passage suggests that the stones there were free-standing and did not support a heavy roof. Rather, they demarcated a small entrance area comparable to the first section of the Bryn Celli Ddu tomb. Barclodiad y Gawres is therefore like those known as court tombs (see Fig. 38).

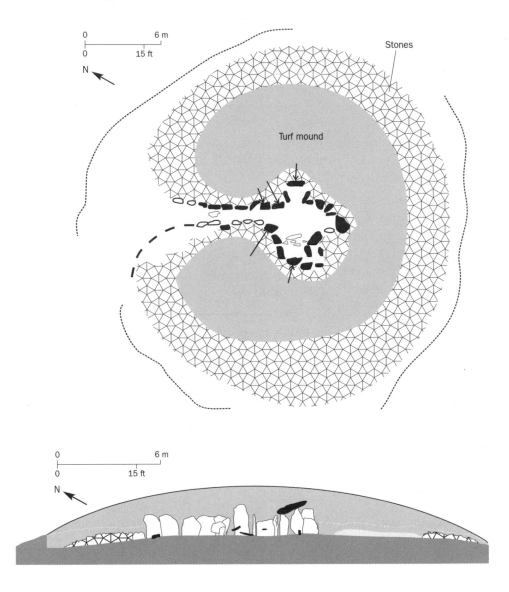

40 *The Barclodiad y Gawres tomb is situated on a headland overlooking the Irish Sea.*
In the centre of the chamber the excavators found a hearth with the remains of a strange
and symbolic 'stew' that contained the bones of frog, toad, grass snake and other species.
The arrows in the upper diagram indicate the positions of decorated stones.

The chamber at the end of the Barclodiad y Gawres passage is more complex than that at Bryn Celli Ddu. It has three side chambers that give it an overall cruciform plan (Fig. 40). Including these alcoves, the whole chamber is about 6.1 m (20 ft) across.

Because the chamber was too large to be covered by a single capstone, the Neolithic builders used the corbel technique to form layers of overlapping stones until the opening was small enough to be covered by a single capstone. The archaeologists who reconstructed Barclodiad y Gawres estimated that the vault was probably about 2.7 m (9 ft) high. The covering mound, 27.4 m (90 ft) in diameter, was constructed by piling sections of turf on top of each other and by an outer ring of tightly packed stones, rather than large kerb-stones as at Bryn Celli Ddu.

The western side chamber, which would have had its own capstone but no corbelling, had a small annexe on the south side and had been closed off from the central chamber with slabs of stone that rested against three uprights. The cremated bones of two men were found in this chamber, together with the remains of charred bone or antler pins. Pins of this kind are frequently found along with Neolithic human remains; they were probably used to hold cloth-ing together around the corpse. There was some bone in the opposite side chamber as well, though most had unfortunately been dug out long before the archaeological excavation.

Symbolic Stew

No human bone was found in the central chamber, but there were even more interesting finds. Excavations showed that a wood fire that was lit in the centre had burned for a considerable time. The hearth was about 0.9 m (3 ft) in diameter and, in the middle, 15.2 cm (6 in) deep. While it was still glowing, a strange concoction was poured over it. The fire was then extinguished by covering it with small flat stones, smooth pebbles, earth and shells. Many of the pebbles were of quartzite. This layer covered the whole of the central area of the hearth but did not extend to the edges. It was clearly distinguishable from the infill of cairn stones that later cascaded through the roof into the tomb.[43] In short, the fire became a circle of glowing embers around the cov-ered central part. Indeed, fires were commonly lit, not only outside tombs, as we have seen, but also in the chambers.[44]

The 'stew' that was poured over the fire included tiny bones of eel, whiting, wrasse (a brightly coloured, rock-haunting fish), frog, toad, natterjack (a striped species of toad), grass snake, mouse, shrew and rabbit.[45] The bones are of such a kind that, if the stew had been allowed to stand, they might have remained in suspension and been poured off from the sediment that would have remained at the bottom of the container. The stew seems unlikely to have been prepared for human consumption, at least as part of a regular diet.

We should not dismiss such finds as being connected with vague 'magical practices' and leave it at that. Instead, we should consider the possible symbolism of the types of creatures that constituted the ingredients. They were not randomly selected: each one meant something and was in some (perhaps not immediately evident) way related to the others. Each was part of a system of symbols.

Initially, the Barclodiad y Gawres recipe recalls the brew that the witches prepared prior to their second meeting with Shakespeare's Macbeth.[46] They called for a seemingly endless list of disgusting items: eye of newt, adder's fork (tongue), toe of frog, blind worm's sting, witches' mummy, slips of yew and so forth. Did they have a common theme for Shakespeare's audience beyond being vile things that witches would find congenial? The people of his time entertained beliefs that Edward Topsell recorded in his *History of Serpents* (1658). He identified various creatures as poisonous and asserted that

toads, both of the earth and of the water, are venomous, although it be held that the toads of the earth are more poysonful than the toads of the water... But the toads of the land, which do descend into marishes [marshes], and so live in both elements, are most venomous [parenthesis added].[47]

In addition to toads, other ingredients thought at that time to be poisonous included snakes ('fenny snake', those that lived in fens), yew trees (especially those that grow in churchyards), blind worms, hemlock and newts. Indeed, Shakespeare's witches emphasize venom: they speak of 'poison'd entrails' and 'Sweltered venom'. The Barclodiad y Gawres pot-pourri could therefore be taken to be a magical poison, a death-inflicting brew. Of course, these beliefs about what was thought to be poisonous probably date from the Middle Ages and thus long post-date the Neolithic. It is possible, though we cannot now know, that they were held so long before Shakespeare's time as during the Neolithic.

Another significant feature of the Barclodiad y Gawres 'gruel thick and slab', to borrow Shakespeare's phrase, is, however, probably closer to the truth. Certainly, it accounts for all, rather than just some, of the ingredients and thus gets at the system of symbols that the makers manipulated. As Topsell astutely pointed out, some creatures (frog, toad and natterjack) 'do descend into marishes, and so live in both elements' – that is, land and water, two elements of a tiered cosmos. 'Marishes' (marshes) may be seen as transitional between land and water. The toad, moreover, is transitional in another way. It is a creature of the twilight, a mysterious, liminal time between darkness and light. Darkness is associated with the nether world, and light with the upper. Toads were also closely associated with the Devil and medieval witches. Some species are indeed poisonous, though mildly so; others contain hallucinogenic substances.[48] In German traditions, toads are believed to lurk in hemlock and to assimilate the plant's poison, and hallucinogenic mushrooms are also associated with toads – hence 'toadstools'.[49] Nor are such beliefs restricted to Europe. In South America, the Amahuaca apply toad poison to self-inflicted burns to induce a state of trance in which they believe themselves to fly and to be in contact with spirits of animals and the forest.[50] Associations with mind-altering substances of course suggest the experiences we have noted (flight and the vortex) and thus transcosmological travel.

Other creatures in the Barclodiad y Gawres stew inhabit a nether realm – water, the sea. There were three species of fish. Moreover, eels (aquatic snakes) combine the symbolism of water and serpents. Still other creatures that went into the brew are transitional in a comparable but somewhat different way: they move from the surface of the land to underground areas. These are rabbits, shrews, mice and snakes that live on the surface of the land but also beneath it in burrows and holes.[51] They are therefore also creatures that move between levels of the tiered cosmos. Indeed, the association of all these creatures with funerary rites in the Barclodiad y Gawres tomb tells us something about this 'system of symbols'. Overall, the ingredients of the Barclodiad y Gawres concoction were not randomly assembled. We suggest that the key to their symbolism is cosmological mediation and movement, and may represent both death and revivification. The way in which cosmological mediation is symbolized is often through taxonomy.

The systematic ways in which Neolithic people categorized creatures would have differed from the Linnaean taxonomy that is in use today, but would have been meaningful in terms of Neolithic cosmology and mythology. People in non-Western societies often classify creatures by features that may seem irrelevant to Westerners. For example, some people in South America classify eagles as creatures, not of the sky as we would readily think, but of the underworld because they dive down from the heavens to the land. It is therefore necessary to examine taxonomies in the light of a people's cosmology.

When we do, we find that the fit between the Barclodiad y Gawres brew and the cosmological themes we are developing is striking. Movement between cosmological levels is always steeped in ritual and religious beliefs and is, moreover, often symbolically represented by selected creatures that, in the local taxonomy, are related by behaviour or other characteristics. For example, the way in which snakes live below and above ground and, more-over, shed their skins can be taken to represent transition and resurrection. We therefore suggest that, when people placed the cremated dead in the inner chambers of passage tombs, they performed rituals that were appropriate to death as cosmological transition and that involved systematically related symbolic creatures – as the Barclodiad y Gawres brew ingredients imply.

The possible symbolic implications of the ingredients of the stew may relate to the position of the site on a promontory overlooking the sea. In his analysis of Neolithic monuments in northwest Brittany, Chris Scarre empha-sizes the liminality of many sites: they are placed close to intertidal zones: 'the nature of islands and ideas about land, sea and shoreline played a crucial role in forming the beliefs and attitudes of these prehistoric communities'.[52] Prox-imity to water, he persuasively suggests, reflected 'a real concern with this symbolic divide, a metaphor perhaps for life and death'.[53] The point that Scarre makes shows how what we have said about neurology, cosmology, architecture and mythology with all its interrelated symbols came together to form a seamless, yet variable and changing, system that lay at the heart of the Neolithic. The combination of terrestrial and marine creatures is therefore telling.

CARVED SYMBOLS

Further cosmological mystery is supplied by the five decorated stones at Bar-clodiad y Gawres (Pl. 19; Fig. 41). Three are situated at the end of the passage where it enters the chamber (a transitional zone) and there is one in each of the two side chambers. The lightly pecked motifs include zigzags, lozenges and spirals. Others are known from the Bend of the Boyne in Ireland, and from Brittany and Iberia. They point to the Neolithic relationship between art, architecture and cosmology that we explore in Chapter 9.[54]

Dead, but not gone

Our discussion of Bryn Celli Ddu shows that an earlier henge monument gave way to an anachronistic megalithic passage tomb that probably rep-resented a resurgence of old beliefs in Anglesey. Barclodiad y Gawres takes us further and allows us to glimpse something of the beliefs that people enter-tained and the practices that took place within and around the tombs. We now need to think more carefully about the reasons for the change from tombs to henge monuments and then, at Bryn Celli Ddu, a change back to

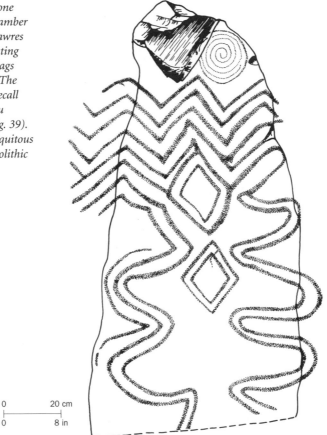

41 A decorated stone from inside the chamber at Barclodiad y Gawres has carved undulating lines, a spiral, zigzags and two lozenges. The undulating lines recall the Bryn Celli Ddu standing stone (Fig. 39). The spiral is a ubiquitous west European Neolithic motif.

chambered tombs. Why did Neolithic people switch to new kinds of structures? We hazard some suggestions.

During the earliest phases of the Neolithic there was

– a growing attachment to specific parts of the landscape by groups of incipiently agricultural people,

– a concomitant emphasis on long-term, durable occupation of specific land and hence

– attachment to significant, founding ancestors rather than generic 'spirits of the dead'.

These conditions would have led to a need to perpetuate the influence of earlier generations. It was now not just the living who were the centre of the cosmological circle. More importantly, it was the dead, those who, by their early tenure, provided legitimacy to their descendants' occupation of the land – and no doubt other benefits and protection as well. This conceptual shift thus placed changing and increasing importance on the dead. The function of the dead had to be reformulated.

Before the building of megalithic tombs, the dead were probably associated with a nether world that was only vaguely placed in the people's notions of the cosmos. Now, with more restricted relationships to specific tracts of agricultural land, they had, unequivocally, to mark both the conceptual and the literal placing of the dead. Changing concepts of land ownership therefore came with cosmological shifts and were represented in people's 'existential maps' – their monuments. But that alone was not enough. They had, at the same time, to facilitate and manifest in some way the dead's continued contact with the living; the founding ancestors were dead but not gone. How did they accomplish this?

We argue that the evidence points to a Neolithic belief that the chambers of megalithic tombs were *underground* in a cosmological sense. The passages between the huge orthostats led from the outside world deep in to the nether world. The Neolithic people of Atlantic Europe began to construct replicas of caves above ground where they had complete control of their topography. Because of the nature of land ownership, they had to place their legitimizing dead precisely on the landscape in clear relationship to their fields, pastures and villages. Unlike mobile hunters and gatherers, the incipient agriculturalists could not work with natural caves that were not tied to their own tracts of land and that were, in any case, rare in Great Britain and Ireland. They could not make do with, and adapt by image-making and other rituals, the given, immutable passages, chambers, diverticules and niches of limestone caves, as did the much earlier Palaeolithic people of France and Spain. In addition to their intractable location, the vagueness implied by the multiplicity of cave topographies had now to be brought under control and formalized as political entities grew in complexity and ascribed their land rights to founding ancestors whose location, both conceptually and literally, was known and who legitimized those rights. The monument builders therefore constructed standardized 'caves'. It does not necessarily follow that the builders of the tombs were directly familiar with limestone caves, though some may well have been. Indeed, in northeast Wales caves were used as Late Neolithic burial places.[55] This instance of cave burial may represent the continuing strength of earlier, perhaps Mesolithic, beliefs.[56]

The tiered cosmos therefore underwent transformation and refinement. The dead who legitimized the present became central to the cosmos and to its reproduction in monuments – as they were in social and political issues. Access to them shaped the three dimensions of religion that we identified in Chapter 1.

- Religious experience: people could experience both the vortex of the mind and the tunnel of the tomb.
- Religious belief: people shared cosmological and religious understandings that were refined by the shape of the tombs, though attitudes to those beliefs were probably not uniform.
- Religious practice: the building of the tombs and their repeated use dramatized social distinctions and made the tiered cosmos seem inescapable.

In thinking about these three dimensions of religion, we must not lose sight of the notion (in addition to the physical experience) of a tunnel leading to, and opening out into, another realm. It is wired into the human brain and may be entertained independently of any real caves. In religious experience, the dead were approached via the neurologically wired tunnel (Pl. 1). People, very probably specialists in religious experience, could enter that mental vortex and journey through it to the realm of the dead, which, we suggest, was now conceived of as lying at or near the centre of the circular cosmos as well as underground. The Neolithic 'existential map' in the form of passage tombs was becoming more complex. Ritual specialists could *repeatedly* traverse the megalithic passage and return to the land of the living. They became closely associated with transitions. Indeed, in visiting the dead they may also have 'died' (in an expanded sense of that word) and returned to life.

So, too, in religious practice, other people could also pass through the megalithic tunnel to reach the remains of the dead, though there were probably restrictions on who could do this. These people need not have had any profound religious experience created by a major shift in consciousness. For them, dreams and ritual euphoria would have been sufficient confirmation of the spiritual realm, though the sensory deprivation afforded by prolonged periods in the dark, silent tombs may well have shifted their consciousness to a sense of Absolute Unitary Being, if not to full-blown hallucinations. In this way, the megalithic passage tombs facilitated a visual, experiential dramatization of spiritual journeys. Megalithic tombs, prominent on the landscape, spoke to everyone of

- the reality and closeness of the dead,
- the specialists who had spiritual access to them, and
- others who were permitted to take part in religious practices.

Then came changes. At some point in the later Neolithic, people began to close up their tombs and to construct open-air, circular henges.[57] Why did they retain the circular plan of many (but not all) megalithic passage tomb mounds? As we have suggested, it seems likely that henge monuments continued, like their predecessors, the tombs, to be maps *and* constructions of the cosmos. They, too, had routes – causeways instead of passages – that led into them to replicate cosmological traversal.

Why are they shaped as they are? The circularity of henges was persistent: at Stonehenge, for instance, rebuilding over some 1,500 years preserved and repeatedly emphasized the circularity of the monument. (In some regions, long, rather than circular, mounds suggest a different version of the relationship between tombs and the cosmos.)

The circularity of henges and rings of standing stones or wooden posts, and indeed the older round tomb mounds, may have been suggested by a number of observations that Neolithic people could easily have made.[58] First, the horizon is circular. Standing on a rise, people see a circle of terrain surrounding them. Then, too, the paths of heavenly bodies through the sky are circular, an arc above and, presumably, a complementary arc beneath the earth (cf. Barasana longhouses, Chapter 4). Colin Richards adds a further point: henges are frequently (but not always) in natural basins surrounded by mountains.[59] These observations tend to place *people* (the viewers) at the centre of the cosmos.

These are fairly straightforward suggestions and may indeed have some truth in them. We, however, wish to draw attention to a key association. The tiered cosmos is frequently also circular. We saw this link in the Desana concept of the universe and their longhouses (Chapter 4). The combination of tiers with circularity seems to be a welding of the neurologically generated cosmos on to observations such as those we noted in the previous paragraph: two different concepts come together. Sometimes, it has to be said, this combination was rather uncomfortable, as in complex medieval notions of the divinely created, tiered and circular cosmos. Then, too, we must not lose sight of the circular vortex that takes seers from one tier to another, from one realm or dimension to another (see Fig. 9). We argue that the west European Neolithic cosmos was something along these lines: tiers linked by circular vortices, all within an encompassing circularity that was plainly evident in the movements of heavenly bodies.

Within this concept of the cosmos, people moved their activities from tombs to open enclosures that preserved the overall shape of the cosmos and so provided ritual continuity. In some ways, ritual time masked social changes and gave people a sense of eternal naturalness whereas, in fact, society and power relations were changing. Yet, paradoxically, those changes were aided by the building of new monuments or the transforming of old ones.[60] What were these changes?

Perhaps there came a time when the elite felt that the entombed ancestors constituted a special class of entitling being (that is, which granted or legitimized land rights or title) that was not perpetuated in the lengthening lineages that soon merged with myth and semi-divine beings like Gilgamesh and Enkidu. The time had come to mark off the 'founding fathers' in the tombs from their latter-day (also deceased) descendants. Some sort of apotheosis of those special ancestors entrenched the long-term rule of the elite. There were now different kinds of ancestors:[61] the ones who guaranteed the authority of the elite and those to whom ordinary people could feel some connection. It is possible that rituals relating to 'founding fathers' then began to be performed in cosmologically structured henges, often but not always near to tombs. The long-dead themselves were now less visible (though their tombs remained prominent), and, as a result, perhaps more pervasive across the landscape and more exalted. The living no longer dared to handle their bones.

At the same time, henges may have been sites of negotiation between the long-dead and the recently dead, and between the increasingly hierarchical living and their hierarchy of ancestors and spiritual beings. A new, more complex social order was emerging, one that was underwritten in the mythic past by a class of extremely powerful ancestors or 'beings'. The social order in the material world was paralleled by a hierarchy of spirit beings in the 'other world'. Particular hierarchies, both 'here' and 'there', were 'naturalized', made to seem an integral, inescapable part of the landscape and the cosmos.

During the Neolithic, there was thus an evolving social hierarchy that was part of an overall cosmology, a framework that simultaneously made sense of religious experience, belief and practice, as well as land rights. Religion, embedded in cosmology, validated land rights and the authority of those who managed the construction of monuments and their use. This new heaven and new earth, as Blake might have expressed it, this new, post-Mesolithic cosmos, is spectacularly manifest in the valley of the Boyne River in Ireland. With what we learned from the two Anglesey tombs in mind, we can now approach these impressive and richly decorated monuments.

CHAPTER 8

Brú na Bóinne

Brú na Bóinne, 'The Bend of the Boyne', a river well known from Irish history, embraces one of the most striking archaeological landscapes in western Europe (Fig. 42). Some 16 km (9.9 miles) upstream from the mouth, the Boyne begins to curve south from its generally west–east course and then north again before continuing on its easterly way to the Irish Sea at the port of Drogheda, another 8 km (4.9 miles) to the east. It was in the loop formed by the Boyne that the notorious Battle of the Boyne took place in 1690.[1]

Two years earlier, England had deposed its last Catholic king, James II. Then, in 1689, Mary, James II's daughter, and her husband, William, the Protestant Prince of Orange and ruler of the Dutch Republic, were crowned joint monarchs. Following complex political machinations, William resolved to bring the whole of Ireland under his control. Eventually, he confronted James II's army at the Boyne, the last natural barrier before Dublin, the capital of Catholic Ireland. There he defeated James II, secured his control of the English throne and entrenched bloody religious and political conflicts in Ireland that were to endure into the 21st century.[2]

Heightened competition

Without knowing it, the Protestant and Catholic armies clashed over land rich in Neolithic sites.[3] We suspect that the late 17th-century conflict in some ways, though with greater loss of life, echoed much earlier Neolithic religious and political struggles. It seems likely that the building of Neolithic monuments often took place within a context of religious dissent, linked to political ascendancy and decline. Religion and political control of land are always an explosive combination.

When viewed northeastwards from Rosnaree, the Bend of the Boyne rises like an island surmounted by, from west to east, the Knowth, Newgrange and Dowth ridges (Fig. 42).[4] Each of the three large tombs, Knowth, Newgrange and Dowth, has small satellite passage tombs and is on the summit of one of these ridges; they are intervisible. There are also standing stones, a cursus (processional way) and a number of henges within the Bend.

Although it may not point unequivocally to strife, archaeological evidence shows that an early passage tomb, probably the first of the great Bend of the Boyne structures, was dismantled. At least 15 decorated stones from it were used in two subsequent tombs, Knowth and Newgrange, the principal foci of this chapter.[5] The motifs carved on the stones from the old monument are rectilinear, whereas those in the two more recent tombs are contrastingly curvilinear. Moreover, the re-used stones were placed so that their decorated surfaces were, apart from one exception, either wholly or partially obscured; some that became orthostats were inverted, decorated portions going into dug sockets.[6]

It is, of course, possible that the earlier tomb was amicably dismantled to make space for the large Knowth tomb that we see today, but the ways in which the 'borrowed' stones were used suggests that there was some estrangement between the early tomb people and the builders of the second. Exactly what the dispute was about no one knows. Nevertheless, it is highly unlikely that such a major change in religious practice (dismantling a passage tomb and building another as a new ritual centre) could be accomplished without a certain amount of debate and friction between groups of people. A state of affairs of this kind may account for both continuity and change. Another passage tomb, similar in overall shape and structure, though much more impressive and requiring a great deal of labour, was built. There was thus some continuity. But parts of the old one were incorporated in ways that downgraded their status. The motifs on these stones retained some of their

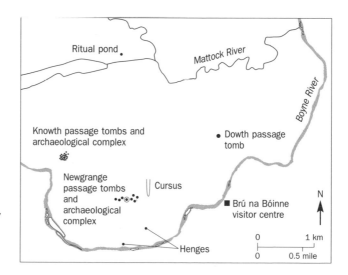

42 *The Bend of the Boyne River embraces Neolithic sites of many kinds. Together the rivers form a virtual island.*

'power' (they were not obliterated), but their influence was diminished. This subordination probably paralleled a decline in the influence of those who controlled the old tomb.

Another point worth noting is that the highly decorated kerb around the large Knowth mound (somewhat later than the tomb)[7] suggests a public face intended to be seen and perhaps processed around by many people, whereas the inner sanctum would be visited by the few. It is all very well to see such a distinction as being between, on the one hand, the general populace and, on the other, loved and respected elders whose every word is a beatific revelation.[8] It seems more likely that distinctions of that kind would be, at least intermittently, contested. As Marx and Engels dramatically proclaimed (not without reason), 'The history of all hitherto existing society is the history of class struggles.'[9]

The notion of endemic Neolithic conflict is not new. In a seminal article, Colin Renfrew saw developments in the Wiltshire Neolithic as the result of competition between growing chiefdoms or polities.[10] Julian Thomas and Alasdair Whittle have put forward a similar explanation for changes in the use of the West Kennet long barrow (chambered passage tomb) in Wiltshire. They write about 'heightened competition', a 'progressively more restricted segment of society', 'continued group differentiation in the area' and, from our present point of view most aptly, 'the closing down of a redundant monument, redolent with powerful associations and which offered competition to new traditions'.[11] In Denmark, too, changing Neolithic burial practices have been interpreted as negotiation of social relations rather than an attempt at a prehistoric revolution.[12] The events at Knowth are also comparable to those that led to the building of the Bryn Celli Ddu passage tomb on a henge, though in Anglesey the new structure seems to have reflected a resurgence of old beliefs and power.

No different from any other society, Neolithic political and religious groups were probably conflictual rather than consensual. But this strife was not automatic and impersonal: groups do not act blindly, without leaders who are fully aware of what they are doing. With parallels frequently evident in present-day societies, the past was, in Julian Thomas's phrase, 'manipulated and recreated in order to support social change'.[13] Neolithic leaders manipulated the social contracts of the time, and, as their focus on tombs and religion shows, associated consciousness contracts as well. The political influence and range of the Bend of the Boyne and the monumental elements within it waxed and eventually waned.[14]

These brief remarks provide a background against which we can view the astounding concentration of Neolithic achievement within the Bend of the Boyne.

A moated grange

Viewed from the tombs, the Boyne forms a semicircular 'moat'. Just to the north of the loop, a smaller river, the Mattock, flows west–east to a confluence with the Boyne at the eastern end of the Bend. A point that does not seem to receive sufficient attention is that virtually all the Neolithic monuments of the immediate area are within this two-river moat. No significant Neolithic monuments are known on the immediate southern side of the river. To the north of the Mattock, near Townleyhall, is a single passage tomb. Within the northern part of the Bend (as defined by both the Boyne and the Mattock) is a 'ritual pond' south of Monknewton. It is on the isthmus leading into the Bend. Probably dating from the Late Neolithic, it comprises a 2-m- (6.6-ft-) high bank enclosing a 30-m- (98.4-ft-) in-diameter area that is filled with water. Close by is an earthen enclosure.

Clearly, the loop of water was, in some way, significant to Neolithic people:[15] it 'contained' a major ritual centre. Probably, the symbolism of water and rivers that we discussed in connection with henges was operating here as well, though on a larger scale and with the added factor that the Boyne provides an easy route to the sea. Water thus demarcated an 'Isle of the Dead' and linked it to the great water, the sea.[16] We have here another suggestion of death (carrying the dead to the tombs) entailing crossing a river[17] and of the realm of the dead being associated with the sea or, more conceptually, a place 'under water'. Ideas of this kind contribute to an explanation of why Neolithic people sometimes disposed of the dead in rivers.[18]

Within the Bend, Neolithic people constructed a range of monuments in an efflorescence of activity paralleled in only a few other places in western Europe. In addition to the great megalithic passage tombs with their high, covering mounds, there are many smaller mounds and tombs, earth enclosures, timber circles, stone circles, pit circles and a cursus. Religious experience and belief, set within complex social parameters, together with what we can call early scientific observation of the heavens, produced a repeatedly resculpted landscape dominated by massive, commanding structures that are visible from afar and – it is hard to avoid the conclusion – proclaimed political power built on a religious foundation. As we have already seen, Rousseau said: 'No state has ever been founded without Religion serving as its base.'[19]

We have argued that spatial divisions in Near Eastern buildings were symbolic of experiential, social and cosmological distinctions. In western Europe, people went further. Not only did individual monuments, such as tombs and henges, relate to cosmology. The people also mapped cosmology and its social and religious implications on to extensive tracts of land.[20] In the great west European centres of Neolithic activity the conceptual cosmos came down to earth in ways that still amaze those who walk over a terrain that was, in those times, a map, or replica, of the people's evolving conception of the whole universe and their place within it. Walk along the great avenue of standing stones that leads to the Avebury henge in Wiltshire, or up the sloping, earth-banked avenue that leads from a shallow valley to the heelstone that marks one's arrival at the (until that dramatic moment) hidden Stonehenge. You will begin to appreciate, though perhaps not understand, the vastness and subtlety, ingenuity and technical brilliance, socio-political labyrinth and conceptual intricacy of the Neolithic world – and, above all, of the drama of Neolithic landscapes. You will realize why Neolithic monuments have had such an impact on Western thinking and art.[21]

Before the tombs

Prior to the Neolithic, during Mesolithic times, the Bend of the Boyne was heavily forested. The rich environment with its animal and aquatic life afforded the hunter-gatherers of the time a comfortable living. Today the stone tools of this period turn up in ploughed fields: arrowheads, burins, scrapers and artefacts apparently used for making holes in leather. Although archaeologists who have systematically walked across fields have found concentrations of stone artefacts, they have not been able to locate any indisputable Mesolithic settlements within the Bend.[22] Nor is there any sign of religious practices.

There is more evidence for Early Neolithic activity. The remains of timber houses from this period were preserved under the later tomb mounds. They have been dated to between 3900 BC and 3500 BC.[23] Nine of the houses were circular, perhaps a pre-echo of the great circular tombs to come.[24] Studies of these and other Irish Neolithic houses have suggested that the nature of settlement varied during the period. At some times there was more mobility than at others, and there was also a tendency for houses to cluster together.

Towards the end of the Early Neolithic, there are indications of social differentiation within settlement sites.[25]

The date of the earliest Bend of the Boyne Neolithic settlement (3900–3500
BC) should be compared with the earliest evidence for farming in Ireland as a
whole, which points to a date of about 4200 BC, or perhaps a few centuries
later.[26] Whether they were immigrants or local Mesolithic communities of
hunter-gatherers, the first Neolithic people settled in Ireland in clusters of
houses; they practised mixed farming – cereals, cattle and sheep, all of which
were imported from Europe and, of course, ultimately from the Near East.
The artefacts of these pioneering communities suggest some continuity with
Mesolithic life-ways, though the break is distinct: the Neolithic was indeed
'new', though not an invasion, not a full-scale population replacement. One
can say that the Neolithic 'arrived' here, whether as a group of people, a package of life-ways or, as now seems more likely, piecemeal, whereas it 'developed'
much more slowly in the Near East.[27]

Gradually or not, the west European Neolithic impacted heavily on the
environment. We saw that in some Near Eastern localities, early farming led
to soil erosion; in the west, Early Neolithic people began to clear the forests
and thus to change and mould the landscape – a process that continued into
the later period of the passage tombs and mounds. Indeed, forest destruction
continued through to, and after, Elizabethan times. At the same time, the people moulded the landscape conceptually, giving meaning to special
locations.[28]

The extensive human settlement in the Bend of the Boyne that forest
clearance permitted was of long duration. It extended from those early
houses through periods of massive tomb-building in the Middle and Late
Neolithic down to 2500 BC and beyond.[29] What we see today is a pile of semi-
transparent pages, the texts of each superimposed on and partly obliterating
earlier pages. Disentangled, the evidence suggests the general progression
shown in Table 2.

A full discussion of every monument in the Bend of the Boyne is not our
aim. Instead, we focus on two tombs: Knowth and, the most famous of all
Irish passage tombs, Newgrange. Our focus on these two monuments takes us
on from the previous chapter by casting further light on what happened in
and around Neolithic tombs. It also develops two themes at which we have so
far barely hinted, but that tell us much about Neolithic religious belief and
practice: the importance of stone as a substance and the power of carved
motifs to integrate architecture and religious experience.

Table 2 The archaeological and historical sequence in the Bend of the Boyne

20th century	The Bend of the Boyne becomes a focus of Irish pride in a rich past.
AD 1690	Battle of the Boyne.
AD 1400	Knowth becomes a quiet hillock in the Irish countryside.
c. AD 1175	Norman settlement.
9th–10th centuries AD	Important political centre for the Kings of Northern Brega.
9th–12th centuries AD	A small village; defences abandoned.
c. AD 800	Early Christian settlement. Thirteen rectangular houses, nine souterrains, bronze- and iron-working areas.
Iron Age (c. 800 BC)	A series of burials. Mound transformed into a well-protected ring-fort with an encompassing ditch and another at the top of the mound.
Bronze Age (from c. 2500 BC)	Four settlements of Beaker people.
Late Neolithic (3100–2500 BC)	Construction of henges and avenues.
Middle Neolithic (3600 to 3100 BC)	Construction of passage tombs.
Early Neolithic (4000–3600 BC)	Farming settlements; rectangular houses, palisades.
Late Mesolithic (c. 7000 BC)	Artefacts left by mobile hunting/gathering communities.

Knowth

Knowth is much more than a prominent mound. It is a cluster of 20 sites (Fig. 42). Newgrange, a larger mound than Knowth, has only three smaller satellite sites, and Dowth, farther to the east, has two smaller attendant sites. Despite the fame of Newgrange, it is Knowth that has the richer legacy. Why are so many burials clustered around the mound of Knowth and so markedly fewer around Newgrange and Dowth? Our wonder at this impressive congregation of tombs must be deemed insignificant if compared with that experienced by the archaeologist who first explored Knowth.

We have remarked on the excitement that Klaus Schmidt felt as he opened up Göbekli Tepe. A similar experience happened to George Eogan, later to be Professor of Archaeology at University College, Dublin. His interest in Neolithic tombs began in the 1950s, but it was not until 11 July 1967 that, working with colleagues and students, he made a sensational discovery. But, again, like Göbekli Tepe, some sites do not reveal their secrets all at once. In 1968, Eogan made a second discovery that was of equal, or perhaps of even more, importance.

The first discovery was of a hitherto unknown passage that led from the west into the great mound of Knowth (the mound covers about an acre of ground). Eogan and his team had begun to work on one of the smaller satellite tombs (Tomb 12; see Fig. 43) to the northwest of the main Knowth mound. Their work extended to the adjacent large mound and eventually

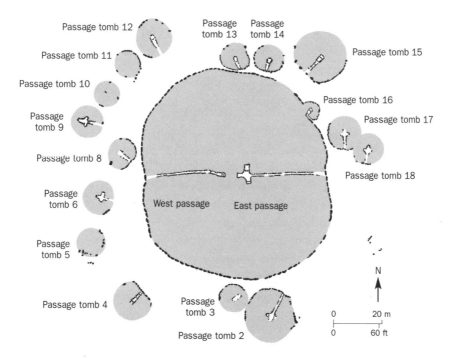

43 *The great Knowth tomb has two passages, one of which is cruciform, and a number of satellite tombs. More than a quarter of the Neolithic art in Western Europe is found at this site, most of it on the kerbstones around the great tomb and in its chambers.*

uncovered a souterrain[30] and a line of decorated kerbstones that curved inwards towards an unusually carved stone: it had nested rectangles and a central vertical line. Clearly, it served some significant function. Soon a capstone came to light behind this stone. Beneath it was an infill of stoneless earth. After about a metre of this had been removed, a cavity appeared. In Eogan's own words:

I asked the youngest and smallest workman on the site, Martin Colfer of Slane, to try and look in. Getting his head and shoulders through, and using a torch, he announced that he could 'see for 20 yards'. As the news seemed too good to be true, it was accepted with caution.[31]

But Colfer was right. By evening, an entrance of about 70 by 70 cm (27.6 x 27.6 in) was visible. Eogan could easily look in and see that the passage led far – perhaps indeed 'for 20 yards'. It was built with huge orthostats, at least one of which bore carved designs. By now it was 6.30 pm and time for the workmen to return home. Eogan continues the story:

Student helpers were told of the discovery and, with Quentin Dresser in the fore, we soon set out on our hands and knees to investigate. It proved to be a thrilling, if also worrying, experience. About 10 m from the entrance, we had to crawl under an orthostat that had partly fallen inward. Next it was necessary to wriggle through a pool of muddy water on the floor beneath a couple of leaning orthostats. Loose stones on the floor made our crawling rather uncomfortable, and it grew difficult to judge how far we had gone, yet there was no sign of an end to the passage.

Eventually the roof began to rise in height and we could almost stand upright. Nearly all the orthostats appeared to be decorated, and the whole structure was much more impressive. At one point a stone basin lay in the passage. Then, coming to a stone sill, we illuminated the orthostat on its inner right side and beheld what seemed to be an anthropomorphic figure with two large, staring eyes [our Fig. 44]. This ghostly guardian suggested that we were approaching the inner sanctum. But we still had several metres to go, now walking erect and easily except for some boulders on the floor. The end of the passage was finally reached: an undifferentiated chamber with two sillstones. The outer sill and the rear stone of the chamber were decorated, apart from the vertical line, in a manner similar to that of the kerbstone before the entrance – with concentric rectangles.

We remained speechless for some time and marvelled at the achievement of these anonymous passage-tomb builders. Here was truly one of their great enterprises of close to 5000 years ago … What a day![32]

That seemed to be as much as any archaeologist could hope for. But the following year the team discovered a second passage, this one on the opposite (east) side of the mound. Its existence came to light on 30 July 1968. At first it seemed to be part of a complex souterrain of four passages dating from the Early Christian period. After some propping up of dangerously leaning orthostats, Eogan began to explore. Could this be another, entirely unexpected tomb? After crawling for some yards, he was able to stand up again.

I noticed a cracked capstone and, flashing my lamp to check its trustworthiness, saw that it was elaborately decorated with a chevron ornament (No. 43). The orthostats to left and right were also decorated. For the first time I was certain that we had found another tomb.[33]

Encountering more leaning orthostats Eogan was obliged to crawl in a small space above them and just below the capstones. Then he stopped,

as if in mid-air. Before me in the lamp's beam was the most amazing sight of my life. About 2.5 m below lay a large chamber, whose great corbelled roof rose around me, spanned by a single capstone up to 4 m above … After a while I dropped down into the chamber, noticing its cruciform plan with a number of decorated orthostats. The right-hand recess in this plan was 'guarded' by two large jambstones. Looking between them, I saw a uniquely ornamented stone basin, with horizontal and vertical scorings on the outside and, just opposite the

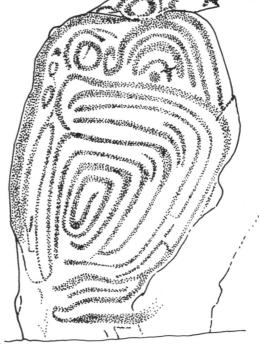

44 A carved stone (OR 49) half way down the western passage at Knowth. Some researchers believe it represents a human face. On the other hand, this impression may be created by a chance configuration of circular, semicircular and spiral motifs.

recess opening, a composition of concentric circles with flankers at the bottom. The inside of the basin, and the rear stone of the recess, were decorated as well.

What a structure and what a surprise! Since the previous year's great discovery, I had never expected a second tomb in the main mound, let alone a much more impressive one. And, having wriggled through some of the difficult parts in the passage on my way in, my presence in the tomb – despite its massiveness – gave me a sense not of isolation, but of security.[34]

And all this construction work took place centuries before the pyramids were built in Egypt. No wonder that Eogan spent the next four decades working at Knowth. We have given his account in his own words because they convey, much more vividly than any dry academic discourse, the wonder of Knowth. We cannot improve on his recollections of those heady days of discovery.

Anyone who enters the Knowth (or other) passages will be struck by the similarity between these Neolithic tombs and the embellished Upper Palaeolithic caves of western Europe. The tomb builders were, as we have suggested (Chapter 7), making their own caves, entrances to the nether realms of their own cosmos and consciousness.[35] Interestingly, the few Mesolithic cave burials that have been found in Ireland are in areas that lack early megalithic tombs.[36]

Entering constructed megalithic 'caves', Eogan felt 'a sense not of isolation, but of security'. Yet the sensory deprivation afforded by Neolithic tombs is inescapable. If one stays still for long enough the silence and darkness envelope one; they seep deeper and deeper into one. There is, it is true, security, but that security seems to derive from an absence of sensation, a settling, palpable calm. Neolithic people may not have entered the tombs in great numbers nor often, but, when they did, sensory deprivation, probably only one of their ways of altering consciousness, awaited them.

One of the most amazing points about Knowth is that the whole tomb with its 9.9-m (32.5-ft) high mound must have been constructed around the large, carved stone basin in the side chamber of the eastern tomb. Does this mean that the basin was in place on the summit of the ridge before the tomb was built? Did the tomb develop, in a spectacular fashion, a pre-existent ritual place, as the Bryn Celli Ddu tomb took over the earlier henge? Perhaps the basin served an open-air function for those smaller tombs that pre-date the large mound. Then, at a certain time, the people thought it necessary to build a tomb around the basin, thus exalting its status and placing it securely in the underworld. It seems likely that such an action would have been implicated in refinements of religious belief, together with ideas about how those beliefs related to the cosmos. As time passes, religious leaders try to make beliefs more formal and explicit, sometimes in dogma, sometimes in scriptures, sometimes in ritual and structures, but almost always with schismatic results.

So, the basins may originally have been places of cremation, or receptacles for cremated bones before the remains were moved into the small tombs. Then, as competing groups of people negotiated details of the consciousness contract and religious belief, the emerging group decided that the receptacle of cremation – and hence transformation – should itself be in the underworld, a built underworld that they could more rigidly control and to which they could restrict access. The circular shape of the stone basins that cradled human remains was then replicated in the shape of the circular mounds. As with the circular and spiral art motifs (Chapter 9), there are circles within circles. There is continuity within change.

If this suggested sequence approximates to what actually happened, we must go on to note that Knowth and Newgrange were probably contemporary, or nearly contemporary, structures. Perhaps, then, the building of the Knowth tomb over the basin resulted from competitive social relations between two groups of people – the 'Knowthians' and the 'Newgrangers'.[37] Yet, the construction of so massive a tomb as Knowth may have had the opposite of the desired effect: the vast amount of debilitating labour required may have weakened, not strengthened, the polity. When Knowth was complete, or nearing completion, the Newgrangers began to increase their power and demonstrated their ascendancy by building an even larger tomb with its own basins and access to the underworld. A similar fate awaited them. Newgrange was eventually closed, and different (though not entirely so) rituals with different social and religious implications were performed in newly constructed henges and along the cursus. The tombs became silent witnesses to the past, by now very probably a mythical past with its tales of creation, heroes, and neurological building-blocks of transcosmological travel and transformation (Chapter 6).

Following the course that we adopted in describing Bryn Celli Ddu and Barclodiad y Gawres, we now discuss some aspects of Knowth, starting at the kerb and working inwards.

AN ENCOMPASSING RING OF STONE

We argued that the ring of kerbstones at Bryn Celli Ddu (and those at other tombs as well) were there to carefully delineate the perimeter of the covering mound, not just to contain any slippage of the piled-up stone and turf (Fig.

43). That view is confirmed at Knowth by the ways in which the stones were selected and placed, as well as by their elaborate decoration: their purpose is clearly more than simply structural. They were 'saying' something. Part of that 'something' may have been a reflection of the encompassing loop of the Boyne and the Mattock.[38] In the same way that one had to cross a swirling, eddying river to enter the Bend, so too one had to cross a circle of decorated stones to enter the tomb, especially the entrance stone with its distinctive motifs that, we later argue, had water and eddies as part of their connotations.

There were 127 kerbstones (three are now missing). They are oblong and average 2.5 m (8.2 ft) in length: they are considerable objects (Fig. 45). When the builders set them in place, they ensured that the tops were aligned. To facilitate this uniformity, some stones were set more deeply into the ground than others and some were placed on built-up smaller stones. Together, they present a regular, symbol-filled profile. The building of the kerb seems to have started at the tomb entrances. As one moves farther away from them, the kerbstones are smaller. The style of image on the kerbstones suggests that the kerb may have been constructed quite some time after the tomb itself.[39] More-over, differences in engraving expertise suggest that stones may have been contributed by different groups of people.

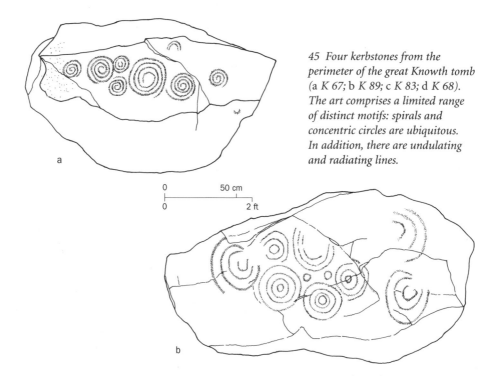

45 Four kerbstones from the perimeter of the great Knowth tomb (a K 67; b K 89; c K 83; d K 68). The art comprises a limited range of distinct motifs: spirals and concentric circles are ubiquitous. In addition, there are undulating and radiating lines.

The original entrances to both Knowth passages were destroyed during the Iron Age and at the beginning of the Early Christian era when a large ditch was dug around the mound. Later, still in the Early Christian period, around the 9th to 11th centuries, what remained of the entrances became parts of settlements. Some orthostats were removed and deposited in the ditch, where Eogan and his team found them. In the eastern passage, a thick layer of dark earth accumulated in the chamber and passage, and the tomb became part of a souterrain complex. Nevertheless, some important observations can be made.

We saw that the kerb at Bryn Celli Ddu bent inwards at the entrance to the passage. At Knowth, there are also slight inward curves at the entrances to the eastern and western tombs, but not as noticeable as at the Anglesey tomb. Though slight, the recessed areas at the two entrances were nevertheless the focus of considerable attention. A kerbstone with nested rectangles and a vertical line was placed directly across the entrance to the western tomb (Fig. 46). To enter the tomb, Neolithic people would probably have had to clamber over the stone, thus passing 'along' the vertical line, 'through' the concentric rectangles and in to the circular mound. A comparable massive stone, this one with two opposed sets of nested rectangles, was placed across the entrance to

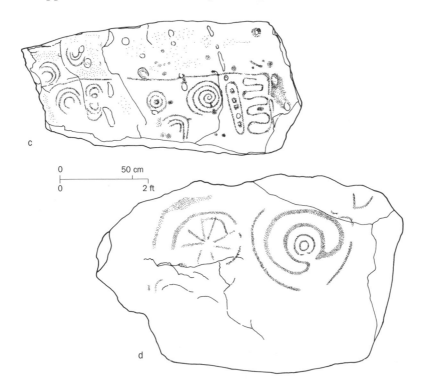

c

0   50 cm

0   2 ft

d

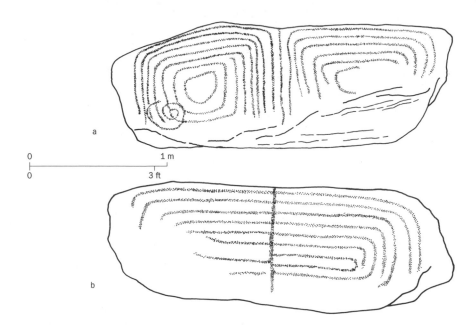

46 *Entrance stones at the openings to the eastern (a K 11) and western (b K 74) passages at Knowth. Each stone is a variation on the theme of nested rectangles, spiral and vertical lines.*

the eastern passage. Here, there is a vertical line between the rectangles that continues over on to the top surface of the stone, where there are further nested rectangles and concentric circles (Fig. 46).

We suggest that, at both entrances, the rectangles are actually concentric circles that have been distorted so that they will fill and also reflect the oblong shapes of the entrance stones. Concentric circles and spirals are, as we shall see, common motifs carved on kerbstones and on orthostats within the tombs, but here the builders felt it necessary for concentric motifs to fill the oblong kerbstones completely, not simply to be engraved on them. Image and stone became a single entity, a point that will be clarified in the next chapter. Further, enlarged and distorted, and bisected by a vertical line, the motif was emphatically associated not just with the entrances to the tombs but also with trajectories that led from the outside world, through the kerb, into the depths of the tombs and then on to the human remains placed there. The stones imply not merely barriers but also movement through them, a cosmological route.

We now look at other features: first, the eastern and, then, the western tomb.

At the entrance to the eastern passage (Fig. 47), there are seven stone settings. The individual stones making up these demarcations were placed on edge and end-to-end to form roughly circular enclosures, except for four that abut kerbstones and are consequently U-shaped. The setting known as No. 1 is the most elaborate. It is directly opposite the entrance to the tomb. Saucer-shaped, it is about 4.5 m (14.8 ft) from the entrance kerbstone, 4.2 m (13.8 ft)

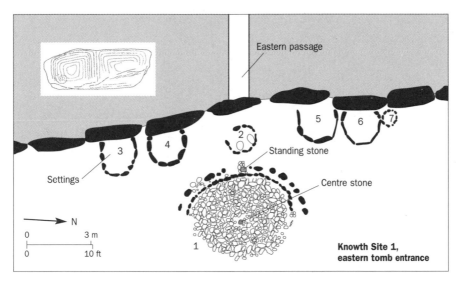

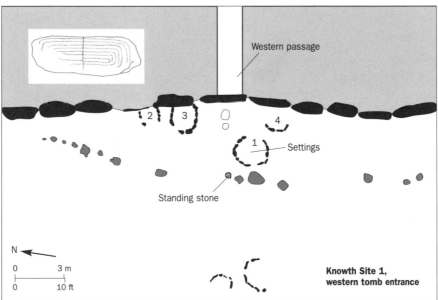

47 Intricate stone settings at the entrances to the eastern and western passages at Knowth. These settings, along with standing stones and the large paved area (eastern passage entrance), suggest that complex rituals took place at these locations.

in diameter and was about 22 cm (8.7 in) below the old ground surface. It was scooped out of the ground. The interior of this setting was paved with small stones averaging about 15 by 10 cm (5.9 x 3.9 in). In the centre of the circle was a larger square piece of grey limestone; it was firmly secured in the ground. Overlying the paving and the centre stone was a scatter of small quartz chips. The whole setting was surrounded by two rows of stones, one of which, the inner, was composed of glacial erratics; the outer row comprised clay ironstone nodules.[40]

Again we find that a circle and its centre (here the piece of grey limestone) were important to Neolithic people. We therefore wonder if a circular setting like No. 1 with its marked centre derived from a conceptual template that also informed the round mound with its two (almost) central chambers and the circular motifs engraved on to the stones. There does seem to be some kind of homology. We also wonder if setting No. 1 was in fact a large 'basin' designed to hold water and to be a conceptual analogue for the whole tomb and thus of the cosmos. Then, at another level, the setting may have been an analogue of the carved stone basins in the eastern and western tombs. If so, was the symbolism of quartz related to that of water?[41] To that question we add another: Was there in the Neolithic mind a connection between a round pool, concentric, circular ripples widening from a dropped stone and nested circular and spiral motifs? Perhaps we can imagine a ritual at the eastern entrance to Knowth during which one or more pieces of quartz were tossed into the pool to create a water-constituted replica of carved motifs. The thrown stone would, literally, pass through the centre of the concentric ripples. Nevertheless, we do not think that concentric motifs merely represent water ripples; there is much more to them. We discuss their probable origin in the next chapter.

In addition to these settings, there is a thick, lunate scatter of what Eogan calls 'unusual stones' – quartz, water-rolled granite, banded ocean-rolled stones and local quarried stone.[42] Two explanations can be advanced. One is that the builders laid down this material to form a 'platform'. Another is that the exotic stone was formerly on the face of the mound around the tomb entrance and that it slipped down to its present position as a result of natural erosion. If the second is the case, as we suspect it is, quartz must have been placed on both the face of the mound *and* in setting No. 1. Noting what seems to be a widespread Neolithic metaphorical association between stone and water (including pebbles from beaches and streams, and shells from tidal zones), Chris Fowler and Vicki Cummings have argued that 'the interplay between water and stone was one of the ways of exploring and expressing' the transformation of 'human bodies both in life and after death'.[43] As we shall see, there was a similar interplay at Newgrange.

Here is one of the points at which we have hinted but which we have not fully explored. The type of stone was important to the builders – in setting No. 1, glacial erratics, ironstone nodules and quartz.[44] Further, the kinds of stone were grouped together in the surrounding edges; in the case of quartz, it was used to characterize the space within the setting. More examples of this use of special, selected stone will come to light as we proceed.

Another key feature of the entrance to the eastern passage is a standing stone, 1.6 m (5.2 ft) long and 23 cm (9.1 in) wide by 20 cm (7.9 in) thick. The excavators found it lying next to a roughly square pit that had been dug to support it. It had been placed so that it aligned with the vertical line that runs through the two opposed sets of rectangular motifs on the entrance stone (Fig. 46) and, beyond that, the passage into the tomb. The standing stone was an addition to the other features at the entrance that signalled a transcosmological route. We now move to the other side of the mound.

The arrangement of features at the western passage largely duplicated those at the entrance to the eastern tomb (see Fig. 47). There are six roughly circular settings of stones. Three of them (Nos 1, 5 and 6) were filled with quartz fragments. Two other settings (Nos 2 and 4) were hollowed out and held 'dark earth'.[45] Perhaps they too were water-containing basins. Either way, the different kinds of infill suggest that different activities were performed at different settings.

There was also a 2.56-m (8.4-ft) high standing stone at the western entrance. It was erected more or less in the centre of a line of stones running almost from the kerb away to the south; some stood upright, some were placed flat on the ground (see Fig. 47). The standing stone aligns with the prominent vertical groove on the entrance stone, the passage and the tomb chamber, on the back wall of which are more concentric rectangles, but no central vertical line. The absence of a vertical line at this point suggests that the alignment, or route, terminates here – that is, at the chamber of the dead – at least temporarily.

As at the eastern passage entrance, there is another spread of stones, including quartz, granite and banded cobbles. Here, the stones were found on top of the fallen standing stone. This relationship suggests that they cascaded down from the mound rather than that they were intentionally laid on the surface. Quartz and special stone were again associated with the entrance.

It is clear that all these features at both passage entrances were not scatters of disparate items. On the contrary, they were vital constituents of a repeated conceptual, symbolic and architectural complex. Again, we are brought back to the notion of a system – or 'grammar' – of symbols that is a feature of all religions (Chapter 1). That grammar articulated with both the structure of the tombs and the cosmos.

Art

The motifs at Knowth were made by two techniques: incision and pecking. As these terms imply, the first was made by drawing a pointed instrument along the surface, and the second by hammering with, very possibly, a hammer and a punch. No such tools have so far come to light.[46]

The main Knowth tomb and its satellites have more than a quarter of the known megalithic art of western Europe. Even the total number of motifs in Brittany, an area noted for its megalithic art, is exceeded by Knowth alone. Moreover, Knowth exceeds by about 100 the total number of decorated stones in all the other monuments within the Bend of the Boyne. More than 300 large decorated stones have been found in the main mound alone. Newgrange may be bigger than Knowth, but the smaller tomb exceeds it in the sheer quantity of its art.

There is a strange anomaly here. Although abundant at Knowth, and within the Bend of the Boyne in general, megalithic art is not found throughout Ireland. Beyond County Meath, passage-tomb art is both rare and rather crudely made.[47] One possible explanation for this limited distribution is that the stones used elsewhere were rougher than those obtained by the Bend of the Boyne builders and were therefore unsuitable for the making of art. Eogan suggests that these undecorated tombs may have been draped with textiles or animal skins, or even painted.[48]

Another explanation, one that we tend to favour, is that the Bend of the Boyne (and other County Meath tombs, such as Fourknocks) were in some way special. They were the seat of Neolithic religious and political power in Ireland and so warranted greater elaboration. Comparisons of motifs with those in Brittany suggest that the practice of intensive image-making on monuments may have originated in France and travelled to eastern Ireland, where it flowered as the polity responsible for the tombs acquired prestige. Image-making became a feature of an east Ireland Neolithic sphere of influence. From here, that polity seems to have touched Anglesey, as the comparable motifs at Barclodiad y Gawres suggest (see Fig. 41).

At Knowth, motifs were placed on kerbstones, orthostats, capstones, sills, lintels and on the corbels above the chambers. Sometimes motifs overlap one another; sometimes they completely fill a surface; sometimes they cover only a small portion of a surface. It is easy for researchers to concentrate on the most beautiful and finished motifs, but Eogan makes an important point. He notes that what seems to be random, scattered pecking, not forming any recognizable motifs, probably did not result from desultory doodling. This conclusion is demonstrated by such pecking being repeatedly found on stones in key positions.[49] Eogan does not offer an explanation for this seemingly meaningless feature. We think that, far from being meaningless, it resulted from a highly significant ritual practice. We suggest that the *act* of pecking a motif, together perhaps with the repetitive sound that this entailed, was meaningful. The technique, not just the resulting motif, was significant. Image-making was a complex religious practice. An implication of this suggestion is that the stone (the substance) on which the motifs were placed was also significant: stone was not a meaningless support. Hammering on a stone (whether to make neat motifs or simply scatters of peck marks) was a way of 'connecting with' the stone as a significant substance, perhaps even of releasing, activating or giving form to some inherent potency within the stone. As we have seen, Aaron Watson describes how sound, including drumming, was probably associated with transitions in Neolithic tombs: 'The process of entering these monuments effectively separated participants from the outside world … Using certain vocal frequencies … it is possible to induce enormous stones to appear to shake and become alive.'[50]

We consider the problems posed by megalithic art motifs in Chapter 9. For the moment, all we need note is that they are an integral part of the tombs, not merely added decoration – as our discussion of the two decorated entrance stones, the standing stones and their joint alignment with the passage that leads to the chamber has shown.

Passages and Chambers

Overall, the two passages in the Knowth mound were oriented along an east–west line (see Fig. 43). The significance of this duality of passages is hard to determine, but, as we shall see, a similar concept was implied at Newgrange that shows that some sort of bisection of the circular mound was part of the thinking of Neolithic builders in the Bend of the Boyne.

Most of the eastern passage, originally approximately 40 m (131 ft) long, was about 1.6 m (5.2 ft) high and 85 cm (33.5 in) wide, but some 11 m

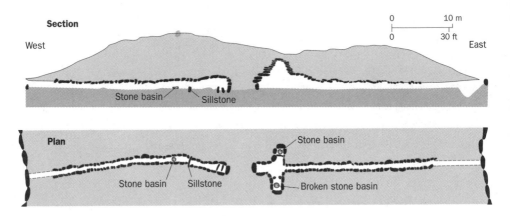

48 *The two passages at Knowth almost meet at the centre of the mound. The eastern passage, with its cruciform chamber, basins and corbelled roof, is the more elaborate of the two.*

(36.1 ft) before the chamber the roof of capstones becomes higher and higher until the innermost capstone is 2.7 m (8.9 ft) above the floor. To increase the height of the capstones, the builders used larger orthostats and, near to the chamber, drystone walling. This arrangement meant that, in this final section, each capstone is higher than the one nearer to the entrance, the structure giving a corbelled effect. The passage roof thus merges with the corbelled roof of the chamber (Fig. 48).

The architecture of the passage and the chamber together gives one the experience of coming out of a constricting passage into a widening funnel and then into the high-roofed chamber itself: after 'descent' into a 'cave' there is a view upwards to a realm above (Fig. 48). This is a significant point. Constriction followed by release into a new space is the fundamental experience of passage tombs. It is, we argue, no accident that this experience replicates the mental vortex that leads from the second stage of our neuropsychological model into the third stage of hallucinations and another existential realm, often interpreted as an underworld that the dead and other spirit beings occupy. The 'cave' in the tomb replicated the cave in the mind.

In the western passage, there is a bend a few metres from the end (see Figs 43 and 48). At this point a sillstone lies across the visitor's path, and the orthostats are dramatically decorated. One (see Fig. 44) bears the carving that gave Eogan the impression of a 'ghostly guardian'. Although we doubt that this motif was intentionally anthropomorphic, it is clear that a concentration of imagery was placed at a certain point in the tunnel. It is in fact not uncommon to find a cluster of motifs, a bend or other feature approximately halfway down a passage (e.g., Newgrange, Knowth, Dowth, Bryn Celli Ddu and tombs in Brittany, such as Gavrinis). They seem to mark stages in the route from the outside world to the chamber of the dead. If so, we suspect that they would also have had social significance. Perhaps certain classes of seers could penetrate only so far down a passage, the remaining few metres being reserved for special seers. Perhaps these points in the passages were a final *Lasciate ogni speranza* ('Abandon hope all ye who enter here').

Beyond these 'signposts', the chambers of the two Knowth Site 1 tombs are of different kinds. The eastern tomb has a cruciform chamber: a central area with two side recesses (see Figs 43 and 48). The western tomb is of the undifferentiated kind: it has a chamber but no side recesses. As we saw in the previous chapter, these end chambers and recesses are the principal, though not the only, places for the deposit of human remains.

Virtually every Irish passage tomb that has been excavated had within it human remains.[51] Both sexes and all age-groups are represented. Interestingly, at one Irish tomb, the Mound of the Hostages (Tara) cremated burials were found in small chambers under the mound but not in the tomb itself. Perhaps they were of people who died during the construction of the tomb. At a cruciform tomb, Belmore (Moylehid), burnt human bones were found in a small angle between the left recess and the end recess. They were mixed with animal bones, boars' tusks and an unburnt human skull. The theme of people and animals being united in death emerges, as it did in our consideration of Near Eastern sites. At a tomb known as Carrowmore 7, burnt human bones were built, apparently at the time of construction, into the drystone walling between the orthostats at the four corners of the chamber. These bones were accompanied by pieces of charcoal and burnt seashells – another reference to the sea. Some deposits of burnt bone were covered by stones, and one deposit by a basin (Loughcrew L).[52] At another Carrowmore site the bones of children were placed on top of an orthostat that did not quite reach to the roofstone. These are just a few of the instances where human remains have been found in Irish passage tombs.

Knowth was no exception. The excavators discovered multiple burials. Cremation makes it difficult to tell how many individuals were represented in a single deposit, but it seems that the number of dead in a tomb could vary from one to, at Tara, over 100. In both tombs in the large Knowth mound, cremated remains were found on the old ground surface and on the flagstone floors of recesses.[53]

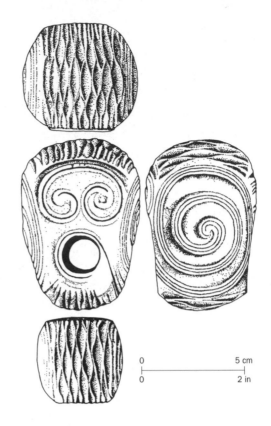

49 The decorated macehead found at the entrance to the right-hand recess of the eastern passage at Knowth (Pl. 21). Once again, it is decorated with a combination of spiral and lozenge shapes.

0   5 cm

0   2 in

Associated with these human remains was a remarkable object. It is a 7.9-cm (3.1-in) long macehead made of flint (Fig. 49). Eogan called it 'One of the finest works of art created by the passage-tomb builders of western Europe.'[54] It was found on the old floor surface at the entrance to the right alcove at Knowth (eastern) between the two jambstones, that is, in front of the stone basin.[55] It was covered by a layer of shale. The distinctive motif carved on it is not found in Irish megalithic art; some researchers believe that it originated in Orkney, Wales or Scotland.[56]

Clearly, the macehead was not a practical object but rather a symbol of status. It is elaborately carved on all its surfaces (Pl. 21; Fig. 49). On one side, there are double, linked spirals that look rather like eyes. On each of the sides is a single spiral; on the 'back' surface sets of lines are on one side of the hole for the handle; other lines are engraved around the hole and trail round to become one of the side spirals. The ends have tightly packed lozenge motifs. Curiously, these images are in relief: the rest of the surface was laboriously and very carefully carved away. Another, undecorated, macehead was found in the western tomb at Knowth. Another example of particular interest was found in the Early Bronze Age site in Wiltshire known as Bush Barrow. Unless it is a relic, which is possible, it is therefore later than the Knowth find. It seems to have had a flint head, and the shaft was decorated with five bands of bone carved in zigzags (Pl. 26).[57]

Eogan believes that the depositing of the Knowth macehead may have been part of the 'dedication ceremony of the great site, after which it was withdrawn forever from human sight, becoming the first object deposited in the tomb'.[58] He is probably correct. From our perspective, however, the really significant aspect of the Knowth macehead is the association of spirals on what is, in all probability, a symbol of political power. The spiral motif, an intimate, repeated feature of the tombs, suggests that political power was founded on religion. The owner (or owners) of the mace exercised political power over other people, and that power was posited on a particular cosmology and the continuing influence of the dead. There was, the Neolithic maces tell us, a close relationship between access to spiritual realms and control of people. Politics and religion went hand in hand.

Overall, we argue that the passages of megalithic tombs were not culs-de-sac, ending in chambers. Rather, the stones that formed the backs and sides of the chambers were themselves doorways to the rest of the journey on which the dead had embarked. The motifs engraved on them suggest that, like the entrance stones, they were barriers that could be passed on appropriate occasions.

THE BASINS

The stone basins are surely among the most wonderful items of Neolithic material culture that have come down to us(Fig. 50). Within the Bend of the Boyne, there are three examples in Knowth (two in the eastern and one in the western tomb), four in the large Newgrange tomb (in the eastern recess, two basins were placed one on top of the other), another in the small passage tomb known as Newgrange Z, and one in Dowth. Approximately six are known from other Irish tombs. In cruciform tombs, such as Knowth east, the basins were found in the recesses of the chambers; in Knowth west, the chamber of which does not have side recesses, and in other undifferentiated sites, the bowls are usually in the chamber. It is clear that much skilled labour went into the making of some of the basins. Others are largely natural in shape, but pecked into a neater form. Most researchers believe that the basins were receptacles for cremated human remains, and human remains were indeed found in the Newgrange Z basin.

The most elaborately decorated (and therefore revealing) basin is the roughly circular one that Eogan so dramatically came across in the right-hand recess of the eastern tomb chamber (Pl. 22). When it was found, there were no human remains in it, though, as we have seen, cremated burials are frequently found in the recesses of cruciform tombs.

The sides of this basin are embellished with deeply cut horizontal lines. These lines stop short of a set of five concentric circles that were facing the entrance to the recess when Eogan first entered the tomb – as they still are. The image-makers left a dot in the centre of the circles. Comparable designs appear on Grooved Ware pottery, a widespread type of vessel that, in Orkney, dates as far back as 3000 BC.[59] Inside the Knowth basin are nested curves and radiating lines (Fig. 50); one of the kerbstones (Fig. 51) has a comparable set of radiating lines emanating from a central hole. The wall behind the basin is also richly decorated with radiating lines, nested curves and a chequerboard pattern (Figs 52, 53).

So, if the Knowth (eastern) basin was made to hold human remains, what can we infer from that conclusion about the decoration on the sides and within it? The motifs must surely have had relevance to the dead. Bearing in mind what we have said about the tunnel, or vortex, experience, we suggest that the motifs on the basin also had cosmological and religious significance. Indeed, we argue that this Knowth basin epitomizes in one small-scale model the message that the entire tomb conveys. What, then, could the motifs on the basin, individually and in combination, signify? This is a matter that we take up in Chapter 9, but we make three preliminary points here.

First, we suggest that the horizontal lines on the outside of the basin may have represented tiers of the cosmos through which the dead (and ritual specialists) travelled. Secondly, the concentric circles, placed so that they link the

50 The decorated interior of the Knowth basin from the right-hand recess of the eastern passage (Pl. 22). The carved lines focus on the spot where human remains were probably placed.

51 A richly decorated kerbstone (K 15) at Knowth. Compare the radiating line and spiral with the motifs shown in Figures 41, 45, 49, 50 and Plates 21–24.

upper- and lowermost horizontal lines, probably represented the vortex that provides a way through the levels of the cosmos. Thirdly, the radiating lines on the inner surface of the basin[60] and the associated curves are probably other ways (each with its own nuances) of representing the vortex. Any cremated human remains placed in the basin would be, appropriately enough, at the focus of the lines and curves, that is, the remains would be on their route through the cosmos. In this way, the stone basins would have epitomized a complex *system of symbols* that embraced

 – the circular kerb,
 – the mound,
 – the entrance complexes with, at the eastern tomb, a circular 'paved basin' with a carefully marked centre point,
 – the nested rectangles on the entrance stones,
 – the passages,
 – the chambers at the ends of the passages, and
 – the complex permutations of various motifs, both outside and within the tomb.

Architecture and art thus coalesced to represent, facilitate and induce religious experience, belief and practice – the three dimensions of religion

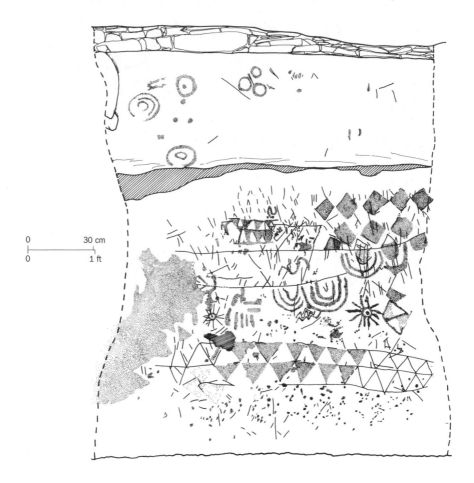

52, 53 (Left) The elaborately decorated back wall of the right-hand alcove of the eastern passage at Knowth. (Opposite) The position of the carved basin in relation to the back wall of the alcove (Fig. 50, Pl. 22). Note the concentric design on the front of the basin.

that we have identified. And, at the same time, to reproduce social relations between individuals and groups that were distinguished and demarcated by the overall form of the tomb. All components were embedded in a complex, and probably fissive, political regimen.

Newgrange

Having discussed Knowth in some detail, we need refer to only a few relevant aspects of the great Newgrange tomb, the one that most tourists visit. They are led from a visitors' centre tucked, appropriately enough, out of sight on

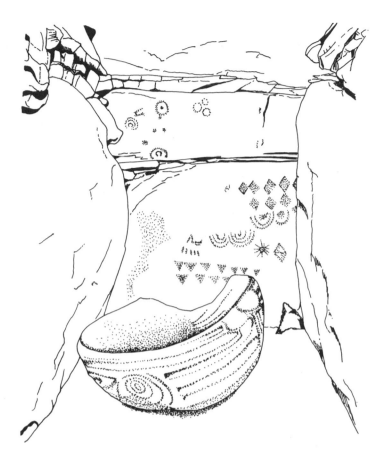

the south bank, over a bridge across the Boyne and so into the Bend, and then conveyed by bus to the tomb.

The mound is huge, the largest within the Bend of the Boyne: its average diameter is about 80 m (262.5 ft); it stands 13 m (42.7 ft) high. Around the mound are the remains of a stone circle that recall the smaller one at Bryn Celli Ddu. There are now only 12 stones, but the sockets that were dug to receive many more have been found. The stone ring probably post-dates the closure of the tomb in Late Neolithic times.

The first feature of the tomb that strikes visitors is the brilliantly white façade. Is it a genuine reconstruction or is it a controversial figment of the restorer's imagination? Michael O'Kelly, Professor of Archaeology at University College Cork, was the highly skilled excavator and restorer of Newgrange. The hazards of his task were abundantly evident to him. On the dedication page of his definitive book he inscribed a warning that must have haunted him:

To be a restorer of ancient monuments one should be sheltered by a triple coat of brass, but even a repairer of such required a coat of mail. DR E. P. WRIGHT, PRESIDENTIAL ADDRESS TO THE ROYAL SOCIETY OF ANTIQUARIES OF IRELAND, DELIVERED 30 JANUARY 1900. (*JOURNAL OF THE ROYAL SOCIETY OF ANTIQUARIES OF IRELAND*, 30:7).[61]

When he chose the quotation about 'a triple coat of brass' that restorers would be prudent to don, O'Kelly was probably thinking principally of the shining face that Newgrange now presents to visitors. This white wall, apart from omissions left to allow the entrance of large numbers of visitors, was, he believes, the aspect that the tomb presented around 2000 BC when Neolithic people approached it from the river.

THE QUARTZ FAÇADE

As far as we can judge, O'Kelly was right to embellish the façade with the vast amount of gleaming quartz that he found, along with rounded granite boulders, lying in front of it. That he did not need to import any quartz for his reconstruction shows just how much of this stone there was. (The positioning of the dark granite boulders in the quartz revetment is frankly conjectural.) The quartz was, he believed, part of a revetment that, on the south, or entrance, side of the mound, stood above the impressive circle of kerbstones (in all, there are 97 kerbstones; none is missing) and helped to contain the slope of the mound. Where a kerbstone had fallen over and outwards, there was no quartz beneath it; the quartz must therefore have come from above the kerbstones and cascaded down after they had fallen over.[62] But that is not the whole story. The fact that the quartz did not continue all around the mound but was associated with the entrance shows that it was more than simply a structural feature. The white quartz face must have had some meaning.[63]

About 2.5 m (8.2 ft) from the kerbstone immediately to the right of the entrance stone there was a complex cairn that sustained the emphasis on quartz. It was oval and approximately 4 x 3.4 m (13.1 x 11.2 ft). It comprised 607 quartz pebbles, each 'about the size of a potato', 103 pieces of granite rounded by water action and 612 fragments of quartz.[64] Within and under it was an oval setting of thin slabs, 3 x 2 m (9.8 x 6.6 ft), which was paved. As part of the pavement, there was 'a highly polished piece of sandstone, 24 cm [9.5 in] in length, oval in cross section, 7.4 cm x 4.5 cm [2.9 x 1.8 in], and displaying a fractured surface at one end and a blunt polished point at the other'.[65] Wondering if this piece represents a phallus, O'Kelly went on to compare the setting with those at Knowth and another rich Neolithic site of passage tombs, Loughcrew. As he points out, all these settings are associated with quartz pebbles: 'It must be taken as certain that the settings are associated with the primary use of the monuments.'[66]

Where did all this quartz come from? It was not local in origin. There must therefore have been organized groups of workers who found, gathered or extracted, and then transported the stone. Research has shown that the New-grange quartz, characterized by flecks of white mica, came from the Dublin/Wicklow Mountains, at least 60 km (37.3 miles) to the south of the Bend of the Boyne (Fig. 54).[67] The ice sheets did not, of course, move from south to north, so the quartz could not have been conveyed from the moun-tains by natural means. It is more likely that it was brought by boat, first by sea and then up the Boyne River – an astonishing feat.

The dark, rounded granodiorite cobbles that were mixed with the quartz probably came from the Mourne Mountains to the north of the Bend of the Boyne. Gabbro cobbles came from a stretch of the northern shore of Dunkald Bay, some 40 km (25 miles) to the northeast. The shore was proba-bly, for Neolithic people, the meeting place of what Knut Helskog, a rock art expert at Tromsø University, calls 'the three natural zones and three cosmological worlds': water, land and sky.[68] The sandstone (greywacke) orthostats and kerb-stones were quarried about 10 km (6.2 miles) to the north.[69]

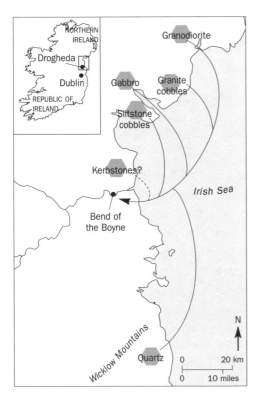

54 The builders of Newgrange transported raw materials from a number of distant sources. The various kinds of rock came together to create the tomb. The importance of the different types of stone related to their distant origins.

The building materials brought to the Bend of the Boyne thus reflected a wide social network, though it should be added that the influence of the Boyne cluster of monuments probably extended much farther than the sources we have mentioned. There is an even more astonishing instance of Neolithic transport. The bluestone that was brought all the way from at least ten different sources within the Preseli Mountains in Wales to Stonehenge in Wiltshire shows just how far Neolithic religious and political contacts could extend. In the absence of any convincing west to east glaciation beyond the Bristol Channel, we must conclude that, however they managed the formidable task, people transported the bluestones to Stonehenge.[70] The importation of 'foreign' stone that must have held special significance for people in western Europe recalls the taking of stalagmitic material from the limestone caves of the Taurus Mountains to Çatalhöyük (Chapter 4).

We defer further discussion of quartz and its significance to the next chapter. But it is necessary to mention the association of this special kind of stone with a unique feature at Newgrange that has attracted much comment and speculation.

A Window to the Heavens

The 18.95-m (62.17-ft) long Newgrange passage opens to the southeast.[71] The orthostats that form its sides average 1.5 m (4.9 ft) in height above the floor level, though, as at Knowth, they are higher near to the chamber where the passage roof is 3.6 m (11.8 ft) high: the same widening funnel effect is thus created. At the outer end of the passage, excavators found the entrance was blocked by a large slab (it is now just to the right of the entrance). All this is typical of passage tombs.

Then, in 1963, O'Kelly discovered a unique feature. The decorated front edge of the top stone of this comparatively small feature was known from at least the 1830s, and was thought to be a 'false lintel'. O'Kelly's excavations revealed its true nature. It is a stone-built box, resting on the first two roofstones of the passage. It is 90 cm (35.4 in) high, 1 m (3.3 ft) wide and 1.2 m (3.9 ft) deep. It is set back from the entrance below it by about 2.5 m (8.2 ft) (Pl. 24). During the excavations, O'Kelly and his team referred to this small structure as the 'roof-box', a name it has retained ever since.[72]

The roof-box was complexly constructed. While the inner part opened into the passage, the sides were built up with drystone walling that supported a large flat stone known as the back corbel. It has circular motifs, each with a central dot, and a set of six radiating lines, likewise focused on a central dot.

Around the outer curve of the 'rays' are two arcs of pecked dots, the inner arc comprising eight and the outer, ten dots (Fig. 55). This corbel supports the decorated lintel.[73] The front edge of the lintel, the part that was known in the 1830s, is expertly made (Fig. 55). It is decorated with a series of crosses (often called 'lozenges') set within a containing line above and at the ends; each cross is separated from its neighbours by vertical lines. To the left, where the edge of the lintel narrows, the design is adapted to fit the available space. Pecking gives the whole decorated surface a uniform texture.

The opening of the roof-box was 'lightly closed by two blocks of quartz, one of which was in situ' when the excavators studied the feature.[74] Scratch marks on the stone below the opening show that the blocks of quartz had been repeatedly slid in and out of the gap. Ridges on the underside of one of the blocks were worn smooth by this action.

What was the purpose of this remarkable feature?

O'Kelly wondered if it was a receptacle for offerings after the tomb had been closed when the large entrance slab was set in place. Or was the slit between the outside world and the passage a 'soul-hole' through which the spirits of the dead could pass when the quartz blocks were slid back?[75] Or was the opening intended to afford communication between the living and the dead?[76] As a result of persistent suggestions made by visitors, probably thinking of Stonehenge and its summer solstice alignment, O'Kelly and his team decided to investigate the possibility of a solar alignment. On 21 December 1969, they recorded the following observations on tape:

At exactly 8.45 hours GMT the top edge of the ball of the sun appeared above the local horizon and at 8.58 hours, the first pencil of direct sunlight shone through the roof-box and along the passage to reach across the tomb chamber floor as far as the front edge of the basin stone in the end recess. As the thin line of light widened to a 17-cm band and swung across the chamber floor, the tomb was dramatically illuminated and various details of the side and end recesses could be clearly seen in the light reflected from the floor. At 9.09 hours, the 17-cm band of light began to narrow again and at exactly 9.15 hours, the direct beam was cut off from the tomb. For 17 minutes, therefore, at sunrise on the shortest day of the year, direct sunlight can enter Newgrange, not through the doorway, but through the specially contrived slit which lies under the roof-box at the outer end of the passage roof.[77]

Because the entrance to the passage is down slope from the back recess, light does not reach from it to the chamber; it was therefore necessary to build a special opening at a higher level – the roof-box (Fig. 56).

Some critics, citing what they deem unpleasant Irish weather, have doubted the practicality of the device. But, despite variable weather at this time of the year, O'Kelly observed the phenomenon annually for at least 11 consecutive years 'on one or more of the three or four days centring on 21 December'.[78] Overcast weather is not the only objection that has been raised. Why, critics ask, is the Newgrange roof-box the only structure of its kind? It may not have been. In the nature of things, it is always the entrances to passage tombs that are most damaged by natural erosion and by human depredations. Frances Lynch suspects that there may have been something similar at Bryn Celli Ddu in Anglesey. In any event, there are numerous unique Neolithic structures: because there is only one Stonehenge, no one argues that it does not exist.

Despite critics' reservations about the weather and the uniqueness of the Newgrange roof-box, it does work. At the winter solstice the sun does indeed reach into the depths of the tomb and light up the innermost chamber. During this short period of annual illumination a solitary carved motif in the end recess of the cruciform chamber is lit by reflected light. It is not on the back wall, as might be expected, but, almost hidden, on the right-hand orthostat. It is the now well-known triple, interlinked spirals that have become a logo for the whole Boyne complex of sites (Pl. 23). Each of the three spirals comprises a double line. It is a highly complex image that must have encoded complex and sophisticated beliefs.

The effect of this 'revelation' of the triple spiral motif is markedly more pronounced on the morning of the solstice than on the few adjacent days when the sun's rays also reach the back stone. To see the spirals clearly, one has

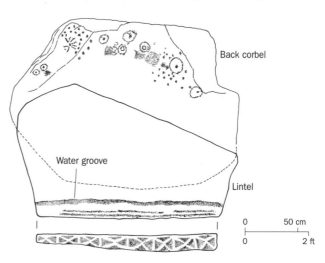

Back corbel

Water groove

Lintel

55 A lintel stone with a narrow decorated edge is above the back corbel of the roof-box at Newgrange. Placed in a position in which they would not have been readily visible, the motifs on the back corbel include radiating lines, circles and dots.

0   50 cm

0   2 ft

actually to enter the deepest alcove of the tomb or, at the very least, to lean into the space. This difficulty suggests that comparatively few people would have seen the illumination of the spirals; those who did manage to do so would have had to avoid blocking the rays, perhaps by sitting in the alcove. It was thus the illumination of the spirals that mattered, not whether the moment was witnessed by many people. The illumination of the spirals may have signalled the 'opening' of the chamber to other levels of the cosmos above the mound, even as the sliding away of the quartz blocks opened the roof-box to the rays of the sun.

Much debate has, of course, centred on the supposed celestial alignments of Neolithic monuments. Some writers, it is now thought, carried their conclusions concerning multiple alignments too far.[79] But some alignments, like Newgrange (winter solstice) and Stonehenge (summer &/or winter solstice), do seem unassailable. That being so, we should allow that many Neolithic

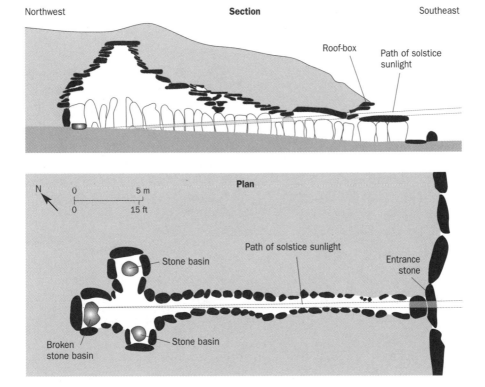

56 *At the winter solstice the rising sun shines through the roof-box and down the passage at Newgrange. At this climactic moment the depths of the tomb were linked to the all-embracing cosmos.*

builders may not have been as technically proficient in their work as modern archaeologists desire for really convincing alignments. Some tombs may well be aligned, but only roughly, to important solar, lunar or astral events. There is also the possibility that some tombs may be aligned on celestial events that today seem of no importance. The amount of observation, calculation and building accuracy necessary to achieve alignments would have been considerable. Yet some Neolithic people did manage it. This is what we may call the 'scientific' component of Neolithic religion. We can draw a key conclusion from these alignments: the dead were linked not only to the underworld but also to events in the sky.

A huge question remains: *Why* did Neolithic people build monuments that – scientifically, rather than just symbolically – related to celestial events? A quick, off-the-cuff response that they 'worshipped' the sun or moon must be treated with scepticism (*pace* some New Agers). As we saw in the case of the Barasana (Chapter 4), the movements of heavenly bodies can be important to people and can feature in myths without any notion of 'worship'. 'Worship' is a culturally constructed concept, not a human universal.

A somewhat more attractive answer to the question is that, with the advent of agriculture, people necessarily became more concerned with the changing seasons. This may be true, but it is not the whole answer. We doubt if 'priests' demonstrated their power by 'controlling' the seasonal movements of the sun at places like Stonehenge and Newgrange, and, consequently, the reason for building the monuments was to demonstrate this power to the gullible. It is unlikely that Neolithic people were so naive as to accept that the round of seasons was entirely in the hands of their ritual specialists. They are more likely to have seen that the cycle of the seasons was inevitable, a simple fact of life. Nor did Neolithic people need massive 'celestial calendars' to tell them when the seasons were about to change. Throughout the world, people in small-scale societies detect the subtle signs of nature and thus know when summer is just around the corner. In fact, the winter solstice does not tell farmers who may observe it anything useful. A bitter January still lies ahead, and any significant seasonal change in the weather cannot be accurately projected from the solstice.

That being so, we think that aligned monuments emphasized *continuity*. There were certain verifiable events in the upper realm of the sky that happened regularly – again and again, year after year. The continuity to which these events pointed concerned not just seasonal time, but also social structure because society dovetailed with the cosmos. In this way, the monuments

15 Stonehenge has become a symbol of ancient British archaeology. Today, the monument attracts worshippers of different kinds. Although much about the site remains unknown, its alignment to the summer solstice is widely accepted.

16 (Right) The Rollright standing stones, Oxfordshire, were the first ancient monument to capture William Stukeley's attention in 1710. Similar stone circles are found in parts of Atlantic Europe.

17 (Below) The entrance to Bryn Celli Ddu burial mound. The ditch surrounding the tomb has been preserved. Originally, there was also a ring of standing stones. An ox burial was discovered in front of the entrance.

18 (Opposite below left) The replica of the decorated standing stone at Bryn Celli Ddu (see also Fig. 39). The original stone stood in the centre of the ring and was buried when the mound was constructed.

19 (Opposite below right) One of the five decorated stones at Barclodiad y Gawres (see also Fig. 41). The spiral in the upper right portion is a motif that also occurs frequently in the Irish megalithic tombs (see Plates 21, 23, 24).

20 (Above) The corbelled roof above the chamber in the Knowth eastern tomb. The corbelling gives the appearance of a passage spiralling upwards. Similar roofs are found in other Irish Neolithic tombs.

21 (Right) The macehead found at the entrance to the right-hand recess of the eastern passage at Knowth. The details of the elaborate carving on the macehead can be seen in Figure 49.

22 (Above) The decorated stone basin in the right-hand alcove of the Knowth eastern passage. The striking pattern engraved within the bowl is shown in Figure 50. Bowls like this one may have contained human remains.

23 (Right) The interlinked triple spiral in the depths of the Newgrange tomb. At the mid-winter solstice the sun shines down the passage and is reflected onto this pattern.

24 The entrance to the Newgrange tomb: the huge, elaborately carved entrance stone dominates the foreground (see also Figure 70). Above the entrance is the roof-box, and the stone that originally closed the entrance rests on the ground to the right. Researchers believe that the brilliant white quartz originally covered the whole face of the mound.

25 (Above) Silbury Hill, the largest Neolithic human-made mound in western Europe, seen from the West Kennet long barrow. The flat summit of the hill rises above the surrounding countryside.

26 (Right) A reconstructed mace found in the Bush Barrow, Wiltshire. It has an elaborate zigzag design made from bone on its handle.

27 (Below) Neolithic polished stone axes. Often made of special stone, axes were traded over extensive areas. They probably had much more than functional value.

28 (Opposite) One of three niches in the interior of the tomb at Fourknocks, Ireland (see also Figure 69). The lintel and other stones in this tomb are decorated with lozenge motifs.

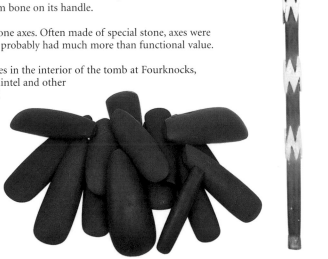

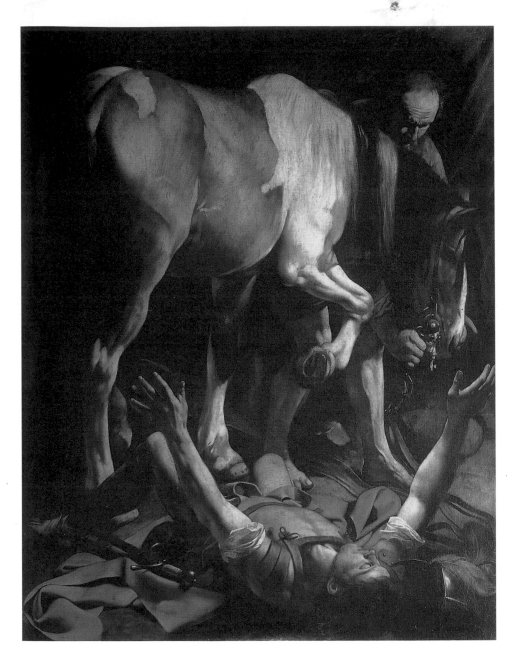

29 Caravaggio's *Conversion of St Paul* (1600–01): 'And suddenly there shined round about him a light from heaven; And he fell to the earth, and heard a voice saying unto him, Saul, Saul, why persecutest thou me? … And he, trembling and astonished, said Lord, what wilt thou have me to do?' (ACTS 9:3–4, 6.)

obliquely underwrote the power of political and religious elites (if there was such a distinction).[80] As far as most Neolithic people were concerned, the monuments were constructed in response to awesome religious beliefs enshrined in myths, rituals and the terrifying visions of seers. They treasured the 'dream', whatever the terror. They also acted – massively – upon the demands of the 'dream'. But 'society' was not a puppet of the 'dream'. We suspect that those in power not only accepted their and other people's different positions in a tiered cosmos that could be reified in monuments. They were at the same time able to see that the whole belief system served their own political purposes. When they elected to build a new monument or to alter an old one, they believed that they knew exactly what the social consequences would be for them: whatever benefits may accrue to the whole community, new structures would enhance their own prestige. In the long run, they may, of course, have been shown to be mistaken.

The roof-box with all these complex, far-reaching social implications is not the only remarkable feature at the entrance to Newgrange.

THE ENTRANCE STONE

The elegantly carved entrance stone (K 1) is especially well known (Pl. 24). It even appeared on an Irish postage stamp in 1983.[81] It is about 3 m (9.8 ft) long and about 2.5 m (8.2 ft) of it stands above ground level. As with the entrance stones at the openings to the two Knowth 1 tombs, it seems that, in Neolithic times, those wishing to enter Newgrange would have had to clamber over the entrance stone. (Raised walkways now render such an approach unnecessary.) Most of the decorated stones in the tombs were carved before they were put in place. This sequence is, for example, shown by the decorated corbels in the chamber: the designs on them extend round into the cairn. The Newgrange entrance stone was, by contrast, carved in situ. The exact positions of the motifs were determined after it had been hauled into place.[82] The careful synthesis of motifs on the stone suggests that the overall pattern must have been sketched out before the pecking work began.

The whole outer surface of the stone is covered with double spirals. The lower and upper spirals are truncated by the edges of the stone. The lower ones do not extend below ground level, though their completion below ground level is implied: they link above and below realms. At the two ends there are diamond-shaped forms that are in some cases (e.g., on the right) created by the spaces between adjacent spirals. That those on the left are not created in this way but are independent motifs suggests that the diamond (lozenge) motif is not merely a spandrel but rather a symbol with its own meaning, even if that meaning was closely related to that of spirals.

There is also a prominent central vertical groove that (we believe highly significantly) becomes part of one of the central spirals: the spiral *unwinds* to become the line, and the line leads to the centre of the spiral. The link between the unwinding spiral motif and the tomb beyond the entrance stone is unmistakable. This line, similar to those on the Knowth entrance stones, seems to be clearly part of a conceptual nexus:

– alignment of the passage to the winter solstice,
– entrance into the tomb,
– the ray of light that, at the solstice, shines all the way down the passage to the chamber, and
– the significance of spirals (to which we come in Chapter 9).

All of which adds up to a complex statement about spiritual travel through the cosmos.

The kerbstone (K 52) on the other side of the mound, directly opposite the entrance to Newgrange, deserves comment (Fig. 57). The elaborate decoration is divided into halves. To the left of a central line, or channel, are a chequerboard, or net, pattern (made up of multiple diamond shapes similar to the five on the entrance stone) and abutting double spirals. The lower row of four lozenges is truncated by ground level so that they look like triangles. To the right, there are nested U-shapes, abutting each other and three oblongs containing holes in the stone.[83] There is no actual, constructed entrance behind K 52, despite the vertical line. Perhaps the builders of Newgrange

57 The 'false' entrance stone (K 52) at Newgrange does not lead to a passage. The bold central line is similar to the line of the 'unwinding' spiral on the tomb's entrance stone (K 1).

envisaged a spiritual passage through the 'back' of the tomb, so that there were in fact two entrances, one real, one imaginary. As we have seen, there are indeed two aligned passages at Knowth. We suggest another possible function for this 'false entrance stone' in a moment. Neolithic concepts and representations of the cosmos were flexible.

HIGH AND LIFTED UP

Thinking of this kind of flexibility and considering the overall structure of corbelled chambers and covering mounds, we wonder if researchers have not focused too tightly on the chambers of tombs like Knowth and Newgrange as the ritual centres of the monuments. We think it probable that the flat tops of some – not necessarily all – mounds were also important, probably complementary, ritual places. As we have said, hills upon hills.[84]

The notion of a raised Neolithic platform is particularly evident at Silbury Hill (Wiltshire), the largest prehistoric mound in Europe. This huge enigmatic 'hill' was constructed in phases over a period of many years, perhaps even a couple of centuries.[85] Begun in 2750 BC, it became the Empire State Building of the Neolithic.[86] Numerous excavations have revealed no sign of any interior structure – no passages, no chambers. It is what it appears to be: a flat-topped hill that is visible from afar and that rises above the horizon from whatever direction it is viewed (Pl. 25). John Barrett, an archaeologist at the University of Sheffield, goes to the heart of the matter and sees the structure in terms of religious practice and the ways that rituals fashion society and, at the same time, are fashioned by society.[87] All the organized labour went towards the literal and figurative raising of a few people: 'a relatively few people were, quite literally, elevated and placed beyond reach, but in full view of those who had given them the means to occupy that position'.[88]

Something similar probably happened in the Bend of the Boyne. But here the mounds are not 'empty': they contain tombs. There was, we argue, a multi-stage *ritual route* that led from the outside world, across the ring of dark water, up the ridge, through the quartz-clad entrance, into the tomb and, still following the line of the solstitial sun, down the passage to the bowls that probably received human remains. And then another leg of the journey into death took the deceased (sometimes via a corbelled cone or through the image-embellished walls of the recesses; Pl. 20) up from the chamber, through the mound (already built on the summit of a ridge) to the sky, the realm above, where the dead, now revivified, joined the cyclic sun and, very likely, a god or gods associated with it in the eternal round of cosmological

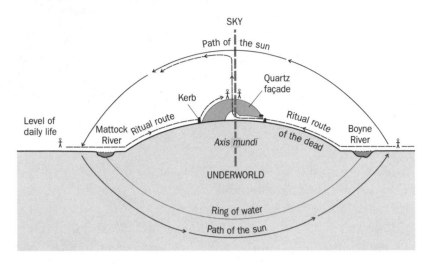

58 The Newgrange tomb is a model of the tiered Neolithic cosmos. At this spot, people's constructions and rituals bridged the tiers of the universe.

life, death and rebirth (Fig. 58). Thus the ritual journey may well have followed the route of the sun across a subterranean river, through the dark underworld and eventually back to eternity in the sky. As in Egyptian belief, the placing of human remains in a tomb was not an endpoint. Rather it marked a stage in the probably hazardous journey that the deceased undertook.

We suggest that the 'false entrance stone' on the opposite side of the mound from the real entrance may have marked the exact point in the kerb from which seers made their way, not down into the 'underground' tomb, but up to the summit of the mound. The vertical groove in the centre of the stone thus pointed to the *axis mundi*, as did the one on the entrance stone, but to an upper section of it that led to the sky realm. The need to climb over entrance or kerbstones, to us an undignified procedure, probably emphasized the demarcatory function of the stones: crossing them was for the few, not for society at large; and the effort required to clamber over the stones may have dramatized the danger inherent in cosmological transition, whether into the depths or to the sky-neighbouring summit. As people were obliged to scramble over entrance stones to enter the passages, so too some special seers may have clambered over the kerb to reach the place nearest to the sky, which was, after all, indubitably the focus of the alignment of the Newgrange passage. The integrity of the kerb may simply have emphasized the sanctity of the summit. Journeys through the cosmos were not for the faint-hearted.

These thoughts recall the Maya pyramidal temples that enabled what Linda Schele and David Freidel call the king's 'ecstatic performance' and journey into the sacred world to be enacted in the public space on top of the pyramid so that the full community could witness and affirm the event.[89] Pakal, a king of Palenque in Mexico, ensured that his specially built funerary pyramid would rise from the 'cave' of his sarcophagus to the temple on top of the mound (Figs 59, 60). Deep under the pyramid, Pakal recorded the deaths of his ancestral kings, and his son later extended the list back to the founders of the dynasty: continuity with the dead was important.[90] Parallels with Neolithic passage tombs are uncanny.

Upper temple with double galleries and glyphic panels

Vaulted stair

Entry door

59, 60 The Maya Temple of Inscriptions at Palenque – the funerary pyramid of king Pakal – links the underworld to the sky. This impressive structure (section diagram above) actualizes the cosmos in a way that is comparable with the Newgrange tomb (see Fig. 58).

The Bend of the Boyne tombs were thus not solely underground affairs. More comprehensively, they referred to the *whole* cosmos, both below and above the level on which people lived.[91] And in doing so, they raised up and emphasized the bravery and spiritual supremacy of the elite who, in the first place, had organized the building of the structure.

Processions

There is one further feature at the Newgrange end of the Bend of the Boyne that requires comment and that concerns the same cosmological and social issues as those raised by ritual platforms. It is a cursus about 100 m (328.1 ft) east of the Newgrange mound.[92] Today it is barely visible on the ground. Aerial photographs nevertheless show that it extends from the Mattock valley, to the north of the Bend of the Boyne, to just over the crest of the Newgrange ridge, and there ends in a transverse bank that seems to round it off. The side banks of the cursus, now eroded away, were about 20 m (65.6 ft) apart. It was at least 100 m (328.1 ft) long – not a great distance compared with similar monuments in England. The Stonehenge greater cursus is just short of 3 km (1.9 miles); the Dorset cursus is 10 km (6.2 miles) long. As many as thirty such monuments are known in southern England.[93] The multiple stone alignments in Brittany, such as those at Carnac (Fig. 61), should probably be grouped with cursuses as monuments of procession across the landscape.

There is now some doubt as to the age of these earth monuments. The general consensus seems to be that people constructed them after the megalithic tombs, rather than before, but this view may change. There is a growing suspicion among some researchers that henge earthworks are later than the features they sometimes enclose. They may have limited access to older monuments or even have brought their use to an end.[94]

Still, the Newgrange cursus may be younger than the tomb; it seems to have been built at more or less the same time as the four henges in the lower part of the Bend. We suggest that the lower slopes of the ridge close to the 'moat' of the Boyne (or even on the other side of the river) had long been gathering places for people whose status did not permit them to approach the glistening, quartz-protected mound on the hill. Their humble presence near the river did not, at that time, merit any structures. The interwoven social and consciousness contracts kept the community at large away from the summit of political power and intense religious experience. Cosmologically, they were close to the 'moat'; members of the upper hierarchy were close to the sky.

61 *Long lines of standing stones at Le Ménec, Carnac (Brittany). This is one of the most impressive Neolithic sites in France. The lines of stones probably guided religious processions.*

When the tomb was finally closed, there was a shift in, perhaps a slight democratization of, religion, and henges were constructed on the lower land that had long been a gathering place. As the top of the ridge had probably been a 'sacred' place before the tombs were built, so, too, was the lower land nearer to the river socially and religiously significant before the henges were constructed. When these changes took place, the great tomb did not 'disappear'. There was, more complexly, an intensification of land demarcation within the Bend that gave formal expression to and, at the same time, controlled developing social and religious distinctions.

The cursus, then, may have been an approach to one or more of these post-Newgrange monuments, though there is some distance between its end and the henge most directly in line with it.[95] If this was the case, pilgrims or 'priests' would have started their course in the valley to the north of the Newgrange ridge, come up the slope to the top and from there been able to see not only the massive passage tomb (by this time closed) on their right but also the henges below them and nearer to the embracing river. For those waiting below, this processing group would have been silhouetted against the sky and close to the already ancient Newgrange mound. Another possibility is that the cursus was used in the opposite direction. People who had completed their ritual activities at the cluster of Newgrange monuments may have proceeded down the cursus, away to the north and out of the Bend of the Boyne, perhaps via the Monknewton ritual pond. Both uses were, of course, simultaneously possible.

It seems highly likely that monuments of this kind were used for processions across the landscape. A moment ago we used the word 'pilgrim'. Religious processions or journeys are globally ubiquitous. A common theme in pilgrimages is that the people who undertake them are, at the end, different from what they were at the beginning – as pilgrims to Santiago de Compostela aver.[96] Although some writers emphasize the sense of 'communitas' created by pilgrimages, others have pointed out that pilgrimages are sometimes, perhaps always, implicated in religious contestation.[97] Progress across the land is homologous with progress through spiritual states; the movement thus confronts social distinctions.

Processions also imply social order. As Barrett points out, it is necessary for people to move through built (or otherwise demarcated) spaces for social distinctions to operate, to become visible. He suggests that those who led processions, perhaps eventually to occupy the summits of mounds, 'held the focus of the many. That elite did not simply initiate the building of Avebury or Stonehenge but was, instead, created out of the realization of these projects'.[98] At the terminus of a procession groups of people are marked off. At Knowth, Newgrange and other tombs, a few crossed the image-embellished kerb and entered the passage; perhaps some stopped in the passage, alerted by specially placed imagery or other features; a few went on in to the actual chamber, while others stood on the flat summit of the mound. Outside the tombs, especially those that have forecourts, there were probably other distinctions marked off by distance from the centre of the tomb.[99] Many researchers recognize this social function of Neolithic monuments. We add that control of altered states of consciousness and parallels with the structure of the cosmos went hand in hand with those distinctions. Cosmos and consciousness underwrote social discrimination. Power resided in control of consciousness and transition through the cosmos, and was epitomized by megalithic monuments.

The deep substance of religion

This chapter has been an overview of just two Irish megalithic passage tombs, albeit the most spectacular pair. We have tried to show how Neolithic consciousness and social contracts came together within the Bend of the Boyne to produce an astounding landscape. Those contracts and their interactions differ from the ones we encountered in the Near East; yet, if we look below the surfaces of the two regions, we can detect similar neurologically generated building-blocks.

We have by no means exhausted the topic. Two outstanding issues remain to be discussed. They are, first, the nature of the substance we call 'stone', which west European Neolithic people sometimes thought worthy of transport over considerable distances and of special treatment. Thereafter, we need to consider in closer detail the enigmatic motifs that Neolithic people dredged up from their consciousness and carved into their megalithic monuments: images were inseparable from stone. It is here that we shall find a final synthesis of the principal ideas we have been developing.

CHAPTER 9

Religion de Profundis

Our penultimate chapter stands back from the specifics of selected sites and examines components of west European Neolithic religion that are at one and the same time abstract and concrete. Especially, it takes us back to the closely interwoven consciousness and social contracts of that time and also to universal ways of cosmological thinking that emerge from a unity of the two kinds of contracts. In doing so, this chapter highlights the neuropsychological foundation that underlay – and was so differently expressed in – both Near Eastern and west European Neolithic life.

The trope of 'depth' is ubiquitous in Westerners' and, indeed, other people's thought. It is one of the metaphors we all live by.[1] Myths are said to have deep meanings. In the Hellenic world, myths were said to have a *hypnoia*, an 'underthought'.[2] Myths themselves are often built on notions of symbolic depth. For instance, we are told that, after Gilgamesh's death, 'In nether-earth the darkness will show him a light.'[3] Here the vertical up : down dimension parallels, as it frequently does, the light : darkness opposition. We see this parallel again in the *Inferno*. Moving through circles and hemispheres, Dante and Virgil ascend from the depths of horror until they see 'a circular opening in the cave: Thence issuing we again beheld the stars.'[4] Then, too, Milton's very human Satan, tormented by doubt as to his destructive enterprise, sees 'in the lowest deep a lower deep' threatening to devour him.[5] Depth and sleep constitute another parallel: Abou Ben Adhem awoke from 'a deep dream of peace' to behold a vision.[6] Coleridge 'continued for about three hours in profound sleep, at least to the external senses' before his 'vivid confidence … rose up before him as *things*' (his emphasis).[7] As Gerard Manley Hopkins put it:

> O the mind, mind has mountains; cliffs of fall
> Frightful, sheer, no-man-fathomed.[8]

Why is this 'no-man-fathomed' trope so ubiquitous? Because, we suggest, it derives from human consciousness and the sense of 'sinking away', of 'falling', into sleep and hence mysterious realms where – sometimes – we feel we can grasp truths, but all too often we struggle to make sense of it all, 'whatever the terror' – or perhaps *because* of the terror. That is why the notion of depth permeated Neolithic thought even as it does our own. Their brains functioned in the same ways as ours do.

From this foundation, we explore all-embracing Neolithic versions of the trope by considering depth in two senses: first, the depth of the earth beneath us, and, then, the depth of our own minds, in Coleridge's phrase, the 'profound sleep' in which a 'vivid confidence' can seem a *thing* (Chapter 1). Because of the way in which human consciousness functions it is difficult to keep these two senses separate: the one invades the other with serious emotional consequences. Our two examples are related keys to understanding some of the 'profundities' of Neolithic thought. Though at first glance so different, *stone* and *images* were both associated with these two senses of depth, cosmological and mental: stone axes are, in some instances, 'buried' in the 'depths' of carved tomb imagery. And the carved imagery of the tombs is inseparable from its support – stone.

'Isolation and separation'

In Norfolk, England, there is a Neolithic site known as Grimes Graves. Over 433 craters are scattered over an area of some 7.6 ha (18.8 acres). More probably await discovery. Each hollow represents the top of a buried shaft. Between 1868 and 1870, after decades of fanciful explanations, a certain Canon Greenwell correctly surmised that the ancient 12-m (39.4-ft) shafts cut down into the chalk were made for the purpose of extracting good quality flint. At about the same time, Colonel Augustus Lane Fox advanced a similar explanation for the Cissbury shafts, Sussex.[9]

When more modern archaeologists took over the study of these sites, they found that they dated to between 3000 and 2200 BC.[10] Older dates have been obtained from other mining sites, such as Blackpatch and Harrow Hill (both in Sussex). They show that flint mining in southern England began about 4000 BC.

The flint in these ancient mines is found in seams. Flint from the upper two layers, known as topstone and wallstone, is of poorer quality than the deeper floorstone layer, and it was this deep seam that Neolithic miners mostly exploited by digging side galleries that extended for about 9 m (29.5 ft) from the shaft. Some of these galleries connected up with those from other shafts. Finds in the shafts and galleries suggest that red deer antlers were the principal mining tool.

For some decades, archaeologists tended to place sites like Grimes Graves and Cissbury in the same category as modern-day mines. They knew that flint was an important trade item during the Neolithic and assumed that the mines were utilitarian, without the luxury of any symbolism or 'meaning'. But the British Neolithic was a vastly different place from the land from which so many 19th-century British miners and entrepreneurs emigrated to make their fortunes in the colonies. In Neolithic western Europe, everything was multi-dimensional.[11]

Recognizing the complexity of Neolithic thought, Miles Russell of Bournemouth University notes that incised patterns are known in some of the mines. For instance, at Harrow Hill, excavators discovered a 'chessboard design' incised into the entrance to a side gallery (Fig. 62).[12] Elsewhere, series of dots, lines and cup-shaped marks have been found. In one of the Church Hill shafts (also in Sussex) circular cuts were identified above three of the five side galleries. Writers have advanced various prosaic explanations for these marks, but Russell points out that similar pieces of engraved stone have been found in the ditches of enclosure sites and at the entrances to passageways at the rich Skara Brae Neolithic site in the Orkney Islands off the north coast of Scotland. None of these is an extraction site. Russell concludes that the 'carvings may perhaps indicate a form of social, tribal or community identifier'.[13]

62 Linear carvings found deep underground in a gallery in the Neolithic Harrow Hill flint mine. It seems unlikely that this complex grid pattern was mere doodling (see also Fig. 64).

Other finds in flint-mining shafts include animal and human bones. In one case the remains of an adult and two juveniles were found. With them were a cattle skull and a deer antler pick.[14] Noting that the siting of Neolithic flint mines probably related to 'spiritual, tribal or "ancestral" ways', Russell comments:

As faunal remains appear to occur in significant numbers in shaft fill when human remains are present, it is possible that there was originally a link between the two types of deposit … though the desire to generate good quality stone certainly provided one of the reasons for cutting shafts, the range of nonfunctional finds and features suggests that ceremonial activity was just as important … Vertical shafts cannot be treated as simple industrial features in the same way that one may today view a modern coal, tin or gold mine.[15]

We agree and add that, given a tiered cosmos, it seems highly likely that Neolithic people would have thought that flint mines delved into a nether realm. The trope of depth with all its connotations inevitably takes over. Russell puts his finger on an important corollary. He says that a sense of 'dislocation' from normal society would have been created by climbing down into a shaft:

Even today, once in the deep galleries of Neolithic shafts, the sense of isolation and separation from the 'real world' is immense. Galleries are dark, damp and cold. Anyone today who manages to crawl to the end of a gallery at Grimes Graves will appreciate just how alien their environment suddenly becomes. It is the Neolithic equivalent of a sensory deprivation tank (a similar sense having already been noted for the stone chambers of structured mounds). There are no familiar noises, what sounds there are being muffled and distorted. One cannot feel the sun, wind or rain on one's face. There are no bright colours. There is often no real sense of day or night … it is possible that the act of descending into shafts and the extraction of flint in the Neolithic formed a rite of passage [original parenthesis].[16]

Whether Russell is correct about a rite of passage we do not know. But we feel sure that he has rightly identified the nature of those shafts: they are indeed like the chambers of passage tombs and may well have induced a shift of consciousness in those who remained long enough in those cramped conditions. For Neolithic people they were experientially in another level of the cosmos. Gabriel Cooney sums up this position: 'Extracting stone from the earth can be seen, then, as providing a contact with the spirit or ancestral world.'[17] In other words, we have depth in both senses of the trope.

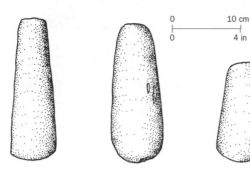

63 *Polished Neolithic stone axes (see also Pl. 27). Axes like these, which were traded over long distances, were probably symbols of power and authority and, at the same time, situated that power in a spiritual underworld.*

In the other cosmological direction – upwards – it is worth noting that axe 'factories' are often situated in spectacular upland locations. In the case of the largest group, those in Cumbria, there is evidence that people ignored the readily accessible rock and preferred to exploit exposed, high and dangerous locations. Indeed, there are axe-production sites within a few metres of Scafell Pike, the highest point in England. In these precipitous locations, on narrow ledges, Neolithic people opened out fissures, thus creating 'a series of shallow caves or adits'.[18] Neolithic people seem to have been concerned with the extremities of the *axis mundi*.

If flint came from a place of 'isolation and separation', did it carry its special 'spiritual' qualities over into the world of daily life? Did traded flint have more than economic significance? Did other kinds of stone, also wrested from the earth, have innate powerful qualities?

Petrological analysis has greatly assisted research into these questions.[19] It is now possible to determine with a good degree of accuracy the points of origin of stone axes (Pl. 27; Fig. 63). But beyond such hi-tech methods, certain kinds of stone are identifiable simply by their colour and texture. Axes that Neolithic people exchanged, often over considerable distances, were not always made of the best kind of stone for practical purposes: colour and exotic origin seem to have been important.[20] These special axes were easily distinguished from axes made of local stone. People wanted objects that clearly came from distant places and that were associated with the realm beneath their feet.

One of these special stones is porcellanite. Although there are only a few sources in Ireland (in the extreme northeast), over half of the known Irish axes were made from it.[21] Moreover, Irish porcellanite axes crop up throughout Britain. This kind of distribution – it also applies to distinctive types of pottery – suggests widespread contacts during Neolithic times. There is, for instance, no doubt that Neolithic exchange took place across the Irish Sea, between northern Ireland and Scotland, and, a little farther south, between Ireland, the Isle of Man and Wales. Neolithic people were not as parochial as we may at first think. Some researchers have tried to discover the boundaries of trade-connected areas, but it seems better to think of them as overlapping networks with important nodes. Boundaries may not have been a prominent part of Neolithic thinking. The concept of territorial, political boundaries may have been completely foreign to Neolithic ideas about geography: it was ritual *locations* that mattered.

Throughout western Europe, there were nodes, or centres, of Neolithic activity, places where a number of monuments and other structures formed a pattern on the landscape. Probably, people processed through them and thereby contacted spirit beings, ancestors and non-material tiers of the cosmos. Within these centres, there were exotic elements: kinds of stone, axes, pottery and, very possibly, recognizably imported designs engraved on monuments. In books on the subject, wider Neolithic networks are depicted on maps of western Europe with, often, arrows indicating exchange routes. Although it is unavoidable, we must remember that this way of representing Neolithic activity is embedded in Western concepts of space and the conventions of representing space by means of maps, lines (boundaries) and arrows. If Neolithic people themselves had no concepts of that kind, how, then, did they comprehend local centres studded with exotic elements? How did they, for instance, picture the source of the flint macehead found at Knowth? Or the quartz on the façade of Newgrange? Or, for that matter, the source of the famous bluestones at Stonehenge that came all the way from Wales?

To answer those questions we return to the multiple realms, or dimensions, that are integral to the electro-chemical functioning of the human brain. We believe it likely that Neolithic people thought of those realms as 'places' in their cosmos, probably vaguely situated.[22] The distinction between 'places' whence axeheads came and 'realms' where ancestors existed was probably at best poorly developed, more probably non-existent. The realm of ancestors was therefore paralleled by the realm-place from which axes came. If Neolithic people were asked to draw a diagram of their cosmos (assuming they knew what the question meant), they would probably have indicated the place where they lived, the places from which axes and other exotic items came, and the places where supernaturals lived *all by the same conventions*.

This notion of geographic and spiritual intermeshing partially explains why spirals are engraved on the Knowth macehead. The object came from a spirit realm – possibly the one where ancestors and mythic beings lived – that was reached via a vortex or passage tomb. (We return to the question of spirals in a moment.) Here we have an answer to the problem of why possession of exotic items, such as the spiralled macehead and porcellanite or polished flint axes, bestowed power, political *and* spiritual; indeed, why political power was really indistinguishable from spiritual power. What are to modern Westerners distinct kinds of power were to Neolithic people one and the same: a status, or mechanism of influence, rooted in their belief in realms/places, a belief that was, in turn, informed by the functioning of their brains.

This view of a geographic, yet multi-dimensional, world provides one of the ways in which we can begin to build up an integrated picture of life and thought in the Neolithic, not only in western Europe but in the Near East as well. It was a blurring of any distinction between transcendence and immanence that structured people's lives and decision-making. Rational decision-making, as we argued in our discussion of the domestication of the aurochs, was not set aside from ritual and beliefs in the supernatural.

Stealing light from the dawn

We have reserved the significance of quartz for special discussion because it was imported in such vast quantities to embellish the Newgrange façade and, as we saw in the previous chapter, was associated with many other Neolithic tombs as well. Like flint, it was 'of the earth'.[23]

Writers have shown that the importance of quartz continued after the end of the Neolithic[24] and that, throughout that long period, it seems to have been associated with cosmology. The early Christian Church, Timothy Darvill argues, consciously took over the symbolic use of quartz, often scattered on graves, to provide continuity with the pagan past.[25] He suggests that quartz, even as far back as the Neolithic, may have symbolized the soul; for the living, quartz may have represented 'the gateway to other dimensions through which they negotiate with the spirit world'. Further, water and the moon may have been linked to the white stone.[26] But, as Chris Scarre rightly points out, colour is not the only property of a kind of stone.[27] We note some others in a moment. Our principal point now is to take up Darvill's observation about a 'gateway to other dimensions' and to see how quartz fits into the kind of cosmology and associated consciousness and social contracts that we have described. An understanding of the full spectrum of human consciousness opens up a way to further understandings of the symbolic role of quartz.

Throughout the world, quartz crystals and similar sorts of stone are associated with spiritual beliefs. As Piers Vitebsky puts it, 'Crystals are used by
shamans from America to Borneo.'[28] The importance of quartz in societies
that accord altered states of consciousness a central position is an empirical
observation we support now by giving examples from three widely separated
regions of the globe: Australia, South America and North America.

In his book *Aboriginal Men of High Degree*, first published in 1945, the Australian anthropologist Peter Elkin describes people 'of high degree' whom he
calls 'doctors' or 'medicine men'. He reports that, in many parts of Australia,
crystals play a prominent role in beliefs about these practitioners. Often,
they carry quartz crystals around with them.[29] Then, too, Elkin reports that
Wiradjeri shamans spoke of quartz as being solidified 'sacred powerful water',
which was sprinkled on neophytes. 'The water spread all over the postulant
and was completely absorbed. Then feathers emerged from the latter's arms,
which grew into wings in the course of two days'.[30] Quartz brought about a
transformation that facilitated transcosmological flight.

Ronald Rose tells us more and gives a dramatic description of two young
Australian Aboriginal men being initiated into the mysteries of, as they are
also known, 'clever men'. At a moment of great emotion, a vision of an old
man showed them 'a large, bright crystal that stole the light from the dawn
and dazzled their eyes'.[31] Soon the boys felt strange things moving on their
bodies, 'things that felt like snakes and spiders ... He thought he felt the sharp
stab of fangs in his leg and it went numb'.[32] The sensations of insects or small
animals crawling on or under the skin (known as 'formication'[33]) and of sharp
pricking are common in altered states of consciousness.[34]

One of the boys began to tremble, perspire and become tense; he failed the
test and was led away. Then the other sank into 'a state of repose that was
almost sleep'. In this state the boy saw strange and wonderful things. Some of
the doctors seemed to walk into eucalyptus trees; they melted into the trees
and a moment later appeared on the other side.[35] The doctors then 'produced
from within themselves great numbers of gleaming quartz crystals ... Each
old doctor formed a small pile of crystals beside him. These, too, were part of
his power, symbols of the sacred water that each had acquired during his making as a clever-man.'[36] The Wiradjeri believe that a supernatural being known
as Baiame 'sings a piece of quartz crystal into their foreheads so that they will
have X-ray vision'.[37] Again, along with this accomplishment comes an ability to
'fly'. Quartz comes from the depths of the earth to catch the light that comes
from above. Quartz mediates the tiers of the cosmos, as does flight.

Working in Arnhem Land (northwest Australia), Rhys Jones and Neville White found that the power believed to be inherent in shiny stone can be released as stone is flaked in the making of tools.[38] The Yolngu liken this quality to shining animal fat and believe that stone points made from quartzite have special killing power. The quarry where the special stone was obtained and trade of artefacts made from it were controlled by a designated clan. We suspect that Jones and White's next remark also applied to the Wicklow Mountains (see Fig. 54) whence the Newgrange quartz came: 'Visits to the site were both utilitarian industrial ones to obtain armatures for weapons, and there were also mystical experiences to reunite the bonds between the place, the stone and its role in a broader religious system'.[39] This sort of trade, Jones and White argue, 'was part of a higher level integration of society, articulated through a web of reciprocal obligations and responsibilities in the religious sphere'.[40] Later, also in Arnhem Land, Paul Taçon found a widespread link between certain stone tools and 'Ancestral power': 'quartzite and quartz tools at times shimmer with bright reflected light or are almost iridescent'. This 'most important quality … [is] associated with both life and Ancestral beings.'[41]

Comparable reports come from North America where David Whitley and four colleagues discovered the importance of quartz crystal at a Mojave Desert site known as Sally's Rock Shelter.[42] Here, they found that people had taken at least six quartz cobbles and thrust them into cracks in the rock; other pieces of quartz had been worked into artefacts or were resulting debris. No quartz crystals, veins or outcrops are present at the site or in its immediate vicinity: the quartz had been carried to the site. In the shelter itself is a panel of rock engravings that Whitley and colleagues interpret as being derived from visions. Drawing on Numic ethnography, they show that rock art in that region was made by shamans as part of their vision quests. The images served a number of functions: they were instrumental in the acquisition of power and, at the same time, marked transitional phases of life.

Abundant ethnography also shows that offerings of various kinds were left at such sites, some being thrust into cracks that were considered portals to the supernatural realm where spirits resided.[43] Numic shamans also used quartz as part of their paraphernalia for weather control.[44] Indeed, shamanistic use of quartz crystals was widespread in North America, and Whitley and his colleagues cite so much ethnography to support this conclusion that it cannot be gainsaid; their evidence is overwhelming.[45]

In South America, Geraldo Reichel-Dolmatoff found that a Desana *payé*, or shaman, wears 'a polished cylinder of white or yellowish quartz' suspended from his neck and carries smaller pieces in his purse.[46] For the Desana, hexagonal crystals provide a model of the cosmos that, by extension, structures a wide range of activities and beliefs.[47] Crystals also symbolize 'sacred space' wherein 'all essential transformations are thought to take place'.[48] The way in which such stones reflect and refract light is, for the Desana, 'an image of dynamic change'.[49] The notion of transformation from one state to another is echoed in the Desana custom of burying their dead in a canoe that has been cut in half, one half serving as a lid; the space thus created is, like a quartz crystal, hexagonal.[50]

More specifically, quartz is associated with lightning and semen, especially the semen of the Sun.[51] A Desana shaman can throw lightning in the form of a quartz crystal at people.[52] Small pieces of quartz are considered pathogenic if they penetrate one's body. A shaman is believed to cause illness by sending such splinters into a person and to cure the sick by sucking the quartz out. Having removed a pathogenic quartz fragment, he shows it to the person he has healed.[53]

Reichel-Dolmatoff's research provides a pivotal hint as to why there is such a widespread association between quartz and spiritual states.[54] He draws on neuropsychological studies of altered consciousness. The Desana say that they see bright geometric forms (entoptic phenomena) in altered states of consciousness induced by the hallucinogenic vine *yajé*. Some of these percepts are, like crystals, angular and hexagonal, and they glisten and appear to shine with their own light. It is easy to see how people can associate entoptic phenomena with crystals. Reichel-Dolmatoff also points out that 'Colombian shamans will fix their sight on the multicoloured reflections of a rock crystal to induce certain psychic states'.[55] Crystals are not only associated with entoptic phenomena: they can also be used to induce altered states of consciousness.

In all these accounts from Australia, North America and South America, we can see a key commonality: altered states of consciousness constitute a foundation for religious experience, and those states are frequently associated with quartz and shiny crystals. We ask: *Why* is quartz believed to have these properties? Two answers come to mind.

First, we suggest that it may be a visual parallel between glistening, reflecting eyes and shiny crystals that often leads people to associate crystals with visionary experience. Sight and visions are both intimately associated with light. Secondly, Whitley and his colleagues point out that, when rubbed together, quartz rocks 'generate a bright, lightning-like flash of light' known as triboluminescence.[56] (It is worth noting that a significant proportion of the Newgrange quartz façade had been modified.[57]) As long ago as 1880, Pierre and Jacques Curie discovered that certain crystals, including quartz, produce electrical voltage known as piezoelectricity ('pressure electricity'). There are thus scientific grounds for accepting that quartz possesses rather unusual properties.

Clearly, it was some expression of those properties that led to the embellishment of the Newgrange façade with quartz. We suggest a symbolic system that included: light, the sun and supernatural power. Raised from the depths of the earth, quartz greeted each dawn and drew power from the sun. Then, in front of the roof-box, two blocks of quartz guarded the passage of light into the tomb. They could, on appropriate occasions, be moved by those who had the authority to do so to allow light to reach the depths of the tomb and human remains.

For the people who built and used Newgrange, the light that the façade caught at dawn and that, at the winter solstice, shone down the passage to the dead was locked up in quartz. And that quartz had to be transported from the Wicklow Mountains, some 60 km (37.3 miles) away. The influence of Newgrange was far more than local.

Motifs of the mind

Another source of information on Neolithic geographic and spiritual networks is the carvings on the tombs.[58] We have seen, for example, that Barclodiad y Gawres in Anglesey has motifs that have affinities with art in the Bend of the Boyne. Further, motifs in Newgrange and Knowth seem to point to Neolithic art in Brittany.[59] Another persuasive link in motifs is between Newgrange and Knowth and the distant tomb of Maes Howe in Orkney.[60]

The exchange of stone axes is easily understandable: people could hold them, display them and, in the end, place them in graves or other ritual places so that they could return to the nether sphere whence they came.[61] Axes surely had some reference to both political power and the nether realms. Can the same be said of the motifs? They are more elusive and seem to function more abstractly. Were they 'abstract' (that is, they did not represent things in the material world but rather concepts and beliefs) and so open to wider, more diverse interpretations by the Neolithic people who made and saw them? What, we may ask, did they mean, even in the most general terms?

Neolithic art and its patchy scatter across western Europe is, whether we know its meanings or not, one of the glories of the period – and one of the toughest nuts that researchers have to crack.[62] Axes, we can understand without any trouble, came from a lower level of the tiered cosmos. Where did the motifs come from? If it can be shown that some Neolithic motifs derived from geometric entoptic phenomena, can those motifs be labelled 'abstract'? Probably not. Then we need to ask: Was their origin cosmologically located in Neolithic thought? If we can answer some of these questions, even partially, we shall gain significant insight into Neolithic religion in all three of its dimensions – experience, belief and practice. To achieve that insight, we return to aspects of the consciousness contract.

In the mid-1970s, Joseph Eichmeier and Oskar Höfer, two researchers at the Technical University, Munich, argued that the 'abstract' motifs of megalithic art (and many other arts) derived from the hard-wired geometric mental imagery[63] that we have called 'entoptic phenomena' and that we located in the first stage of our neuropsychological model of shifting human consciousness. Their survey of a wide range of art, however, gave an impression of superficiality: it seemed that almost any geometric motif could be declared entoptic, and most readers were unimpressed. After the 1988 publication of the neuropsychological model and its relevance to Upper Palaeolithic cave and mobile art,[64] Richard Bradley used it to highlight a persuasive set of formal correspondences between entoptic phenomena and megalithic art motifs.[65] Then, following Bradley, Mark Patton developed a diachronic perspective with particular reference to the megalithic monuments of southern Brittany.[66]

In 1993, one of us explored the application of the neuropsychological model to Neolithic art.[67] That article took up a point that we have made more fully in this book: the spectrum of human consciousness can be a site of struggle. People who manage to control access to the 'deep' end of the spectrum and who define the different values to be placed on segments of that spectrum are in a powerful position. They are able to make their constructed, historically situated definitions and controls appear natural and immutable. A potential part of this strategy is to accord specific entoptic phenomena meanings and thereby to focus on them to the (comparative) exclusion of others. This, we saw, is what happens among the South American Tukano (Chapter 2).

As an introduction to our present argument about the role of mental imagery in megalithic art we emphasize a number of preliminary points that

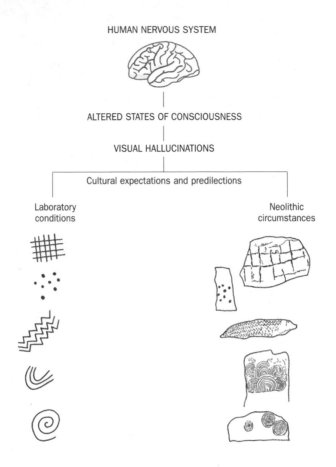

64 *Certain distinctive motifs are complexly derived from the structure and function of the human brain. This diagram shows that human beings are not unthinking photocopiers. Cultural expectations control what people make of their hallucinations.*

are summarized in Figure 64. In altered states of consciousness, the human nervous system generates geometric visual percepts. But human beings are not insensate photocopying machines. We again emphasize that there is nothing deterministic about the neuropsychological model. It simply presents a *potential* source of mental imagery in a way that uncovers the progression of that imagery. People's cultural environment leads them to select percepts from a wide range and then standardize them, also in culturally specific ways, thus creating what some writers call 'styles'. This means that the entoptic forms we see illustrated in neuropsychological publications and that derive from laboratory research are standardized by Western volunteers who are familiar with geometry and are adept at using a pencil on a piece of paper in formal, neat ways. They work in unemotional, clinical conditions, whereas Neolithic people exploited the imagery of altered states in highly charged emotional circumstances, as is the case among many shamanistic societies. We should therefore not expect people in other cultures, such as the Neolithic, to produce motifs in their depictions of entoptic phenomena that are *identical* with laboratory subjects' drawings. Yet, as Figure 64 shows, fundamental forms are recognizable.

After publication of this work,[68] some archaeologists felt that the lookalike argument was, by itself, insufficient. It was at this point that Jeremy Dronfield, then a Cambridge Ph.D. student, undertook an important study.[69] When he published key parts of his work in the *Cambridge Archaeological Journal*, the editor invited comments from a range of researchers. Looking back now at that 1996 debate, we find it instructive to examine the different tones and stances that the commentators adopted. One was extremely sceptical, stating his views in a forthright, uncompromising manner. Others were much more receptive and asked for clarifications – which Dronfield was able to supply in his response. Yet, although a leading and perceptive researcher like Julian Thomas could write that Dronfield's argument that Neolithic people used mind-altering techniques to 'gain access to other-worldly dimensions' was 'an attractive hypothesis', curiously few researchers have followed up the potential that neuropsychology holds for understanding those mental states.

Tightening up an argument

Dronfield's starting point was to establish 'highly specified diagnostic shapes and patterns' that could be indicators of the association of an art with altered states of consciousness. The categories of shapes that he used are:
 – general undiagnostic,
 – endogenous diagnostic,
 – non-endogenous diagnostic.

The purpose of his 'general undiagnostic' category of motifs was to investigate the extent of commonality in all abstract arts, and thus to address the worry that some researchers rightly have about the possibility of any geometric form being declared entoptic. His term 'endogenous' refers to what we call 'entoptic', that is, elements that are wired into the human nervous system. The diagnostic shapes he identified were meanders, fortification (zigzag arcs, as in migraine scotoma), arc-spirals, filigrees, arcs, spirals and small circular, scattered U-shapes. He derived these forms principally from neuropsycho-logical laboratory research in which people after an altered state were asked to draw their mental percepts, either during or after the altered state.

Dronfield then investigated the distribution of these diagnostic shapes in two different types of art:

- Category S arts are known to be associated with various ways of altering human consciousness; we know that the artists represented subjective visual phenomena. The arts used were: laboratory experimental draw-ings; Tukano (South America), Huichol (Central America) and Chumash (California).
- Category N arts are known to have no connection with such practices. The arts used were: Roman, Nubian, Benin and Chilkat.

The results of his analysis showed that his selected range of motifs (spirals, zigzags, meanders and so forth) is indeed diagnostic of whether an art is asso-ciated with altered states of consciousness or not – if they are present to a statistically verifiable degree. He found that they are common in Category S and uncommon in Category N arts.

Having thus gained confidence in the diagnostic potential of the set of motifs, Dronfield saw that the next step was to test them against Irish passage-tomb art. Into which category, S or N, would megalithic art fall? Dronfield worked with five groups of passage tombs, omitting those where we cannot be sure that we have a full (or virtually full) range of motifs preserved. The tombs he selected were: Knockmany and Sess Kilgreen, Loughcrew, and the ones in the Bend of the Boyne that we have discussed, Newgrange, Knowth and Dowth. The match he found was persuasive. The motifs are common in the tombs – as they are in Category S arts. But he was still not satisfied. So he went on to test his results statistically. Finally, citing his statistical tests, he was able to conclude:

we can say – with approximately 80% confidence – that Irish passage-tomb art is *funda-mentally* similar to (as opposed to merely resembling) arts derived from endogenous subjective vision and fundamentally dissimilar to arts not so derived. Therefore, we can confidently say that Irish passage-tomb art was itself derived from endogenous visual phenomena.

Thus, the basic conclusions already reached by Bradley (1989) and Lewis-Williams & Dowson (1993) are vindicated (at least so far as Ireland is concerned), by using a more substantive and reliable analytical process … Irish passage-tomb art was apparently derived from endogenous visions associated with some form of mind-altering practice [original emphasis].[70]

The importance of this conclusion can hardly be overestimated. The art shows that Irish Neolithic religion indeed entailed causing the level of consciousness to slide towards the introverted end of the spectrum, and then by placing meaning and value on selected mental percepts perceived in those states. Neolithic people carved those meaningful percepts on tombs, in the process standardizing them. Careful, statistically tested research thus supports the overall theme of this book, at least in Ireland: a consciousness contract lay at the heart of Neolithic people's religion and view of the cosmos.[71]

More was to come. Dronfield went on to use statistical techniques to study the distribution of motifs within tombs. In terms of the concepts we have been using, we can say that, because various motifs were derived from the human nervous system and carved on to monuments, they probably constituted a *system* of symbols. In other words, each motif had a meaning or meanings, and those meanings may well have governed where motifs were placed in relation to other motifs and in relation to the significance of various parts of the tombs.

Most obviously, Dronfield wondered if the spiral motif was related to the passages in megalithic tombs. In Chapter 2 we gave numerous examples of the mental spiral being seen as a passage or tunnel. We recall one of them in more detail now because it shows how an image can proliferate in meaning, yet remain tied to the fundamental spiral form. Geraldo Reichel-Dolmatoff was the first researcher to appreciate the potential that laboratory work on entoptic phenomena held for anthropological studies. This relevance was especially great for the northwest Amazonian people with whom he worked because their whole cosmology and religion was built on altered states of consciousness induced by the hallucinogenic vine *Banisteriopsis* (*yajé*). The Desana Indians use this hallucinogen to 'induce visionary experiences which are believed to offer glimpses of a reality that lies beyond this world and to which the shaman is a spiritual guide'.[72] As a result of studying drawings that the Desana and Tukano Indians made of their visionary experiences, Reichel-Dolmatoff realized that entoptic forms, such as the spiral, were fundamental building-blocks in Amazonian art and thought. Following up this idea, he discovered fascinating beliefs that the Desana Indians hold about twin-conical pot stands (Fig. 65):

The twisted cone is compared with the concept of a spiraling whirlpool, with a devouring and birth-giving element related to the *día oréri* spiral concept. But when seen in profile, as an hourglass, the object can be interpreted as a cosmic model, the two cones connected by a circular 'door', an image that leads to others such as 'birth', 'rebirth', the passage from one 'dimension' (*turí*) to another while under the influence of a narcotic, and to similar shamanistic images. It is not surprising, then, that shamans will use this artefact in curing rituals as a stand, a '*mesa*', for medicinal preparations. As an abstract geometrical outline the hourglass design can also come to represent the constellation of Orion, an image that leads to further elaborations such as the structure of the sacred central part of the longhouse or the particular pattern of ritual dances at the equinoctial dates … In sum, the hourglass shape contains a great amount of shamanistic imagery concerned with cosmic structures and with transformative processes.[73]

The fundamental form, the vortex, as experienced in altered states, becomes an image of passage from one existential dimension to another. Its similarity to whirlpools also invokes the depth metaphor: one goes 'down' into a whirlpool. The hourglass shape of the pot stands reflects this psychic transitional movement and, we believe, recalls the narrow megalithic passages that leave the wide, outside world, constrict the movement of those who pass through them, and that then open up into the chambers of, especially, corbelled tombs. At Newgrange and Knowth the conical corbelled roof of the chamber seems to spiral upwards in stark contrast to the narrow passage (Pl.

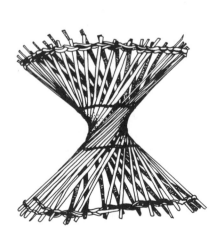
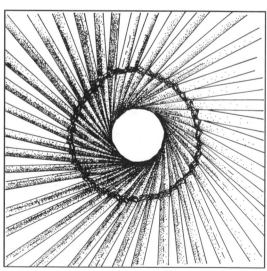

65 A South American Desana shaman's pot stand in the form of a vortex. Viewed from above (right) the spiral vortex is distinct (see also Fig. 8). The Desana themselves explain that many of their motifs derive from hallucinations.

20). The notions of 'birth' and 'rebirth' also recall the Samoyed shamanistic narrative that we analysed in Chapter 6, and the whole complex concept of 'birth' that we examined in Chapter 5. Being born and dying, the beginning and the end of life on earth by transition between realms, both entail passage through a 'tunnel' – the uterus and the vortex. As Inuit people see exit from an igloo as 'birth' (Chapter 5), so too may west European Neolithic people have seen parallels between birth, death and passage tombs.

Then there is a further suggestion in the Amazonian beliefs. The double cone and its basic vortex are related to the stars and to equinoctial ritual dances – that is, to the tier of the cosmos that is above the diurnal level of life. The Newgrange passage, we know, points to a solar event (the winter solstice); carved spiral motifs may have done the same (at least as part of their significance), though not as literally. The Amazonian chain of meanings that leads on from the vortex is complex; the situation in the west European Neolithic was probably similarly complex. As we have seen, one of the spirals on the Newgrange entrance stone unwinds to become the vertical line that points to the passage beyond the entrance; in the other direction, the line leads into the spiral, eventually to its very centre. It may also be that the vertical lines on that stone, on the 'false' Newgrange entrance stone and on the two Knowth entrance stones point not only to the passages but also skywards to an upper realm. The spiral experience may have led both down into the tomb *and* up into the heavens. If so, the spiral was at the centre of the Irish Neolithic cosmos; it represented the *axis mundi* that linked all the cosmological levels and also passage through that axis.

To test these thoughts we need to ask if there is any statistical evidence for a link between spirals and tomb entrances?

To tackle this question, Dronfield first divided the tombs into three areas. Area A was the passage itself. Area B comprised surfaces associated with the passage, and which could be seen by a viewer looking along the passage. Area C comprised surfaces not associated with the passage. Using rigorous analytical methods at Newgrange, Knowth Site 1 and Loughcrew, he found significant correlations. At Newgrange, 'concentric patterns' (including spirals), unlike arcs, have their highest concentrations in Area B, that is, they are associated with the passage. All other shapes are most common in Area C, that is, away from the passage.[74]

At Knowth, analytical work is complicated by the presence of not one but two passages and 17 smaller satellite tombs. Still, Dronfield was able to show that art in general concentrated on the Knowth passages. (In Chapter 8 we saw that attention to passage entrances was suggested by the arrangement of the embellished kerbstones, the larger ones being nearer to the entrances.) Concentric motifs again turned out to be a special category that was associated with the passages, though the association was less clear-cut than at Newgrange.

At Loughcrew, Dronfield again had to adjust his approach because of the rarity of kerbstones with art, as well as other factors. So he tested possible correlations between passage lengths and concentric motifs. He found 'further confirmation of a conceptual association between curvilinear concentrics and passages'.[75]

It seems clear, then, that the spiral motif was associated in Neolithic people's minds with the passages in megalithic tombs and with the sort of transcosmological travel that death implied. This is most clearly seen on the Newgrange entrance stone where, as we have noted, one of the central spirals unwinds to form a line that parallels the passage behind the stone (Pl. 24, and see Fig. 70). Another feature of the decoration on this stone, one on which we have not seen comment, is that multiple nested curves rise up from the ground just to the right of the centre of the stone (the carvings do not extend below ground level), thus giving the impression of deriving from an underground region. The one on the left swirls round to become a spiral; the one on the right becomes more angular and gives form to lozenges.

We are therefore almost certainly correct in the overall view of megalithic tombs that we have developed in this and the previous two chapters:

- Neolithic tombs were replicas of a tiered cosmos.
- The passages were seen as routes between dimensions of the cosmos.
- Neolithic art motifs constituted a system of symbols with cosmological and experiential referents.
- The spiral motif was associated with the architectural passage of the tomb and with mental travel between cosmological realms.

Can we reach any further conclusions about the meanings of the motifs? Dronfield tried his quantitative and statistical approach on the lattice motif. He found that 'lattices are most highly concentrated in the chambers'.[76] He thus confirmed Claire O'Kelly's and George Eogan's observation that 'angular' and 'rectilinear' motifs are concentrated inside tombs.[77] Dronfield concludes: 'This implies that lattices are associated with mortuary deposition.'[78] But within the chambers and side chambers at Knowth, the placing of lattices is ambiguous. Dronfield sees the significance of this point: 'The distinctiveness of each recess in terms of size, structure and deposits suggests

that they were also intended to be functionally and conceptually distinct, perhaps representing different rites or phases of the same rite'.[79] These phases
may have entailed moving remains from, first, the basin in the right recess to
the back recess and, then, to the recess on the left, each movement taking place
after a fixed time.

Inscribing experience

The curves, spirals and lozenges on the Newgrange entrance stone and on
other megaliths in western Europe enable us to observe the inscription of
visual and spiritual experiences, not, we repeat, as photocopy machines
duplicate images, but as human beings reach compromises between mercurial experiences and a desire to fill spaces. Clues to this simultaneously
experiential and materializing process are to be found in the images that
South American Tukano people derive from their *yajé*-induced mental percepts.

Figures 66 and 67 show drawings that Yebá, a 45-year-old Tukano shaman,
made at the request of Geraldo Reichel-Dolmatoff.[80] The anthropologist
recorded that Yebá was 'practically untouched by civilization' and spoke no
Spanish.[81] Like other older Tukano, he worked 'with a deep intentness' and
'always tried to explain or, at least, to *name*, each individual design element';
he was 'greatly concerned about discovering transcendental rules or messages
in the visions [he] had' (emphasis in original).[82] The drawings thus reconsti-
tute and organize visions that Yebá himself considered important.

Figure 66 shows, to the left and to the right, two anthropomorphic figures
that are 'abstract representations of Pamurí-mashë', who was 'a superhuman
helmsman ... [who] steered the serpent-shaped canoe of the first settlers'.[83]
The way in which geometric entoptic images combine with and actually constitute anthropomorphic figures shows that Yebá's vision was part of a Stage-3
experience. Of especial interest to us is the way in which Yebá packed the
repeated entoptic images (polyopsia, Chapter 2) into the available space. Similarities with the placing of motifs on west European Neolithic megaliths are
striking. In the central column the spaces between the semicircular curves
form what we have called lozenge shapes; Yebá identified these 'star-shaped
patterns' and the informing arcs as emblems of 'fertility and increase'.[84]

The way in which spandrels created between adjacent spirals become
meaningful elements in themselves is again evident in Figure 67. In the
second level from the top there are unwinding double spirals (said to be

66 *A Tukano drawing of yajé-induced hallucinations. To the left and right repeated entoptic motifs are construed as 'abstract representations' of Pamurí-mahsë, who steered the first humans' canoe. The arcs of the upper register indicate interaction between humankind and the superhuman sphere.*

imprints that ritual trumpets leave in the sand) and concentric circles (imprints of ritual flutes that suggest the importance of sound). In this level, the spandrels are left untouched. The top level shows two flanking double spirals with elongated curves between them; here the spandrel is emphasized by a motif with a central dot. Another informant, Biá, said that 'perforated lozenges' in other drawings, represented exogamic groups.[85] Again pointing to the importance of social relations in visions, Yebá said that his overall design emphasized 'the law of exogamy'.[86] Visions are always socially situated.

67 *A Tukano shaman's drawing of a vision. He explained that the top panel shows a 'door'; it is flanked by spirals. Compare this drawing with Figs 64, 68 and 70.*

Perhaps most interestingly, he said that the top level with its double spirals and central semi-lozenge spandrel represented a 'door'.[87] For Tukano, spiral and curved entoptic elements were associated with transitions between realms. The very nature of neurologically generated and therefore universal entoptic spirals and vortex experiences suggests 'passage'. It seems highly likely that Neolithic spirals similarly had movement between realms as part of their meaning, and that they were combined in ways that conveyed complex and, probably, open-ended messages.

We believe that these and other Tukano drawings that Reichel-Dolmatoff collected help us to understand how Neolithic people recalled their visions and then inscribed them on stone. The meanings of individual Neolithic motifs (which could be displayed in isolation) would, in most cases, have been different from those that the Tukano attach to them, but neurologically generated spirals and tightly packed curves probably have the potential to attract universal meanings. Dronfield's finding that Newgrange spirals are associated with passages is borne out on a general, neurological level.

Deliberate errors

An important point needs to be made about Dronfield's use of quantitative analysis and statistical tests. Techniques of this kind seem to imply a rigidity in human behaviour that we know is not the case. As he freely admits, his analysis works better at Newgrange than it does at Loughcrew. But the Loughcrew results do not cancel out what he established at Newgrange; those findings remain untouched. In fact, discrepancies are what we should expect in human behaviour. People are not puppets of deterministic systems, political, neurological or any other kind. Those systems are resources that people manipulate at given times in particular social circumstances. What may statistically seem to be 'errors' were probably results of deliberate choices that people made to achieve particular ends that seemed necessary at specific times. The deliberate breaking of a rule also says something.

This point is illustrated by the kerbstone on the opposite side of the Newgrange mound from the entrance to the passage, stone K 52 (see Fig. 57). Here, on the left of the vertical groove that parallels the one on the entrance stone, are three spirals (two of them double) along with a set of four U-shapes that are connected to the spirals (which, in turn, are joined to each other) and that seem to disappear beneath the lower right spiral. Many U-shapes seem to be 'half-hidden' spirals, but the form is a recognized entoptic element in its own right (Chapter 2, repeated form type 5). A point we have not so far mentioned is that there is a 'black hole', a 'blind spot', within the entoptic curves that blots out veridical perception. In this respect, the nested curves are comparable to the spiral (type 7; and the vortex).

To the right of the vertical groove are more U-shapes. Now, if Dronfield is correct about lattices being associated with deposited human remains, that 'rule' (or convention) is broken by a set of rectilinear lozenges below the spirals on the left. But we must not lose sight of the fact that we are dealing with an integrated *system* of symbols. As the entrance stone shows, angular diamond shapes can be created by, and are closely associated with, spirals. Thus the passage and the dead are, in terms of Dronfield's analysis, closely connected. Kerbstone K 52 seems, in a way that we do not fully understand, to be making a statement that was occasioned, at least in part, by the *absence* of a passage behind it, despite its vertical groove. We wonder if the rectilinear lozenges were, in some way, taking the place of the dead who lay down the passage from the real entrance stone. If, as we suggested in the previous chapter, this 'false entrance stone' leads not to the 'underground' chamber but up to the sacred summit of the mound, we may tentatively infer that the dead have left their remains behind in the tomb and are now disembodied – trans-formed – in the upper realm of the sky (see Fig. 58).

Dynamic experience and hidden power

All in all, it now seems certain that the Neolithic people who built and used the tombs in the Bend of the Boyne selected certain geometric visual percepts from the full range that the human nervous system generates, accorded them complex meanings and deployed them within the tombs so that they articu-lated with notions of the cosmos that the tombs themselves epitomized. Now we need to go a step further and see if the mercurial ways in which that sort of mental imagery is experienced had any influence on the art.

The neuropsychological model has a component that we have reserved for detailed comment at this point, where it is directly relevant. The dynamic ways in which entoptic phenomena (and the hallucinations of Stage 3) are experienced may be categorized as a number of transformational principles. The images do not appear in the (mental) visual field as a series of motionless, discrete 'pictures' apprehended in grand isolation and which snap from one to the next. We now consider two of those principles, polyopsia and integra-tion.[88]

The first, *polyopsia*, is one that we briefly noted in Chapter 2: a single image may suddenly multiply into a series of repeated images, rather like infinite reflections in parallel mirrors. A laboratory subject experienced Stage-3 poly-opsia like this: 'One toy soldier is duplicating and becoming a whole army of toy soldiers'.[89] An examination of megalithic art with this principle in mind is compelling. While some panels comprise a range of different geometric forms, others, such as some of the orthostats at Gavrinis (Brittany; Fig. 68), lintels at Fourknocks (Pl. 28; Fig. 69),[90] and the entrance stone at Newgrange (Pl. 24; Fig. 70) repeat a single entoptic element. We argue that polyopsia explains these tightly packed, repetitive motifs. Megalithic image-carvers were duplicating one of the ways in which seers experienced the mental imagery of altered states because it added something to the significance of a single motif. What was that added significance? We suggest it was *proliferating* access to other dimensions and hence to power in this world.

Another transformational principle is *integration*. In Stage 1, different entoptic images become integrated to form more complex geometric halluci-nations.[91] This principle explains the origin of Tukano barkcloth paintings of mental imagery that show curvilinear forms outlined by or in other ways

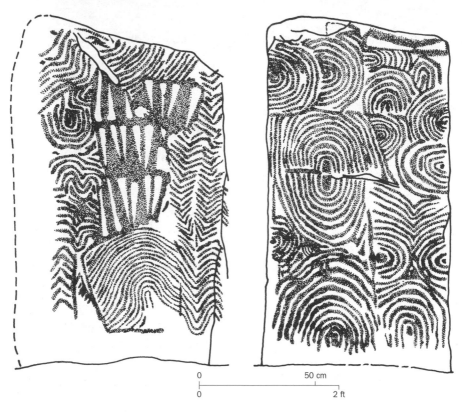

68 (Above) Two highly decorated stones (L 9, L 10) in the passage of the Gavrinis tomb (Brittany). The motifs on orthostat L 9 surround depictions of stone axes. L 10 shows how repeated motifs are packed together.

69 (Below) A decorated lintel above one of the alcoves in Fourknocks burial mound, Ireland. The lintels above all the alcoves are heavily decorated (see also Plate 28).

associated with dots (Fig. 71).[92] Another kind of integration occurs in Stage 3, when iconic hallucinations of people, animals and objects fuse with or are surrounded by geometric elements. In a Stage 3 hallucination, a laboratory subject reported seeing 'pulsating stars outlining the shape of a dog overlaying a spiral-tunnel of lights' (Fig. 72).[93] In South American *yajé* rituals, iconic Stage 3 hallucinations, such as canoes and people involved in mythical events, are surrounded by geometric motifs.[94]

Comparable integrations of 'naturalistic' images and entoptic elements occur in megalithic art. For instance, at Gavrinis, a bow, arrows and axes are embedded in nested curves, spirals and curving lines (Fig. 73).[95] Indeed, as many as five orthostats at Gavrinis have integrated images of axes; in all, there are 32 axe images. Among these integrated images are the kind of 'from-the-depths' axes that we have discussed. The large numbers of these axes that have been found in burial mounds around the Gulf of Morbihan, Brittany, led Bradley to propose a 'powerful symbolic link' between the carvings and the artefacts in the burial mounds.[96] We agree.

We have seen that stone axes (and the macehead from Knowth) were probably symbols of political power and that their origin in a nether realm added 'depth' to that significance: they and the power they stood for were indissolubly linked to the cosmos – more specifically, to a lower and probably terrifying tier.[97] Ritual and political power went hand in hand.[98] We have repeatedly argued that Neolithic life was not as idyllic as some people tend to

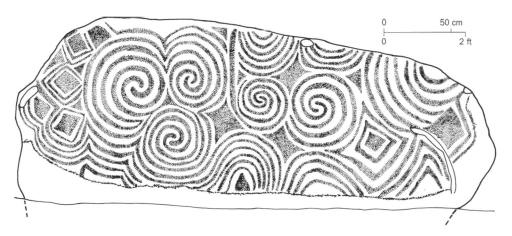

0   50 cm

0   2 ft

70 The entrance stone (K 1) at Newgrange (see also Plate 24). The central spiral 'unwinds' to form a vertical line that points in the direction of the passage. This magnificent stone shows how the lozenge motif is created by the spaces between spirals.

71 (Left) Barkcloth drawings of South American Tukano mental imagery. The double spirals are outlined with dots.

72 (Below) A Western laboratory subject's hallucination of a dog outlined by brilliant dots of light and superimposed on a vortex of larger 'stars' against a dark background.

imagine; it was not a pastoral epic. Like all other societies, there were within it competing groups of people.

There were also divisions that cross-cut the ones that most readily spring to mind. The evidence of the tombs and their art suggests another kind of distinction, one that depended on 'seeing the cosmos': seers were different from ordinary people. All too often researchers omit this kind of power when they consider prehistoric societies. As Andrew Sherratt pithily put it: 'Any account of prehistoric Europe which omits a consideration of [mind altering] substances is likely to be incomplete.'[99] Marx and Engels recognized that appropriating the material means of production (food resources; and including instruments of production, such as axes) entails appropriating what they call the 'mental means of production' as well.[100] Altered states of consciousness are an oft-ignored part of the mental means of production, but they can assume political importance in a variety of circumstances.[101] In the Neolithic, the imposing tombs with their hallucinatory imagery were probably implicated in an ideology that justified and negotiated an elite's control of resources, labour and the fruits of that labour. There was thus a reciprocal relationship: guarded neurologically based experiences were a foundation from which seers commanded labour that led to the building of the massive tombs, which, in turn, presented exploitative material relations as eternal and immutable (though, of course, they were not in the long run).

Why, then, are the Gavrinis axes 'hidden' in amongst polyopsic entoptic imagery? One explanation is that the makers of the images were simply reproducing the way in which emotionally charged iconic imagery of Stage 3 is sometimes surrounded by entoptic phenomena. But, as we have said, image-makers do not unthinkingly produce exact facsimiles of their visions: they select and modify them in meaningful ways. Because a certain amount of skill is required to disentangle the iconic elements embedded in the parallel curving lines, nested arcs and spirals, a more penetrating explanation may be that these carvings point to the generation of arcane knowledge to mark and reproduce social distinctions. The axes are clearly associated with nested U-shapes and thus with cosmological transition. Over and above that relationship is their hidden nature: they are set in the interstices between entoptic forms. The carvings may thus have been a cryptographic 'text', the correct exegesis of which was controlled by the elite and taught to selected

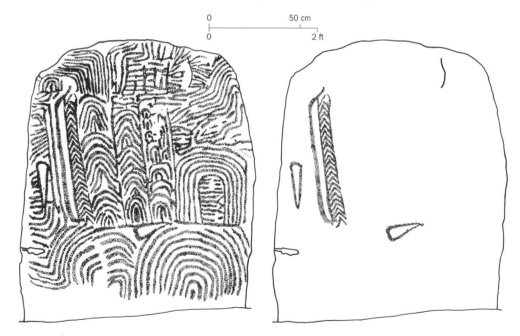

73 A densely decorated orthostat (L 6) in the passage at Gavrinis (Brittany). Two axes and a bow are hidden among nested arcs. A column of chevrons is adjacent to the bow string.

novices, whose growing command of trance experience provided hallucinatory and deeply emotional guarantees of the truths they were learning. It may even have been that the image-makers were the novices, in the same way that comparatively junior members of a medieval monastery were the ones who laboriously copied manuscripts. They may not themselves have seen spirals, lattices and nested curves, but they may have hoped to do so some day in the future when they would be higher up the hierarchy of seers.

Earth and sky

The monuments and their imagery were, then, as Julian Thomas puts it, constructed to 'orchestrate the encounter with the ancestral remains' in such a way as to define, reproduce and manipulate asymmetrical power relations and arcane knowledge.[102] Sometimes researchers speak of a Neolithic 'cult of the dead'. We can see why they do so. But we suggest that the dead were but one element in a much grander 'cult'. The importance of the dead was that they moved through the cosmos. Like the sun, they were a dynamic element, a mediating factor between levels of the cosmos. Therein lay their power and the power of those who managed to associate themselves with the dead and their cosmological travels: the dead placed the living – or rather *some* of the living – at the point of transition, the vortex, and thus in positions of power. The seers probably said that they were taking care of the dead, but it was actually the dead who were taking care of the seers.

As we have argued, the journey of the dead was almost certainly from one level of a multi-tiered cosmos to another, assisted at each transition by rituals that the living performed. The dead moved from the outside world, through the passage (vortex) to the underground realm of the chambers where, as numerous researchers suggest, seers performed various rituals with the (usually cremated) remains of the dead. At an appropriate time, the next leg of their journey was, we suggest, upwards, through the cone of the corbelled roof (or capstone), through the mound and up into the sky, their final abode where they consorted with the sun and became closely associated with solar events, such as the winter solstice. On the summit of the mound, with the nether realm of death beneath their feet, seers reached for the sky and stood as close as any human being could to the puissant essence of the universe. Along this multi-stage route, carved motifs were oriented not just to the living but, more importantly, to the dead. It seems highly likely that motifs within the tombs were so placed to guide the dead on their post-mortem journey, to remind them of complex mythological and cosmological beliefs, and, perhaps, to empower them to face the hazards that awaited them.

The tombs, and probably the Bend of the Boyne in general, were thus an *axis mundi*, a centre of the universe, a place of political and religious power for a considerable geographical area. It was *the* place in eastern Ireland where major transcosmological transitions were enacted. It was much more than a cemetery. People thus performed rituals

- outside tombs (e.g., processions around the carved kerbstones, and rituals performed at the ponds and settings),
- in passages as selected people passed significant, marked points,
- in the chambers where the cremated remains were manipulated, and
- on top of the mound whence released spirits of the dead flew to the path of the sun.

These were ritual cycles that related to solar events that, in turn, related to the passing of the sun through the tiers of the cosmos by means of the vortices that linked those realms. Perhaps it was especially at the winter solstice that seers entered Newgrange to perform rituals with the remains of the deceased or scaled the mound to stand between earth and 'heaven'. Later, after the tomb had been sealed, they may have moved the quartz blocks at the opening of the roof-box to complete a cosmic circle of light: light from the sun entered the tomb, travelled to the underworld, illuminated the chamber with its triple spirals, looped upwards through the corbelled vault, and left the top of the mound to reconnect with the sun – the very route that the dead themselves followed. Certainly, the winter solstice was, at Newgrange, a significant event for the dead, as well as for the living: it signalled the swing of the sun back to natural and human life.

Tombs like Newgrange were blends of architecture and iconography. The structures themselves presented an iconographic image of a tiered cosmos that underwrote social distinctions. Many researchers today accept that the tombs, stone circles, cursuses and avenues of stones were socially generative structures; they created, reproduced and modified society. We add that the structures and the ways in which they acted within society were even more complex. We argue that the functioning of the human nervous system within fractious Neolithic society underwrote the conception, construction and modification of monuments and, in some instances, their embellishment with motifs that likewise derived from the human brain.

An unlikely unity

We submit that there was a Neolithic homology between, on the one hand, the depths of the cosmos (the lower tier or tiers to which the dead travelled before their ascent to the sky and the source of powerful substances, such as quartz and the materials from which symbolic axes were fashioned), and, on the other hand, the depths of the human mind out of which came images of transition, such as spirals, and vivid experiences of trans-tier journeys. We need to abandon our conceptual categories (Chapter 5). In other categorizations stone is not necessarily different from human beings. Stones could 'cry out', as they did in the Samoyed shamanistic narrative (Chapter 6, part 3: 'The stones spoke to him one after the other'). Once we realize that such a taxonomy (for us, hardly conceivable) is indeed possible, some of the key problems that the Neolithic presents us with begin to dissolve – perhaps not altogether disappear, but certainly become more comprehensible.

If Neolithic people cried from the depths, they did so from the deep tiers of their cosmos and from the depths of their minds – and the difference between the two was negligible.

CHAPTER 10
East is East and West is West

The past is indeed another country. No one doubts that people did things differently there. But they were, in large measure, the same things. People were born, they laboured, procreated, died and their bodies became the focus of ritual attention – even as they do today in simple interments or elaborate state funerals. Always, we see the past through a glass, darkly. But the images we see in the glass are hauntingly familiar as well as different from what we know and experience today. That is the great fascination of archaeology. Walter De La Mare's Traveller left his horse to 'champ the grasses/Of the forest's ferny floor' as he knocked on the moonlit door. He called out, 'Is there anybody there?' Silence. The Listeners, he knew, were there, but they did not respond, and, as he left, 'the silence surged softly backward'.[1] The silence of the past is what intrigues.

In our attempt to engage with that silence, we chose two temporal and geographic poles of the Neolithic – Early Neolithic settlements in the Near East, and the societies that created the great monuments of Atlantic Europe. We compared and contrasted them to show people doing the same things differently. The difficult question is: What inherent mental processes framed both the glowering bucrania of Çatalhöyük and the richly carved kerbs, passages and chambers of the Bend of the Boyne? Our answer is not simple and unitary. We do not assert that *this* or *that* factor was the sole drive that led to skeletons beneath the floors of Çatalhöyük dwellings and to the dark passages into which the ancient people of the west carried the cremated and disarticulated remains of their dead. Rather, we point to complex, interlinked social and psychological pacts (or 'contracts') that *all* societies must forge in one way or another. The specifics of these dual pacts differ from place to place and from time to time, but the complex generating interaction of their elements must take note of – indeed, be fashioned from – human universals.

Since the 1960s when James Mellaart published his haunting reconstructions of Çatalhöyük, indeed since the earliest speculation about megalithic monuments, no one has doubted that, in both instances, human endeavours were spurred on by deeply held beliefs that researchers could reasonably call

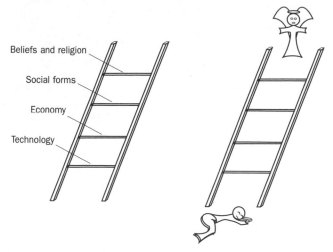

Beliefs and religion

Social forms

Economy

Technology

74 Christopher Hawkes's degrees of difficulty in archaeological explanations parallel Jacob's vision of a ladder. Traditionally, archaeologists have seen beliefs and religion to be virtually out of the reach of researchers.

religious. The people were building this world in order to contact another, unseen, world, and it was rituals performed in these structures that made contact with that other realm. But that general explanation is insufficient. We need more detail. And that is where researchers come up against a stone wall. Is it, they wonder, conceivable that we could understand the religious beliefs of people who lived so long ago? Unlike stone tools, buildings and tombs, beliefs do not 'fossilize'. You can't dig up beliefs. They have been silenced.

It was this view that led Christopher Hawkes to propose a metaphor for archaeological research that has long moulded researchers' expectations.[2] It continues to do so, even though few archaeologists would today express undivided loyalty to the trope. Though seldom fully articulated, it became one of those almost invisible metaphors by which archaeologists live and work. Hawkes envisaged a ladder of archaeological inference leading from technology to economy to social forms and, finally, to beliefs and religion (Fig. 74). Like Jacob's ladder, it led from the material, the stone on which the visionary laid his head, to the immaterial, the realm from which angels descended. Indeed, Hawkes's ladder recalls the transcosmological ladder we have discussed (Chapter 4).

Hawkes considered the lower rungs fairly safe: ancient technology, he believed, was easily inferred from stone tools and other artefacts. In stone arrowheads archaeologists can almost see the hunting process. From that process they can infer something about ancient technology and also about the type of economy that the makers of arrowheads practised, though 'technology' and 'economy' are of course abstract concepts, not things that researchers can hold in their hands. The higher rungs of the ladder, Hawkes argued, are much less secure. The social structures within which people made artefacts, distributed the spoils of the hunt and lived their daily and political lives are abstract rather than concrete things that can be excavated. Even more so, whereas archaeologists can literally lay their hands on artefacts (though not on 'technology' and 'economy'), beliefs are more elusive. The inferential distance between, say, megalithic tombs and the religion that underwrote their construction is greater than that between stone artefacts and hunting techniques. We acknowledge a certain truth in what Hawkes claimed, but there are approaches to ancient belief systems of which he, in the 1950s, could have had no idea.

Beyond the ladder

Our choice of the Near East and western Europe enabled us to point to both differences and similarities between the two regions. The Neolithic was not a single, homogeneous, unchanging entity. So east may well be east, and west west, but there is neither east nor west in the final analysis, or as Rudyard Kipling put it, 'when earth and sky stand presently at God's great judgement seat' (and also in somewhat jingoistic, testosterone-filled situations involving 'strong men').[3] Turning away from Kipling's apocalyptic vision, we have argued that 'the final analysis' is neurological. East and west, in their different Neolithic embodiments, were the results of different ways of handling neurological resources within incipient and also more developed farming communities.

Julian Thomas puts the point rather differently. He writes about the Neolithic as 'an interrelated set of material and symbolic resources'.[4] He comes to this conclusion partly as a result of the study of stable isotopes in human bones. Stable isotope analysis can tell if the people whose bones are being analysed subsisted principally on plants or animals; it can also determine if people ate fish or land animals during the final ten years of their lives. The results of this research show that, at the start of the Neolithic in southern Britain, people stopped eating fish. Yet seashells occur, sometimes in large quantities, in Neolithic tombs in Ireland, Wales and Scotland.[5] The argument that edible grave goods were simply intended to sustain the deceased on their way to the spirit world needs rethinking. It may, however, not be absolutely wrong: marine foods may have been considered more appropriate to nether-realm nutrition than to material life. Either way, there was a significant change.

Thomas sees this anomaly – turning away after many millennia from marine foods yet placing them in funerary contexts – as 'a positive rejection' caused by a new cultural prohibition on marine foods. From material remains (fishbones) he infers abstract beliefs. Socially sanctioned rejection of certain foods is a way of manifesting one's identity. Thomas goes on to say that the shift in diet 'implies a fundamental change in the relationship between human beings and the sea at the beginning of the Neolithic'.[6] What was that new, cosmological relationship? Neolithic dead were frequently placed in rivers that, of course, eventually find their way to the sea.[7] The sea seems to have become part of the underworld in a way that earlier Mesolithic people did not accept. Although Thomas does not put it quite like this, he is speaking about a change in cosmology, a rethinking of the nether realm of a tiered cosmos and its relationship to the living.

Just how Neolithic communities should relate to a nether realm and its occupants (including deceased generations) is a problem that people from the Near East to western Europe had to face. The past, partly embedded in a neurologically generated cosmos, is both a necessary confirmation of the present and, because people's conception of it requires continual adjustment to suit changing social and political circumstances, an embarrassment. Both the past and the cosmos must therefore be constantly reworked. In the Near East itself there were different ways of dealing with the dead, of separating them from daily life yet keeping them 'alive' as a guarantee of the 'naturalness' – the inevitability – of the contemporary social order. At Çatalhöyük, people lived in their built 'domestic' version of the cosmos and placed (some of) the dead beneath their floors. At certain times in western Europe, people placed the dead in megalithic tombs, powerful monuments on the landscape. The dead, at least those in the tombs, were probably not an intimate part of mundane life: more probably, they were exalted above daily tribulations. But in certain circumstances (such as personal bereavement or economic disaster) that separation could seem at least partly unsatisfactory: people needed the influence of the dead in their daily lives, as well as – on a grander scale – to sustain society and cosmos. If the cosmos is in the hands of a pantheon, there is always the implication that individuals on earth must find a way to relate to the gods. Because they experience another realm at the inwards-directed end of the consciousness spectrum, they have a passage to the beings of the cosmos.

If we allow the neurological foundation and the socially discriminatory divisions of the consciousness spectrum, we must clearly examine the nature and functioning of human consciousness – as we have done. How else can we ascend to the upper rungs of the ladder where immaterial beliefs and beings hold sway?

We are, of course, aware that some archaeologists entertain reservations about references to human neurology in studies of the past. Old misunderstandings are brought up again and again. Neurological determinism, for which as far as we are aware no one has argued, is still a straw man who is given an occasional outing. Perhaps this book will contribute towards a better understanding of how the human nervous system is a resource, not a puppeteer. Human beings are sentient. They know what is going on around them. They are marionettes of neither their environment, nor their culture, nor their neurology. An understanding of consciousness gives us a *framework* that makes sense of otherwise apparently disparate and meaningless elements of Neolithic religious experience, belief and practice. Fortunately, the tide is turning. Some writers are attempting more sophisticated neurological understandings of religious experience and the varied relationships between that kind of experience and religious belief and practice.[8]

The three dimensions of religion that we have distinguished (experience, belief and practice) help us to atomize the complexity of religion and so move towards a better understanding of what we mean by 'religion' in its social and cosmological contexts. Religion is, ultimately, embedded in neurology, as is pre-scientific cosmology: the two are hardly separable. We have argued that, fundamentally, religion is based on belief in supernatural realms and non-material entities. Perceptions of those invisible realms derive from the electro-chemical functioning of the brain. Whether people are animists, ancestor worshippers, polytheists, monotheists or believers in a Great Something that underlies the universe, they accept that there is a supernatural realm that is immune to scientific study. Contact with that realm is what we designate religious experience. People achieve that kind of experience by exploring the introverted end of the consciousness spectrum.

As we have seen, religious experience comes in varying degrees. Some people have blinding, life-changing hallucinations, like St Paul (until then known as Saul of Tarsus) on the road to Damascus (Pl. 29). Among the South American Tukano and other peoples whom we have considered, visions are induced by ingesting psychotropic substances. We have also seen that others depend solely on chanting, rhythmic driving, sensory deprivation and so forth. Still others, probably including Paul, suffer from hallucination-inducing pathological conditions. They believe they actually *see* parts and aspects of the supernatural that are invisible under ordinary circumstances.

Over and above religious experiences, all these people, whether they believe in the supernatural or not, may experience what has been called Absolute Unitary Being, a sense of melding with the cosmos, such as Wordsworth experienced 'a few miles above Tintern Abbey'. He wrote of

> that serene and blessed mood,
> In which the affections gently lead us on,—
> Until, the breath of this corporeal frame
> And even the motion of our human blood
> Almost suspended, we are laid asleep
> In body, and become a living soul:
> While with an eye made quiet by the power
> Of harmony, and the deep power of joy,
> We see into the life of things.[9]

The body is held in suspended animation and what Wordsworth called the 'affections', the emotions, take over. In that AUB state, subjects feel released from 'this unintelligible world' and believe that they have access to knowledge, rather vague, it must be admitted, of 'the life of things'. The experiences of altered consciousness seem to be inextricably bound up with notions of exceptional understanding, of beyond-the-ordinary insight. This theological or non-theological experience (it can be interpreted as either), this sense of revelation or what some call 'heightened consciousness', is, we now know, explicable in terms of neurology.[10]

Others experience the simpler calm and euphoria induced by prayer, meditation, chanting, sensory deprivation and participation in rituals. Then, as we have repeatedly pointed out, all people have the potential to interpret their dreams as being essentially of the same kind as other, more spectacular, experiences and visions. Dreams become common, demotic intimations of spiritual dimensions.

It is true that some people do not experience any of these states of mind (apart from dreams, which they dismiss), yet they describe themselves as religious. They are willing to take the experience of others as indicative of a supernatural realm and to concern themselves with religious belief and practice. The reasons why they accept the testimony of others to the existence of a supernatural realm are complex and varied. In some societies it is impossible not to be a believer. Such was probably the case in medieval Europe. Almost certainly it was the case during the Neolithic.

Beyond environment

We can now draw together two of our principal points. We can envisage how religion with its three dimensions and its tiered cosmos relates to social and consciousness contracts, not just in the Neolithic but also throughout history. We try to formulate a model that reflects the changing balance between religion and society and, in doing so, we try to throw some light on changes in present-day society and belief. We develop the diagram we gave in Figure 3 by providing a context for the three dimensions of religion. Religion is not a free-floating add-on to society. We therefore envisage the three dimensions of religion superimposed on interlinked consciousness and social contracts (Fig. 75). Principally, the diagram emphasizes the point that all three dimensions are embedded in those contracts. But the relationships implied by this diagram are not frozen. Through time there are shifts in balance. Towards the left of the diagram lies belief in the supernatural; in some societies, beliefs in supernatural beings and forces are paramount. To the right is a rational, materialist view of life; in some societies, the products of the introverted end of the consciousness spectrum are not considered influential. But, always, there are degrees.

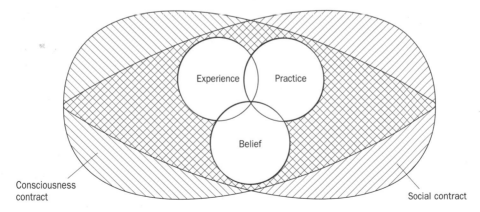

75 The three dimensions of religion are set within social and consciousness contracts. Some people veer to the left and emphasize experience, others to the right and emphasize intellectual belief and ritual practice.

Within the central three, interacting dimensions there is also shifting emphasis. For some individuals, and also societies as a whole, altered states are supreme not just for spiritual enlightenment, being able to 'see into the life of things', but also for political ends. Those who claim that sort of insight can wield enormous power. That is why we superimpose the three dimensions of religion on the two interlocking contracts. Arcane knowledge and an ability to explore the cosmos can have major political implications.

Today in the West, the swing of the pendulum is towards the right of Figure 75. The social contract is linked to a new, science-based consciousness contract that denies the reality of supernatural insight. Of course, that view is not shared by everyone. There are still those who believe that the West should be a theocracy, as are numerous predominantly Muslim countries, but, by and large, a claim to divine revelation is not accepted in Western political and economic affairs. During the Neolithic (and later periods as well) the pendulum was swinging in the opposite direction. It was religious experience that gave people the power to command the construction of megalithic monuments and to sacrifice animals and very probably human beings in order to keep the cosmos in good order. Another way of putting that point is, of course, to say that animal and human sacrifices – mastery of enforced cosmological transition – kept the elite in power.

For archaeologists, there is now evidence that we must consider new types of explanation that do not assume humankind's impotence in the face of environment. We return to the distinction between etic and emic explanations (Chapter 3). Etic explanations are those formulated from without a society. An archaeologist who proposes that certain political changes were a reaction to climatic change is putting forward an etic explanation. It is, however, highly unlikely that individuals in the changing society would have described what was happening to them in terms of ecological theory. They would have had an emic explanation, one that made sense in the context of their own understanding of causality, their religion and system of symbols. This sort of explanation has not attracted archaeologists. Like Gordon Childe and other Marxists, most researchers place the material base of society, the infrastructure, at the point of change. Changes in belief were, in their view, simply folk beliefs, superstitions that had no real impact on change.

The time has now come for archaeologists to consider emic explanations.[11] What was, understandably enough, seen as insubstantial flight of fantasy must now, in the light of inescapable, interlinked consciousness and social contracts, be re-evaluated. Within the context of the interrelationships shown in Figure 75, people formulate beliefs that, independently of their environment, lead to social, political, architectural and artistic change. The power for change that an emic view can wield needs to be taken seriously.

Beyond eternal sadness

Although we have used the pendulum metaphor to describe changing emphases on experiences at the introverted end of the consciousness spectrum, we think it inappropriate if we take a long view of intellectual history.

In Classical antiquity, schools of Greek philosophy expressed reservations about the gods and their impact on human life. Placing their emphasis on reason not revelation, thinkers like Aristotle had grasped the principles of inductive and deductive logic. Reason, not the gods, was considered supreme and, importantly, open to all. All authority was open to question.

Later, those reservations were swept aside as Platonic philosophy with its beliefs about ideal Forms in a supernatural realm was embraced and reworked by the Christian Church after the Emperor Constantine committed the Roman Empire to Christianity. Now imperial edict and supposed revelation, not reason, settled disputes. If, as Plato taught, there is a realm of ideal Forms, revelation, not observation of imperfect replicas of those Forms on earth, must be the ultimate source of authority. Indeed, Plato went so far as to say, 'We shall approach astronomy, as we do geometry, by way of problems, and ignore what is in the sky if we intend to get a real grasp of astronomy.'[12] Here we have an early parallel to the view taken by Copernicus's and Galileo's ecclesiastical opponents: mathematical formulations that fit observed celestial events are not necessarily representations of the truth (Chapter 3).

By medieval times, disbelief in received dogma was virtually impossible. The pendulum had swung back again, though schoolmen and, especially, Thomas Aquinas (c. 1225–1274), tried to reinstate logic in theology. But speculation was not for everyone. Early on, Origen (c. 185–c. 253) put it like this: 'we accept [faith] as useful for the multitude, and that we admittedly teach those who cannot abandon everything and pursue a study of rational argument to believe without thinking out their reasons'.[13] A chilling instance of knowledge being the foundation of power. But he was merely echoing Paul's advice to the Corinthians (1 CORINTHIANS 2:5): 'your faith should not stand in the wisdom of men, but in the power of God'. And again: 'For the wisdom of this world is foolishness with God' (1 CORINTHIANS 3:19). To the Colossians (COLOSSIANS 2:8) he wrote: 'Beware lest any man spoil you through philosophy.'

Perhaps the resurgence of the supernatural and the authority of revelation was possible because the earlier Greek reservations were philosophical rather than the outcome of scientific research on the human brain and the universe. Once we get into the functioning of the brain as the generator of belief and logic we are in a very different area of enquiry. Speculations as to whether the soul is part of the body or not become as meaningless as the problem of how many angels can be accommodated on the point of a pin.

Once the trend to recognition of the supernatural as a product of the human brain is firmly established, there is probably no way to turn back, no matter how fiercely reactionary some believers may be. True, the rise of fundamentalism with its desire to control scientific research in some parts of the West must give us pause, but it seems unlikely that, in the long run, scientific advance with its rejection of supernatural agency can be stopped. Attempts to achieve a rapprochement between science and religion are today common, but they inevitably end in adjustments to religious belief, not to scientific findings.

In immediately post-Darwin decades people heard the 'melancholy, long, withdrawing roar' of the Sea of Faith as it retreated 'down the vast edges drear And naked shingles of the world.' Today the ebb tide continues. But, more than a century on from Matthew Arnold's glum reflections on Dover Beach, there is no 'eternal note of sadness'. Twenty-first-century people need not lament the loss of the 'bright girdle' of faith that once lay 'round earth's shore'.[14] The ebbing tide reveals the 'naked shingles of the world' and their 'grating roar' for what they are – pebbles, pieces of stone, flung back and forth by the waves. They are not mysterious, minatory beings lurking in a nether realm that can be contacted through induced states of mind.

Is it possible to have a religion that does not entail belief in the supernatural? Does the archaeology of religion, as we have pursued it in this book, have anything to say to 21st-century people as they face the great anachronism, belief in supernatural realms and beings? We believe it does.

Notes

PREFACE (PAGES 6–12)
1 Pinker (2002, viii–ix).
2 On human universals, see Brown (1991).
3 For a discussion of analogy see Lewis-Williams (1991).
4 Writers who recognize the importance of altered states include Furst (1972, 1976); Harner (1973a); La Barre (1975); Garwood et al. (1991); Goodman et al. (1995); Devereux (1997); Winkelman (2002); as well as writers we cite in subsequent chapters.
5 Lewis-Williams (2002a).

1 THE REVOLUTIONARY NEOLITHIC (PAGES 13–36)
1 Kenyon (1957, 60).
2 Kenyon (1957, 61).
3 Kenyon (1957, 61).
4 Kenyon (1957, 61).
5 Kenyon (1957, 62).
6 Kenyon (1957, 72).
7 Kenyon (1957, 72); on sacrifice and dismemberment see Hill (2003).
8 Schmandt-Besserat (1998, 7).
9 Kenyon (1957, 62).
10 Pfeiffer (1982).
11 Mellars & Stringer (1989).
12 McBrearty & Brooks (2000).
13 Lewis-Williams (2002a).
14 Greene (1999).
15 Marx & Engels (2002 [1848], 219).
16 Childe cited in McGuire (1992, 69).
17 It is sometimes said that Central and South American 'liberation theology' shows that Marx and Engels were wrong about the masking nature of ideology. But liberation theology merely substitutes one form of domination (that of capitalism) for another (domination by the Catholic Church and its hierarchy).
18 For a review of traditional explanations for the origins of agriculture see Flannery (1973); see also Sherratt (1983); Kohler-Rollefson (1989); Clutton-Brock (1999); for a recent and detailed analysis of the domestication of various species see Haber & Dayan (2004).
19 Toynbee (1946).
20 On this point see Cauvin (2000a).
21 E.g., Lee & De Vore (1968).
22 Sahlins (1968, 85).
23 Marshall (1961, 243).
24 Cauvin (2000a, 2000b).
25 Cauvin (2000a, 240, 245).

26 Sullivan (1988, 115, 124).
27 Whitehouse (1995, 2000).
28 Geertz (1966, 4); see also Geertz (1973).
29 d'Aquili & Newberg (1993, 1999); see also Ramachandran & Blakeslee (1998).
30 See, for example, Spiro (1966).
31 Whitehouse (2000).
32 Berger (1973).
33 Hauptmann (1999).
34 Hauptmann (1999, 75); Schmidt (2000, 2004); Peters and Schmidt (2004).
35 Hauptmann (1999, 75).
36 Hauptmann (1999, 76).
37 Schmidt (1995, 1996, 1999, 2000, 2001, 2004); Kromer & Schmidt (1998); Peter & Schmidt (2004)
38 On complex hunter-gatherers see Hayden (1990, 2003).
39 http://catal.arch.cam.ac.uk/catal/TAG_papers/#Lewis-Williams, accessed 1996; Cauvin (2000a); Lewis-Williams (2004a).
40 Heun et al. (1997).
41 Mithen (2003, 67).
42 Dixon & Grierson (1909, 359–60).

2 THE CONSCIOUSNESS CONTRACT (PAGES 37–59)
1 Rousseau (1997 [1762], 53).
2 Rousseau (1898, 226).
3 Rousseau (1997 [1762], 148).
4 Rousseau (1997 [1762], 146).
5 Rousseau (1997 [1762], 147).
6 Rousseau (1997 [1762], 140).
7 Kingsley (1848).
8 Rousseau (1997 [1762], 140).
9 Rousseau (1997 [1762], 146).
10 Lewis-Williams (2002a).
11 Renfrew (1994, 3). For less hide-bound archaeological research see, for example, Lewis-Williams & Dowson (1994); Renfrew & Zubrow (1994); Helskog & Olsen (1995); Mellars & Gibson (1996); Mithen (1996, 2003); Chippindale & Taçon (1998); Clottes & Lewis-Williams (1998); Whitley (1998, 2001); Helskog (2001); Price (2001); Lewis-Williams (2002a, 2002b); Hayden (2003).
12 Bleek & Lloyd (1911, 335).
13 See Lewis-Williams (2004b) for a discussion of this point.
14 Mavromatis (1987, A: p. 24; B: p. 20; C: p. 21; D: p. 23).
15 Fox (2003, 57–58); see also Newberg &

d'Aquili (1994).
16 F: Wasson, in Narby & Huxley (2001, 144); G: Siegel (1992, 17–18).
17 Siegel (1992, 31).
18 In the order quoted, Keeney (2003, 105–8, 127, 80).
19 Mavromatis (1987, 8).
20 Mavromatis (1987, 31).
21 Mavromatis (1987, 71).
22 Mavromatis (1987, 34).
23 Cytowic (1994).
24 McKellar (1995, 35).
25 Mavromatis (1987, 209–10).
26 McKellar (1995, 36).
27 Siegel (1980, 911).
28 On music and altered states of consciousness see Becker (1994).
29 Crocker (1985, 291).
30 Crocker (1985, 292).
31 The sources for the following paragraphs include: Horowitz (1964, 1975); Reichel-Dolmatoff (1969, 1978); Zuckerman (1969); Brindley (1973); Eichmeier & Höfer (1974); La Barre (1975); Siegel & Jarvik (1975); Siegel (1977, 1978); Harner (1982); Noll (1985); Asaad & Shapiro (1986); Winkelman (1986, 2002); Cardeña (1988, 1992, 1996); Lewis-Williams & Dowson (1988); Bean (1992); Cytowic (1994); Goodman et al. (1995); ffytche et al. (1998); ffytche & Howard (1999); Hutton (2001); Lewis-Williams (2001a); ffytche (2002); Pearson (2002); on neurological and mystical states, see d'Aquili & Newberg (1993); on hallucinogenic plants see Furst (1976); Emboden (1979); Wilbert (1987); Dobkin de Rios (1990); Rudgley (1993); Hutton (2001).
32 Lewis-Williams & Dowson (1988).
33 Helvenston & Bahn (2002, 2003) have questioned the induction of all three stages by means other than certain drugs. The literature in fact shows that all three stages may be induced by rhythmic driving, sensory deprivation and so forth (Lewis-Williams 2004b). For further reaction to Helvenston & Bahn see Clottes (2004); Pearce (2004); Wilson (2004).
34 E.g., Klüver (1966).
35 E.g., Oster (1970).
36 Dronfield (1995, 1996).
37 Tyler (1978, 1633); Lewis-Williams & Dowson (1988).
38 Walker (1981).
39 Sacks (1997).
40 Reichel-Dolmatoff (1971, 1978, 32–34).
41 Rose, in Narby & Huxley (2001, 123).
42 Horowitz (1964, 514, 1975, 177, 178, 181).
43 Heinze (1986).
44 Horowitz (1975, 177).
45 Siegel (1977).
46 E.g., Siegel (1980); Drab (1981); Blackmore (1982); Fox (2003).
47 Moody, quoted in Fox (2003, 17). Although Moody collected a number of near-death accounts, his analysis of them is highly suspect (Siegel 1980, 920–21).
48 Moody, quoted in Fox (2003, 17).
49 Moody, quoted in Fox (2003, 21).
50 Vitebsky (1995, 70).
51 Eliade (1972 [1951]).
52 Eliade (1972 [1951], 234).
53 Eliade (1972 [1951], 240).
54 Halifax (1979, 38).
55 Freidel et al. (1993, 151).
56 Fernandez (1972, 251).
57 Reichel-Dolmatoff (1971, 27).
58 Reichel-Dolmatoff (1985, 33); on South American Warao tunnel experience, see Wilbert (1997).
59 Gow (2001, 58).
60 Cohen (1964, 76–77).
61 Moody, quoted in Fox (2003, 21).
62 Halifax (1979, 38).
63 Biesele (1993, 71).
64 Sullivan (1988, 122).
65 Eliade (1972 [1951], 235).
66 Bressloff et al. (2001).
67 Siegel & Jarvik (1975, 104–05).
68 Klüver (1966, 71–72).
69 For more on the consciousness spectrum see Lewis-Williams (2002a).
70 On dreams worldwide, see Bourguignon (1972).
71 Atkinson (1992); for recent examples see Lewis-Williams & Pearce (2004a, 2004b).
72 Schulman et al. (1999); Price-Williams (1987).
73 Lewis-Williams (2002a).

3 Seeing and Building a Cosmos (pages 60–87)

1 Losee (1980, 43–50).
2 Freeman (2002).
3 Vastokas & Vastokas (1973, 38).
4 Vastokas & Vastokas (1973, 38).
5 Zimmerman (1996, 118).
6 Hultkrantz (1987, 20).
7 Vitebsky (1995, 112–13).
8 Vitebsky (1995, 17).
9 Vitebsky (1995, 17).
10 Hutton (2001, 61).
11 Vitebsky (1995, 10).

12 Vitebsky (1995, 10).
13 Shirokogorov (1935, 125).
14 Bogoras (1907, 330).
15 Bogoras (1907, 330–31).
16 C. Hugh-Jones (1979, 209).
17 Read & Gonzalez (2000, 20–24, and *passim*); see also Freidel *et al.* (1993).
18 Schele & Freidel (1990, 105).
19 Harner (1973b, 158–60); Sullivan (1988, 412).
20 Narby & Huxley (2001, 99).
21 Crocker (1985, 201).
22 Some researchers believe these may represent a hanging bear skin (Sutherland 2001, 138–40).
23 Jordan (2001, 92).
24 Bleek (1935, 18); unpublished Bleek MS L.V.8.4701 rev., Jagger Library, University of Capetown.
25 Pearson (2002, 75).
26 Eliade (1972 [1951], 140).
27 Halifax (1982, 23).
28 Vitebsky (1995, 11).
29 Moody, quoted in Fox (2003, 17).
30 Keeney (2003, 105).
31 Bressloff *et al.* (2001).
32 Siegel (1992, 17–18).
33 Blanke *et al.* (2002).
34 Gow (2001, 38).
35 Vitebsky (1995, 15).
36 Halifax (1979, 1).
37 S. Hugh-Jones (1979, 121).
38 Bogoras (1907, 281–82).
39 Bogoras (1907, 416).
40 Turner (1996, 132).
41 Turner (1996, 132).
42 Narby & Huxley (2001, 49).
43 Narby & Huxley (2001, 105).
44 Narby & Huxley (2001, 200, 203).
45 Bleek (1933, 390).
46 Bleek (1933, 390).
47 Bleek & Lloyd (1911, 187); Lee (1967, 35); Katz (1982, 101, 115, 227, 229); Biesele (1993, 111); Katz *et al.* (1997, 25); Guenther (1999, 187); Marshall (1999, 238).
48 Reichel-Dolmatoff (1971, 137).
49 Sullivan (1988, 244), quoting N. Fock.
50 Schmandt-Besserat (1998, 1).
51 Schmandt-Besserat (1998, 2).
52 http:www.art.man.ac.uk/ARTHIST/ay2091/ainghazal.htm, accessed 2003.
53 Schmandt-Besserat (1998, 3).
54 Schmandt-Besserat (1998, 3).
55 Schmandt-Besserat (1998, 6).
56 Schmandt-Besserat (1998, 6).
57 Schmandt-Besserat (1998, 6).
58 Fagan (1998, 81).
59 Cauvin (2000b, 247).
60 Schmandt-Besserat (1998, 11).
61 McCall (1989, 54); Schmandt-Besserat (1998, 11).
62 McCall (1989, 54); Schmandt-Besserat (1998, 11).
63 Denning-Bolle (1992, 41), in Schmandt-Besserat (1998, 12).
64 For a review of plastered skulls, see Bienert (1992).
65 Goren *et al.* (2001, 671).
66 Goren *et al.* (2001, table 1).
67 Goren *et al.* (2001, 673).
68 Goren *et al.* (2001, 681).
69 Goren *et al.* (2001, 688).
70 Kenyon (1957, 72).
71 Mellaart (1966, 190, pls LXII–LXIII).
72 Russell & McGowan (2002).
73 Hauptmann (1999, 76).
74 See, for example, Goring-Morris (2000).
75 E.g., Kuijt (1996).
76 For a fuller explanation of the problems with functionalism see Friedman (1974).
77 Cauvin (2000a, 91).
78 Özdogan & Özdogan (1998, 581–93).
79 The views that the skulls were of old people who had lost their teeth and that the plastered skulls had their teeth removed are no longer tenable; Bonogofsky (2002).
80 Hayden (2003, 198).
81 Wason (1994, 157).
82 Hill (2003).
83 Kenyon (1957, 72).
84 See Otte *et al.* (1995) on caves in southern Turkey.
85 Lewis-Williams (2002a).
86 What may appear to be an exception to this rule has recently come to light. There are radiocarbon-dated (25,120 ± 120 BP) Upper Palaeolithic human skeletons in the newly discovered Cussac cave in France, but they are near the entrance to this long passage cave (Aujoulat *et al.* 2001).
87 Kuhn (1957, 181).
88 Crocker (1985).
89 S. Hugh-Jones (1996).

4 CLOSE ENCOUNTERS WITH A BUILT COSMOS (PAGES 88–122)
1 Richard Bradley (2002, 18–19) has also noted the relevance of this source to Neolithic structures.
2 C. Hugh-Jones (1979); S. Hugh-Jones (1979).
3 S. Hugh-Jones (1979, 3).

4 Reichel-Dolmatoff (1971, 173–74).
5 S. Hugh-Jones (1979, 151).
6 C. Hugh-Jones (1979, 265–66).
7 C. Hugh-Jones (1979, 264).
8 Reichel-Dolmatoff (1979).
9 S. Hugh-Jones (1979, 153).
10 C. Hugh-Jones (1979, 112).
11 S. Hugh Jones (1979, 125).
12 S. Hugh-Jones (1979, 124–25).
13 Crocker (1985, 33).
14 Rollefson (2000, 187).
15 http://www.art.man.ac.uk/ARTHIST/ay
2091/ainghazal.htm, accessed 11/2003.
16 cf. Cauvin (2000b, 246).
17 Rollefson & Kafafi (1994, 20–23).
18 http://link.lanic.utexas.edu/menic/ghazal/
intro/int.html, accessed 2003.
19 Verhoeven (2002, 239).
20 Verhoeven (2002, 238, 239).
21 Goren et al. (2001, 675).
22 http://link.lanic.utexas.edu/menic/ghazal/
intro/int.html, accessed 2003.
23 http://www.art.man.ac.uk/ARTHIST/ay
2091/ainghazal.htm, accessed 2003.
24 Mellaart (1967, 27).
25 Mellaart (1967, 27).
26 Mellaart (1967, 16).
27 Hodder (1996a, 366).
28 Lewis-Williams (2004a).
29 Hamilton (1996); Hodder & Cessford
(2004).
30 http://Çatalhöyük.arch.cam.ac.uk/
Çatalhöyük/Archive_rep02/a01.html, accessed
2003.
31 Hodder (1996b, figs 1.8–1.17).
32 When referring to specific rooms that
Mellaart identified as shrines we nevertheless
retain an upper case S before the Roman
numeral that designates the layer and the Arabic
numeral that signifies the room. This
convention enables the rooms to which we refer
to be located easily on Mellaart's maps; Mellaart
(1967, figs 4–10); reproduced in Hodder (1996b,
8, figs 1.8–1.17).
33 Last (1998, 373).
34 Otte et al. (1995).
35 Hamilton (1996, 217).
36 E.g., S.VIA.10.
37 Mellaart (1967, 178).
38 Métraux, in Narby & Huxley (2001, 99, 101).
39 Vitebsky (1995, 17).
40 Shirokogoroff (1935, 310).
41 Eliade (1972 [1951], 487).
42 Eliade (1972 [1951], 487–88).
43 Mellaart (1967, 34).
44 Levels X–VI A.
45 Mellaart (1967, 64).
46 S.VIB.44.
47 Mellaart (1967, fig. 31).
48 S.VI.10.
49 S.VII.10.
50 Mellaart (1967, caption to pls 9, 10); Hodder
(1996a, 366).
51 Mellaart (1967, figs 14, 17, 19, 20, 24, 28, 32,
38, 39).
52 It may not be a female figure at all; S.VI.14;
Mellaart (1967, fig. 32).
53 Mellaart (1967, 101).
54 See Hamilton (1996, 225–27).
55 S.VI.8.
56 S.VIB.44.
57 Mellaart (1967, 118–20).
58 Mellaart (1967, 132).
59 X.1; Mellaart (1967, 104).
60 Bégouën & Clottes (1981).
61 Clottes & Lewis-Williams (1998); Lewis-
Williams (2002a).
62 In S.E.VIA.14; Mellaart (1967, 83).
63 Mellaart (1967, 180).
64 Mellaart (1967, 82).
65 Mellaart (1967, 202).
66 Forest (1983).
67 Douglas (1966).
68 Hodder (1990, 10).
69 Voigt (2000, 288).
70 S.VII.23; Mellaart (1967, colour plate VII,
pp. 113–14).
71 Some scholars now believe that this image
may represent a reptile; Hodder pers. comm.,
2003.
72 S.VII.45.
73 Mellaart (1967, 114).
74 Lewis-Williams (1996a, 2002a).
75 Vitebsky (1995, 70).
76 Haaland & Haaland (1995) and Meskell
(1995) have explored other possible
significances.
77 In S.A.III.1.
78 Mellaart (1967, 173–74).
79 Oppitz (1992); Vitebsky (1995, 78, 80–81);
Manker (1996); Potapov (1996).
80 Mellaart (1967, 174).
81 Mellaart (1967, 175).
82 Lewis-Williams & Biesele (1978); Lewis-
Williams (1981); Lewis-Williams & Dowson
(1999).
83 Mellaart (1967, 175).
84 In S.VIIB.8; Mellaart (1967, pls 46–49) and
S.VII.21; Mellaart (1967, figs 14, 15, pp.
166–68).

85 Hauptmann (1999, 75).
86 Mellaart (1967, 166); see also Hamilton (1996, 257–58); Hodder pers. comm., 2003.
87 Mellaart (1967, 82, figs 14, 15).
88 Vitebsky (1995); Hayden (2003).
89 E.g., Eliade (1972 [1951]).
90 Katz (1982, 235).
91 Katz (1982, 235).
92 Level VII; about 8,500 years ago.
93 Mellaart (1967, 164–65).
94 S.A.III.8.
95 S.E.VIA.7; Mellaart (1967, 83).
96 S.E.VIB.10.
97 S.VIB.8.
98 Mellaart (1967, figs 41, 42).
99 Lewis-Williams (1995, 2002a).
100 Lewis-Williams & Blundell (1997); Clottes & Lewis-Williams (1998); Lewis-Williams (2002a, 216–20).
101 S.VIB.10.
102 Mellaart (1967, figs 14, 34–36).
103 S.VIB.44; Mellaart (1967, fig. 31).
104 S.VIA.66; Mellaart (1967, figs 39–40).
105 S.VII.8; Mellaart (1967, fig. 43).
106 S.A.III.8; Mellaart (1967, figs 33, 34).
107 A.III.8; Mellaart (1967, fig. 31).
108 S.VIII.21; Mellaart (1967, colour plate VIII).
109 Hamilton (1996, 270).
110 On 'focused polysemy' and 'multivocality' see Lewis-Williams (1998, 2001b).

5 DOMESTICATING WILD NATURE (PAGES 123–148)
1 Katz (1982, 116).
2 Katz (1982, 100). Katz omits clicks from San words, such as !Kung.
3 Katz (1982, 100).
4 Katz (1982, 106).
5 Katz (1982, 116).
6 Gow (2001, 64).
7 Gow (2001, 135).
8 E.g., Level VIIB.
9 Hubert & Mauss (1964 [1898]).
10 Turner (1967).
11 Freidel et al. (1993, 204).
12 Hill (2003).
13 Eliade (1972 [1951], 190–92); cf. Vitebsky (1995, 37).
14 Vitebsky (1995, 61); see Siikala & Hoppál (1992, 33).
15 Vitebsky (1995, 61).
16 Vitebsky (1995, 61).
17 For a trenchant exposé of this position see Sandall (2001).
18 Hodder (1990, 11).
19 Hodder (1990, 5).

20 Hodder (1990, 5).
21 Hodder (1990, 12).
22 Whitley (2002, 120).
23 S.A.III.1.
24 Smith (1992).
25 For a still-useful review of the origins of agriculture see Bender (1975); see also Ingold (1986, 1993); Mithen (2003).
26 Mellaart (1967, 19).
27 Summarized by Isaac (1962, 198); see Hahn (1896, 1909).
28 Isaac (1962, 198).
29 Isaac (1962, 203).
30 Hodder, pers. comm., 2003.
31 For more on these important verbatim manuscripts see Deacon & Dowson (1996); Lewis-Williams (2000); Hollmann (2004).
32 The clicks of the southern African Khoisan languages are represented by signs such as !, ≠, ? and /.
33 Bleek (1936, 144).
34 Lewis-Williams & Dowson (1999, figs 16d, 28, 41a, 45, 46, 49a, 72); Lewis-Williams (2003, figs 23, 39, 55).
35 Bleek (1935, 46).
36 Bleek (1935, 45).
37 Unpublished Bleek & Lloyd MS L.V.4729 rev., Jagger Library, University of Cape Town.
38 Bleek (1935, 47).
39 Unpublished Bleek & Lloyd MS L.V.10.4742–4743. Jagger Library, University of Cape Town.
40 Unpublished Bleek & Lloyd MS L.V.10.4742–4743. Jagger Library, University of Cape Town.
41 See Lewis-Williams & Pearce (2004a, 2004b) on San egalitarianism.
42 Mellaart (1967, 223).
43 Hodder pers. comm., 2003.
44 Mellaart (1967, 172).
45 Mellaart (1967, 173).
46 Mellaart (1967, 175).
47 Hayden (2001, 2003).
48 Cauvin (2000a).
49 Mithen (2003).
50 Bradley (1989); Patton (1990); Lewis-Williams & Dowson (1993); Dronfield (1995).

6 TREASURE THE DREAM WHATEVER THE TERROR (PAGES 149–168)
1 On this and other explanations see Banton (1966); Cohen (1969); Maranda (1972); Kirk (1974); d'Aquili (1978); Hunt (1997); d'Aquili & Newberg (1999). For a recent and brilliant analysis of a myth see Gow (2001).

2 Hodder (1996a, 366).
3 See, for example, Lewis-Williams (1996b, 1997a); Lewis-Williams & Pearce (2004a).
4 On narrative structure, see Propp (1968).
5 Lévi-Strauss (1968).
6 Gow (2001, 56).
7 Lévi-Strauss (1968, 206–31); see also the four volumes of *Mythologiques*, especially Lévi-Strauss (1970).
8 Leach (1969).
9 E.g., Lévi-Strauss (1967).
10 Lévi-Strauss (1968, 229).
11 Leach (1970, 56).
12 Pinker (2002).
13 Eliade (1972 [1951], 38–43); first published by Popov (1936) and Lehtisalo (1937).
14 George (1999, 2003).
15 Sandars (1960, 21).
16 George (2003, vol. 2, 713).
17 After George (1999, 1–99).
18 George (1999, 1).
19 Sandars (1960, 25).
20 Sandars (1960, 82).
21 Sandars (1960, 30).
22 cf. Kirk (1974, 206).
23 Sandars (1960, 69).
24 Sandars (1960, 30–31).
25 Sandars (1960, 96, 101, 103, 106).
26 Sandars (1960, 80).
27 Goren *et al.* (2001, 675); Verhoeven (2002, 238).
28 Sandars (1960, 89).
29 Sandars (1960, 92).
30 Sandars (1960, 77–79).
31 Sandars (1960, 92).
32 George (1999, xxxix).
33 Sandars (1960, 35–36).
34 George (2003[2], 898–901).
35 George (2003[2], 899).
36 Douglas (1957, 1966).
37 Eliade (1972 [1951], 39).
38 Eliade (1972 [1951], 40).
39 Halifax (1982, 15); cf. Price (2003, 208, 320–23) on horses and Viking shamanism.
40 Eliade (1972 [1951], 40–41).
41 Watson (2001a, 188).
42 Eliade (1972 [1951], 41).
43 Lewis-Williams (2001a).
44 Eliade (1972 [1951], 41).
45 Eliade (1972 [1951], 41).
46 Eliade (1972 [1951], 41).
47 Eliade (1972 [1951], 41–42).
48 Eliade (1972 [1951], 41–42).
49 Hodder (1996, 366).
50 Sandars (1960, 93).
51 Mellaart (1967, 16).
52 Hodder (1996a, 366).
53 Lewis-Williams (2002a).
54 See, for example, Hodder (1990); Sherratt (1990); on dating the transition, see Gkiasta *et al.* (2003).

7 THE MOUND IN THE DARK GROVE
(PAGES 169–197)

1 Blake (1933, 999).
2 Beaufort (1828), quoted in Eogan (1986, 18).
3 Stukeley (1776, 48).
4 Renfrew (1982).
5 Renfrew (1973). Twelve years after he devised the phrase, Renfrew felt constrained to say, 'Cognitive archaeology – the study of past ways of thought as inferred from material remains – still presents so many challenges that it seems if not a novel, at any rate, an uncertain endeavour' (Renfrew 1994, 3). Now, another decade and more on, many archaeologists, especially those who study the Neolithic, accept that there was more to ancient life than wresting a living from a hostile Nature.
6 Hemp (1930); see also O'Kelly (1969); Eogan (1983); Lynch (1991); Lynch *et al.* (2000).
7 Bradley pers. comm., 2004.
8 See Pitts (2000) for an entertaining and stimulating account of henge monuments. See also Wainwright (1989).
9 This view has been challenged, but not conclusively (Eogan 1983).
10 Pitts (2000, 38–39).
11 The tongues and grooves on some of the bluestones at Stonehenge suggest that they may have been lintels at an earlier monument.
12 Chippindale (1994, 187–88); see also Edmonds (1993).
13 Lynch (1991, 95).
14 Richards (1996a); see also Condit (1997); Connolly & Condit (1998).
15 Eliade (1959, 20–68); Richards (1996a, 315, 1996b, 206); Watson (2001b).
16 Connolly & Condit (1998, 9).
17 Connolly & Condit (1998, 10).
18 Connolly & Condit (1998, 9).
19 Richards (1996a, 313).
20 Sandars (1960).
21 See Burl (1999, 9–31) for an account of legends relating to Rollright.
22 Quoted in Castleden (1992, 156); see also Burl (1999).
23 Quoted in Castleden (1992, 156).
24 For more on Thom's work see Chippindale (1994, 225 ff.).

25 George (1999, 79).

26 Sandars (1960, 102).

27 George (1999, 79). Square brackets indicate words restored with confidence; italics signal restorations that are not certain (George 1999, liv.).

28 Lynch (1991, 95).

29 Bender (1989).

30 cf. Richards (1996a, 320). This has been true of rock art research as well (cf. Lewis-Williams 1990), where we find that, as understanding of the significance and function of images grows, so emphasis on classification diminishes.

31 Davis & Payne (1993).

32 Boujot & Cassen (1993); see also Thomas (1988, 549–50); Grant (1991).

33 Thomas (1988, 549); see also Thomas & Whittle (1986).

34 Lévi-Strauss (1970).

35 Chesterman (1977).

36 Lynch (1991, 96).

37 Chesterman (1977).

38 Pitts (2000, 38).

39 The stone presently at the site is a replica of the original, which is in the National Museum and Gallery in Cardiff, Wales.

40 Lynch (1991, 94–95).

41 Thomas (1988, 555).

42 Powell & Daniel (1956); Powell et al. (1969); Lynch (1991, 70–79).

43 R. J. Pumphrey, in Powell & Daniel (1956, 16–18).

44 See, for example, Renfrew (1979); Davidson & Henshall (1989).

45 Powell & Daniel (1956, 17).

46 Powell & Daniel (1956, 17).

47 Quoted in Muir (1962, 109).

48 Rudgley (1993, 71–73, 96).

49 Devereux (1997, 102).

50 Rudgley (1993, 72); see also Furst (1976, 158–65).

51 On snakes as links between cosmological levels in South America, see Wilbert (1997).

52 Scarre (2002a, 38).

53 Scarre (2002a, 38).

54 Powell & Daniel (1956, 27–30).

55 Aldhouse-Green (1996).

56 Lynch (2000, 75–77).

57 In other regions communities changed ritual structures in different ways (e.g., Damm 1991; Shee Twohig 2001).

58 Bradley (1998, 104–9).

59 Richards (1996b).

60 Bradley (1998, 86–100).

61 Whittle (1998).

8 BRÚ NA BÓINNE (PAGES 198–249)

1 The name of the river is much older than the 17th-century conflicts. In AD 150 Ptolemy, famous for placing the earth at the centre of the universe, recorded in his geography of Ireland the names of places, rivers and tribes. What we know as the river Boyne was then called Buvinda. A literal translation of this Celtic word is 'illuminated cow', vind meaning white, brightness and wisdom. We wonder if there is here a distant echo of the shining white quartz façade of Newgrange.

2 Stout (2002).

3 See, amongst others, Shee Twohig (1981); O'Kelly (1982); Eogan (1986); Cooney (2000); Stout (2002). All references to O'Kelly (1982) are to M. J. O'Kelly unless otherwise stated.

4 Cooney (2000, 153).

5 Eogan (1998, 1999).

6 On the inclusion of decorated Bretton menhirs in later tombs see L'Helgouac'h (1996). On style and image sequence in the Bend of the Boyne tombs see O'Sullivan (1989); Eogan (1997, 1999); Shee Twohig (2000).

7 Eogan (1997, 232).

8 Cooney (2000, 213–19) gives a persuasive, frankly imaginative, but highly insightful history of events within the Bend of the Boyne. He does not, though, allow for social friction.

9 Marx & Engels (2002 [1848], 219). Marx and Engels specified 'all written history' (p. 219), but later Engels followed Lewis Henry Morgan and considered the breakdown of pre-literate 'primitive communism'.

10 Renfrew (1973); see also Thomas (1984); Bradley & Chapman (1986); Renfrew (1986).

11 Thomas & Whittle (1986, 153).

12 Damm (1991).

13 Thomas (1988, 557).

14 Eogan (1999).

15 See, for example, Tilley (1994); Scarre (2001a, 2002b).

16 cf. Scarre (2002b); Fowler & Cummings (2003).

17 cf. Scarre (2002a).

18 Bradley & Gordon (1988); Parker Pearson (2000).

19 Rousseau (1997 [1762], 146).

20 See, for example, Parker Pearson & Ramilisonina (1998a); Watson (2001b); see also debate by Barrett & Fewster (1998), and Whittle (1998), with response from Parker Pearson & Ramilisonina (1998b): Antiquity 72: 847–56.

21 Michell (1982); Chippindale (1994). On Neolithic landscapes, see Sheridan (1985/6);

Hodder (1990); Thomas (1991); Barrett (1994); Harbison (1994); Bradley (1998); Russell (2002). Our discussion of the monuments in the Bend of the Boyne depends principally on the work of George Eogan (1986), Michael O'Kelly (1982), Gabriel Cooney (2000), David Sweetman (1985, 1987), Elizabeth Shee Twohig (1981, 2000), Geraldine Stout (2002) and numerous other researchers who have produced astounding archaeological insights into this 'constructed landscape'.

22 Cooney & Brady (1998).

23 Stout (2002, 21); for more on Neolithic houses in Ireland see Grogan (1996).

24 Roche (1989); Eogan & Roche (1997a).

25 Grogan (1996, 59–60).

26 Monk (1993); Stout (2002, 22).

27 Thomas (2003).

28 This cognitive process has been a focus of recent archaeological research, e.g., Tilley (1996); Bradley (1998, 2002).

29 Cooney (2000, 30).

30 A tunnel, probably a refuge, built up with drystone walling; made by early Christians.

31 Eogan (1986, 32).

32 Eogan (1986, 32–34).

33 Eogan (1986, 34).

34 Eogan (1986, 34–35).

35 cf. Bradley (1999).

36 Bradley pers. comm., 2004.

37 On the use of space and the placing of tombs see Fraser (1998).

38 cf. Tilley (1996).

39 Eogan (1997, 232–34).

40 The eastern side of this feature was destroyed by an early Christian cobbled area.

41 cf. Fowler & Cummings (2003).

42 Eogan (1986, 48).

43 Fowler & Cummings (2003, 16).

44 Scarre (2002a).

45 Eogan (1986, 48).

46 Eogan (1986, 148).

47 Eogan (1986, 147).

48 Eogan (1986, 148).

49 Eogan (1986, 149–50).

50 Watson & Keating (2000, 261); see also Scarre (1989); Watson & Keating (1999); Watson (2001a).

51 Eogan (1986, 135–36).

52 Eogan (1986, 137).

53 For the locations of cremation deposits in Knowth, see Eogan (1986, figs 19, 20).

54 Eogan (1986, caption to plates 34–37).

55 Eogan & Richardson (1982); Eogan (1986, 42–43, 179–80, pls 34–37, pl. X).

56 Bradley pers. comm., 2004.

57 Clarke et al. (1985, fig. 4.42).

58 Eogan (1986, 180).

59 Wainwright (1989, 32, fig. 4); Bradley pers. comm., 2004.

60 Eogan (1986, b&w pls 22, 24).

61 O'Kelly (1982).

62 O'Kelly (1982, 68).

63 When David prepared to build the temple in Jerusalem, he gathered 'glistering stones' (I Chronicles 29:2).

64 O'Kelly (1982, 75).

65 O'Kelly (1982, 76, 186, fig. 56).

66 O'Kelly (1982, 76).

67 Mitchell (1992); Eogan (1999); Cooney (2000, 136); Meighan et al. (2002); Stout (2002, fig. 25, p. 30).

68 Helskog (1999); see also Scarre (2001a).

69 Eogan (1986, 113–14).

70 Thomas (1923); Thorpe et al. (1991); Scourse (1997); Pitts (2000, 198–204); for a dissenting view see Burl (1999). On the complex history of the construction of Stonehenge see Chippindale (1994); Lawson (1997).

71 O'Kelly (1982, 21).

72 O'Kelly (1982, 93).

73 O'Kelly (1982, pls 40–42).

74 O'Kelly (1982, 96).

75 O'Kelly (1982, 123).

76 Lynch (1973).

77 O'Kelly (1982, 123–24).

78 O'Kelly (1982, 124).

79 E.g., Thom (1967, 1978); North (1996); for critiques, see Ruggles (1999); Pollard & Ruggles (2001); on worldwide alignments see Krupp (1997).

80 Bender (1989); Bradley (1991); Pollard & Ruggles (2001).

81 Stout (2002, fig. 7, p.195).

82 O'Kelly (1982, 149).

83 For a photograph see O'Kelly (1982, fig. 28) or Stout (2002, fig. 18, p. 46).

84 Fraser (1998).

85 Malone (1989, 99).

86 Castleden (1992, 228).

87 Barrett (1994, 29–32).

88 Barrett (1994, 31–32).

89 Schele & Freidel (1990, 105).

90 Schele & Freidel (1990, 317–18).

91 cf. Richards (1996b) on Orkney Neolithic structures.

92 Stout (2002, fig. A, p.82, fig. 5, p. 66). Good aerial photo in Stout (2002, fig. 32, p. 34).

93 Wainwright (1989, 47).

94 Bradley pers. comm., 2004.

95 O'Kelly (1982, pl. 1, Site A).
96 Turner & Turner (1978); see also Morinis (1992); Scarre (2001b).
97 Eade & Sallnow (1991, 2).
98 Barrett (1994, 29).
99 Lewis-Williams & Dowson (1993).

9 RELIGION DE PROFUNDIS (PAGES 250–280)
1 The phrase comes from the title of Lakoff & Johnson (1980).
2 Manuel & Manuel (1972, 97).
3 Sandars (1960, 118).
4 Dante (1998, 147).
5 Beeching (1946, 183).
6 Milford (1923, 93).
7 Dixon & Grierson (1909, 359).
8 Gardner (1953, 61).
9 Russell (2002, 97).
10 Castleden (1992, 143); Russell (2002, 98).
11 cf. Russell (2002, 109).
12 Russell (2002, 105, fig. 61).
13 Russell (2002, 106).
14 Russell (2002, 108).
15 Russell (2002, 108–9).
16 Russell (2002, 110–11).
17 Cooney (2000, 190).
18 Bradley & Edmonds (1993).
19 Clough & Cummins (1988); Mandal & Cooney (1996).
20 E.g., Le Roux (1998).
21 Cooney (2000, 200).
22 cf. Robb (2001, 190).
23 For discussions of quartz and colour in archaeological research see Jones & MacGregor (2002); Scarre (2002a).
24 E.g., Darvill (2002).
25 Darvill (2002, 85).
26 Darvill (2002, 85); Burl (1981, 93) also argued for associations with the moon.
27 Scarre (2002a, 238).
28 Vitebsky (1995, 82).
29 Elkin (1994 [1946], 13).
30 Elkin (1994 [1946], 87).
31 Rose (1957, 95). Rose adopts a parapsychological approach, from which we dissociate ourselves.
32 Rose (1957, 95–96).
33 Asaad (1980).
34 Siegel (1978, 313, 1992, 29); Lewis-Williams (1997b), reprinted in Lewis-Williams (2002b).
35 Rose (1957, 96).
36 Rose (1957, 96).
37 Berndt & Berndt (1992, 308–9).
38 Jones & White (1988).
39 Jones & White (1988, 84).
40 Jones & White (1988, 54).
41 Taçon (1991, 198).
42 Whitley et al. (1999).
43 Whitley et al. (1999, 234).
44 Driver (1937, 59); Vogelin (1938, 64); Zigmond (1986, 406).
45 See also Whitley (2000).
46 Reichel-Dolmatoff (1971, 16, 118).
47 Reichel-Dolmatoff (1979).
48 Reichel-Dolmatoff (1979, 121).
49 Reichel-Dolmatoff (1979, 127).
50 Reichel-Dolmatoff (1979, 127).
51 Reichel-Dolmatoff (1979, 119, 129).
52 Reichel-Dolmatoff (1979, 177).
53 Reichel-Dolmatoff (1979, 176, 177, 181).
54 Reichel-Dolmatoff (1978, 1985).
55 Reichel-Dolmatoff (1988, 22).
56 Whitley et al. (1999).
57 Bradley pers. comm., 2004.
58 Eogan (1999).
59 O'Sullivan (1996).
60 Eogan (1992).
61 Patton (1991, 67–68).
62 Eogan (1999).
63 Eichmeier & Höfer (1974, 151–60).
64 Lewis-Williams & Dowson (1988).
65 Bradley (1989).
66 Patton (1990).
67 Lewis-Williams & Dowson (1993).
68 Lewis-Williams & Dowson (1993).
69 Dronfield (1993, 1994, 1995, 1996).
70 Dronfield (1995, 545, 548).
71 The early incised linear motifs in the Boyne valley and Orkney do not seem to conform with entoptic elements; they may call for a separate explanation (Bradley et al. 2000).
72 Reichel-Dolmatoff (1985, 2).
73 Reichel-Dolmatoff (1985, 33).
74 Dronfield (1996).
75 Dronfield (1996, 45). See also Shee Twohig (1996).
76 Dronfield (1996, 47).
77 C. O'Kelly (1982, 147); Eogan (1986, 181–95).
78 Dronfield (1996, 47).
79 Dronfield (1996, 48).
80 Reichel-Dolmatoff (1978, pls VIII, XVI).
81 Reichel-Dolmatoff (1978, 49).
82 Reichel-Dolmatoff (1978, 49).
83 Reichel-Dolmatoff (1978, 1).
84 Reichel-Dolmatoff (1978, 64).
85 Reichel-Dolmatoff (1978, 54).
86 Reichel-Dolmatoff (1978, 80).
87 Reichel-Dolmatoff (1978, 80).
88 For others see Lewis-Williams & Dowson (1988).

89 Siegel & Jarvik (1975, 114).
90 Shee Twohig (1981, fig. 247B).
91 Klüver (1942, 177); Siegel (1977, 134).
92 Reichel-Dolmatoff (1978, pls K–M).
93 Siegel & Jarvik (1975, 132).
94 Reichel-Dolmatoff (1978, pl. 10).
95 Bradley (1989, fig. 5).
96 Bradley (1989, 72); cf. Patton (1990, 556, 1991).
97 Patton (1991) has argued that Neolithic Brittany axes had male associations and may have represented phalli. Axe exchange inextricably linked the 'sacred' and the 'secular' components of Neolithic life.
98 Renfrew (1973); Shanks & Tilley (1982); Bradley & Chapman (1986, 36).
99 Sherratt (1991, 52); see also Sherratt (1997, 376–402).
100 Marx & Engels (2002 [1848], 39).
101 E.g., Lewis (1971); Stephen (1979); Hayden

(1987); Thomas & Humphrey (1996).
102 Thomas (1990, 175).

10 EAST IS EAST AND WEST IS WEST (PAGES 281–290)
1 De La Mare (1969).
2 Hawkes (1954).
3 Kipling (1940, 268).
4 Thomas (1991, 2003, 72).
5 Thomas (2003).
6 Thomas (2003, 70).
7 Bradley & Gordon (1988); Parker Pearson (2000).
8 E.g., Dornan (2004).
9 Hayden (1977, 358–59).
10 d'Aquili & Newberg (1999).
11 cf. Swenson (2003).
12 Quoted in Freeman (2002, xvii).
13 Quoted in Freeman (2002, 145).
14 Tinker & Lowry (1950).

Bibliography and Guide to Further Reading

Aldhouse-Green, S. H. R. 1996. Hoyle's Mouth and Little Hoyle caves. *Archaeology in Wales* 36, 70–71.

Asaad, G. 1980. *Hallucinations in Clinical Psychiatry: A Guide for Mental Health Professionals.* New York: Brunner/Mazel.

Asaad, G. & Shapiro, B. 1986. Hallucinations: theoretical and clinical overview. *American Journal of Psychiatry* 143, 1088–97.

Atkinson, J. M. 1992. Shamanisms today. *Annual Review of Anthropology* 21, 307–30.

Aujoulat, N., Geneste, J.-M., Archambeau, C., Barraud, D., Delluc, M., Duday, H. & Gambier, D. 2001. The decorated cave of Cussac. *INORA* 30, 3–9.

Banton, M. (ed.) 1966. *Anthropological Approaches to the Study of Religion.* London: Tavistock.

Barrett, J. C. 1994. *Fragments From Antiquity: An Archaeology of Social Life in Britain, 2900–1200 BC.* Oxford: Blackwell.

Barrett, J. C. & Fewster, K. J. 1998. Stonehenge: *is* the medium the message? *Antiquity* 72, 847–52.

Bean, L. J. (ed.) 1992. *California Indian Shamanism.* Meno Park: Ballena Press.

Beaufort, L. C. 1828. An essay upon the state of Architecture and Antiquities, previous to the landing of the Anglo-Normans in Ireland. *Transactions of the Royal Irish Academy* 15, 101–242.

Becker, J. 1994. Music and trance. *Leonardo Music Journal* 4, 41–51.

Beeching, H. C. (ed.) 1946. *The English poems of John Milton.* Oxford: Oxford University Press.

Bégouën, R. & Clottes, J. 1981. Apports mobiliers dans les cavernes du Volp (Enlène, Les Trois-Frères, Le Tuc d'Audoubert). *Altamira Symposium*, pp. 157–87.

Bender, B. 1975. *Farming in Prehistory: From Hunter-Gatherer to Food-Producer.* London: John Baker.

Bender, B. 1989. The roots of inequality. In Miller, D., Rowlands, M. & Tilley, C. (eds) *Domination and Resistance*, pp. 83–93. London: Unwin and Hyman.

Berger, P. L. 1973. *The Social Reality of Religion.* London: Penguin.

Berndt, R. M. & Berndt, C. H. 1992. *The World of the First Australians: Aboriginal Traditional Life: Past and Present.* Canberra: Aboriginal

Studies Press (first published 1964, Sydney: Ure Smith).

Bienert, H.-D. 1992. Skull cult in the prehistoric Near East. *Journal of Prehistoric Religion* 5, 9–23.

Biesele, M. 1993. *Women Like Meat: The Folklore and Foraging Ideology of the Kalahari Ju/'hoan.* Johannesburg: Witwatersrand University Press.

Blackmore, S. 1982. *Beyond the Body: An Investigation of Out-of-the-body Experiences.* London: Heinemann.

Blake, W. 1933. Jerusalem. In *The Methodist Hymn-book.* London: Methodist Conference Office.

Blanke, O., Ortigue, S., Landis, T. & Seeck, M. 2002. Stimulating illusory own-body perceptions: the part of the brain that can induce out-of-body experiences has been located. *Nature* 419, 269–70.

Bleek, D. F. 1933. Beliefs and customs of the /Xam Bushmen. Part VI: Rain-making. *Bantu Studies* 7, 375–92.

Bleek, D. F. 1935. Beliefs and customs of the /Xam Bushmen. Part VII: Sorcerers. *Bantu Studies* 9, 1–47.

Bleek, D. F. 1936. Beliefs and customs and the /Xam Bushmen. Part VIII: More about sorcerers and charms. *Bantu Studies* 10, 131–62.

Bleek, W. H. I. & Lloyd, L. C. 1911. *Specimens of Bushman Folklore.* London: George Allen.

Bogoras, W. 1907. *The Chukchee, Part II: Religion.* Memoirs of the American Museum of Natural History, vol. 11.

Bonogofsky, M. 2002. Reassessing dental 'evulsion' in Neolithic plastered skulls from the Levant through use of computed tomography, direct observation, and photographs. *Journal of Archaeological Science* 29, 959–64.

Boujot, C. & Cassen, S. 1993. A pattern of evolution for the Neolithic funerary structures of the west of France. *Antiquity* 67, 477–91.

Bourguignon, E. 1972. Dreams and altered states of consciousness in anthropological research. In Hsu, F. L. K. (ed.) *Psychological Anthropology*, pp. 403–34. Cambridge, Mass.: Schenkman.

Bradley, R. 1989. Deaths and entrances: a contextual analysis of megalithic art. *Current Anthropology* 30, 68–75.

Bradley, R. 1991. Ritual, time and history. *World Archaeology* 23, 209–19.

Bradley, R. 1998. *The Significance of Monuments: On the Shaping of Human Experience in Neolithic and Bronze Age Europe.* London: Routledge.

Bradley, R. 1999. The stony limits: rock carvings in passage graves and in the open air. In Harding, A. (ed.) *Experiment and Design: Archaeological Studies in Honour of John Coles*, pp. 30–36. Oxford: Oxbow Books.

Bradley, R. 2002. *The Past in Prehistoric Societies.* London: Routledge.

Bradley, R. & Chapman, R. 1986. The nature and development of long-distance relations in Later Neolithic Britain and Ireland. In Renfrew, C. & Cherry, J. F. (eds) *Peer Polity Interaction and Socio-Political Change*, pp. 127–36. Cambridge: Cambridge University Press.

Bradley, R. & Edmonds, M. 1993. *Interpreting the Axe Trade: Production and Exchange in Neolithic Britain.* Cambridge: Cambridge University Press.

Bradley, R. J. & Gordon, F. 1988. Human skulls from the River Thames, their dating and significance. *Antiquity* 62, 503–9.

Bradley, R., Phillips, T., Richards, C. & Webb, M. 2000. Decorating the houses of the dead: incised and pecked motifs in Orkney chambered tombs. *Cambridge Archaeological Journal* 11, 45–67.

Bressloff, P. C., Cowan, J. D., Golubitsky, M., Thomas, P. J. & Wiener, M. C. 2001. Geometric visual hallucinations, Euclidean symmetry and the functional architecture of the striate cortex. *Philosophical Transactions of the Royal Society, London, Series B* 356, 299–330.

Brindley, G. S. 1973. Sensory effects of electrical stimulation of the visual and paravisual cortex in man. In Jung, R. (ed.) *Handbook of Sensory Psychology*, vol. 7, pp. 583–94. New York: Springer-Verlag.

Brown, D. E. 1991. *Human Universals.* Philadelphia: Temple University Press.

Burl, A. 1981. *Rites of the Gods.* London: Dent.

Burl, A. 1999. *Great Stone Circles.* New Haven: Yale University Press.

Cardeña, E. 1988. Deep hypnosis and shamanism: convergences and divergences. In Heinze, R.-I. (ed.) *Proceedings of the Fourth International Conference on the Study of Shamanism and Alternate Modes of Healing*, pp. 289–303. Madison: A-R Editions.

Cardeña, E. 1992. Trance and possession as dissociative disorders. *Transcultural Psychiatric Research Review* 29, 287–300.

Cardeña, E. 1996. 'Just floating in the sky': a comparison of shamanistic and hypnotic phenomenology. In Quekelberge, R. & Eigner, D. (eds) *Sixth Yearbook of Cross-cultural*

Medicine and Psychotherapy, pp. 367–80. Berlin: Verlag für Wissenschaft und Bildung.

Castleden, R. 1992. *Neolithic Britain: New Stone Age Sites of England, Scotland and Wales.* London: Routledge.

Cauvin, J. 2000a. *The Birth of the Gods and the Origins of Agriculture.* Cambridge: Cambridge University Press.

Cauvin, J. 2000b. The symbolic foundations of the Neolithic Revolution in the Near East. In Kuijt, I. (ed.) *Life in Neolithic Farming Communities: Social Organization, Identity, and Differentiation*, pp. 235–51. New York: Kluwer.

Chesterman, J. T. 1977. Burial rites in a Cotswold long barrow. *Man* (n.s.) 12, 22–32.

Chippindale, C. 1994. *Stonehenge Complete.* London & New York: Thames & Hudson.

Chippindale, C. 2004. *Stonehenge Complete.* Third edition. London & New York: Thames & Hudson.

Chippindale, C. & Taçon, P. S. C. (eds) 1998. *The Archaeology of Rock-art.* Cambridge: Cambridge University Press.

Clarke, D. V., Cowie, T. G. & Foxon, A. 1985. *Symbols of Power at the Time of Stonehenge.* Edinburgh: National Museum of Antiquities of Scotland.

Clottes, J. 2004. Hallucinations in caves. *Cambridge Archaeological Journal* 14(1), 81–82.

Clottes, J. & Lewis-Williams, J. D. 1996. *Les Chamanes de la Préhistoire: Trans et Magie Dans les Grottes Ornées.* Paris: Le Seuil.

Clottes, J. & Lewis-Williams, J. D. 1998. *The Shamans of Prehistory: Trance and Magic in the Painted Caves.* New York: Harry Abrams.

Clough, T. H. McK. & Cummins, W. A. (eds) 1988. *Stone Axe Studies II: The Petrology of Prehistoric Stone Implements from the British Isles.* London: Council for British Archaeology, Research Report 67.

Clutton-Brock, J. 1999. *A Natural History of Domesticated Animals.* Cambridge: Cambridge University Press.

Cohen, P. S. 1969. Theories of myth. *Man* (n.s.) 4(3), 337–53.

Cohen, S. 1964. *The Beyond Within: The LSD Story.* New York: Atheneum.

Condit, T. 1997. Monknewtown ritual pond. In Condit, T. & Cooney, G. (eds) *Brú na Bóinne.* Dublin: Royal Irish Academy.

Connolly, M. & Condit, T. 1998. Ritual enclosures in the Lee Valley, Co. Kerry. *Archaeology Ireland* 46, 8–12.

Cooney, G. 2000. *Landscapes of Neolithic Ireland.* London: Routledge.

Cooney, G. & Brady, C. 1998. The Red Mountain transect: the results of a pilot fieldwalking study in the Boyne Valley area, unpublished report, Department of Archaeology, University College, Dublin.

Crocker, J. C. 1985. *Vital Souls: Bororo Cosmology, Natural Symbolism, and Shamanism.* Tucson: University of Arizona Press.

Cytowic, R. E. 1994. *The Man who Tasted Shapes: A Bizarre Medical Mystery offers Revolutionary Insights into Emotions, Reasoning, and Consciousness.* London: Abacus.

Damm, C. B. 1991. Burying the past: an example of social transformation in the Danish Neolithic. In Garwood, P., Jennings, D., Skeates, R. & Toms, J. (eds) *Sacred and Profane: Proceedings of a Conference on Archaeology, Ritual and Religion, Oxford, 1989*, pp. 43–49. Oxford: Oxford University Committee for Archaeology.

Dante, A. 1998. *Inferno.* (Trans. Henry Francis Cary). Ware: Wordsworth Editions.

d'Aquili, E. 1978. The neurological basis of myth and concepts of deity. *Zygon* 13, 257–75.

d'Aquili, E. & Newberg, A. B. 1993. Religious and mystical states: a neuropsychological model. *Zygon* 28, 177–99.

d'Aquili, E. & Newberg, A. B. 1999. *The Mystical Mind: Probing the Biology of Religious Experience.* Minneapolis: Fortress Press.

Darvill, T. 2002. White on blonde: quartz pebbles and the use of quartz at Neolithic monuments in the Isle of Man and beyond. In Jones, A. & MacGregor, G. (eds) *Colouring the Past: The Significance of Colour in Archaeological Research*, pp. 73–91. Oxford: Berg.

Davidson, J. L. & Henshall, A. S. 1989. *The Chambered Cairns of Orkney.* Edinburgh: Edinburgh University Press.

Davis, S. & Payne, S. 1993. A barrow full of cattle skulls. *Antiquity* 67, 12–22.

Deacon, J. & Dowson, T. A. (eds) 1996. *Voices From the Past: /Xam Bushmen and the Bleek and Lloyd Collection.* Johannesburg: Witwatersrand University Press.

De La Mare, W. 1969. *The Complete Poems of Walter De La Mare*, p. 126. London: Faber and Faber.

Denning-Bolle, S. 1992. *Wisdom in Akkadian Literature: Expression, Instruction, Dialogue.* Mededelingen en verhandelingen van het Vooraziatisch-Eqypisch Genootschap 'Ex Orient Lux' 28. Leiden: Ex Oriente Lux.

Devereux, P. 1997. *The Long Trip: A Prehistory of Psychedelia*. London: Penguin.

Dixon, W. M. & Grierson, H. J. C. (eds) 1909. *The English Parnassus: An Anthology of Longer Poems*. Oxford: Clarendon Press.

Dobkin de Rios, M. 1990. *Hallucinogens: Cross-cultural Perspectives*. Bridport: Prism Press.

Dornan, J. L. 2004. Beyond belief: religious experience, ritual, and cultural neuro-phenomenology in the interpretation of past religious systems. *Cambridge Archaeological Journal* 14, 25–36.

Douglas, M. 1957. Animals in Lele religious symbolism. *Africa* 27, 47–58.

Douglas, M. 1966. *Purity and Danger: An Analysis of Concepts of Pollution and Taboo*. London: Routledge & Kegan Paul.

Drab, K. J. 1981. The tunnel experience: reality or hallucination? *Anabiosis* 1, 126–52.

Driver, H. E. 1937. Culture element distributions, part 6: southern Sierra Nevada. *University of California Anthropological Records* 1(2), 53–154.

Dronfield, J. C. 1993. Ways of seeing, ways of telling: Irish passage tomb art, style and the universality of vision. In Lorblanchet, M. & Bahn, P. (eds) *Rock Art Studies: The Post-stylistic Era*, pp. 179–93. Oxford: Oxbow.

Dronfield, J. C. 1994. Subjective Visual Phenomena in Irish Passage Tomb Art: Vision, Cosmology and Shamanism. Unpublished Ph.D. dissertation, University of Cambridge.

Dronfield, J. C. 1995. Subjective vision and the source of Irish megalithic art. *Antiquity* 69, 539–49.

Dronfield, J. C. 1996. Entering alternative realities: cognition, art and architecture in Irish passage-tombs. *Cambridge Archaeological Journal* 6, 37–72.

Eade, J. & Sallnow, M. J. 1991. Introduction. In Eade, J. & Sallnow, M. J. (eds) *Contesting the Sacred: The Anthropology of Christian Pilgrimage*, pp. 1–29. London: Routledge.

Edmonds, M. R. 1993. Interpreting causewayed enclosures in the past and the present. In Tilley, C. (ed.) *Interpretative Archaeology*, pp. 99–142. London: Berg.

Eichmeier, J. & Höfer, D. 1974. *Endogene Bildmuster*. Munich: Urban and Schwarzenberg.

Eliade, M. 1959. *The Sacred and the Profane: The Nature of Religion*. New York: Harcourt, Brace Jovanovich.

Eliade, M. 1972 [1951]. *Shamanism: Archaic Techniques of Ecstasy*. New York: Routledge & Kegan Paul.

Elkin, A. P. 1994 [1946]. *Aboriginal Men of High Degree: Initiation and Sorcery in the World's Oldest Tradition*. St Lucia: University of Queensland Press.

Emboden, W. 1979. *Narcotic Plants*. New York: Macmillan.

Eogan, G. 1983. Bryn Celli Ddu. *Antiquity* 57, 135–36.

Eogan, G. 1986. *Knowth and the Passage Tombs of Ireland*. London & New York: Thames & Hudson.

Eogan, G. 1992. Scottish and Irish passage tombs: some comparisons and contrasts. In Sharples, N., Sharples, A. & Sheridan, A. (eds) *Vessels for the Ancestors*, pp. 120–27. Edinburgh: Edinburgh University Press.

Eogan, G. 1997. Overlays and underlays: aspects of megalithic art succession at Brugh na Bóinne, Ireland. In Bello Diéguez, J. M. (ed.) *III Coloquio Internacional de Arte Megalítico: Actes*, pp. 217–34. A Coruña: Brigantium 10.

Eogan, G. 1998. Knowth before Knowth. *Antiquity* 72, 162–70.

Eogan, G. 1999. Megalithic art and society. *Proceedings of the Prehistoric Society* 65, 415–46.

Eogan, G. & Richardson, H. 1982. Two maceheads from Knowth, County Meath. *Journal of the Royal Society of Antiquaries of Ireland* 112, 123–38.

Eogan, G. & Roche, H. 1997a. Pre-tomb Neolithic house discovered at Knowth, Co. Meath. *Archaeology Ireland* 40, 31.

Eogan, G. & Roche, H. 1997b. *Excavations at Knowth, 2*. Dublin: Royal Irish Academy.

Fagan, B. 1998. *From Black Land to Fifth Sun: The Science of Sacred Sites*. Reading, Mass.: Helix Books.

Fernandez, J. W. 1972. Tabernanthe iboga: narcotic ecstasis and the work of the ancestors. In Furst, P. T. (ed.) *Flesh of the Gods: The Ritual use of Hallucinogens*, pp. 237–60. London: Allen and Unwin.

ffytche, D. H. 2002. Cortical bricks and mortar. *Journal of Neurology, Neurosurgery and Psychiatry* 73, 472.

ffytche, D. H. & Howard, R. J. 1999. The perceptual consequences of visual loss: positive pathologies of vision. *Brain* 122, 1247–60.

ffytche, D. H., Howard, R. J., Brammer, M. J., David, A., Woodruff, P. & Williams, S. 1998. The anatomy of conscious vision: an fMRI study of visual hallucinations. *Nature Neuroscience* 1, 738–42.

Flannery, K. V. 1973. The origins of agriculture. *Annual Review of Anthropology* 2, 271–310.

Forest, J.-D. 1983. *Les pratiques funéraires en Mésopotamie du 5e millénaire au début du 3e: étude de cas.* Délégation archéologique française en Iraq, URA 8 du CRA du C.N.R.S.

Fowler, C. & Cummings, V. 2003. Places of transformation: building monuments from water and stone in the Neolithic of the Irish Sea. *Journal of the Royal Anthropological Institute* (n.s.) 9, 1–20.

Fox, M. 2003. *Religion, Spirituality and the Near-death Experience.* London: Routledge.

Fraser, S. 1998. The public forum and the space between: the materiality of social strategy in the Irish Neolithic. *Proceedings of the Prehistoric Society* 64, 203–24.

Freeman, C. 2002. *The Closing of the Western Mind: The Rise of Faith and the Fall of Reason.* London: Heinemann.

Freidel, D., Schele, L. & Parker, J. 1993. *Maya Cosmos: Three Thousand Years on the Shaman's Path.* New York: William Morrow.

Friedman, J. 1974. Marxism, structuralism and vulgar materialism. *Man* (n.s.) 9, 444–69.

Furst, P. T. (ed.) 1972. *Flesh of the Gods: The Ritual use of Hallucinogens.* London: Allen and Unwin.

Furst, P. T. 1976. *Hallucinogens and Culture.* Novato, Ca: Chandler and Sharp.

Gardner, W. H. (ed.) 1953. *The Poems and Prose of Gerard Manley Hopkins.* Penguin: London.

Garwood, P., Jennings, D., Skeates, R. & Toms, J. (eds) 1991. *Sacred and Profane: Proceedings of a Conference on Archaeology, Ritual and Religion, Oxford, 1989.* Oxford: Oxford University Committee for Archaeology.

Geertz, C. 1966. Religion as a cultural system. In Banton, M. (ed.) *Anthropological Approaches to the Study of Religion,* pp. 1–46. London: Tavistock.

Geertz, C. 1973. *Interpretation of Cultures.* New York: Basic Books.

George, A. 1999. *The Epic of Gilgamesh: The Babylonian Epic Poem and other Texts in Akkadian and Sumerian.* London: Penguin.

George, A. 2003. *The Babylonian Gilgamesh Epic.* Two volumes. Oxford: Oxford University Press.

Gkiasta, M., Russell, T., Shennan, S. & Steele, J. 2003. Neolithic transition in Europe: the radiocarbon record revisited. *Antiquity* 77, 45–62.

Goodman, J., Lovejoy, P. & Sherratt, A. (eds) 1995. *Consuming Habits: Drugs in History and Anthropology.* London: Routledge.

Goren, Y., Goring-Morris, A. N. & Segal, I. 2001. The technology of skull modeling in the Pre-Pottery Neolithic B (PPNB): regional variability, the relation of technology and iconography and their archaeological implications. *Journal of Archaeological Science* 28, 671–90.

Goring-Morris, N. 2000. The quick and the dead: the social context of aceramic Neolithic mortuary practices as seen from Kfar HaHoresh. In Kuijt, I. (ed.) *Life in Neolithic Farming Communities: Social Organization, Identity, and Differentiation,* pp. 103–36. New York: Kluwer.

Goring-Morris, A. N., Goren, Y., Horwitz, L. K. & Bar-Yosef, D. 1995. Investigations at an Early Neolithic settlement in Lower Galilee: results of the 1991 season at Kfar HaHoresh. *Antiqot* 27, 37–62.

Gow, P. 2001. *An Amazonian Myth and its History.* Oxford: Oxford University Press.

Grant, A. 1991. Economic or symbolic? Animals and ritual behaviour. In Garwood, P., Jennings, D., Skeates, R. & Toms, J. (eds) *Sacred and Profane: Proceedings of a Conference on Archaeology, Ritual and Religion, Oxford, 1989,* pp. 109–14. Oxford: Oxford University Committee for Archaeology.

Greene, K. 1999. V. Gordon Childe and the vocabulary of revolutionary change. *Antiquity* 73, 97–109.

Grogan, E. 1996. Neolithic houses in Ireland. In Darvill, T. C. & Thomas, J. S. (eds) *Neolithic Houses in Northwest Europe and Beyond,* pp. 41–60. Oxford: Oxbow.

Guenther, M. 1999. *Tricksters & Trancers: Bushman Religion and Society.* Bloomington: Indiana University Press.

Haaland, G. & Haaland, R. 1995. Who speaks the goddess's language? Imagination and method in archaeological research. *Norwegian Archaeologica Review* 37(2), 105–21.

Haber, A. & Dayan, T. 2004. Analyzing the process of domestication: Hagoshrim as a case study. *Journal of Archaeological Science* 31, 1587–601.

Hahn, E. 1896. *Die Haustiere und thre Beziehungen zur Wirtschaft des Menschen.* Leipzig: Duncker and Humbolt.

Hahn, E. 1909. *Die Entstehung der Pflügkultur.* Heidelberg: Winter.

Halifax, J. 1979. *Shamanistic Voices: A Survey of Visionary Narratives.* London: Penguin.

Halifax, J. 1982. *Shaman: The Wounded Healer.* New York: Crossroad.

Hamilton, N. 1996. Figurines, clay balls, small

finds and burials. In Hodder, I. (ed.) *On the Surface. Çatalhöyük 1993–95*, pp. 215–63. Cambridge: McDonald Institute for Archaeological Research.

Harbison, P. 1994. *Pre-Christian Ireland: From the First Settlers to the Early Celts*. London & New York: Thames & Hudson.

Harner, M. (ed.) 1973a. *Hallucinogens and Shamanism*. New York: Oxford University Press.

Harner, M. J. 1973b. Common themes in South American Indian *yajé* experiences. In Harner, M. J. (ed.) *Hallucinogens and Shamanism*, pp. 155–75. New York: Oxford University Press.

Harner, M. 1982. *The Way of the Shaman*. New York: Bantam.

Hauptmann, H. 1999. The Urfa Region. In Özdogan, M. (ed.) *Neolithic in Turkey*, pp. 65–86. Istanbul: Arkeoloji ve Sanat Yayinlari.

Hawkes, C. 1954. Archaeological theory and method: some suggestions from the Old World. *American Anthropologist* 56(1), 155–68.

Hayden, B. 1987. Alliances and ritual ecstasy: human responses to resource stress. *Journal for the Scientific Study of Religion* 26, 81–91.

Hayden, B. 1990. Nimrods, piscators, pluckers, and planters: the emergence of food production. *Journal of Anthropological Archaeology* 9, 31–69.

Hayden, B. 2001. Fabulous feasts. In Dietler, M. & Hayden, B. (eds) *Feasts*, pp. 23–64. Washington: Smithsonian Institution Press.

Hayden, B. 2003. *Shamans, Sorcerers and Saints: A Prehistory of Religion*. Washington: Smithsonian Books.

Hayden, J. O. (ed.) 1977. *William Wordsworth: The Poems*. Vol. 1. New Haven: Yale University Press.

Heinze, R.-I. 1986. More on mental imagery and shamanism. *Current Anthropology* 27, 154.

Helskog, K. 1999. The shore connection: cognitive landscape and communication with rock carvings in northernmost Europe. *Norwegian Archaeological Review* 32, 73–94.

Helskog, K. (ed.) 2001. *Theoretical Perspectives in Rock Art Research*. Oslo: Novus Forlag.

Helskog, K. & Olsen, B. (eds) 1995. *Perceiving Rock Art: Social and Political Perspectives*. Oslo: Novus Forlag.

Helvenston, P. A. & Bahn, P. G. 2002. *Desperately Seeking Trance Plants: Testing the 'Three Stages of Trance' Model*. New York: R. J. Communications.

Helvenston, P. A. & Bahn, P. G. 2003. Testing the 'three stages of trance' model. *Cambridge Archaeological Journal* 13(2), 213–24.

Hemp, W. J. 1930. The chambered cairn of Bryn Celli Ddu. *Archaeologia* 80, 179–214.

Herity, M. 1974. *Irish Passage Graves*. Dublin: Irish University Press.

Heun, M., Schafer-Pregl, R., Klawan, D., Castagna, R., Accerbi, M., Borghi, B. & Salamini, F. 1997. Site of einkorn wheat domestication identified by DNA fingerprinting. *Science* 278, 1312–14.

Hill, E. 2003. Sacrificing Moche bodies. *Journal of Material Culture* 8, 285–99.

Hodder, I. 1990. *The Domestication of Europe: Structure and Contingency in Neolithic Societies*. Oxford: Blackwell.

Hodder, I. 1996a. Conclusions. In Hodder, I. (ed.) *On the Surface: Çatalhöyük 1993–95*, pp. 359–66. Cambridge: McDonald Institute for Archaeological Research.

Hodder, I. 1996b. Re-opening Çatalhöyük. In Hodder, I. (ed.) *On the Surface: Çatalhöyük 1993–95*, pp. 1–18. Cambridge: McDonald Institute for Archaeological Research.

Hodder, I. (ed.) 1996c. *On the Surface: Çatalhöyük 1993–95*. Cambridge: McDonald Institute for Archaeological Research.

Hodder, I. (ed.) 2000. *Towards Reflexive Method in Archaeology: The Example at Çatalhöyük*. Cambridge: McDonald Institute for Archaeological Research.

Hodder, I. (ed.) 2005a. *Inhabiting Çatalhöyük: Reports from the 1995–99 Seasons*. Cambridge: McDonald Institute for Archaeological Research.

Hodder, I. (ed.) 2005b. *Changing Materialities at Çatalhöyük: Reports from the 1995–99 Seasons*. Cambridge: McDonald Institute for Archaeological Research.

Hodder, I. & Cessford, C. 2004. Daily practice and social memory at Çatalhöyük. *American Antiquity* 69(1): 17–40.

Hollman, J. (ed.) 2004. *Customs and Beliefs of the /Xam Bushmen*. Johannesburg: Witwatersrand University Press.

Horowitz, M. J. 1964. The imagery of visual hallucinations. *Journal of Nervous and Mental Disease* 138, 513–23.

Horowitz, M. 1975. Hallucinations: an information-processing approach. In Siegel, R. K. & West, L. J. (eds) *Hallucinations: Behaviour, Experience, and Theory*, pp. 163–95. New York: Wiley.

Hubert, H. & Mauss M. 1964 [1898]. *Sacrifice: Its Nature and Function*. (Trans. W. D. Halls.) Chicago: University of Chicago Press.

Hugh-Jones, C. 1979. *From the Milk River:*

Spatial and Temporal Processes in Northwest Amazonia. Cambridge: Cambridge University Press.

Hugh-Jones, S. 1979. *The Palm and the Pleiades: Initiation and Cosmology in Northwest Amazonia.* Cambridge: Cambridge University Press.

Hugh-Jones, S. 1996. Shamans, prophets, priests, and pastors. In Thomas, N. & Humphrey, C. (eds) *Shamanism, History, and the State.* Ann Arbor: University of Michigan Press.

Hultkrantz, A. 1987. *Native Religions of North America: The Power of Visions and Fertility.* San Francisco: Harper & Row.

Hunt, E. 1997. *The Transformation of the Hummingbird: Cultural Roots of a Zinacantecan Mythical Poem.* Ithaca: Cornell University Press.

Hutton, R. 2001. *Shamans: Siberian Spirituality and the Western Imagination.* London: Hambledon and London.

Ingold, T. 1986. *The Appropriation of Nature: Essays in Human Ecology and Social Relations.* Manchester: Manchester University Press.

Ingold, T. 1993. The reindeerman's lasso. In Lemonnier, P. (ed.) *Technological Choices: Transformation in Material Cultures since the Neolithic,* pp. 108–25. London: Routledge.

Isaac, E. 1962. On the domestication of cattle. *Science* 137, 195–204.

Jones, A. & MacGregor, G. (eds) 2002. *Colouring the Past: The Significance of Colour in Archaeological Research.* Oxford: Berg.

Jones, R. & White, N. 1988. Point blank: stone tool manufacture at the Ngilipitji Quarry, Arnhem Land, 1981. In Meehan, B. & Jones, R. (eds) *Archaeology with Ethnography: An Australian Perspective,* pp. 51–93. Canberra: Australian National University.

Jordan, P. 2001. The materiality of shamanism as a 'world-view': Praxis, artefacts and landscape. In Price, N. (ed.) *The Archaeology of Shamanism,* pp. 87–104. London: Routledge.

Katz, K. 1982. *Boiling Energy: Community Healing Among the Kalahari Kung.* Cambridge, Mass.: Harvard University Press.

Katz, R., Biesele, M. & St. Denis, V. 1997. *Healing Makes our Hearts Happy: Spirituality and Cultural Transformation Amongst the Kalahari Ju/'hoansi.* Rochester: Inner Traditions.

Keeney, B. 2003. *Ropes to God: Experiencing the Bushman Spiritual Universe.* Philadelphia: Ringing Rocks Press.

Kenyon, K. 1957. *Digging Up Jericho.* London: Ernest Benn Limited.

Kingsley, C. 1848. Letters to the Chartists 2. *Politics for the People,* May 27.

Kipling, R. 1940. *Rudyard Kipling's Verse.* Inclusive edition. London: Hodder & Stoughton, Ltd.

Kirk, G. S. 1974. *The Nature of Greek Myths.* London: Penguin.

Klüver, H. 1942. Mechanisms of hallucinations. In McNemar, Q. & Merrill, M. A. (eds) *Studies in Personality,* pp. 175–207. New York: McGraw-Hill.

Klüver, H. 1966. *Mescal and Mechanisms of Hallucination.* Chicago: University of Chicago Press.

Kohler-Rollefson, I. 1989. Changes in goat exploitation at 'Ain-Ghazal between the Early and Late Neolithic: a metrical analysis. *Paleorient* 15, 141–46.

Kromer, B. & Schmidt, K. 1998. Two radiocarbon dates from Göbekli Tepe, South Eastern Turkey. *Neo-Lithics* 3/98, 8–9.

Krupp, E. C. 1997. *Skywatchers, Shamans and Kings: Astronomy and the Archaeology of Power.* New York: John Wiley.

Kuhn, T. S. 1957. *The Copernican Revolution: Planetary Astronomy in the Development of Western Thought.* New York: Random House.

Kuijt, I. 1996. Negotiating equality through ritual: a consideration of Late Natufian and Prepottery Neolithic A period mortuary practices. *Journal of Anthropological Archaeology* 15, 313–36.

La Barre, W. 1975. Anthropological perspectives on hallucination and hallucinogens. In Siegel, R. K. & West L. J. (eds) *Hallucinogens: Behaviour, Experience, and Theory,* pp. 9–52. New York: John Wiley.

Lakoff, G. & Johnson, M. 1980. *Metaphors We Live By.* Chicago: University of Chicago Press.

Last, J. 1998. A design for life: interpreting the art of Çatalhöyük. *Material Culture* 3(3), 355–78.

Lawson, A. J. 1997. The structural history of Stonehenge. *Proceedings of the British Academy* 92, 15–37.

Le Roux, C.-T. 1998. Specialised Neolithic production, diffusion and exchange in western France. In Edmonds, M. & Richards, C. (eds) *Understanding the Neolithic of North-western Europe,* pp. 370–84. Glasgow: Cruithne Press.

Leach, E. 1969. *Genesis as Myth and Other Essays.* London: Jonathan Cape.

Leach, E. 1970. *Lévi-Strauss.* London: Fontana.

Lee, R. B. 1967. Trance cure of the !Kung Bushman. *Natural History* 76(9), 31–37.

Lee, R. B. & De Vore, I. (eds) 1968. *Man the Hunter*. Chicago: Aldine.

Lehtisalo, T. 1937. Der Tod und die Wiedergeburt des künftigen Schamanen. *Journal de la Société Finno-Ougrienne* 48, 1–34.

Lévi-Strauss, C. 1967. The story of Asdiwal. In Leach, E. (ed.) *The Structural Study of Myth and Totemism*, pp. 1–47. London: Tavistock.

Lévi-Strauss, C. 1968. *Structural Anthropology*. (Trans. Claire Jacobson and Brooke Grundfest Schoepf.) London: Penguin.

Lévi-Strauss, C. 1970. *The Raw and the Cooked*. (Trans. John and Deirdre Weightman.) London: Jonathan Cape.

Lewis, I. M. 1971. *Ecstatic Religion*. London: Penguin.

Lewis-Williams, J. D. 1981. *Believing and Seeing: Symbolic Meanings in Southern San Rock Paintings*. London: Academic Press.

Lewis-Williams, J. D. 1990. Documentation, analysis and interpretation: dilemmas in rock art research. Review of Pager (ed.) *The rock paintings of the Upper Brandberg*. Part 1: *Amis Gorge. South African Archaeological Bulletin* 45, 126–36.

Lewis-Williams, J. D. 1991. Wrestling with analogy: a problem in Upper Palaeolithic art research. *Proceedings of the Prehistoric Society* 57(1), 149–62.

Lewis-Williams, J. D. 1995. Modelling the production and consumption of rock art. *South African Archaeological Bulletin* 50, 143–54.

Lewis-Williams, J. D. 1996a. Harnessing the brain: vision and shamanism in Upper Palaeolithic Western Europe. In Conkey, M. W., Sopher, O., Stratmann, D. & Jablonski, N. G. (eds) *Beyond Art: Pleistocene Image and Symbol*, pp. 321–42. Berkeley: University of California Press.

Lewis-Williams, J. D. 1996b. 'A visit to the Lion's house': the structure, metaphors and socio-political significance of a 19th century Bushman myth. In Deacon, J. & Dowson, T. A. (eds) *Voices From the Past: /Xam Bushmen and the Bleek and Lloyd Collection*, pp. 122–41. Johannesburg: Witwatersrand University Press.

Lewis-Williams, J. D. 1997a. The Mantis, the Eland and the Meerkats: conflict and mediation in a nineteenth-century San myth. In McAllister, P. (ed.) *Culture and the Commonplace: Anthropological Essays in Honour of David Hammond-Tooke*, pp. 195–216. Johannesburg: Witwatersrand University Press.

Lewis-Williams, J. D. 1997b. Agency, art, and altered consciousness: a motif in French (Quercy) Upper Palaeolithic art. *Antiquity* 71, 810–30.

Lewis-Williams, J. D. 1998. *Quanto?* The issue of many meanings in southern African San rock art research. *South African Archaeological Bulletin* 53, 86–97.

Lewis-Williams, J. D. (ed.) 2000. *Stories that Float from Afar: Ancestral Folklore of the /Xam San*. Cape Town: David Philip.

Lewis-Williams, J. D. 2001a. Brainstorming images: neuropsychology and rock art research. In Whitley, D. S. (ed.) *Handbook of Rock Art Research*, pp. 332–57. Walnut Creek: Altamira.

Lewis-Williams, J. D. 2001b. Monolithism and polysemy: Scylla and Charybdis in rock art research. In Helskog, K. (ed.) *Theoretical Perspectives in Rock Art Research*, pp. 23–39. Oslo: Novus Forlag.

Lewis-Williams, J. D. 2002a. *The Mind in the Cave: Consciousness and the Origins of Art*. London & New York: Thames & Hudson.

Lewis-Williams, J. D. 2002b. *A Cosmos in Stone: Interpreting Religion and Society Through Rock Art*. Walnut Creek: Altamira.

Lewis-Williams, J. D. 2003. *Images of Mystery: Rock Art of the Drakensberg*. Cape Town: Double Storey.

Lewis-Williams, J. D. 2004a. Constructing a cosmos: architecture, power and domestication at Çatalhöyük. *Journal of Social Archaeology* 4, 28–59.

Lewis-Williams, J. D. 2004b. Neuropsychology and Upper Palaeolithic art: observations on the progress of altered states of consciousness. *Cambridge Archaeological Journal* 14, 107–11.

Lewis-Williams, J. D. & Biesele, M. 1978. Eland hunting rituals among northern and southern San groups: striking similarities. *Africa* 48, 117–34.

Lewis-Williams, J. D. & Blundell, G. 1997. New light on finger-dots in southern African rock art: synesthesia, transformation and technique. *South African Journal of Science* 93, 51–54.

Lewis-Williams, J. D. & Dowson, T. A. 1988. The signs of all times: entoptic phenomena in Upper Palaeolithic art. *Current Anthropology* 29, 201–45.

Lewis-Williams, J. D. & Dowson, T. A. 1993. On vision and power in the Neolithic: evidence from the decorated monuments. *Current Anthropology* 34, 55–65.

Lewis-Williams, J. D. & Dowson, T. A. (eds)

1994. *Contested Images: Diversity in Southern African Rock Art Research.* Johannesburg: Witwatersrand University Press.

Lewis-Williams, J. D. & Dowson, T. A. 1999. *Images of Power: Understanding San Rock Art.* Cape Town: Struik.

Lewis-Williams, J. D. & Pearce D. G. 2004a. *San Spirituality: Roots, Expressions, and Social Consequences.* Walnut Creek: Altamira, and Cape Town: Double Storey.

Lewis-Williams, J. D. & Pearce, D. G. 2004b. Southern African San rock painting as social intervention: a study of rain-control images. *African Archaeological Review* 21(4), 199–227.

L'Helgouac'h, J. 1996. De la lumière aux tenèbres. In L'Helgouac'h, J., Le Roux, C.-T. & LeCornec, J. (eds) *Art et Symboles du Megalithisme Européen,* pp. 107–23. Rennes: Revue Archéologique de l'Ouest, Supplément 8.

Losee, J. 1980. *A Historical Introduction to the Philosophy of Science.* Oxford: Oxford University Press.

Lynch, F. 1973. The use of the passage in certain passage graves as a means of communication rather than access. In Daniel, G. & Kjærum, P. (eds) *Megalithic Graves and Ritual,* pp. 147–61. Copenhagen: Jutland Archaeological Society.

Lynch, F. 1991. *Prehistoric Anglesey: The Archaeology of the Island to the Roman Conquest.* Second edition. Llangefni: The Anglesey Antiquarian Society.

Lynch, F. 2000. The Earlier Neolithic. In Lynch, F., Aldhouse-Green, S. & Davies, J. L. *Prehistoric Wales,* pp. 42–78. Stroud: Sutton.

Lynch, F., Aldhouse-Green, S. & Davies J. L. 2000. *Prehistoric Wales.* Stroud: Sutton.

McBrearty, S. & Brooks, A. 2000. The revolution that wasn't: a new interpretation of the origin of modern human behavior. *Journal of Human Evolution* 39, 453–563.

McCall, H. 1989. *Mesopotamian Myths.* Austin: University of Texas Press.

McGuire, R. H. 1992. *A Marxist Archaeology.* New York: Academic Press.

McKellar, P. 1995. Creative imagination: hypnagogia and surrealism. *Journal of Mental Imagery* 19, 33–42.

Malone, C. 1989. *Avebury.* London: Batsford.

Mandal, S. & Cooney, G. 1996. The Irish stone axe project: a second petrological report. *Journal of Irish Archaeology* 7, 41–64.

Manker, E. 1996. *Seite* cult and drum magic of the Lapps. In Diószegi, V. (ed.) *Folk Beliefs and Shamanistic Traditions in Siberia,* pp. 1–14. Budapest: Akadémiai Kiadó.

Manuel, F. E. & Manuel F. P. 1972. Sketch for a natural history of Paradise. *Dædalus* Winter, 83–128.

Maranda, P. (ed.) 1972. *Mythology.* London: Penguin.

Marshall, L. 1961. Sharing, talking and giving: relief of social tensions among !Kung Bushmen. *Africa* 31, 231–49. (Revised reprint in Marshall, L. 1976. *The !Kung of Nyae Nyae,* pp. 287–312. Cambridge, Mass.: Harvard University Press.)

Marshall, L. 1999. *Nyae Nyae !Kung: Beliefs and Rites.* Cambridge, Mass.: Harvard University Press.

Marx, K. & Engels, F. 2002 [1848]. *The Communist Manifesto.* London: Penguin.

Mavromatis, A. 1987. *Hypnagogia: The Unique State of Consciousness Between Wakefulness and Sleep.* London: Routledge & Kegan Paul.

Meighan, I., Simpson, D. & Hartwell, B. 2002. Newgrange: sourcing of its granitic cobbles. *Archaeology Ireland* 16, 32–35.

Mellaart, J. 1966. Excavations at Çatal Hüyük, 1965: fourth preliminary report. *Anatolian Studies* 16, 165–91.

Mellaart, J. 1967. *Çatal Hüyük: A Neolithic Town in Anatolia.* London & New York: Thames & Hudson.

Mellars, P. & Gibson, K. (eds) 1996. *Modeling the Early Human Mind.* Cambridge: McDonald Institute for Archaeological Research.

Mellars, P. & Stringer, C. (eds) 1989. *The Human Revolution: Behavioural and Biological Perspectives on the Origin of Modern Humans.* Edinburgh: Edinburgh University Press.

Meskell, L. 1995. Goddesses, Gimbutas and 'New Age' Archaeology. *Antiquity* 69, 74–86.

Michell, J. 1982. *Megalithomania: Artists, Antiquarians and Archaeologists at the Old Stone Monuments.* London & New York: Thames & Hudson.

Milford, H. S. (ed.) 1923. *The Poetical Works of Leigh Hunt.* London: Oxford University Press.

Mitchell, G. F. 1992. Notes on some non-local cobbles at the entrances to the passage-graves at Newgrange and Knowth, County Meath. *Journal of the Royal Society of Antiquaries of Ireland* 122, 128–45.

Mithen, S. 1996. *The Prehistory of the Mind: A Search for the Origins of Art, Religion and Science.* London & New York: Thames & Hudson.

Mithen, S. 2003. *After the Ice: A Global Human History 20,000–5000 BC.* London: Weidenfeld and Nicolson.

Monk, M. A. 1993. People and environment: in search of the farmers. In Shee Twohig, E. & Ronayne, M. (eds) *Past Perceptions: The Prehistoric Archaeology of South-west Ireland*, pp. 35–52. Cork: Cork University Press.

Morinis, A. (ed.) 1992. *Sacred Journeys: The Anthropology of Pilgrimage*. Westport: Greenwood Press.

Muir, K. (ed.) 1962. *Macbeth*. Arden Edition. London: Methuen.

Narby, J. & Huxley, F. (eds) 2001. *Shamans Through Time: 500 Years on the Path to Knowledge*. London & New York: Thames & Hudson.

Nash, G. & Chippindale, C. (eds) 2002. *European Landscapes of Rock-art*. London: Routledge.

Newberg, A. B. & d'Aquili, E. G. 1994. The near death experience as archetype: a model for 'prepared' neurocognitive processes. *Anthropology of Consciousness* 5(4), 1–15.

Noll, R. 1985. Mental imagery cultivation as a cultural phenomenon: the role of visions in shamanism. *Current Anthropology* 26, 443–61.

North, J. 1996. *Stonehenge: Neolithic Man and the Cosmos*. London: HarperCollins.

O'Kelly, C. 1969. Bryn Celli Ddu, Anglesey: a re-interpretation. *Archaeologia Cambrensis* 118, 17–48.

O'Kelly, C. 1982. Part V: Corpus of Newgrange art. In O'Kelly, M. J. *Newgrange: Archaeology, Art and Legend*, pp. 146–85. London & New York: Thames & Hudson.

O'Kelly, M. J. 1982. *Newgrange: Archaeology, Art and Legend*. London & New York: Thames & Hudson.

O'Sullivan, M. 1989. A stylistic revolution in the megalithic art of the Boyne valley. *Archaeology Ireland* 3, 138–42.

O'Sullivan, M. 1996. Megalithic art in Ireland and Brittany: divergence or convergence? In L'Helgouac'h, J., Le Roux, C.-T. & LeCornec, J. (eds) *Art et Symboles du Megalithisme Européen*, pp. 81–96. Rennes: Revue Archéologique de l'Ouest, Supplément 8.

Oppitz, M. 1992. Drawings on shamanic drums. *RES: Anthropology and Aesthetics* 22, 62–81.

Oster, G. 1970. Phosphenes. *Scientific American* 222(2), 83–87.

Otte, M., Yalcinkaya, I., Leotard, J.-M., Kartal, M., Bar-Yosef, O., Kozlowski, J., Bayón, L. & Marshack, A. 1995. The Epi-Palaeolithic of Öküzini cave (SW Anatolia) and its mobiliary art. *Antiquity* 69, 931–44.

Özdogan, M. & Özdogan, A. 1998. Buildings of cult and the cult of buildings. In Arsebuk, G., Mellink, M. & Schirmer, W. (eds) *Light on Top of the Black Hill*, pp. 581–93. Istanbul: Ege Yayinlari.

Parker Pearson, M. 2000. Ancestors, bones and stones in Neolithic and Early Bronze Age Britain and Ireland. In Ritchie, A. (ed.) *Neolithic Orkney in its European Context*, pp. 203–14. Cambridge: McDonald Institute for Archaeological Research.

Parker Pearson, M. & Ramilisonina. 1998a. Stonehenge for the ancestors: the stones pass on the message. *Antiquity* 72, 308–26.

Parker Pearson, M. & Ramilisonina. 1998b. Stonehenge for the ancestors: part two. *Antiquity* 72, 855–56.

Patton, M. 1990. On entoptic images in context: art, monuments and society in Neolithic Brittany. *Current Anthropology* 31, 554–58.

Patton, M. 1991. Axes, men and women: symbolic dimensions of Neolithic exchange in Armorica (north-west France). In Garwood, P., Jennings, D., Skeates, R. & Toms, J. (eds) *Sacred and Profane: Proceedings of a Conference on Archaeology, Ritual and Religion, Oxford, 1989*, pp. 65–79. Oxford: Oxford University Committee for Archaeology.

Pearce, D. G. 2004. 'Testing' and altered states of consciousness in Upper Palaeolithic art research. *Cambridge Archaeological Journal* 14(1), 82–85.

Pearson, J. L. 2002. *Shamanism and the Ancient Mind: A Cognitive Approach to Archaeology*. Walnut Creek: Altamira.

Peters, J. & Schmidt, K. 2004. Animals in the symbolic world of Pre-Pottery Neolithic Göbekli Tepe, south-eastern Turkey: a preliminary assessment. *Anthropozoologica* 39(1), 179–218.

Pfeiffer, J. E. 1982. *The Creative Explosion: An Inquiry into the Origins of Art and Religion*. New York: Harper & Row.

Pinker, S. 2002. *The Blank Slate: The Modern Denial of Human Nature*. London: Allen Lane.

Pitts, M. 2000. *Hengeworld*. London: Arrow.

Pollard, J. & Ruggles, C. 2001. Shifting perceptions: spatial order, cosmology, and patterns of deposition at Stonehenge. *Cambridge Archaeological Journal* 11, 69–90.

Popov, A. A. 1936. *Tavgytzy: Materialy po Etnografi Avanskikh I Vedeyevskikh Tavgytzev*. Moscow: Trudy Instituta Anthropologii I Etnografii.

Potapov, L. P. 1996. Shamans' drums of Altaic ethnic groups. In Diószegi, V. (ed.) *Folk Beliefs and Shamanistic Traditions in Siberia*, pp. 97–126. Budapest: Akadémiai Kiadó.

Powell, T. G. E. & Daniel, G. E. 1956. *Barclodiad y Gawres: The Excavation of a Megalithic Tomb in Anglesey*. Liverpool: Liverpool University Press.

Powell, T. G. E., Corcoran, J. X. W. P., Scott, J. G. & Lynch, F. M. 1969. *Megalithic Enquiries in the West of Britain*. Liverpool: Liverpool University Press.

Price, N. (ed.) 2001. *The Archaeology of Shamanism*. London: Routledge.

Price, N. 2003. *The Viking Way: Religion and War in Late Iron Age Scandinavia*. Uppsala: University of Uppsala.

Price-Williams, D. 1987. The waking dream in ethnographic perspective. In Tedlock, B. (ed.) *Dreaming: Anthropological and Psychological Interpretations*, pp. 246–62. Cambridge: Cambridge University Press.

Propp, V. 1968. *Morphology of the Folktale*. Austin: University of Texas Press.

Ramanchandran, V. S. & Blakeslee, S. 1998. *Phantoms in the Brain: Probing the Mysteries of the Human Mind*. New York: HarperCollins.

Read, K. A. & Gonzalez, J. J. 2000. *Mesoamerican Mythology: A Guide to the Gods, Heroes, Rituals, and Beliefs of Mexico and Central America*. Oxford: Oxford University Press.

Reichel-Dolmatoff, G. 1969. El contexto cultural de un Alucinogeno Aborigen, *Banisteriopsis Caapi*. *Academia Colombiana de Ciencias Exactas, Fisicas y Naturales* 13(51), 327–45.

Reichel-Dolmatoff, G. 1971. *Amazonian Cosmos: The Sexual and Religious Symbolism of the Tukano Indians*. Chicago: University of Chicago Press.

Reichel-Dolmatoff, G. 1978. *Beyond the Milky Way: Hallucinatory Imagery of the Tukano Indians*. Los Angles: UCLA Latin America Center.

Reichel-Dolmatoff, G. 1979. Desana shamans' rock crystals and the hexagonal universe. *Journal of Latin American Lore* 5, 117–28.

Reichel-Dolmatoff, G. 1985. *Basketry as Metaphor: Arts and Crafts of the Desana Indians of the Northwest Amazon*. Los Angeles: Museum of Cultural History, University of California.

Reichel-Dolmatoff, G. 1988. *Goldwork and Shamanism: An Iconographic Study of the Gold Museum*. Medellín: Compañía Litográfica Nacional S. A.

Renfrew, C. 1973. Monuments, mobilization, and social organization in Neolithic Wessex. In Renfrew, C. (ed.) *The Explanation of Culture Change: Models in Prehistory*, pp. 539–58. London: Duckworth.

Renfrew, C. 1979. *Investigations in Orkney*. London: Society of Antiquaries.

Renfrew, C. 1982. *Towards an Archaeology of Mind*. Cambridge: Cambridge University Press.

Renfrew, C. 1986. Introduction: peer polity interaction and socio-political change. In Renfrew, C. & Cherry, J. F. (eds) *Peer Polity Interaction and Socio-political Change*, pp. 1–18. Cambridge: Cambridge University Press.

Renfrew, C. 1994. Towards a cognitive archaeology. In Renfrew, C. & Zubrow, E. B. W. (eds) *The Ancient Mind: Elements of Cognitive Archaeology*, pp. 1–12. Cambridge: Cambridge University Press.

Renfrew, C. & Zubrow, E. B. W. (eds) 1994. *The Ancient Mind: Elements of Cognitive Archaeology*. Cambridge: Cambridge University Press.

Richards, C. 1996a. Henges and water: towards an elemental understanding of monumentality and landscape in Late Neolithic Britain. *Journal of Material Culture* 1(3), 313–36.

Richards, C. 1996b. Monuments as landscape: creating the centre of the world in Late Neolithic Orkney. *World Archaeology* 28, 190–208.

Robb, J. 2001. Island identities: ritual, travel and the creation of difference in Neolithic Malta. *European Journal of Archaeology* 4(2), 175–202.

Roche, H. 1989. Pre-tomb habitation found at Knowth. C. Meath, spring 1989. *Archaeology Ireland* 3, 101–3.

Rollefson, G. O. 2000. Ritual and social structure at Neolithic 'Ain Ghazal. In Kuijt, I. (ed.) *Life in Neolithic Farming Communities: Social Organization, Identity, and Differentiation*, pp. 165–90. New York: Kluwer.

Rollefson, G. O. & Kafafi, Z. 1994. The 1993 season at 'Ain Ghazal: preliminary report. *Annual of the Department of Antiquities of Jordan* 38, 11–32.

Rose, R. 1957. *Living Magic: The Realities Underlying the Psychical Practices and Beliefs of Australian Aborigines*. London: Chatto & Windus.

Rousseau, J.-J. 1898. *The Social Contract or Principles of Political Right*. London: Swan Sonnerschein & Co.

Rousseau, J.-J. 1997 [1762]. *The Social Contract and Other Later Political Writings*. (Ed. and trans. Victor Gourevitch). Cambridge: Cambridge University Press.

Rudgley, R. 1993. *The Alchemy of Culture: Intoxicants in Society*. London: British Museum Press.

Ruggles, C. L. N. 1999. *Astronomy in Prehistoric Britain and Ireland*. New Haven: Yale University Press.

Russell, M. 2002. *Monuments of the British Neolithic: The Roots of Architecture*. Stroud: Tempus.

Russell, N. & McGowan, K. J. 2002. Dance of the cranes: crane symbolism at Çatalhöyük and beyond. *Antiquity* 77, 445–55.

Sacks, O. 1997. Scotoma: forgetting and neglect in science. In Silvers, R. B. (ed.) *Hidden Histories of Science*, pp. 141–87. London: Granta Books.

Sahlins, M. D. 1968. Notes on the original affluent society. In Lee, R. B. & DeVore, I. (eds) *Man the Hunter*, pp. 85–89. Chicago: Aldine.

Sandall, R. 2001. *The Culture Cult: Designer Tribalism and Other Essays*. Boulder: Westview Press.

Sandars, N. K. 1960. *The Epic of Gilgamesh*. London: Penguin.

Scarre, C. 1989. Painting by resonance. *Nature* 338, 382.

Scarre, C. 2001a. A place of special meaning: interpreting pre-historic monuments in the landscape. In David, B. & Wilson, M. (eds) *Inscribed Landscapes: Marking and Making Place*, pp. 154–75. Honolulu: University of Hawai'i Press.

Scarre, C. 2001b. Pilgrimage and place in Neolithic western Europe. In Smith, A. T. & Brookes, A. (eds) *Holy Ground: Theoretical Issues Relating to the Landscape and Material Culture of Ritual Space*, pp. 9–20. Oxford: BAR International Series 956.

Scarre, C. 2002a. Epilogue: Colour and materiality in prehistoric society. In Jones, A. & MacGregor, G. (eds) *Colouring the Past: The Significance of Colour in Archaeological Research*, pp. 227–42. Oxford: Berg.

Scarre, C. 2002b. A pattern of islands: the Neolithic monuments of north-west Brittany. *European Journal of Archaeology* 5(1), 24–41.

Schele, L. & Freidel, D. 1990. *A Forest of Kings: The Untold Story of the Ancient Maya*. New York: William Morrow.

Schmandt-Besserat, D. 1998. 'Ain Ghazal 'Monumental' Figures. *Bulletins of the American School of Oriental Research* 310, 1–17.

Schmidt, K. 1995. Investigations in the Upper Mesopotamian Early Neolithic: Göbekli Tepe and Gücütepe. *Neo-lithics* 2/95, 9–10.

Schmidt K. 1996. The Urfa-Project 1996. *Neo-Lithics* 2/96, 2–3.

Schmidt K. 1998. Beyond daily bread: evidence of Early Neolithic ritual from Göbekli Tepe. *Neo-Lithics* 2/98, 1–5.

Schmidt K. 1999. Boars, ducks and foxes – the Urfa-project 99. *Neo-Lithics* 3/99, 12–5.

Schmidt, K. 2000. Göbekli Tepe and the rock art of the Near East. *Turkish Academy of Sciences Journal of Archaeology* 3, 1–14.

Schmidt, K. 2001. Göbekli Tepe, southeastern Turkey. A preliminary report on the 1995–1999 excavations. *Paléorient* 26, 45–54.

Schmidt, K. 2004. Frühneolithische zeichen vom Göbekli Tepe. *Turkish Academy of Sciences Journal of Archaeology* 7, 93–105.

Schulman, D., Stroumsa, G. G. & Stroumsa, G. A. G. (eds) 1999. *Dream Cultures: Explorations in the Comparative History of Dreams*. Oxford: Oxford University Press.

Scourse, J. D. 1997. Transport of the Stonehenge bluestones: testing the glacial hypothesis. In Cunliffe, B. & Renfrew, C. (eds) *Science and Stonehenge*, pp. 271–314. Oxford: Oxford University Press.

Shanks, M. & Tilley, C. 1982. Ideology, symbolic power, and ritual communication: a reinterpretation of Neolithic mortuary practices. In Hodder, I. (ed.) *Symbolic and Structural Archaeology*, pp. 129–54. Cambridge: Cambridge University Press.

Shee Twohig, E. 1981. *The Megalithic Art of Western Europe*. Oxford: Clarendon Press.

Shee Twohig, E. 1990. *Irish Megalithic Tombs*. Princes Risborough: Shire Publications.

Shee Twohig, E. 1996. Context and content of Irish passage tomb art. *Revue archéologique de l'Ouest*, supplement 8, 67–80.

Shee Twohig, E. 2000. Frameworks for the megalithic art of the Boyne Valley. In Desmond, A., Johnson, G., McCarthy, M., Sheehan, J. & Shee Twohig, E. (eds) *New Agendas in Irish Prehistory: Papers in Commemoration of Liz Anderson*, pp. 89–105. Bray: Wordwell.

Shee Twohig, E. 2001. Changes and continuity: post passage tomb ceremonial near Loughcrew, Co Meath. *Revue archéologique de l'Ouest*, supplement 9, 113–24.

Sheridan, A. 1985/6. Megaliths and megalomania: an account, and interpretation, of the development of passage tombs in Ireland. *Journal of Irish Archaeology* 3, 17–30.

Sherratt, A. 1983. The secondary exploitation of animals in the Old World. *World Archaeology* 15(1), 90–104.

Sherratt, A. 1990. The genesis of megaliths: monumentality, ethnicity and social complexity in Neolithic north-west Europe. *World Archaeology* 22, 147–67.

Sherratt, A. G. 1991. Sacred and profane substances: the ritual use of narcotics in Later Neolithic Europe. In Garwood, P., Jennings, D., Skeates, R. & Toms, J. (eds) *Sacred and Profane: Proceedings of a Conference on Archaeology, Ritual and Religion, Oxford, 1989*, pp. 50–64. Oxford: Oxford University Committee for Archaeology.

Sherratt, A. G. 1997. *Economy and Society in Prehistoric Europe: Changing Perspectives.* Edinburgh: Edinburgh University Press.

Shirokogorov, S. M. 1935. *Psychomental Complex of the Tungus.* London: Kegan Paul, Trench, Trubner.

Siegel, R. K. 1977. Hallucinations. *Scientific American* 237, 132–40.

Siegel, R. K. 1978. Cocaine hallucinations. *American Journal of Psychiatry* 135, 309–14.

Siegel, R. K. 1980. The psychology of life after death. *American Psychologist* 35, 911–31.

Siegel, R. K. 1992. *Fire in the Brain: Clinical Tales of Hallucination.* New York: Dutton.

Siegel, R. K. & Jarvik, M. E. 1975. Drug-induced hallucinations in animals and man. In Siegel, R. K. & West, L. J. (eds) *Hallucinations, Behaviour, Experience, and Theory*, pp. 81–161. New York: John Wiley.

Siikala, A.-L. & Hoppál, M. 1992. *Studies on Shamanism.* Budapest: Akadémiai Kiadó.

Smith, N. W. 1992. *An Analysis of Ice Age Art: Its Psychology and Belief System.* New York: Peter Lang.

Spiro, M. E. 1966. Religion: problems of definition and explanation. In Banton, M. (ed.) *Anthropological Approaches to the Study of Religion*, pp. 85–126. London: Tavistock.

Stephen, M. 1979. Dreams of change: the innovative role of altered states of consciousness in traditional Melanesian religion. *Oceania* 50, 3–22.

Stout, G. 2002. *Newgrange and the Bend of the Boyne.* Cork: Cork University Press.

Stukeley, W. 1776. *Itinerarium Curiosum*, I. London.

Sullivan, L. E. 1988. *Icanchu's Drum: An Orientation to Meaning in South American Religions.* New York: Macmillan.

Sutherland, P. D. 2001. Shamanism and the iconography of Palaeo-Eskimo art. In Price, N. (ed.) *The Archaeology of Shamanism*, 135–45. London: Routledge.

Sweetman, P. D. 1985. A Late Neolithic/Early Bronze Age pit circle at Newgrange, County Meath. *Proceedings of the Royal Irish Academy, C,* 85, 195–221.

Sweetman, P. D. 1987. Excavations of a Late Neolithic/Early Bronze Age pit circle at Newgrange, County Meath. *Proceedings of the Royal Irish Academy, C,* 87, 283–98.

Swenson, E. R. 2003. Cities of violence: sacrifice, power and urbanization in the Andes. *Journal of Social Archaeology* 3(2), 256–96.

Taçon, P. S. C. 1991. The power of stone: symbolic aspects of stone use and tool development in western Arnhem Land, Australia. *Antiquity* 65, 192–207.

Thom, A. 1967. *Megalithic Sites in Britain.* Oxford: Clarendon Press.

Thom, A. 1978. *Megalithic Remains in Britain and Brittany.* Oxford: Clarendon Press.

Thomas, H. 1923. The source of the stones at Stonehenge. *Antiquaries Journal* 3, 239–60.

Thomas, J. 1984. A tale of two polities: kinship, authority and exchange in the Neolithic of south Dorset and north Wiltshire. In Bradley, R. & Gardiner, J. (eds) *Neolithic Studies: A Review of Some Current Research*, pp. 161–76. Oxford: British Archaeological Reports, 133.

Thomas, J. 1988. The social significance of Cotswold-Severn burial practices. *Man* (n.s.) 23, 540–59.

Thomas, J. 1990. Monuments from the inside: the case of the Irish megalithic tombs. *World Archaeology* 22, 168–89.

Thomas, J. 1991. *Rethinking the Neolithic.* Cambridge: Cambridge University Press.

Thomas, J. 2003. Thoughts on the 'repacked' Neolithic Revolution. *Antiquity* 77, 67–74.

Thomas, J. & Whittle, A. 1986. Anatomy of a tomb – West Kennet revisited. *Oxford Journal of Archaeology* 5(2), 129–56.

Thomas, N. & Humphrey, C. (eds) 1996. *Shamanism, History, and the State.* Ann Arbor: University of Michigan Press.

Thorpe, R. S., Williams-Thorpe, O. & Watson, J. S. 1991. The geological sources and transport of the 'bluestones' of Stonehenge, Wiltshire, UK. *Proceedings of the Prehistoric Society* 57, 103–58.

Tilley, C. 1994. *A Phenomenology of Landscape.* Oxford: Berg.

Tilley, C. 1996. The power of rocks: topography and monument construction on Bodmin Moor. *World Archaeology* 28, 161–76.

Tinker, C. B. and Lowry, H. E. (eds) 1950. *The Poetical Works of Matthew Arnold.* London: Oxford University Press.

Toynbee, A. 1946. *A Study of History.*

(Abridgement by D. C. Somervell.) Oxford: Oxford University Press.

Turner, E. 1996. *The Hands Feel It: Healing and Spirit Presence Among a North Alaskan People.* DeKalb: Northern Illinois University Press.

Turner, V. 1967. *The Forest of Symbols: Aspects of Ndembu Ritual.* Ithaca: Cornell University Press.

Turner, V. W. & Turner, E. 1978. *Image and Pilgrimage in Christian Culture: Anthropological Perspectives.* New York: Columbia University Press.

Tyler, C. W. 1978. Some new entoptic phenomena. *Vision Research* 18, 1633–39.

Vastokas, J. & Vastokas, R. 1973. *Sacred Art of the Algonkians: A Study of the Peterborough Petroglyphs.* Peterborough: Mansard Press.

Verhoeven, M. 2002. Ritual and ideology in Pre-Pottery Neolithic B of the Levant and southeast Anatolia. *Cambridge Archaeological Journal* 12, 233–58.

Vitebsky, P. 1995. *The Shaman: Voyages of the Soul, Ecstasy and Healing from Siberia to the Amazon.* London: Macmillan.

Vogelin, F. W. 1938. Tubatulabal ethnography. *University of California Anthropological Records* 2, 1–90.

Voigt, M. M. 2000. Çatalhöyük in context: ritual at early Neolithic sites in central and eastern Turkey. In Kuijt, I (ed.) *Life in Neolithic Farming Communities: Social Organization, Identity, and Differentiation*, pp. 253–93. New York: Kluwer.

Wainwright, G. 1989. *The Henge Monuments: Ceremony and Society in Prehistoric Britain.* London & New York: Thames & Hudson.

Walker, J. 1981. The amateur scientist: about phosphenes. *Scientific American* 255, 142–52.

Wason, P. K. 1994. *The Archaeology of Rank.* Cambridge: Cambridge University Press.

Watson, A. 2001a. The sounds of transformation: acoustic, monuments and ritual in the British Neolithic. In Price, N. (ed.) *The Archaeology of Shamanism*, pp. 178–92. London: Routledge.

Watson, A. 2001b. Composing Avebury. *World Archaeology* 33, 296–314.

Watson, A. & Keating, D. 1999. Architecture and sound: an acoustic analysis of megalithic monuments in prehistoric Britain. *Antiquity* 73, 325–36.

Watson, A. & Keating, D. 2000. The architecture of sound in Neolithic Orkney. In Ritchie, A. (ed.) *Neolithic Orkney in its European Context*, pp. 259–63. Cambridge: McDonald Institute for Archaeological Research.

Whitehouse, H. 1995. *Inside the Cult: Religious Innovation and Transmission in Papua New Guinea.* Oxford: Oxford University Press.

Whitehouse, H. 2000. *Arguments and Icons: Divergent Modes of Religiosity.* Oxford: Oxford University Press.

Whitley, D. S. (ed.) 1998. *Reader in Archaeological Theory: Post Processual and Cognitive Approaches.* London: Routledge.

Whitley, D. S. 2000. *The Art of the Shaman: Rock Art of California.* Salt Lake City: University of Utah Press.

Whitley, D. S. (ed.) 2001. *Handbook of Rock Art Research.* Walnut Creek: Altamira.

Whitley, D. S., Dorn, R. I., Simon, J. M., Rechtman, R. & Whitley, T. K. 1999. Sally's rock shelter and the archaeology of the vision quest. *Cambridge Archaeological Journal* 9, 221–47.

Whitley, J. 2002. Too many ancestors. *Antiquity* 76, 119–26.

Whittle, A. 1998. People and the diverse past: two comments on 'Stonehenge for the ancestors'. *Antiquity* 72, 852–54.

Wilbert, J. 1987. *Tobacco and Shamanism in South America.* New Haven: Yale University Press.

Wilbert, J. 1997. Illuminative serpents: tobacco hallucinations of the Warao. *Journal of Latin American Lore* 20, 317–32.

Wilson, D. 2004. People talk about heaven … *Cambridge Archaeological Journal* 14(1), 86–90.

Winkelman, M. 1986. Trance states: a theoretical model and cross-cultural analysis. *Ethos* 14, 174–203.

Winkelman, M. 2002. Shamanism and cognitive evolution. *Cambridge Archaeological Journal* 12(1), 71–101.

Zigmond, M. 1986. Kawaiisu. In D'Azevedo, W. (ed.) *Handbook of North American Indians*, vol. 11: *Great Basin*, pp. 398–411. Washington (DC): Smithsonian Institution.

Zimmerman, L. J. 1996. *Native North America.* London: Macmillan.

Zuckerman, M. 1969. Hallucinations, reported sensations, and images. In Zubek, J. P. (ed.) *Sensory Deprivation: Fifteen Years of Research.* New York: Appleton Century Crofts.

Acknowledgments

We are grateful to friends and colleagues who read and so usefully commented on sections of this book: Geoff Blundell, Richard Bradley, Jeremy Hollman, Karim Sadr, Andrew Sherratt, Ben Smith and David Wilson. Chris Chippindale, Jean Clottes, Andrew Lawson, Elizabeth Shee Twohig and Claire Tuffy kindly assisted us in visiting sites. We thank Jean Clottes, Steven Mithen, Chris Scarre and David Wilson for drawing our attention to useful publications and other information. Wendy Voorvelt is thanked for producing excellent illustrations. This project was funded by the South African National Research Foundation under grant number 2053693. The opinions expressed are our own and should not be attributed to the NRF.

Sources of Illustrations

TEXT FIGURES: 1 After Verhoeven (2002), fig. 1; 2 Jericho Excavation Fund; 3 W. Voorvelt; 4, 5 left and centre Salwa Hauptmann-Hamza; 5 right Euphrat-Archiv, Heidelberg; 6 after Cauvin (2000a), fig. 70; 7 Bibliothèque Nationale, Paris; 8 W. Voorvelt; 9 after Siegel (1977), 137; 10 British Museum, London; 11 after Read and Gonzales (2000), fig. 7; 12 after Schele and Freidel (1990), figs, 3, 6; 13 after Schmandt-Besserat (1998), figs 1, 3, 5; 14 after Schmandt-Besserat (1998), figs 4, 6; 15 after Verhoeven (2002), fig. 8 and Goren *et al.* (2001), figs 2, 3, 4; 16 Cayönü Archive, Istanbul University; 17 top after S. Hugh-Jones (1979), fig. 1, and bottom after C. Hugh-Jones (1979), fig. 39; 18 after C. Hugh-Jones (1979), fig. 44; 19 W. Voorvelt; 20 photo B. Degedeh, courtesy Gary O. Rollefson; 21 photo Yusif Zo'bi, courtesy Gary O. Rollefson; 22 after Mellaart (1967), fig. 10; 23 after Mellaart (1967), figs 41, 42; 24, 25 after Mellaart (1967), pl. 49; 26 after Mellaart (1967), pl. 41; 27 after Mellaart (1967), pls 33, 40; 28 J. Schadeberg; 29 Andrea Mantegna, *The Sacrifice of Isaac, c.* 1490/95, Kunsthistorisches Museum, Vienna; 30 T. A. Dowson, RARI; 31 University of Cape Town Libraries; 32 after Mellaart (1967), pls 49, 52; 33 British Museum, London; 34 from William Stukeley, *Stonehenge*, 1740; 35 from William Stukeley, *Abury Described*, vol. 2, 1743; 36 W. Voorvelt; 37 after Lynch *et al.* (2000), fig. 2.14; 38 after Shee Twohig (1990), figs 7, 14, 36; 39 after Lynch (1991), fig. 24; 40 after Lynch *et al.* (2000), fig. 2.14 and Powell and Daniel (1956), fig. 17; 41 after Lynch (1991), fig. 11; 42 after Stout (2002), 1; 43 after Stout (2002), 50, fig. 8; 44 after Stout (2002), 49, figs 13A, 13B; 45 after Eogan (1986), figs 67, 68, 71, 72; 46 after Eogan (1986), figs 83, 84; 47 after Eogan (1986) figs 24, 25; 48 after Stout (2002), 49, fig. 5; 49 after Eogan (1986), fig. 57; 50, 51 D. G. Pearce, RARI; 52, 53 after Eogan (1986), fig. 61; 54 after Stout (2002), 30, fig. 25; 55 after O'Kelly (1982), fig. 52; 56 after Stout (2002), fig. 8; 57 after O'Kelly (1982), fig. 28; 58 W. Voorvelt; 59 after Schele and Friedel (1990), fig. 6.1; 60 Photo AKG Images/ François Guénet; 61 D. G. Pearce, RARI; 62 Sussex Archaeological Society/Curwen Collection; 63 after Bradley (1993); 64 after Lewis-Williams and Dowson (1993), fig. 1; 65 after Reichel-Dolmatoff (1985), pls 74, 75; 66 after Reichel-Dolmatoff (1978), pl. VIII; 67 after Reichel-Dolmatoff (1978), pl. XVI; 68 after Shee Twohig (1981), fig. 113; 69 D. G. Pearce, RARI; 70 after O'Kelly (1982), fig. 24; 71 after Reichel-Dolmatoff (1978), pls K–M; 72 W. Voorvelt; 73 after Shee Twohig (1981) fig. 111 and Bradley (1989), fig. 5; 74, 75 W. Voorvelt.

PLATES: 1 Hieronymus Bosch, *The Ascent of the Empyrean, c.* 1500. Palazzo Ducale, Venice; 2 DAI, Berlin; 3 D. Johannes/DAI, Berlin; 4 I. Wagner/DAI, Berlin; 5 Euphrat-Archiv, Heidelberg; 6 DAI, Berlin; 7 Ashmolean Museum, Oxford; 8 Photo B. Degedeh, courtesy Gary O. Rollefson; 9 Photo P. Dorrell and S. Laidlaw, courtesy Dr Gary O. Rollefson; 10, 11, 12 N. Leibhammer, RARI; 13, 14 Photo James Mellaart; 15 Photo Mike Pitts; 16 Oxford Archaeological Unit; 17, 18, 19, 20 D. G. Pearce, RARI; 21 National Museum of Ireland, Dublin; 22, 23 D. G. Pearce, RARI; 24 Michael Jenner; 25 D. G. Pearce, RARI; 26 Wiltshire Archaeological and Natural History Society, Devizes; 27 Photograph reproduced with the kind permission of the Trustees of the National Museums and Galleries of Northern Ireland. Photograph © Ulster Museum; 28 D. G. Pearce, RARI; 29 Caravaggio, *Conversion of St Paul*, 1600-01, Sta Maria del Popolo, Rome.

Index